FRONTIER:

American Literature and the American West

In quella parte del libro della mia memoria, dinanzi alla quale poco si potrebbe leggere, si trova una rubrica, la quale dice: *incipit Vita Nova*. Sotto la quale rubrica io trovo scritte le parole, le quali è mio intendimento d' assemprare in questo libello, e se non tutte, almeno la loro sentenzia.

(*La Vita Nuova*)

Only a fadograph of a yestern scene.

(*Finnegans Wake*)

Frontier:

American Literature and
the American West

BY EDWIN FUSSELL

Princeton, New Jersey
Princeton University Press
1965

For Jean

Preface

In "The First Official Frontier of the Massachusetts Bay" (1914), Frederick Jackson Turner recorded the fact that "an act of March 12, 1694-5, by the General Court of Massachusetts enumerated the 'Frontier Towns' which the inhabitants were forbidden to desert on pain of loss of their lands (if landholders) or of imprisonment (if not landholders), unless permission to remove were first obtained." Sixty-five years earlier (illustrating Emerson's principle that "the primary use of a fact is low; the secondary use, as it is a figure or illustration of my thought, is the real worth"), Henry David Thoreau was writing: "In 1694 a law was passed 'that every settler who deserted a town for fear of the Indians should forfeit all his rights therein.' But now, at any rate, as I have frequently observed, a man may desert the fertile frontier territories of truth and justice, which are the State's best lands, for fear of far more insignificant foes, without forfeiting any of his civil rights therein." There, in stark contrast, is the difference between factual and imaginative historiography. Needless to say, my historiography is altogether of the imaginative kind, though at the same time I have tried, as Thoreau did, to respect the basic factuality of things. One of the things I have especially tried to respect is the integrity of the individual writers whose varying responses to the idea of the West (so the argument runs) eventuate in the definition and description of a historical and literary epoch; as might be expected, since the West had no single or fixed meaning, each of these writers viewed the West differently, according to his own peculiar mind and mood (Melville's language)—Hawthorne, for example, as ambiguity, Poe as terror. I have also tried to bear in mind that my interpretation of these writers, and of this entire body of literature, is only one out of many possible interpretations, some of which have been handsomely explicated by previous scholars, others of which remain to be explicated by future scholars.

More inclusively still, I should like to think that this volume illustrates two reciprocal principles: that history at its best is always literary (or imaginative) and that literary criticism at its best is always historical (or realistic). As Ernest Fenollosa reminds us: "The primitive metaphors do not spring from arbitrary *subjective* processes. They are possible only because they follow objective lines of relations in nature herself." If that is so, then it is well to remember that the American frontier must have been first of all the simplest of physical conditions and the most ordinary of human behaviors, and only later, as men began to take notice of these conditions and behaviors, a complex image formed of a myriad particularized perceptions and memories. Later still—doubtless, much later—these conditions and behaviors received a name, and the frontier became a metaphor. Conjectures about the origin of the frontier metaphor are found in the Introduction; the literary chapters which comprise the remainder of the book trace the development and decline of that metaphor, and thus constitute a short history—albeit a somewhat specialized one—of the American West impinging upon the American mind, and, to a considerable extent, forming it.

Serious consideration of the Westward Movement of American writing dates from W. H. Venable, *Beginnings of Literary Culture in the Ohio Valley* (Cincinnati, 1891). His most notable successors have been Ralph Leslie Rusk, *The Literature of the Middle Western Frontier* (New York, 1925); Dorothy Anne Dondore, *The Prairie and the Making of Middle America* (Cedar Rapids, Iowa, 1926); Lucy Lockwood Hazard, *The Frontier in American Literature* (New York, 1927); and (much the most distinguished of these studies) Henry Nash Smith, *Virgin Land: The American West as Symbol and Myth* (Cambridge, 1950). On slightly different topics, but equally stimulating to the student of Western literature (by which term, here and elsewhere, I normally mean literature written "about the

West," rather than literature written "in the West") are Roy Harvey Pearce, *The Savages of America: A Study of the Indian and the Idea of Civilization* (Baltimore, 1953), and Arthur K. Moore, *The Frontier Mind: A Cultural Analysis of the Kentucky Frontiersman* (Lexington, 1957). Of books about American literature generally, the most stimulating have been Lewis Mumford, *The Golden Day* (New York, 1926); Constance Rourke, *American Humor* (New York, 1931); Charles Feidelson, Jr., *Symbolism and American Literature* (Chicago, 1953); R. W. B. Lewis, *The American Adam* (Chicago, 1955); and Harry Levin, *The Power of Blackness* (New York, 1958). The best treatment of American literary nationalism is Benjamin T. Spencer, *The Quest for Nationality* (Syracuse, 1957). For mid-nineteenth-century intellectual history, Perry Miller, *The Transcendentalists* (Cambridge, 1950) is the all but inevitable starting point. After the works of Frederick Jackson Turner, the most useful historical background is in Ray Allen Billington, *Westward Expansion: A History of the American Frontier*, 2nd ed. (New York, 1960).

At the very beginning of this project, during a year of research supported by the Fund for the Advancement of Education, I was stimulated and assisted by conversations with Harry Levin, Charles Feidelson, Jr., Willard Thorp, and Norman Holmes Pearson, who subsequently furnished material on Hawthorne. Charles S. Holmes, Frederick Bracher, Ray Frazer, Cecil Y. Lang, Marshall Waingrow, Albert B. Friedman, John Niven, French R. Fogle, Robert H. Fossum, and John Zeigel read portions of the manuscript. Sherman Paul read the chapters on Thoreau, Leon Howard and John D. Seelye the chapters on Melville. James F. Beard generously answered questions about Cooper, and Ray Allen Billington and Wilbur Jacobs answered questions about Turner. Four distinguished American scholars—Roy Harvey Pearce, Edward Weismiller, W. T. Jones, and Douglass G. Adair—read practically the entire manuscript, and some of it more than once. To all of these people, I am deeply indebted for advice, encouragement, dissent, provocation, and criticism. I am also grateful to the staffs of the Honnold Library and the Huntington Library for a variety of courtesies extending over many years; to Catherine Tramz and Parker Palmer for typing; to the Claremont Graduate School for funds in support of research; and to Herbert S. Bailey, Jr., R. Miriam Brokaw, and Harriet Anderson, of the Princeton University Press, for editorial wisdom and kindness. Finally, I wish to thank Marshall Waingrow and W. T. Jones for reading proof, Susan T. Fussell and Paul H. Fussell for helping with the index.

More specific intellectual obligations are of course recorded in the notes. If particular articles—for example, Lawrence Willson, "The Transcendentalist View of the West," *Western Humanities Review*, XIV (1960), 183-191, or Charles Feidelson, Jr., *"The Scarlet Letter,"* in *Hawthorne Centenary Essays*, ed. Roy Harvey Pearce (Columbus, 1964)—are not so recorded, it is because I read them only after the relevant portions of this book were written. Since Professors Willson and Feidelson had no more seen my work than I had seen theirs, our agreements, when I came to know about them, were all the more comforting to me.

"Thoreau's Unwritten Epic" appeared previously in *Thoreau, A Collection of Critical Essays*, ed. Sherman Paul (Englewood Cliffs, N.J., 1962), and portions of the Hawthorne material were published in *Hawthorne Centenary Essays*, ed. Roy Harvey Pearce (Columbus, 1964). They are reprinted with the permission of Prentice-Hall, Incorporated, the Ohio State University Press, and the original editors.

Material in copyright is quoted, with the permission of the publishers or other copyright holders, as follows:

Bald Eagle Press, for *Walt Whitman of the New York Aurora*, ed. Joseph Jay Rubin and Charles H. Brown, copyright 1950 by Bald Eagle Press.

Constable and Company Limited, for *The Works of Herman Melville*, copyright 1922-1924 by Constable and Company Limited.

Doubleday and Company, Incorporated, for *The Uncollected Poetry and Prose of Walt Whitman*, ed. Emory Holloway. Copyright 1921 by Emory Holloway. Reprinted by permission of Doubleday and Company, Inc.

E. P. Dutton and Company, Incorporated, for *Chivers' Life of Poe*, ed. Richard Beale Davis, copyright 1952 by E. P. Dutton and Company, Incorporated.

Ginn and Company, for *The Poems of Edgar Allan Poe*, ed. Killis Campbell, copyright 1917 by Killis Campbell.

Harcourt, Brace and World, Incorporated, for Charles Brockden Brown, *Wieland*, ed. Fred Lewis Pattee, copyright 1926 by Harcourt, Brace and Company, Incorporated; Constance Rourke, *American Humor*, copyright 1931 by Harcourt, Brace and Company, Incorporated; and Jay Leyda, *The Melville Log*, copyright 1951 by Jay Leyda.

Harper and Row, Publishers, Incorporated, for Ray Allen Billington, *The Far Western Frontier, 1830-1860*, copyright 1956 by Harper and Row, Publishers, Incorporated.

Harvard University Press, for *Walt Whitman's Workshop*, ed. Clifton Joseph Furness, copyright 1928 by Clifton Joseph Furness; *Journal of a Visit to London and the Continent by Herman Melville, 1849-1850*, ed. Eleanor Melville Metcalf, copyright 1948 by the President and Fellows of Harvard College; *The Letters of Edgar Allan Poe*, ed. John Ward Ostrom, copyright 1948 by the President and Fellows of Harvard College; *Hawthorne's Doctor Grimshawe's Secret*, ed. Edward H. Davidson, copyright 1954 by the President and Fellows of Harvard College; and Merton M. Sealts, Jr., *Melville as Lecturer*, copyright 1957 by the President and Fellows of Harvard College.

Harvard University Press and The Belknap Press of Harvard University Press, for *The Letters and Journals of James Fenimore Cooper*, ed. James Franklin Beard, copyright 1960 by the President and Fellows of Harvard College, and William Gilmore Simms, *Views and Reviews in American Literature, History and Fiction*, ed. C. Hugh Holman, copyright 1962 by the President and Fellows of Harvard College.

Library of Harvard University, for Melville's manuscript, "The River."

Hendricks House, Incorporated, for the following volumes of Melville: *Collected Poems*, ed. Howard P. Vincent, copyright 1947 by Packard and Company; *The Piazza Tales*, ed. Egbert S. Oliver, copyright 1948 by Hendricks House, Farrar Straus and Company, Incorporated; *Pierre*, ed. Henry A. Murray, copyright 1949 by Hendricks House, Farrar Straus and Company, Incorporated; *Moby-Dick*, ed. Luther S. Mansfield and Howard P. Vincent, copyright 1952 by Hendricks House, Incorporated; *The Confidence-Man*, ed. Elizabeth S. Foster, copyright 1954 by Hendricks House, Incorporated; and *Clarel*, ed. Walter E. Bezanson, copyright 1960 by Hendricks House, Incorporated.

Holt, Rinehart and Winston, Incorporated, for Frederick Jackson Turner, *The Frontier in American History*, copyright 1920 and 1947 by Frederick Jackson Turner.

Houghton Mifflin Company, for *The Journals of Ralph Waldo Emerson*, ed. Edward Waldo Emerson and Waldo Emerson Forbes, copyright 1909-1914 by Edward Waldo Emerson; F. B. Sanborn, *The Life of Henry David Thoreau*, copyright 1917 by Louisa Sanborn; and *Consciousness in Concord; the Text of Thoreau's Hitherto "Lost Journal," (1840-1841)*, ed. Perry Miller, copyright 1958 by Perry Miller.

The Glenn Hughes Estate, for *A Child's Reminiscences, by Walt Whitman*, ed. Thomas O. Mabbott and Rollo G. Silver, copyright 1930 by Glenn Hughes.

Alfred A. Knopf, Incorporated, for Alexis de Tocqueville, *Democracy in America*, translated by Henry Reeve, revised by Francis Bowen, corrected and ed. Phillips Bradley, copyright 1945 by Alfred A. Knopf, Incorporated; William Bradford, *Of Plymouth Plantation, 1620-1647*, ed. Samuel Eliot Morison, copyright 1952 by Samuel Eliot Morison; and Harry Levin, *The Power of Blackness*, copyright 1958 by Harry Levin.

The Macmillan Company, for Gay Wilson Allen, *The Solitary Singer*, copyright 1955 by Gay Wilson Allen.

The Modern Language Association of America, for *The English Notebooks of Nathaniel Hawthorne*, ed. Randall Stewart, copyright 1941 by the Modern Language Association of America and reprinted by its permission.

New Directions, for William Carlos Williams, *In the American Grain*, copyright 1925 by James Laughlin.

The New York Public Library, for "Sketch of Major Thomas Melville By a Nephew" in the Gansevoort-Lansing Collection, Melville Papers, 1802-1845, vol. IV.

Oxford University Press, for Jonathan Swift, *A Tale of a Tub*, ed. A. C. Guthkelch and D. Nichol Smith, copyright 1920 by Oxford University Press.

Norman Holmes Pearson, for material from his forthcoming edition of Nathaniel Hawthorne, *The French and Italian Note-books*.

G. P. Putnam's Sons, for *The Gathering of the Forces*, ed. Cleveland Rodgers and John Black, copyright 1920 by G. P. Putnam's Sons, and James Fenimore Cooper (grandson), *The Legends and Traditions of a Northern County*, copyright 1921 by James Fenimore Cooper.

Scholars' Facsimiles and Reprints, for Daniel Drake, *Discourse on the . . . West*, ed. Perry Miller (1955); *Walt Whitman's Drum-Taps and Sequel to Drum-Taps*, ed. F. DeWolfe Miller (1959); *Battle-Pieces and Aspects of the War*, by Herman Melville, ed. Sidney Kaplan (1960); and John S. Robb, *Streaks of Squatter Life*, ed. John Francis McDermott (1962).

The Sewanee Review, for Walter J. Ong, "Metaphor and the Twinned Vision."

Odell Shepard, for *The Journals of Bronson Alcott*, ed. Odell Shepard, copyright 1938 by Odell Shepard.

William Sloane Associates, Incorporated, for Newton Arvin, *Herman Melville*, copyright 1950 by William Sloane Associates, Incorporated.

The Viking Press, Incorporated, for James Joyce, *Finnegans Wake*, copyright 1939 by James Joyce, and *The Writings of Margaret Fuller*, ed. Mason Wade, copyright 1941 by The Viking Press, Incorporated.

EDWIN FUSSELL

Claremont, California
1 January 1965

Contents

FRONTIER:

American Literature and the
American West

Introduction

FOR AN UNDERSTANDING of early American literature, the word West, with all its derivatives and variants, is the all but inevitable key. Yet no word commonly associated with the American identity and destiny has been, and continues to be, more frequently misused and sentimentalized. As Caroline Kirkland asked well over a century ago about "the 'West'": "How much does that expression mean to include? I never have been able to discover its limits." (The superficial retort would be that an expression which includes everything means nothing.) Mrs. Kirkland's near contemporary George Catlin still more pointedly observed: "Few people even know the true definition of the term 'West;' and where is its location?—phantom-like it flies before us as we travel." And in a review of Charles Fenno Hoffman, *A Winter in the West. By a New-Yorker* (1835), an unknown analyst puzzled the matter out at considerable length:

> "The West," however, is a vague designation of any place in North America. Although there be a distinct meaning in the phrase, well understood by the person using it, yet paradoxical as this is, it points to no locality. Twenty years ago the Alleghany range might, by most people, be considered in these new countries. Ten years ago, the Mississippi was the *ne plus ultra* for five-sixths of Americans. The imaginary line which limited the bounds of the West, has thus been continually changing, till at length it has found a natural correspondence in the "woods where rolls the Oregon," and on the shore laved by the Pacific. Still the phrase has a local meaning. The mind of a citizen of Philadelphia referring to the West, does not now reach beyond the Mississippi. When an inhabitant of Ohio speaks of the West, he means beyond that river; and when one of Missouri talks of this still receding land, he fixes himself, as he

3

geographically is, in the centre of the Union, and locates the West far beyond his Pawnee or Comanche neighbors, along the distant peaks that give rise to the Oregon and Missouri.[1]

Especially in early nineteenth-century American thought and expression, the term West is not only all-inclusive but it perpetually vacillates between what might be called an absolute meaning (location) and what might be called a relative meaning (direction), the first of which is entirely arbitrary while the second is dependent upon the time, the location, and the linguistic habits of the speaker. The word must be interpreted anew for each new use, according to its presumed function in the context, and this function is not always easy to determine, for American speakers normally intend both the absolute and relative senses of the word, however vaguely, together with some sort of doctrinal connection between them, usually implicit. The American West is almost by definition indefinite and indefinable, or at least changing, pluralistic, and ambiguous in signification.

To envisage America's ambiguous civilization in the light of the West is also to become involved with both our difference from, and our continuity with, the Eastern Hemisphere. As Walt Whitman continually reminds us, the germs of American civilization were long harbored in Europe, or even farther East, and therefore American civilization is not a simple malady, although modern Europeans often act as if it were. However much they have been associated with the United States by Europeans and Americans alike, the concepts of the West and the frontier, and nearly every one of their component or sustaining elements, are un-American in origin. In "Walking," Thoreau correctly surmised that "the island of Atlantis, and the islands and gardens of the Hesperides, a sort of terrestrial paradise,

---

[1] *A New Home—Who'll Follow? or, Glimpses of Western Life* (New York, 1839), p. 11. *Letters and Notes on the . . . North American Indians* (London, 1841), I, 62. *American Quarterly Review,* XVII (1835), 178-179.

appear to have been the Great West of the ancients, enveloped in mystery and poetry."[2] (And vice versa, of course.) Thoreau might also have mentioned the poets and philosophers of Renaissance Europe, who likewise looked beyond the Atlantic for their Utopias, cities in the sun, and brave new worlds. Unlike the ancients, they not only looked but saw. And those who came to America not only saw but were seen, not only by those who remained at home but by themselves. American civilization and, within it, American literature, result from the confrontation and reciprocal interaction of Old World predispositions and New World actualities.

Oddly enough, the myth of the West was further reinforced by Christian tradition. Christ Himself (according to St. Matthew) predicted that the Son of Man would spring from the East and flash across to the West. And who can really estimate how much of the continuing emotional charge and nuisance value of such conventional counters as Old World and New World was once derived from analogies with Old and New Testaments, old and new dispensations, prophecy and redemption, order and liberty, Eden lost and (to be) regained? Our bibliolatrous forefathers were well aware of these remotely gratifying sanctions, and if their enlightened children were not, they were fortified to comparable political ends by universal history (from the European point of view), with its delightful teachings about the inevitably progressive and Westward course of empires. In 1807, one of John Adams' friends preserved a tradition that the following lines were "drilled into a Rock on the shore of Monument Bay in our old Colony of Plymouth, and were supposed to have been written and engraved there by some of the first emigrants":

> The Eastern nations sink, their glory ends
> And Empire rises where the sun descends.

[2] *The Writings of Henry David Thoreau* (Boston, 1906), v, 219. See also Arthur K. Moore, *The Frontier Mind* (Lexington, 1957), pp. 30-37.

"However this may be," said Adams of the unlikely tale, "I have heard these verses for more than sixty years. . . . There is nothing . . . more ancient in my Memory than the observation that Arts, Sciences and Empire had travelled Westward: and in Conversation it was always added, since I was a Child that their next Leap would be over the At-lantick into America."[3] Adams' reassuring memory was perhaps overstocked with such verses, for the second line of this couplet appears to have been slightly misquoted from "The Rising Glory of America," a Princeton graduation poem by Philip Freneau and Hugh Henry Brackenridge, and of no more venerable date than 1771.

Interpenetration of the Western myth with the actual events comprising the expansion of the United States from a strip of Atlantic colonies to a continental nation, produced not only American civilization but the complex phenome-non known to historians (though not very clearly under-stood) as the Westward Movement. For the period between the Revolution and the Civil War, these two phenomena—American civilization and the Westward Movement—are to all intents and purposes interchangeable. The Westward Movement is also the inclusive term within which the more limited term the West must always be approached, as the West, so defined, is the inclusive term containing the still more restricted term the frontier. Regrettably, these terms do not become clearer as they shrink in comprehensiveness—neither do they become clearer as time goes on—but on the contrary intensify their inherent ambiguities. From the outset, the American concept of the frontier reveals a shift-ing character and a striking ambivalence; and these are found in all the major American writers through Whitman, and, in a tentative and somewhat inchoate form, in the works of J. Hector St. John de Crèvecœur, writing on the verge of American political independence, and of Charles Brockden Brown, writing soon after.

In Crèvecœur's *Letters From an American Farmer*

[3] *Old Family Letters: Copied From the Originals for Alexander Biddle*, Series A (Philadelphia, 1892), pp. 143-144.

6

(1782), a naïve narrator named James conducts us from idyl ("On the Situation, Feelings, and Pleasures of an American Farmer"), to definition ("What Is An American"), and then through a tour of the colonies to disintegration and disaster ("Distresses of a Frontier Man"). "If they be not elegant," says the local minister of these letters, "they will smell of the woods, and be a little wild," for they come "from the edge of the great wilderness, three hundred miles from the sea."[4] Crèvecœur's frontier farmer catches pigeons which he fancies "breed toward the plains of Ohio, and those about Lake Michigan," and like Franklin and Jefferson imagines that "many ages will not see the shores of our great lakes replenished with inland nations, nor the unknown bounds of North America entirely peopled. Who can tell how far it extends?" Within the verge of this conception, but on the hither edge of a conception which is about to controvert and supplant it, he offers the famous definitions of Americanism: "What then is the American, this new man? . . . *He* is an American, who leaving behind him all his ancient prejudices and manners, receives new ones from the new mode of life he has embraced, the new government he obeys, and the new rank he holds. . . . Americans are the western pilgrims, who are carrying along with them that great mass of arts, sciences, vigour, and industry which began long since in the east; they will finish the great circle."

But this conventional conception of the frontier as cutting edge for happy American progress runs into difficulty when the narrator thinks of actual pioneers. Sharply dissociating himself from their barbarism, he moves to new ground and a new metaphor, the frontier as neutral territory, or middle condition (in middle-class eighteenth-century English parlance). James has subtly changed his place of residence from the edge of the wilderness to "the middle settlements," the "intermediate space" between ocean and woods, where "a sort of resurrection" transcends constitutive opposition, and the idyl of agrarianism naturally occurs. In Crèvecœur's

[4] Crèvecœur quotations are from the Dublin edition of 1782.

triple-tiered civilization, those who live near the ocean are "bold and enterprising" but dull—except Nantucketers who "go to whaling . . . as a landman undertakes to clear a piece of swamp"—while those who live in the woods are horridly fascinating, and are described at length in connection with the Westward Movement. The pioneers are "the most hideous parts of our society. They are a kind of forlorn hope, preceding by ten or twelve years the most respectable army of veterans which come after them. . . . Such is our progress, such is the march of the Europeans toward the interior parts of this continent. In all societies there are off-casts; this impure part serves as our precursors or pioneers." Entirely forgetting what the *Letters* were supposed to smell like, Crèvecœur now tells us of woods which corrupt. "Thus our bad people are those who are half cultivators and half hunters; and the worst of them are those who have degenerated altogether into the hunting state. As old ploughmen and new men of the woods, as Europeans and new made Indians, they contract the vices of both."

At the end, as colonial civilization collapses in Revolution, and Loyalist Crèvecœur's intermediate space is devastated by incursions of Loyalist Indians, the fictive farmer is once more driven to reconceive his frontier. "You know the position of our settlement. . . . To the west it is inclosed by a chain of mountains, reaching to ———; to the east, the country is as yet but thinly inhabited." The distressed frontiersman imagines himself farther West than he actually is and decides to "revert into a state approaching nearer to that of nature," even to the extent of turning half hunter. "You may therefore, by means of anticipation," he warns his correspondent, "behold me under the Wigwham." In the course of a typically French critique of the failing English empire, the new man undergoes a still further metamorphosis. Gladly will James learn from the Noble Savages—previously described as "a race doomed to recede and disappear before the superior genius of the Europeans" —and gladly teach them civilized ways, or "chearfully go even to the Missisippi" in quest of peace. Going native is the same as pioneering, and the only imaginable direction is West.

Post-Revolutionary American writing never more clearly reveals the New World's traumas than when attempting to march toward the interior; perhaps in part because until the 1820's, the only imaginable direction for American literature proved impossible to travel. In a prefatory note to *Edgar Huntly; or, Memoirs of a Sleep-Walker* (1799), Charles Brockden Brown spoke of the need to investigate "sources of amusement to the fancy and instruction to the heart, that are peculiar to ourselves," with special emphasis upon "the incidents of Indian hostility, and the perils of the Western wilderness."[5] As advertised, *Edgar Huntly* contains the famous portrait of Old Deb, a malingering Delaware woman whose tribe has removed after "encroachments." Unfortunately, the border warfare she instigates is operatic to the point of parody, the vaunted wilderness where it occurs is only a nearby suburban desert, and the connection between wilderness warfare and the somnambulistic nightmares otherwise informing the novel is obscure. Yet indirectly and much more significantly Brown shows European emigrants and American natives penetrating the unknown future and unwittingly going savage. "Was I still in the vicinity of my parental habitation, or was I thousands of miles distant?" He was perhaps the first American writer to suspect that the West might more profitably be defined as a condition of the soul than as a physiographical region. In *Ormond; or, The Secret Witness* (1799), the protagonist has mysteriously been outside "the precincts of civilized existence," and among other places "beyond the Mississippi," or "in the heart of desert America"; his ardent sister has fought in the patriot armies "on the frontiers." Their tales enlarge our heroine's little Atlantic seaboard world to include "men, in their two forms, of savage and

[5] Quotations from Brown's novels are from the modern scholarly editions of *Edgar Huntly*, by David Lee Clark (New York, 1928); *Ormond*, by Ernest Marchand (New York, 1937); and *Wieland*, by Fred Lewis Pattee (New York, 1926).

9

refined," for, on the threshold of development, America is neither, or both. The adolescent hero of *Clara Howard; or, The Enthusiasm of Love* (1801) hysterically pictures himself adventuring by canoe to the Pacific Ocean. By this time Brown's ambition had clearly outrun American history and American geographical knowledge.

An earlier novel is still more illuminating. In *Wieland; or, The Transformation. An American Tale* (1798), a European seeking conversion of the Indians emigrates to the New World, and as far inland as "the shores of the Ohio." In the next generation, fanatical piety turns to religious mania in the son, who murders wife and children, and takes his own life, as if he were an Indian in such an atrocity-novel as Mrs. Ann Eliza Bleecker's *History of Maria Kittle* (1797). Evidently the chaos created by young Wieland is in Brown's parable to be thought of as resulting from a reciprocity of forces at the meeting point between savagery and civilization. "It was worthy of savages trained to murder, and exulting in agonies. . . . Surely, said I, it is a dream." (There are many similar passages.) Consequently, Clara Wieland and her uncle decline further participation in the American dream and flee to Europe. " 'I confess I came over with an intention to reside among you,' " the uncle observes, " 'but these disasters have changed my views.' " *Wieland* is an indispensable chapter in the story of Europe mythically projecting the New World and then reacting to the actual creation; ironically, it was published in the year of the Alien and Sedition Acts, and allegedly deals with events "between the conclusion of the French and the beginning of the revolutionary war."

In the supplementary "Memoirs of Carwin, the Biloquist," Brown's "villain" is pointedly identified as a native American—from "a western district of Pennsylvania"—who has been corrupted by prolonged residence in Europe. After helping produce the Wielands' cultural regression, Carwin entertains the idea of burying himself in the wilderness—in order to write!—but finally settles for the tranquilizing pursuit of rural competence, presumably in

Crèvecœur's intermediate space. Had Brown been able to fuse these polar actions within a single unified vision, he might have earned in our literary history approximately the position occupied by Cooper, for the narrative which *Wieland* so inefficiently embodies bears many an anticipatory resemblance to the Leatherstocking Tales. But 1798 was simply too early; not even Thomas Jefferson had a sufficiently clear idea what the continent was like, or what American development might portend. Clara Wieland's self-description is inevitably the description of her creator, his contemporaries, and their yet undefined nation: "My ideas are vivid, but my language is faint; now know I what it is to entertain incommunicable sentiments. . . . What but ambiguities, abruptnesses, and dark transitions, can be expected from the historian who is, at the same time, the sufferer of these disasters?"

The West was won by American literature in the next generation, and it was not an easy victory. As journalistic publicists were always saying: "The American mind will be brought to maturity along the chain of the great lakes, the banks of the Mississippi, the Missouri, and their tributaries in the far northwest. There, on the rolling plains, will be formed a republic of letters which, not governed like that on our seaboard, by the great literary powers of Europe, shall be free, indeed." But even a promotional tract had to concede that in the actual West "the very atmosphere of society is averse to mental culture, and all refinement is so systematically as well as practically decried, as to have fallen into absolute discredit."[6] The apparent paradox is easily explained: a kind of nihilistic and anarchic cultural regression was the immediate local effect of the continually advancing frontier line, and, by the very nature of the process, it was superficial and temporary. Americanization was a delayed reaction in the rear, and a vastly different affair. It probably began in the minds of writers desperately

[6] J. Milton Mackie, "Forty Days in a Western Hotel," *Putnam's*, IV (1854), 630; William Kirkland, "The West, the Paradise of the Poor," *Democratic Review*, XV (1844), 188.

trying to make some kind of provisional sense of their rapidly evolving civilization. From variously brilliant responses to the challenge of the new West, which in at least the geographical sense was plainly to become the greater part of a new America, they developed a genuinely American literature. As Margaret Fuller said in a volume of Western travels: "I trust by reverent faith to woo the mighty meaning of the scene, perhaps to foresee the law by which a new order, a new poetry, is to be evoked from this chaos."[7] The new order of literature evoked from the chaos is a matter of record, and we have no choice but to assume that it tells us the fundamental truth about the Westward Movement. (If it does not, we shall never know it.) Neither have we cause for complaint, for the truth told by American literature is considerably more fascinating, if somewhat less comforting, than the tales of the forest found in our history books.

Of course, it is equally true that without the real and imagined experiences of actual pioneering to serve as informing principle and guiding light, nineteenth-century American literature as we know it would never have come into being. Insofar as it resulted from a series of aesthetic transformations, through which intrinsically meaningless pioneer experiences were elevated to the status of ideas and forms, American literature may in its origins fairly be called an effect of the frontier; re-entering society, it became a continuing cause (a far more important cause than the actual frontier) toward the creation of the American character, nationalism, democracy, or whatever other values (a few of them more elevating than these) are actually found in the literature. Given the American situation, it was perhaps to have been expected that some people would resent the intrusions of a higher truth into literature, that they would attack the truth from the cover of anti-intellectual "realism," and that the attacks would come from the most anti-intellectual of the American sections. Almost

[7] *Summer on the Lakes* (1844), in *The Writings of Margaret Fuller*, ed. Mason Wade (New York, 1941), p. 22.

from the beginning, second-rate writers like Daniel Drake, residing in what they were pleased to consider the real West, fulminated against Cooper, for example, arguing that "in delineating the West, no power of genius, can supply the want of opportunities for personal observation on our natural and social aspects. No western man can read those works with interest."[8] The simple truth is that the American West was neither more nor less interesting than any other place, except in mythology or in the swollen egos of Westerners, until by interpretation the great American writers—all of whom happened to be Eastern—made it seem so. This they did by conceiving its physical aspects (forests, rivers, lakes, clearings, settlements, prairies, plains, deserts) and its social aspects (isolation, simplicity, improvisation, criticism, chaos, restlessness, paradox, irony) as expressive emblems for the invention and development of a new national civilization, and not as things in themselves.

Most Americans preferred an easier progress, and rather mindlessly found it in insignificant puns about different orders of movement. "The expansive future is our arena, and for our history. We are entering on its untrodden space. . . . We are the nation of human progress, and who will, what can, set limits to our onward march? . . . The far-reaching, the boundless future will be the era of American greatness. In its magnificent domain of space and time, the nation of many nations is destined to manifest to mankind the excellence of divine principles."[9] Those exhilarating

[8] *Discourse on the History, Character, and Prospects of the West* (1834), ed. Perry Miller (Gainesville, Fla., 1955), p. 55. "Those works" were Cooper's *Prairie* and Paulding's *Westward Ho!*. Paulding wrote Drake glorifying the West, and repenting his trespasses. *The Letters of James Kirke Paulding*, ed. Ralph M. Aderman (Madison, 1962), pp. 158-159. Of course, this was a game that more than two could play. New England's James Freeman Clarke attacked James Hall—a professional Westerner like Drake—for ignorance of Western character and lack of "western spirit." *North American Review*, XLIII (1836), 2.

[9] "The Great Nation of Futurity," *Democratic Review*, VI (1839), 427. As Caroline Kirkland said in *Forest Life* (New York, 1842):

analogous progressions from East to West and from present to future were surcharged with teleological nationalism cartographically advancing from right to left, Old World to New, reality to beatitude. Yet paradoxically the American West—as chaos, matrix, or embryo—was also "earlier," and therefore the past. By moving his point of observation Eastward, the nationalistic writer commanded a double vision, and conveniently close to home. Under the guise of the past he foretold the future, as under the pretense of describing the Revolutionary colonies he secretly visited the West. Of "The Spy. A Tale of the Revolution," whose setting was Maryland, and which was included in *Tales of the Border*, James Hall explained:

> Although the title which we have chosen for this volume, would seem to confine us, in the selection of our scenes, to an imaginary line which forms the boundary of our settled population, yet, in fact, the limit which it imposes refers rather to time than place, for ours is a moving frontier, which is continually upon the advance. What is now the *border*, has but recently assumed that character, and if we trace back the history of our country to its earliest period, in search of the stirring scenes attendant upon a state of war, we shall find ourselves rapidly travelling towards the shores of the Atlantic. There has been a point in the history of every state in the Union, when a portion of its territory was a wilderness. . . . It is this circumstance which renders the whole of our broad empire so rich in materials for the novelist.[10]

The same time-space equations ambiguously supported American appropriation of Condorcet's social-stages-of-history theory, as posthumously propounded in *Outlines of an Historical View of the Progress of the Human Mind*

"The future—the bright, far-ahead, vague Western future—is to make up for all" (1, 28).
[10] (Philadelphia, 1835), pp. 129-130.

(1795). That optimistic program for egalitarian democracy
supplied a philosophic rationale for expansion of civilization
in the New World—if necessary through obliteration of
"those savage nations still occupying there immense tracts
of country"—and, best of all, it placed the Anglo-Americans, with the French, in the vanguard of progress.[11] Unfortunately, the topography and climate of America practically
prescribed certain physiographical concentrations of economic activity: commerce on the East Coast, cattle-raising
far to the West of the nation's granaries. Condorcet considered the pastoral condition inevitably more primitive than
agriculture, and agriculture more primitive than commerce.
In this view, Westward progress meant cultural regress. It
is not surprising, then, that at the heart of the American
language, radically divergent conceptions of the national
destiny were impounded in conflicting notions of "back"
("backwoodsman") and "front" (frontiersman"), which
reflected the antithetical regressive and progressive readings
of the Westward Movement and, ultimately, the conflicting
European-community vs. isolationist interpretations of
American history. The frontier was the meeting point between these readings. From their interpenetration on the
neutral ground of national becoming, early nineteenth-
century writers zealously looked for a new culture, geneti-
cally European but better, and certainly not a pallid
compromise between our old home and a disheartening
environment.[12] After all, "front" implied not only "back,"

[11] (Baltimore, 1802), pp. 210, 212.

[12] After 1814, American writers had available for imitation and
development Scott's Romantic figuration of the Highlands-Lowlands
border:

> He [Rob Roy] owed his fame in a great measure to his residing
> on the very verge of the Highlands, and playing such pranks in
> the beginning of the 18th century, as are usually ascribed to
> Robin Hood in the middle ages,—and that within forty miles of
> Glasgow, a great commercial city, the seat of a learned univer-
> sity. Thus a character like his, blending the wild virtues, the
> subtle policy, and unrestrained licence of an American Indian,
> was flourishing in Scotland during the Augustan age of Queen
> Anne and George I. Addison, it is probable, or Pope, would

but also a duality of direction, a "fronting both ways," or even an oppositional situation surreptitiously sexual and procreative; as Margaret Fuller incomparably announced: "Male and female represent the two sides of the great radical dualism."[13] Naturally the hopes and fears of the American writer were drawn to this provocative and realistic symbol of the cultural antagonisms which beset him. Somewhere out West, as analogously on the frontier within his own soul, a struggle was being enacted between the failing forms of the paternal civilizations and the threat of absolute formlessness. Through a sort of secular miracle, new forms and values might yet emerge from the deathlock, expressive of the new time and place, and indeed constituting them. And at this point, the anticipated miracle miraculously occurred—not literally on the frontier or magically in the forest, but in the minds and on the tongues of men.

Frederick Jackson Turner carefully called attention to the way that "in American thought and speech the term 'frontier' has come to mean the edge of settlement, rather than, as in Europe, the political boundary," and he also insisted that "the American frontier is sharply distinguished from the European frontier—a fortified boundary line running through dense populations."[14] It is not easy to under-

---

> have been considerably surprised if they had known that there existed in the same island with them a personage of Rob Roy's peculiar habits and profession. It is this strong contrast betwixt the civilized and cultivated mode of life on the one side of the Highland line, and the wild and lawless adventures which were habitually undertaken and achieved by one who dwelt on the opposite side of that ideal boundary, which creates the interest attached to his name.

"Introduction" to *Rob Roy*, in *Waverley Novels* (Edinburgh, 1829), VII, viii. Scott frequently envisaged Highlanders as Indians, and repeatedly called their dwellings "wigwams."

[13] *Writings*, p. 176.

[14] *The Frontier in American History* (New York, 1920), pp. 3, 41. See also Fulmer Mood, "Notes on the History of the Word *Frontier*," *Agricultural History*, XXII (1948), 78-83. Earlier American writers were occasionally sensitive to the possibilities of confusion, and avoided the "frontier" except in its Western meaning. Writing about the Six Nations' boundaries in *League of the . . . Iroquois* (Rochester,

stand how these two significations could have been kept
apart in the early days, and of course they were not. Always
in relationship with each other, the European and Western
meanings of the word together formed a trope, and should
properly be called "the frontier metaphor."[15] Consequently,
what the American frontier means is its genesis: a new situation, vaguely sensed, and requiring designation, was denoted
by an old word with an adaptable meaning. The mingling
of meanings helps explain why the American frontier was
sometimes a line and sometimes a space, as it also helps
explain why it was a militantly nationalistic concept
unrelated to any other nation. Either way, the frontier was
a figure of speech, gradually but never entirely sloughing
European implications as it assumed new functions in a new
context, and thus incidentally a splendid illustration of
the Americanizing process Turner used it to describe. The
frontier was the imaginary line between American civilization and nature, or the uncreated future, and everything
that came to depend upon that line was ironically reversible.

Not merely in this primary sense was the frontier metaphor the leading formal principle of early American literature. A further theshold was crossed when American writers
learned to double their basic metaphor, especially the
frontier-as-space, by involving it with social, psychological,
philosophical, or other situations analogously reconciling
opposites through interpenetration and transcendence. Doubling was easiest in the case of phrases like "neutral ground"
and "debatable land," which originated in the actual conditions of early American history, and were formally and
intentionally the same as Crèvecoeur's "intermediate space."
Gradually they came to signify the Western frontier and

1851), Lewis Henry Morgan nervously side-stepped it for several
pages, and then in desperation succumbed to "the limital line" (pp.
41-46).

[15] "It is a commonplace that in metaphor a term does not abandon
one signification for another but rather stands related to two significations at once." Walter J. Ong, "Metaphor and the Twinned
Vision," *Sewanee Review*, LXIII (1955), 194.

proliferated into a whole series of similar terms. Then by a simple extension of meaning comparable to the extension through which the old word frontier was first applied to conditions in the new West, Cooper could say that in frontier communities gentle and common folk "meet, as it might be, on a sort of neutral ground," and Orestes Brownson could discuss the fluid relations between prose and poetry in terms of the Western border: "No man can define the exact boundary line between them; and it is only when at a considerable distance from the line, that we can tell whether we are in the territory of the one or of the other. On each side of the line, there is and always must be a disputed territory."[16]

As Bronson Alcott revealingly wrote of Emerson's early works, and the criticisms of them: "These I deem first fruits of a new literature. . . . Nature and the Soul are conjoined. The images are American. The portrait is set in a frame of western oak."[17] On the philosophical side, the Western

---

[16] *Home as Found* (Philadelphia, 1838), I, 180, and *The Works of Orestes A. Brownson*, ed. Henry F. Brownson (Detroit, 1882-1907), I, 98. For the actual historical conditions, see "Debatable Land" and " 'Neutral Ground' " in *Dictionary of American History*, ed. James Truslow Adams and R. V. Coleman (New York, 1940), II, 116, and IV, 87; *Prose Writings of William Cullen Bryant*, ed. Parke Godwin (New York, 1901), I, 194; John A. McClung, *Sketches of Western Adventure* (Maysville, Ky., 1832), pp. 49-50. The overwhelming condition was of course the no-man's-land between the advancing Americans and their retreating victims. One writer defined the frontier as "the extreme verge of white population," and another as "that mutual antipathy which has drawn a broad line of separation between the white and red races." "The Last of the Boatmen," *The Western Souvenir*, ed. James Hall (Cincinnati, 1828), p. 118; James Hall, preface to *Tales of the Border*, p. 11. "Neutral ground" and "Debatable Land" are also found in Scott (*Waverley Novels*, I, 130; VII, 222; XX, 26); and "neutral ground" (italicized) in Coleridge (*Biographia Literaria*, ed. J. Shawcross, Oxford, 1907, II, 61).

[17] *The Journals of Bronson Alcott*, ed. Odell Shepard (Boston, 1938), p. 112. For a comparable geographical-metaphysical phenomenon in German thought ("das Volk der Mitte"), see Herman Weigand, *Thomas Mann's Novel, Der Zauberberg* (New York, 1933), esp. ch. 6, "What is German?" and René Wellek, *A History of Modern Criticism: 1750-1950* (New Haven, 1955-), II, 292.

frontier became more and more entangled with Transcendental dialectic imported from Germany by way of British oversimplifications and spatially displayed on the expansive fields of American geographical and spiritual progress. Dialectic was the all-but-universal mode of reconciling opposites, and opposites were rife. In addition to the intrinsic and almost unavoidable opposites (life-death, known-unknown, good-evil), early nineteenth-century thinkers were infatuated with such pairs as civilization-nature (especially popular in the United States), mind-matter, reason-understanding, reason-imagination, imagination-fancy, organism-mechanism, self-society, subject-object, poet-nature, fiction-fact, poetry-prose, heart-head, synthesis-analysis—real or imaginary dichotomies spotting the gray debris of Cartesian confusion and Kantian clarification. For Romantic thought, these pairs rested on a special feeling for duality-in-unity, or the reverse, most vigorously articulated by Teufelsdrökh-Carlyle, whose American vogue in the 1830's amounted to a craze; Thoreau and Whitman judged him essentially Western, as, in a way, he was.[18] "Consider them [two Goethe characters] as the two disjointed Halves of the singular Dualistic Being of ours," he would go on and on, while the Americans gaped, "a Being,

---

Aristotle, as usual, was in the field first: "Those who live in a cold climate and in Europe are full of spirit, but wanting in intelligence and skill. . . . Whereas the natives of Asia are intelligent and inventive, but they are wanting in spirit. . . . But the Hellenic race, which is situated between them, is likewise intermediate in character, being high-spirited and also intelligent." *Politics*, 1327b, 23-30.

[18] *Writings of Thoreau*, IV, 320; *Prose Works 1892*, ed. Floyd Stovall (New York, 1963), I, 254-255. Carlyle wrote Emerson in 1834: "It occasionally rises like a mad prophetic dream in me, that I might end in the Western Woods!"; in 1837: "Whenever I think of myself in America, it is as in the Backwoods, with a rifle in my hand, God's sky over my head"; to which Emerson: "Your genius tendeth to the New, to the West. Come and live with me a year"; and then Carlyle again: "Natty Leatherstocking's lodge in the Western Wood, I think, were welcomer still [welcomer than Rome]." *The Correspondence of Thomas Carlyle and Ralph Waldo Emerson*, ed. Charles Eliot Norton (London, 1883), I, 25, 116, 162, 168.

I must say, the most utterly Dualistic; fashioned, from the very heart of it, out of Positive and Negative . . . everywhere out of *two* mortally opposed things, which yet must be united in vital love, if there is to be any *Life*;—a Being, I repeat, Dualistic beyond expressing."[19] Around 1840 Thoreau reported that a sagacious lecturer—it would have been Emerson or Alcott—was effectively making his point by holding up "one finger to express individuality, and two for dualism."[20]

This central intellectual structure of the age was quite literally a meta-physics. As Emerson retrospectively noted: "The magnet was thrown into Europe, and all philosophy has taken a direction from it."[21] Perhaps the first, and certainly the most influential philosopher who was thought to have taken direction was Kant. His *Versuch, den Begriff der negativen Grössen in die Weltweisheit einzuführen* (1763) contained a tantalizing distinction between "real" and "logical" opposition, and was widely misinterpreted as arguing that universal laws might be derived from electromagnetic polarity. In *Biographia Literaria* (1817), Coleridge propped his theory of imagination with a preliminary discussion of Kant's treatise, whence he transcendentally extracted from the "effective pioneer" a "master-thought," the "inter-penetration of the counteracting powers [any powers], partaking of both." It was an easy step to the famous definition of "the poet, described in *ideal* perfec-

[19] *The Works of Thomas Carlyle* (New York, 1898-1901), XXVII, 452. His early essays were spiced with such phrases as "this strange dualistic Life of ours" (XXVIII, 173), and "the dualisms of man's wholly dualistic nature" (236).

[20] *Consciousness in Concord; The Text of Thoreau's Hitherto "Lost Journal," (1840-1841)*, ed. Perry Miller (Boston, 1958), p. 133.

[21] *Journals of Ralph Waldo Emerson*, ed. Edward Waldo Emerson and Waldo Emerson Forbes (Boston, 1909-1914), VIII, 39. See also *Carlyle-Emerson Correspondence*, II, 28-29; James E. Cabot, *A Memoir of Ralph Waldo Emerson* (Boston, 1887), II, 786; *Journals of Alcott*, p. 171, and "Orphic Sayings—XXXI, Calculus," *The Dial*, I (1840), 93; W. W. Story, "Sympathy and Antipathy," *The Boston Miscellany of Literature*, II (1842), 79.

tion," and especially his unifying esemplastic power revealing itself "in the balance or reconciliation of opposite or discordant qualities." In *The Friend* (1818), Coleridge elicited from "the phænomena of electricity the operation of a law which reigns through all nature, the law of POLARITY, or the manifestation of one power by opposite forces." And his retrospect was the same as Emerson's: the "new light" of the day was "the discovery of electricity," and "the new path, thus brilliantly opened, became the common road to all departments of knowledge."[22]

Unfortunately, the new light illuminated an ancient roadblock. "A believer in Unity, a seer of Unity," Emerson typically confessed, "I yet behold two." Dualism haunted this representative American mind. "All the universe over, there is but one thing, this old Two-Face . . . of which any proposition may be affirmed or denied." He summed up his problem in a *Journal* entry ambivalently headed "*The two Statements, or Bipolarity.*" Emerson was finally unable to share some people's enthusiastic interpretations of Kant as the author of discontinuity: "If, as Hedge thinks . . . the world is not a dualism [!], is not a bipolar unity, but is *two*, is Me and It, then is there the alien, the unknown, and all we have believed and chanted out of our deep instinctive hope is a pretty dream."[23] The national literature being at stake, Emerson rejected the "Infernal Twoness" in favor of the "Supernal Oneness" (Poe's terms), namely a polar, paradoxical, ironic, ambiguous monism which remains to this day the signature of American thought and expression. Unity was the spirit of the age, or as Emerson said in a variety of contexts: " 'T is indifferent whether you say,

[22] *Biographia Literaria*, I, 196, 198; II, 12. (At I, 103-104, Coleridge sees Kant, Schelling, and himself as all followers of Giordano Bruno, inaugurator of "polar logic and dynamic philosophy.") *The Friend* (London, 1818), III, 188; *Hints Towards the Formation of a More Comprehensive Theory of Life*, ed. Seth B. Watson (Philadelphia, 1848; but written before 1834), pp. 31-32; see also pp. 50-52.

[23] *Journals*, IV, 248; *The Complete Works of Ralph Waldo Emerson*, ed. Edward Waldo Emerson (Boston, 1903-1904), III, 245; *Journals*, VIII, 86-87; V, 206.

all is matter, or, all is spirit; and 't is plain there is a tendency in the times to an identity-philosophy,"[24] a magnificent instance of American fascination with form at the expense of content.

For reasons comprehending American history from the Declaration of Independence through the Civil War, the passion for unity was more frenetic in the United States than elsewhere. In 1836, Brownson instructed his compatriots in *New Views of Christianity, Society, and the Church*, where Our Lord was Americanized along the mythical-dialectic border. "We are to reconcile spirit and matter," he declared. "Nothing else remains for us to do. Stand still we cannot. . . . Progress is our law and our first step is Union." Theological in application but philosophical and political in origin, Brownson's argument was shaped by a constitutive opposition comprising the whole experience of mankind: "Spiritualism" (Catholicism, "the Eastern World") vs. "Materialism" (Protestantism, "the Western World"). Having supplied His own dilemma, God triumphantly produced the ecumenical American answer: "This antithesis generates perpetual and universal war. It is necessary then to remove it and harmonize, or unite the two terms. Now, if we conceive Jesus as standing between spirit and matter, the representative of both— God-Man—the point where both meet and lose their antithesis . . . we shall have his secret thought and the true idea of Christianity."[25] By perfect analogy and reciprocal causation, the standpoint between spirit and matter was precisely the point where civilization and nature met and

[24] *Journals*, VIII, 255. Logically, Emerson should have admired Poe's reduction of the universe to matter in *Eureka*, though it is unlikely that he did.
[25] *Works*, IV, 8, 32. So Theodore Parker split the world of mind into "The Rationalistic View, or Naturalism," and "The Anti-Rationalistic View, or Supernaturalism," let them interpenetrate, and emerged where he started, with "The Natural-Religious View, or Spiritualism" (i.e., Transcendentalism). *A Discourse of Matters Pertaining to Religion* (1842), ed. Thomas Wentworth Higginson (Boston, 1907), pp. 174-207.

American life was perpetually reborn. On the frontier, Christ turned into Leatherstocking, Crèvecœur's new man suffered still another forest-change (Turner's phrase), and the Second Coming was subsumed in the Westward Movement. Under auspices so benign, even the minor writer could chant his deep instinctive hopes. Daniel Boone, according to William Gilmore Simms, "was not merely a hunter. He was on a mission. The spiritual sense was strong in him. He felt the union between his inner and the nature of the visible world, and yearned for their intimate communion."[26]

In "The Young American" (1844), Emerson wrote: "Luckily for us, now that steam has narrowed the Atlantic to a strait, the nervous, rocky West is intruding a new and continental element into the national mind, and we shall yet have an American genius." And then, somehow, Emerson's gaze wandered, and when he looked again, his visionary powers were gone. "It is to be remembered that the flowering time is the end," he said in an 1853 lecture: "we ought to be thankful that no hero or poet hastens to be born." After a trip to St. Louis in the same year he wrote Carlyle: "Room for us all, since it has not ended, nor given sign of ending, in bard or hero."[27] In fact, the flowering time was almost over, and the heroic poets hastening to their literal or figurative graves. Just before his death Cooper wrote in a new introduction to *The Prairie*: "Since the original publication of this book [1827] . . . the boundaries of the republic have been carried to the Pacific." Already the end was in sight, for those who had eyes to see. "In 1820, Missouri was the 'far West,' and Independence the boundary of civilization. Now, in 1854, there is no 'far West.' It has been crowded overboard into the Pacific Ocean. . . . Pioneer life and pioneer progress must

---

[26] *Views and Reviews in American Literature, History and Fiction*, First Series (1846), ed. C. Hugh Holman (Cambridge, 1962), pp. 156-157.
[27] *Works*, I, 369-370; Cabot, *Memoir of Emerson*, II, 755; *Carlyle-Emerson Correspondence*, II, 218.

soon pass away for ever, to be remembered only in story."[28]

But the West Coast never was a frontier in the primary metaphorical sense of neutral territory between advancing civilization and nature lying beyond; and when California was admitted to the Union in 1850, with Oregon following in 1859, all the other straggling frontiers to the East were by the same action effectually blocked off. No longer was the West a field of boundless opportunity, but a mopping-up operation. During the 1850's and 1860's the figurative frontier and the teleological West were drained of expressive value, and disappeared from literary currency. The West exerted serious imaginative impact in the United States only so long as it remained a living idea, which was only so long as it survived in real potentiality; the winning of the actual West brought the Westward Movement of American writing to a natural and inevitable end a few years after the closing of the frontier.

Thus, by the time Mark Twain arrived on the scene, the frontier and the West were gone, though their memory left minor, vestigial traces on almost everything he wrote. He exploded the final trace in *A Connecticut Yankee in King Arthur's Court*, where the Wild West show comes to a rude end with the Boss blowing up his own "civilization-factories" on a "kind of neutral ground."[29] This symbolic explosion of the frontier metaphor may perhaps be taken for Mark Twain's signing off as the Buffalo Bill of American literature, a role evidently foisted upon him by the long-held expectation of a Great American Writer emanating from the Great West, and more or less willingly played at in such early books as *Roughing It* (1872) and *The Gilded Age* (1873). After the Civil War, practically no Americans either knew or cared what they meant by the West, though apparently Mark Twain suspected, for the main point of his role as literary Westerner increasingly came to be its ludicrously anachronistic irrelevance—hence

[28] Edward P. Mitchell ("Ralph Roanoke"), "Rambles in the Far West," *The Knickerbocker Gallery* (New York, 1855), p. 147.
[29] (New York, 1889), pp. 543, 554.

such standing jokes as the Arkansas legislature, territorial governments, the backwoods, the Choctaw language, Sherman chasing Indians, or, for that matter, Buffalo Bill—or its sentimental value as an image of youth. Inevitably his deepest desires found expression through a small boy's dwindling dream, nourished by a mythical river running through land settled on both banks and concluding: "And so there ain't nothing more to write about, and I am rotten glad of it. . . . But I reckon I got to light out for the Territory ["for howling adventures amongst the Injuns"] ahead of the rest, because Aunt Sally she's going to adopt me and sivilize me, and I can't stand it. I been there before."[30] And there he would stay, the "Territory" of 1885 not being worth lighting out for, as can be verified in any historical atlas; and as appears in the opening of *Tom Sawyer Abroad* (1894), Huck Finn on second thought decided not to try for it. The geographical axis of *The Adventures of Huckleberry Finn* ("SCENE: THE MISSISSIPPI VALLEY. TIME: FORTY TO FIFTY YEARS AGO.") is conspicuously North-South, and the only realistic direction of escape revealingly lies to the East, the same line of escape taken by the author. Neither was Mark Twain born "on the frontier," as so often alleged, for the frontier, however defined, was in 1835 far West of Florida, Missouri, if, indeed, it was anywhere at all, except as an object of thought or figure of speech.

[30] (New York, 1885), pp. 365, 366.

25

The Leatherstocking Tales of
James Fenimore Cooper

"IT WAS COMPLETELY AN AMERICAN SCENE," wrote James
Fenimore Cooper in *Notions of the Americans*, "embracing
all that admixture of civilization, and of the forest, of the
works of man, and of the reign of nature, that one can so
easily imagine to belong to this country."[1] For all the cam-
paigns and nostrums urged on behalf of a native American
literature, an indigenous expression could hardly have
originated elsewhere. Perhaps it began so easily and
naturally with Cooper—son of an entrepreneurial land-
settler who in 1810 had written a do-it-yourself book called
A Guide in the Wilderness—because he grew up with the
admixture. In 1810, James was just coming of age. Years
earlier, his older sister had said of him and his brothers,
"they are very wild and show plainly they have been bred
in the Woods," and, in the same breath, "they go to school
and are learning Latin."[2] Almost from the beginning, it
might seem, Cooper was destined to be a highly civilized
writer whose personal experience, extended by his father's,
was the national experience of the easily imagined frontier.

The admixture was also easy to imagine because Cooper
so closely identified his role as a writer with the West.

---

[1] (Philadelphia, 1828), I, 248. Cf. the setting of *The Bravo* (Philadelphia, 1831): "On the very confines of that line which separates
western from eastern Europe, and in constant communication with
the latter, Venice possessed a greater admixture of character and
costume, than any other of the numerous ports of that region" (I,
10).
[2] Quoted in James Fenimore Cooper (grandson), *The Legends and
Traditions of a Northern County* (New York, 1921), p. 171.

Whether as novelist or as social critic, his attitude toward American civilization was aggressively creative. In a sense both broad and deep, he was a pioneer himself, as his young competitor Poe was at such pains to deny, and in *Wyandotté; or, The Hutted Knoll* (1843) indirectly described himself in terms of America's most significant activity: "There is a pleasure in diving into a virgin forest and commencing the labours of civilization, that has no exact parallel in any other human occupation. That of building, or of laying out grounds, has certainly some resemblance to it, but it is a resemblance so faint and distant as scarcely to liken the enjoyment each produces. The former [diving into a virgin forest] approaches nearer to the feeling of creating, and is far more pregnant with anticipations and hopes, though its first effects are seldom agreeable, and are sometimes nearly hideous."[3] Cooper's heart was in his writing, and especially in the protracted and fumbling pioneer epic which he rightly believed his best claim upon the attention of the future. Despite his social conservatism, which he often misunderstood and misrepresented, he was a novelist of social transitions. Again and again he returned to the American Revolution, and even in European novels like *The Heidenmauer; or, The Benedictines* (1832), he carried the American viewpoint abroad: "Our object in this tale is, to represent society, under its ordinary faces, in the act of passing from the influence of one set of governing principles to that of another." His best subject was the Western frontier, where American society might be conceived as passing from one set of principles to another in two directions at once.

Cooper's power lay in his assurance that one direction was morally right and the other practically inevitable. His frontier novels were attempts to define, to nourish, and to preserve the emerging idea of a morally and aesthetically estimable America, as first embodied in his own personality, and then in the personalities of Leatherstocking and his

[3] Cooper's novels are quoted from the first editions. I have silently corrected a few obvious misprints.

friends the Noble Savages. Despite a sentimental and literalistic acclaim of these heroic patterns, Cooper's audience was not to be swerved from its course, and he did not live long enough, or perhaps did not read widely enough, ever to realize with what grandeur his intimations were being developed by his successors. From Paris in 1831 he wrote: "Now my longing is for a Wilderness—Cooperstown is far too populous and artificial for me and it is my intention to plunge somewhere into the forest, for six months in the year, at my return. I will not quit my own state"—he did not need to do that—"but I shall seek some unsettled part." Of course, as it turned out—as it always turned out—the plunging was imaginative rather than literal. A little later he was writing wistfully: "There ⟨are⟩ have been already four generations of Coopers at Cooperstown, counting those who are gone! The other day the whole country was a wilderness."[4] The habitual need for recessive withdrawal, of which his prolonged sojourn in Europe was only the most conspicuous example, sprang from Cooper's fundamental alienation from his country, an alienation which was more significantly psychic and ethical than sociological, and which was quite as authentic as the need for creativity sustaining his authority as the first major American writer. Taken together, these motives help explain his ambiguous attitude toward himself, his art, the Westward Movement, and American civilization, as they also help explain why he and the new nation were, in virtues and in defects, to all intents and purposes one.

In 1852, Francis Parkman, who had recently published *The California and Oregon Trail* (1849), and was soon to embark on a many-volume history of the colonial American

---

[4] *The Letters and Journals of James Fenimore Cooper*, ed. James F. Beard (Cambridge, 1960-), II, 89, 109; angle brackets indicate canceled word. Back in America, Cooper wrote: "In the last event, I can return to Europe, and continue to write, for in that quarter of the world I am at least treated with common decency. It is not improbable that such will be the *dénouement.*" *Correspondence of James Fenimore-Cooper*, ed. James Fenimore Cooper (grandson) (New Haven, 1922), I, 334.

forest, reviewed Cooper's collected novels. "Of all American writers," he declared, "Cooper is the most original, the
most thoroughly national." Leatherstocking he especially
praised. "Had Cooper achieved nothing else, this alone
must have insured him a wide and merited renown. There
is something admirably felicitous in the conception of this
hybrid offspring of civilization and barbarism, in whom
uprightness, kindliness, innate philosophy, and the truest
moral perceptions are joined with the wandering instincts
and hatred of restraint which stamp the Indian." In fact,
Parkman nearly always took a dim view of Indians, and a
dimmer view of those who spoke on their behalf. "Cooper
is responsible for the fathering of those aboriginal heroes,
lovers, and sages, who have long formed a petty nuisance
in our literature." Uncas, for example, "does not at all
resemble a genuine Indian. Magua, the villain of the story,
is a less untruthful portrait." And so Parkman went about
reducing Cooper's magnanimous ambiguities to patriotic
platitudes. "Civilization has a destroying as well as a
creating power. It is exterminating the buffalo and the
Indian, over whose fate too many lamentations, real or
affected, have been sounded for us to renew them here. It
must, moreover, eventually sweep from before it a class of
men, its own precursors and pioneers, so remarkable both
in their virtues and their faults, that few will see their
extinction without regret. Of these men Leatherstocking
is the representative. . . . His life conveys in some sort an
epitome of American history."[5] So it does, but in no such
sort as Parkman implies. In Cooper's view, which is in
nearly every respect antithetical to Parkman's, civilization
is destructive only because men are, and extermination of
buffalo and Indian is a moral issue rather than a convenient
necessity. It may be true that Leatherstocking must disappear with the conditions which created him, though we
can hardly say that a man who dies at ninety, the epitome
of his people's history, was swept away; but his virtues—
incomparably more important than the fact that he once

[5] *North American Review*, LXXIV (1852), 147, 150, 151, 155.

hunted and trapped for a living—remain, to be admired and applied to new conditions, as writing a novel is like plunging into a virgin forest. In 1838, Orestes Brownson proposed to the nation an ideal of society clearly drawn from the figurative frontier of the Leatherstocking Tales, but by no means restricted to their literal conditions: "all the individual freedom of the savage state with all the order and social harmony of the highest degree of civilization."[6]

Of the five Leatherstocking Tales, three were composed in the 1820's and two in the early 1840's. The development of the series is usually described as a movement from the realistic to the Romantic; from personal experience to myth (though the last novel reverts to the Cooperstown region of the first); from the hard facts of old age to the pleasing possibilities of youth. Each of these descriptions is true, but it is more comprehensively true that Cooper increasingly generalized his materials, and in doing so advanced from a fairly conventional American account of the Westward Movement to a far more imaginative, complex, and critical view. The first novel opens with an optimistic account of pioneering: "The whole district is hourly exhibiting how much can be done, in even a rugged country, and with a severe climate, under the dominion of mild laws, and where every man feels a direct interest in the prosperity of a commonwealth, of which he knows himself to form a distinct and independent part. . . . Only forty years have passed since this whole territory was a wilderness." The last one ends: "We live in a world of transgressions and selfishness, and no pictures that represent us otherwise can be true; though, happily for human nature, gleamings of that pure Spirit in whose likeness man has been fashioned, are to be seen relieving its deformities, and mitigating, if not excusing, its crimes." As Leatherstocking remarks in the same book: " 'What a thing is power! . . . and what a thing it is, to have it, and not to know how to use it!' " After a trip to Michigan in 1847, Cooper moralized again

[6] *The Works of Orestes A. Brownson*, ed. Henry F. Brownson (Detroit, 1882-1907), xv, 60.

in the preface to *The Oak Openings; or, The Bee-Hunter* (1848): "There is nothing imaginary in the fertility of the west. . . . Time may lessen that wonderful fertility, and bring the whole country more on a level; but there it now is, a glorious gift from God, which it is devoutly to be wished may be accepted with due gratitude, and with a constant recollection of His unwavering rules of right and wrong, by those who have been selected to enjoy it." Moral accountability was the gist of Cooper's letter to his countrymen.

The Pioneers; or, The Sources of the Susquehanna (1823), in which Cooper drew most heavily on memories of his Cooperstown boyhood, stands somewhat apart from the other Leatherstocking Tales. It is not an adventure story, but (as Bryant observed) a pastoral,[7] closer to sketch than to romance, and more expository than narrative. Except toward the end, there is little plot, but rather a series of loosely-connected episodes illustrating the rough charms of life in a frontier community. There is little of the open violence which dominates the later Tales, but instead an almost continuous air of comedy. In *The Pioneers*, Cooper concentrates on the amity and near-amity existing among men joined in a struggle with nature. Despite their fallings out, Leatherstocking and the aristocratic Judge Temple are more often than not on the same side—especially with respect to the conservation of natural resources—and it is difficult to tell which of them is meant by the title. Very likely it refers to both.

Within the relatively simple and apparently innocuous overview of happy pioneering, Cooper is quietly subversive. At the end, the villainous scamp Hiram Doolittle pulls up stakes and departs for the farther West, presumably as one of "that band of Pioneers, who are opening the way for

[7] "I read it with a delighted astonishment. Here, said I to myself, is the poet of rural life in this country—our Hesiod, our Theocritus, except that he writes without the restraint of numbers, and is a greater poet than they." "Discourse on the Life and Genius of Cooper," *Memorial of James Fenimore Cooper* (New York, 1852), p. 47.

the march of our nation across the continent." That phrase, which magniloquently and sentimentally concludes the novel, ostensibly refers to Leatherstocking, who has been driven from his home of forty years by a civilization in which Doolittles thrive, and who has no intention whatever of opening the way for the march of any such people. Throughout *The Pioneers* the Americans are said to have "dispossessed" the Indians, and indeed the novel slyly hints that the Fall of Man and private land ownership are practically coterminous, at least in this country; if so, then further progress will entail further costs. (" 'I never know'd preaching come into a settlement, but it made game scarce, and raised the price of gun-powder.' ") Attempting to defend Judge Temple from the charge of rapacity, the Reverend Mr. Grant blunders into a broader indictment: " 'The wrongs which have been done to the natives are shared by Judge Temple, only, in common with a whole people.' " Temple's daughter Elizabeth enthusiastically declares that " 'the enterprise of Judge Temple is taming the very forests! . . . How rapidly is civilization treading on the footsteps of nature!' "—but she comes to learn that Judge Temple's civilization is not altogether a blessing. She thrills to her father's account of his heroic efforts in the past; she sees with her own eyes the dubious results in the present. Like Christ, Judge Temple once multiplied loaves and fishes for starving tenants; now his disciples recklessly slaughter fish, flesh, fowl, and forests, apparently from some inner compulsion to destroy, and he is helpless to stay them. *The Pioneers* is built on ironies arising from different meanings of the word creation. Ideally, the works of God and the works of man are analogous; in fact, and in the United States, they appear to be in almost total contradiction. This is another reason one can so easily imagine the admixture of civilization and forest.

American development is regularly designated as "magical change," or words to that effect. " 'Every thing in this magical country seems to border on the marvellous,' " says Elizabeth of the district which, in her father's happy language, once " 'lay in the sleep of nature,' " and then " 'awoke to supply the wants of man.' " But this train of images concludes with a forest fire which is also said to be "instantaneous and magical." The instantaneous magic is likewise subverted by another series of images, in which the uncertainties of civilization are repeatedly compared with the transitional, vacillating Templeton weather. An even better image of the civilizing process is the "small and uncertain light [which] was plainly to be seen, though, as it was occasionally lost to the eye, it seemed struggling for its existence." The light proceeds from in front of Leatherstocking's hut into the surrounding "obscurity, which, like the gloom of oblivion, seemed to envelope the rest of the creation." Into this obscurity also obtrude the garish illuminations of Judge Temple's "improvements," for the road to the West is paved with his intentions. The buildings of Templeton "bore not only strong marks of the absence of taste, but also, by the slovenly and unfinished appearance of most of the dwellings, indicated the hasty manner of their construction. . . . The whole were grouped together in a manner that aped the streets of a city." The common style of architectural design, which is also Cooper's commanding emblem for American civilization in its formative stages, is "the composite order," a hilarious melting-pot of incongruous imitative styles concocted by the novel's chief villain (Doolittle) and its chief buffoon (Richard Jones, the Judge's brother-in-law). Everything they plan or build is a failure—nothing fits, nothing meets, nothing works. Inevitably the district already boasts a little band of counterfeiters, whose product "afterwards circulated from one end of the Union to the other." The composite order emigrates Westward with Doolittle.

The Pioneers is for the most part a comic story, and the comedy derives from the incompetence of its presumably civilized citizenry. In the opening scene, the Great Land Chief (Temple) "with a practised eye and steady hand, drew a trigger; but the deer dashed forward undaunted, and apparently unhurt." The deer is killed by Leatherstocking's rifle, whose owner thereupon "drew his bare hand across the bottom of his nose, and again opened his enormous mouth with a kind of inward laugh." This silent, ironic laughter is continuous throughout the Leatherstocking Tales, and signifies the hero's superiority to his betters. As it turns out, Judge Temple has accidentally shot Oliver Edwards. On the way home, Richard Jones cannot manage the horses, and the whole party must be rescued from his jaunty ineptitude by the victim of the first accident. The doctor who dresses Edwards' wound has acquired reputation (and a medical education) by repairing the wounds of woodcutters, on whom the trees they were felling have unaccountably fallen; the same doctor steals his best remedies from Indian John Mohegan, to whom he condescends. There is constant comedy in the religious conversations of Indian John and Mr. Grant, who do not speak the same language; for example, while Mohegan is calmly dying, the minister anxiously inquires if he is " 'sensible of his lost state.' " Judge Temple cannot keep Leatherstocking in jail, unless Leatherstocking consents to be kept, because neither he nor his sycophants are capable of building a jail which can hold him. Leatherstocking's fellow prisoner, Ben Pump, spikes the lock on the cell door to protect its inmates from further depredations by the law.

The farce of incompetence is counterpointed by the tragedy of misunderstanding. Some of the misunderstandings are factitious and remediable, such as the confusions about Edwards' identity and Temple's probity. Through most of the novel, the Judge is viewed in a false light, enabling Cooper perpetually to insult him and then exonerate him in the end. But if Temple's rectitude is ultimately vindicated, his intelligence is not. His overestimation of the law is a serious error in philosophy, and his nearly total inability to assess the character and control the behavior of his underlings is an equally serious defect of moral prudence. Deluded by superficial notions of justice, he relentlessly pursues a course of action whose injustice is apparent to the meanest intelligence. Apparently Cooper already sensed the truth he was to articulate a decade later, upon returning to the United States from Europe: "Every hour I stay at home convinces me more and more that society has had a summerset, and that the *élite* is at the bottom!"[8] Temple's legal proceedings against Natty Bumppo are simply one long train of judicial errors, while Natty Bumppo's indictment of the society which permits such persecution is unanswerable. At the end, with almost inconceivable stupidity, Temple benevolently orders a "pursuit" of Leatherstocking, who, knowing better, has already entered the forest.

But if Judge Temple is not the hero of the book, he is clearly at its center, as the representative American faced with the problem of Leatherstocking; it is not Leatherstocking's failure to adapt himself to American civilization that constitutes the problem, however, as it would have for a conformist like Crèvecœur, but the fact that Leatherstocking's existence prefigures the possibility of a morally higher American civilization. We are told that Marmaduke Temple's knowledge "was eminently practical, and there was no part of a *settler's* life, that he was not familiar with"; in this dimension, Temple is the William Cooper of *A Guide in the Wilderness*, but there, probably, the resemblance ends, for otherwise this fictional guide in the wilderness is hopelessly lost. He defines Leatherstocking as " 'an exception . . . for thou hast a temperance unusual in thy class,' " unwittingly describing the transcendence (of limitation or of contradiction) which is the inner principle of Cooper's hero and the real reason Judge Temple, who has no such talent for development, will never understand him. In a social situation characterized by bewildering change, Temple's steady good sense and fixed good intentions are worthless or worse. While his daughter is imperiled by a forest fire, "the distance was not too great, for the figure of Judge Temple to be seen, standing in his own grounds, and, apparently, contemplating, in perfect unconsciousness of the

[8] *Correspondence of Cooper*, I, 341.

danger of his child, the mountain in flames." His child is rescued by Leatherstocking, to whom she is attracted from the beginning, for Elizabeth Temple is another potential aristocrat of the spirit. For the sake of simple justice and ordinary decency, this witty and ironic girl finally defies family loyalty and invites the fleeing Leatherstocking to use her father's property in escaping her father's unconscious persecution. During the forest fire, Natty Bumppo wraps her in buckskin, an explicit symbol of transcendence through emblematic investiture in the garb of reality.

Ethical transcendence, which is a function of the imagination, is found in all social classes, and often takes the ironic form of social descent. When Oliver Edwards is reduced to poverty, and throws in his lot with Leatherstocking and Mohegan, his future is secured; he has become " 'a man of the woods,' " and will survive his inherited good fortune. Perhaps even more than Leatherstocking, and certainly more than Temple, Edwards exhibits the resilient spirit of the figurative frontier. "His hand that held the cap, rested lightly on the little ivory-mounted piano of Elizabeth, with neither the restraint of rustic timidity, nor with the obtrusive boldness of awkward vulgarity. A single finger touched the instrument, as if accustomed to dwell on such places. His other arm was extended to its utmost length, and the hand grasped the barrel of his long rifle, with something like convulsive energy. The act and the attitude were both involuntary."[9] Two hands, one man: evidently the best American transcendence results from a reconciliation of opposites. Leatherstocking "had imbibed, unconsciously, many of the

[9] Cf. the poem at the head of Emerson's essay, "Civilization":
> . . . Witness the mute all hail
> The joyful traveller gives, when on the verge
> Of craggy Indian wilderness he hears
> From a log cabin stream Beethoven's notes
> On the piano, played with master's hand.
> "Well done!" he cries; "the bear is kept at bay. . . .
> Twirl the old wheels! Time takes fresh start again,
> On for a thousand years of genius more."

The Complete Works of Ralph Waldo Emerson, ed. Edward Waldo Emerson (Boston, 1903-1904), VII, 17.

Indian qualities, though he always thought of himself, as of a civilized being, compared with even the Delawares." Indian John has arrived at nearly the same interesting condition from the opposite direction: "From his long association with the white-men, the habits of Mohegan, were a mixture of the civilized and savage states, though there was certainly a strong preponderance in favour of the latter. In common with all his people, who dwelt within the influence of the Anglo-Americans, he had acquired new wants, so that his dress was a mixture of his native fashions and European manufactures." As early as *The Pioneers*, Cooper introduces, but does not really activate, his conception of the Double Indian—Delaware vs. Mingo—as an obvious allegorical equivalent for the good and evil to be found in all men.

In this first Leatherstocking Tale, Indian John ends his days with pathos and dignity. To be sure, he becomes intoxicated in the local tavern—even more intoxicated than Judge Temple and his genteel friends—and the next day suffers a hangover which prevents his participation in the turkey-shoot. For this and other venial sins he performs more than sufficient penance, since the sins are in every case caused by prolonged commerce on unequal terms with an insensitive race. Mohegan's social decorum and inward integrity are models of heroic virtue, and as conspicuous in this crowd of big talkers as his laconic speech, his innate modesty, his unquestioning loyalty, and his seemingly inexhaustible charity. Mainly he suffers from old age and disuse; no more than Leatherstocking is he what he was or what, in the later Tales, he will become. He dies dreaming of the Indian past and in the glorious hope of an Indian immortality, but he is thoroughly defeated by this world. " 'There will soon be no red-skin in the country. When John has gone, the last will leave these hills.' "

As long as possible, and with considerable eloquence, his lifelong friend Leatherstocking sets himself against American progress. " 'So the old hero beat them back—he beat them back! did he!' " exults Edwards, after one of the old hero's temporary victories. But Leatherstocking does not dominate *The Pioneers*, as he dominates the later Tales, however fervently Cooper may subscribe to his opinions. Whereas in every subsequent Tale the other characters depend on Leatherstocking, in this one he helplessly depends on them, and especially on their intelligence, imagination, and good will, which are not invariably forthcoming. How easily he can be victimized in such a place as Templeton is suggested by the weakness of the people who victimize him. And perhaps as a result of the subsidiary role, his many incipient virtues are adulterated with faults typical of a testy, old, conservative crank; indeed, in several ways, Leatherstocking is a burlesque of Judge Temple's Federalist obsessions. Although in Elizabeth Temple's eyes, he is her knight, Sir Leatherstocking, he is by other people as maliciously slandered as the Judge; but, on the whole, he is too isolated from Templeton to affect its communal life one way or another. Like Indian John, he is a pathetic figure, first in his hut, then in his cave, and finally in his flight from the settlements, their questionable denizens, their wasty ways, and the sound of their axes and hammers. Upon Elizabeth Temple he invokes the blessing of " 'the Lord that lives in clearings as well as in the wilderness,' " a singular concession for him; and then, waving his hand, he disappears. We never see him in the settlements again.

The scene of *The Last of the Mohicans: A Narrative of 1757* (1826) is notably different from the scene of *The Pioneers*. Although "since the period of our tale, the active spirit of the country has surrounded it with a belt of rich and thriving settlements . . . none but the hunter or the savage is ever known, even now, to penetrate its rude and wild recesses." The increase in violence is also notable, for this is "emphatically, the bloody arena, in which most of the battles for the mastery of the colonies were contested"; typically, none of the various contestants was by 1826 in possession of it. Elsewhere, Cooper speaks of "romantic, though not unappalling beauties," and indeed the word for this country, the behaviors it engenders, and the novel which records them, is *implacable*. It is thus at least triply ironic that the woods into which small bands of warriors disappear—and sometimes reappear—seem "as still . . . as when they came fresh from the hands of their Almighty Creator." Of all the Leatherstocking Tales, *The Last of the Mohicans* is most unrelentingly bloody, cruel, and savage.

Superficially considered, forest violence is natural for red men but unnatural for white, as Hawkeye remarks after one of Chingachgook's more sophisticated scalpings. On this assumption, forest violence indirectly reveals the white man's inability to adapt to a realm of existence for which his virtues and experiences have all too inadequately prepared him; throughout the novel, he is portrayed as irrelevant, ineffectual, and irresponsible. Captain Duncan Heyward, the presumed conventional hero, is frequently a comic target not essentially different in function from such an obvious one as David Gamut, the Puritan singing-master. " 'Is there nothing that I can do?' demanded the anxious Heyward," ever eager to assume a heroic role for which he is not cut out. " 'You!' repeated the scout, who, with his red friends, was already advancing in the order he had prescribed; 'yes, you can keep in our rear, and be careful not to cross the trail.' " Another time, Leatherstocking is obliged to warn him: " 'If you judge of Indian cunning by the rules you find in books, or by white sagacity, they will lead you astray, if not to your death.' " Throughout *The Last of the Mohicans*, the respectable white characters commit one act of folly after another, from the consequences of which they must be rescued by Hawkeye, Chingachgook, or Uncas. " 'Natur' is sadly abused by man,' " says Hawkeye, " 'when he once gets the mastery' "; as the novel also shows, things are sometimes worse when he fails to get the mastery. All the white men but Hawkeye conspicuously fail to get the mastery. Montcalm cannot control his Indian allies because he cannot control himself. By contrast, the good Indians are marvels of self-control, whereas the bad Indians, like Magua, resemble the white men by whom they have been corrupted. If Uncas nearly always finds the trail first, while Heyward is unable to tell beavers from Indians, that is because woodcraft is a moral discipline. "Believing himself irretrievably lost, he [Duncan] drew Alice to his bosom, and stood prepared to meet a fate which he hardly regretted, since it was to be suffered in such company." Such company, such heroics, and such sensibilities are of little utility in a war-torn wilderness. Late in the novel, Heyward and the Puritan singing-master are still unable to walk in single file properly.

The genuine heroes are determined both pragmatically (by competence) and ethically (by loyalty to their "gifts"). In a rare moment of insight, Heyward enunciates the official doctrine of moral judgment: " 'As bright examples of great qualities are but too uncommon among Christians, so are they singular and solitary with the Indians; though, for the honour of our common nature, neither are incapable of producing them.' " Uncas is the ultimate hero of this novel, and in nearly every respect Leatherstocking's superior. " 'I, who am a white man without a cross,' " Leatherstocking proudly declares himself, page after tedious page, with no awareness of the ironic pun he always makes on "cross," once even assuring us that his blood is not tainted " 'by the cross of a bear.' " Insofar as miscegenation is a major theme of this tragic novel, the attitudes of Colonel Munro and of his daughter Cora are controlling. Cora's all-too-white half-sister Alice is no more the heroine than Heyward is the hero, as even her language shows (" 'Father! father! . . . it is I! Alice! thy own Elsie! spare, oh! save, your daughters!' "). Cora, on the contrary, commands a style so sharply pertinent that it survives even errors of judgment, such as her initial confidence in Magua: " 'Should we distrust the man, because his manners are not our manners, and that his skin is dark!' coldly asked Cora." She is the only person in the novel who makes the same point with sufficient force about Uncas: " 'Who, that looks at this creature of nature, remembers the shades of his skin!' " Everybody else, it seems. "A short, and apparently an embarrassed, silence succeeded this characteristic remark."

Far from attacking miscegenation, as has often been alleged, Cooper surreptitiously advocates it. On the one hand, *The Last of the Mohicans* presents for our dismayed contemplation example on example of pure and bloody savagery, red and white; on the other hand, it presents for our admiring recognition the noble Uncas nobly in love with the nobly dark Cora. "Uncas stood, fresh and blood-stained from the combat, a calm, and, apparently, an unmoved looker-on, it is true, but with eyes that had already lost their fierceness, and were beaming with a sympathy, that elevated him far above the intelligence, and advanced him probably centuries before the practices of his nation." Death may be the great obliterator, but sex is the great leveler and therefore the principal agent of progress toward human unity.[10] So all may learn from the nervously impassioned conversation about Cora between her father and Heyward. Mistakenly thinking that Heyward's erotic interests center in Cora, Colonel Munro describes her mother: " 'She was the daughter of a gentleman of those isles [the West Indies], by a lady, whose misfortune it was, if you will,' said the old man, proudly, 'to be descended, remotely, from that unfortunate class, who are so basely enslaved to administer to the wants of a luxurious people! . . . Ha! Major Heyward, you are yourself born at the south.' " Heyward admits the charge, "unable any longer to prevent his eyes

[10] Cf. Tocqueville: "I have previously observed that the mixed race is the true bond of union between the Europeans and the Indians; just so, the mulattoes are the true means of transition between the white and the Negro; so that wherever mulattoes abound, the intermixture of the two races is not impossible. In some parts of America the European and the Negro races are so crossed with one another that it is rare to meet with a man who is entirely black or entirely white; when they have arrived at this point, the two races may really be said to be combined, or, rather, to have been absorbed in a third race, which is connected with both without being identical with either." *Democracy in America*, trans. Henry Reeve (1835 and 1840), revised by Francis Bowen (1862), corrected and ed. Phillips Bradley (New York, 1945), I, 374.

from sinking to the floor in embarrassment," and the father resumes the attack. " 'And you cast it on my child as a reproach! You scorn to mingle the blood of the Heywards, with one so degraded,' " he sarcastically continues. Heyward prays Heaven to guard him " 'from a prejudice so unworthy' . . . at the same time conscious of such a feeling." Naturally he prefers and eventually marries Alice, a girl without a cross.

In the course of a long harangue, Magua assures his people that God created Negroes to be slaves, and white men to be exploiters. " 'Some the Great Spirit made with skins brighter and redder than yonder sun,' continued Magua . . . 'and these did he fashion to his own mind.' " If Cooper sometimes seems nearly to espouse Magua's view, it is not only because Cooper has so thoroughly identified himself with Uncas, and with the elegiac tone promoted by Uncas' premature death, but because Cooper is bent on deriving from this tragic and elegiac action as many ominous ambiguities as he can. Uncas is often a surrogate of the author. "The Mohican chief maintained his firm and haughty attitude; and his eye, so far from deigning to meet her [an old squaw's] inquisitive look, dwelt steadily on the distance, as though it penetrated the obstacles which impeded the view, and looked deep into futurity." The ancient Tamenund is another spokesman for the novelist. Sympathetically responding to the appeal of Cora, whose mention of her own tainted blood has touched the old man's heart, Tamenund speaks out until it hurts: " 'I know that the pale-faces are a proud and hungry race. I know that they claim, not only to have the earth, but that the meanest of their colour is better than the Sachems of the red man.' " It is perhaps for this reason that the white man does *not* have the earth, as the novel so abundantly demonstrates. " 'The dogs and crows of their tribes,' continued the earnest old chieftain, without heeding the wounded spirit of his listener, whose head was nearly crushed to the earth, in shame, as he proceeded, 'would bark and caw, before they would take a woman to their wigwams, whose blood was not of the colour of snow. But let them not boast before the face of the Manitto too loud. They entered the land at the rising, and may yet go off at the setting sun!' " In the last paragraph of the book, Tamenund speaks again; the tenor of his speech is the same, the application of it even more mysteriously alarming: " 'The pale-faces are masters of the earth, and the time of the red-men has not yet come again.' " Whatever else this speech is taken to mean, it surely means Cooper's recognition that the nobility of the outraged American Indian is now passing to the major American writer, defined as major by his moral antipathy to the Westward course of American empire and by his acts of enlightened counteraggression against it. According to Leatherstocking, " 'Nothing but vast wisdom and unlimited power should dare to sweep off men in multitudes.' " *The Last of the Mohicans* shows us limited power, and almost no wisdom at all.

The various themes of the novel are joined, and more or less resolved, in the closing chapter. Peace has finally been restored to the wilderness, but Cora, Uncas, and Magua have been killed in the process. (Uncas dies "with a look of inextinguishable scorn.") Of Magua, nothing more is said; of Cora and Uncas, much. Delaware girls strew with forest flowers the corpse of "ardent, high souled, and generous Cora." At "the opposite space of the same area" sits Uncas, "as in life." Soon the Delaware maidens commence "a sort of chant in honour of the dead," in which they observe that Cora's and Uncas' deaths, so nearly coincident, "render the will of the Great Spirit too manifest to be disregarded." Then "they advised her to be attentive to the wants of her companion, and never to forget the distinction which the Manitto had so wisely established between them." The Manitto's distinction is between male and female, not between Indian and white man. "That she [Cora] was of a blood purer and richer than the rest of her nation, any eye might have seen." The Delaware girls allude but briefly to the weeping Alice. "They doubted not that she was lovely in the eyes of the young chief [Heyward], whose skin and whose sorrow seemed so like her own; but, though far from expressing such a preference, it was evident, they deemed her less excellent than the maid they mourned."

Hawkeye piously rejects the Indian view "of the future prospects of Cora and Uncas"; Colonel Munro, who has been unable to follow the exact meaning of the funeral chant, responds with greater magnanimity: " 'Say to these kind and gentle females, that a heart-broken and failing man, returns them his thanks. Tell them, that the Being we all worship, under different names, will be mindful of their charity; and that the time shall not be distant, when we may assemble around his throne, without distinction of sex, or rank, or colour!' " The dubious scout transmits the message in such a form "as he deemed most suited to the capacities of his listeners." Then, as in the beginning, "all the white men, with the exception of Hawk-eye, passed from before the eyes of the Delawares, and were soon buried in the vast forests of that region." And so, "deserted by all of his colour," Hawkeye remains, with Chingachgook, the bereaved father of the last of the Mohicans, who calls himself " 'a blazed pine, in a clearing of the pale-faces.' " But there is one final word. " 'No, no,' cried Hawk-eye . . . 'not alone. The gifts of our colours may be different, but God has so placed us as to journey in the same path. I have no kin, and I may also say, like you, no people. He was your son, and a red-skin by nature; and it may be, that your blood was nearer;—but if ever I forget the lad. . . .' " At the end of the novel, Hawkeye alienates himself from his people, transcends the limits of American civilization (as understood by Parkman and such types), and becomes the true hero of the new American civilization hopefully coming into existence through his renunciation and transcendence. The nobility of Uncas passes to him, as the nobility of Uncas' race passes to Cooper.

American civilization continued to wander Westward, and Cooper with it. Much more explicitly than any other Leatherstocking Tale, *The Prairie* (1827) is dominated by the Westward Movement. The action is latest in time—soon after the Louisiana Purchase—and therefore farthest West, in the absolute sense of the term (location). It is also farthest West, in the relative sense of the term (direction), for in no other Leatherstocking Tale is so much attention paid to emigration. As soon as the United States were in possession of Louisiana, "swarms of that restless people, which is ever found hovering on the skirts of American society, plunged into the thickets. . . . The inroad from the east was a new and sudden out-breaking of a people, who had endured a momentary restraint, after having been rendered, nearly, resistless by success." Following the trail of Daniel Boone and his fictional follower Leatherstocking, settlers from Ohio and Kentucky file "deeper into the land, in quest of that which might be termed, without the aid of poetry, their natural and more congenial atmosphere." It is as one particular exemplification of this general exodus that we first behold the notorious Bush family, "a band of emigrants seeking for the Eldorado of their desires." On first acquaintance, their desires seem to be almost wholly for destruction; making a camp, "they stripped a small but suitable spot of its burden of forest, as effectually, and almost as promptly, as if a whirlwind had passed along the place."

Cooper halfheartedly pays homage to the social-stages-of-history theory. "The march of civilization with us, has a strong analogy to that of all coming events, which are known 'to cast their shadows before.' The gradations of society, from that state which is called refined to that which approaches as near barbarity as connection with an intelligent people will readily allow, are to be traced from the bosom of the states, where wealth, luxury and the arts are beginning to seat themselves, to those distant, and ever-receding borders which mark the skirts, and announce the approach, of the nation, as moving mists precede the signs of day."[11] Traveling Westward, the Bushes almost auto-

[11] "Let a philosophic observer commence a journey from the savages of the Rocky Mountains," wrote urbane ex-President Jefferson in 1824, "eastwardly towards our seacoast." He would find,

matically descend from one social stage to the next lower:
" ' 'Tis time to change our natur's,' he [Ishmael Bush] observed to the brother of his wife . . . 'and to become
ruminators.' " The Indians also descend the social stages,
thanks to "that engrossing people who were daily encroach-
ing on their rights, and reducing the Red-men of the west
from their state of proud independence to the condition of
fugitives and wanderers." As early as 1804, Leatherstocking has reached the Pacific Ocean and recoiled, thus anticipating the achievement and return of Lewis and Clark,
whose expedition is in progress simultaneously with the
action of *The Prairie* and is several times alluded to.

" 'I have seen the waters of the two seas! . . . America
has grown, my men, since the days of my youth, to be a
country larger than I once had thought the world itself to
be.' " As Leatherstocking adds, in a passage worth meditating: " 'I came west in search of quiet. It was a grievous
journey that I made.' " Leatherstocking is also an avatar
of the god Terminus, a deity Western orators were fond
of invoking to allay the fears of the anxious.[12] He is first
seen in *The Prairie* as a man against the sky, outlined "between the heavens and the earth," with the intention and
effect of blocking further American headway. He dies at a
Pawnee village in a scene strongly resembling the scene of
his advent, with "the light of the setting sun" falling "upon

---

in order, "those on our frontiers in the pastoral state," then "our
own semi-barbarous citizens, the pioneers of the advance of civilization, and so in his progress he would meet the gradual shades of
improving man until he reached his, as yet, most improved state
in our seaport towns. This, in fact, is equivalent to a survey, in
time, of the progress of man from the infancy of creation to the
present day." *The Writings of Thomas Jefferson* (Washington, 1904-
1905), XVI, 74-75.

[12] "Even Thomas Benton, the man of widest views of the destiny
of the West, at this stage of his career [1825] declared that along
the ridge of the Rocky mountains 'the western limits of the Republic
should be drawn, and the statue of the fabled god Terminus should
be raised upon its highest peak, never to be thrown down.' " Frederick Jackson Turner, *The Frontier in American History* (New York,
1920), p. 35.

the solemn features." Unquestionably, this is his country, which perhaps partly explains Cooper's confounding prairies, plains, and Great American Desert, a concept recently bequeathed the public through erroneous reports from the Long Expedition. The mere fact of Cooper's misinformation about Western American topography is far less significant than the zeal with which he prosecutes a golden opportunity to frustrate the Great American Ego. "Nature," he is pleased to proclaim, and endlessly to reiterate, "had placed a barrier of desert to the extension of our population in the west." Obviously Cooper thought, as Leatherstocking thinks, that " 'the Lord has placed this barren belt of prairie, behind the states, to warn men to what their folly may yet bring the land!' " As Leatherstocking rhetorically inquires: " 'What will the Yankee Choppers say, when they have cut their path from the eastern to the western waters, and find that a hand, which can lay the 'arth bare at a blow, has been here and swept the country, in very mockery of their wickedness. They will turn on their tracks like a fox that doubles, and then the rank smell of their own footsteps will show them the madness of their waste.' "

As a consequence of Cooper's idiosyncratic view of the Westward Movement, and of his identification of it with Leatherstocking as a sort of moralistic *ne plus ultra*, the West—what remains of it—becomes an idealized neutral territory or testing ground for heroes. Except for Leatherstocking, all the white characters are in the end, by Cooper's dispensation, backtrailers. Following his gift, which is small, the comic pedant Dr. Bat becomes "a *savant* in one of the maritime towns." The Bushes are also turned back, and are last seen "pursuing their course towards the settlements. As they approached the confines of society, the train was blended among a thousand others." Middleton and Inez return home (presumably Louisiana), taking with them Ellen Wade (several times called a girl of the settlements) and Paul Hover. This former borderer, bee-hunter, and gamecock of the wilderness, "is actually at this moment a member of the lower branch of the legislature of the State where he has long resided." In *The Pioneers* a wide variety of types, none of them excessively heroic, was happily engaged in taming the wilderness; *The Prairie* suggests that taming the wilderness is the prerogative of those who have tamed themselves, and that these, paradoxically, neither wish nor need to tame it. Here is an aristocracy for which practically no one will ever desire to qualify, and a vastly different world of assumptions from the property-centered *Pioneers*. From that world, Leatherstocking was exiled to the West as a nuisance; now he takes his revenge. He *is* the West, and the other Americans have not caught up with him. Most of them never will. Those who do will not like it. Cooper's Western landscape—Far Western, in 1827—is flat, treeless, semi-arid, empty, silent; more particularly, it seems to be associated with moonlight, driving clouds, birds of prey, and, in episode after episode, wind. " 'For here may natur' be seen in all its richness, trees alone excepted. Trees, which are to the 'arth, as fruits to a garden; without them nothing can be pleasant or thoroughly useful.' " The landscape of *The Prairie* is the basic metaphorical landscape of the entire series, its special starkness dependent on Cooper's studied removal from it of all signs of fruition.

For the third successive time in the Leatherstocking Tales, there is a Last Survivor, Leatherstocking himself, who dies after announcing: " 'I am without kith or kin in the wide world! . . . When I am gone, there will be an end of my race.' " (Whatever he means by race, it is neither family nor nation.) Perhaps Cooper's desire to mitigate an increasing sense of loss and loneliness explains the extraordinary number of "father images" in the novel, which derive not only from the relations of patriarchal Ishmael Bush with his many sons, but more importantly from Natty Bumppo's attempts to establish a continuous relation with humanity before he dies. He adopts the heroic young Pawnee Hard-Heart (" 'I have no son, but Hard-Heart' "), though to do so he must thwart the rival intentions of an elderly Sioux. " 'I have made him my son,' " Leatherstocking explains, " 'that he may know that one is left behind him.'" (Of course, it is Hard-Heart who is left behind.) And if someone else wants Hard-Heart, someone else wants Leatherstocking; Paul Hover offers to take the aged trapper into the settlements home he proposes to make with Ellen Wade, and to treat him like a father. The offer is graciously declined, Leatherstocking's preferences being what they are. Hard-Heart receives the old man's final benediction, and Middleton returns his only property—rifle, pouch, and horn —to Otsego.

Leatherstocking's death is rendered through symbolism reminiscent of the frontier tableau defining Oliver Edwards in *The Pioneers*. "Middleton [officer and gentleman in the United States Army, and link with Leatherstocking's early career along the frontiers of white civilization] and Hard-Heart [inheritor of the roles of Chingachgook and Uncas] placed themselves on the opposite sides of his seat and watched with melancholy solicitude the variations of his countenance. . . . There were moments, when his attendants doubted whether he still belonged to the living. Middleton . . . fancied he could read the workings of the old man's soul in the strong lineaments of his countenance. Perhaps what the enlightened soldier took for the delusion of mistaken opinion did actually occur, for who has returned from that unknown world to explain by what forms and in what manner, he was introduced into its awful precincts!" Death is inevitably a retroactive definition, and in *The Prairie*, Cooper achieves much his best definition of Leatherstocking so far. Middleton says it: "'Unlike most of those who live a border life, he united the better, instead of the worst qualities, of the two people.'" Here is the heart of the Leatherstocking Tales and of early American literature: the constitutive antithesis of white man and red, civilization and nature (or almost any other antithesis), is mediated and transcended by a figure—a character who is also a figure of speech—who incarnates the best of both worlds, is born of their deathlock, and is very much himself. The series of Tales is the tragic story of this man's life, death, and apparent defeat; alternatively, or simultaneously, it is the heroic story of his eventual triumph in what Romantic writers liked to call "the world of mind."

As in all the Tales after *The Pioneers*, the genteel characters are unimportant. Captain Middleton is only a *deus ex machina* and Inez ("the beau idéal of female loveliness") rather a cause of plot than a person in it. More than ever our interests are enlisted in the fate of Leatherstocking, and then in the affairs of the Bush family, whose sorry mismanagement reminds us that Cooper is again treating his civilization-nature polarities in terms of different kinds of law (prairie or Indian law vs. American law, and then both vs. divine law). Particularly in the first half of the novel, Cooper obviously finds distasteful this crude squatter and his crude family, who live closer to instinct than to reason; this is a severe limitation, as Leatherstocking is forever pointing out, though he is also forever praising instinct. Within the space of three paragraphs, Cooper defines the Bushes as "a race who lived chiefly for the indulgence of the natural wants," defends a "great principle of female nature" (maternal love) in Esther Bush, and then describes her as behaving "with that sort of acuteness which is termed instinct, in the animals a few degrees below her in the scale of intelligence." For all their dullness, the Bushes are frequently spoken of as exceptionally competent within the range of their experience. The Bush girls "promised fairly to become . . . no less distinguished than their mother for their daring, and for that singular mixture of good and evil, which, in a wider sphere of action, would probably have enabled the wife of the squatter to enrol her name among the remarkable females of her time." In many ways the Bushes resemble Leatherstocking, as in Cooper's generic description of them: "It would have been a curious investigation, for one skilled in such an inquiry, to have traced those points of difference, by which the offspring of the most western European [the American] was still to be distinguished from the descendant of the most remote Asiatic [the Indian], now that the two, in the revolutions of the world, were approximating in their habits, their residence, and not a little in their characters."

Surely it is not Cooper's final intention to belabor the brutishness of the Bushes, but rather to demonstrate how in people of almost no education, existing almost entirely outside society, there remains a fund of moral knowledge and a connatural sense of justice. Increasingly Cooper was taking his stand on the bedrock of human dignity, man as a divinely created rather than a socially conditioned being. As he did so, the values of his fiction gradually shifted from one side of the frontier to the other, from civilization to nature. The sequence in which the squatter, who knows no law but family, must assume responsibility to sentence and execute his wife's brother for the murder of his eldest son, and then finds it in his heart not only to forgive the man but through his absolution to help his wife find forgiveness—this sequence is widely held to be Cooper's finest achievement. What the action most memorably says is that the divine attributes of justice and mercy are man's attributes too, and that they are not wholly the result of civilization—which is rather the culture of them—but of nature. Perhaps the particular civilization which assisted in the formation of Ishmael Bush is less than perfect, and perhaps his feelings of claustrophobia arise from a subliminal awareness of the imperfection. He always feels himself confined, and seeks a kind of breathing space he never really understands; in this, and in much else, he is less a foil to Natty Bumppo than a variant on a lower plane.

For emphasis on the Indian, *The Prairie* is among the Leatherstocking Tales second only to *The Last of the Mohicans*. " 'The rightful owners of the country,' " as Leatherstocking regularly calls them, are Plains Indians on horseback, but as Leatherstocking also remarks (more for literary than for anthropological reasons), " 'Red-natur' is red-natur', let it show itself on a prairie, or in a forest!' " The allegory of good and evil continues unchanged by the change of tribes or location. Mahtoree (fundamentally a Mingo) stalks through the Bushes' camp "like the master of evil";

Hard-Heart is "Apollo-like." If Hard-Heart is Uncas resurrected, he is also a red Leatherstocking. " 'Look at that noble Pawnee,' " says Leatherstocking, " 'and see what a Red-skin may become, who fears the Master of Life and follows his laws.' " Red men and white are regularly seen as analogues of one another. After all, "little apology is needed for finding resemblances between men, who essentially possess the same nature, however it may be modified by circumstances." Mahtoree leans from the saddle "like some chevalier of a more civilized race," and speaks "in the haughty tones of absolute power," as if he were an American demagogue. "In a state of society, which admitted of a greater display of his energies, the Teton would in all probability have been both a conqueror and a despot." Escorting Middleton to the Pawnee village, Hard-Heart and his braves "set an example of courtesy, blended with reserve, that many a diplomatist of the most polished court might have strove in vain to imitate." Throwing himself on a horse, Hard-Heart makes a sign "with the air of a prince to his followers." Hard-Heart is richly endowed with the capacity to transcend his circumstances, and even the free-thinker Mahtoree is ambiguously said to be "much in advance of his people in those acquirements which announce the dawnings of civilization."

As Hard-Heart explains, with his usual tact: "The Wahcondah sometimes veiled his countenance from a Red-man. No doubt the Great Spirit of the Pale-faces often looked darkly on his children. Such as were abandoned to the worker of evil could never be brave or virtuous, let the colour of the skin be what it might." Whether the Great Spirit of the Pale-faces was in 1827 looking darkly or brightly on his children is a question that only the Great Spirit can answer; unquestionably, the Pale-faces were a success, and had long since learned to argue from success to desert to virtue. But an aged Indian asks Leatherstocking about the Americans: " 'Why cannot his people see every thing, since they crave all?' " And Hard-Heart tells Leatherstocking: " 'Your warriors think the Master of Life

53

has made the whole earth white. They are mistaken. They are pale, and it is their own faces that they see.' " Only Hard-Heart and Leatherstocking transcend historical conditioning to achieve a relation based on their common humanity. In a witty and moving reversal of Christ's language, Leatherstocking says to his adopted child, who faces torture and death, and who has just given his new father instructions for the burial: " 'My son's will shall be done.' " It might be Judge Temple speaking of his difficult son James.

When he returned to the Leatherstocking Tales thirteen years later, Cooper continued the development implicit in the first three with remarkably little change of direction. *The Pathfinder; or, The Inland Sea* (1840), takes place on and about Lake Ontario, "in the year 175-, or long before even speculation had brought any portion of western New-York within the bounds of civilization." The inland sea enabled Cooper to realize an old idea of writing within one set of covers his two favorite kinds of fiction.[13] "Nature," he says, meaning also himself, "appeared to delight in producing grand effects, by setting two of her principal agents in bold relief to each other." Occasionally lake and surrounding forest fuse in a figure of speech, as when we see "an ocean of leaves," or when we are told that the *Scud* resembles "a man threading the forest alone" and that her meeting with another ship "was like that of two solitary hunters beneath the broad canopy of leaves that then covered so many millions of acres on the continent of America." Pathfinder also finds it reasonable to think that God provided " 'lakes of pure water to the west, and lakes of impure [i.e., salt] water to the east,' " for as usual the local scene is emblematic of the national predicament. "At the period of our tale, and, indeed, for half a century later, the whole of that vast region which has been called the west, or the new countries, since the war of the revolution, lay a comparatively unpeopled desert, teeming with all the living

[13] The idea was at least as old as 1831. See *Letters and Journals*, II, 53, 80, 131-132, 253, 256, 258 (n. 2), 354.

productions of nature, that properly belonged to the climate, man and the domestic animals excepted." Paradoxically, as Cooper remarks in the preface, "there are isolated spots, along the line of the great lakes, that date, as settlements, as far back as many of the older American towns, and which were the seats of a species of civilization, long before the greater portion of even the older states was rescued from the wilderness." The species of civilization to which Cooper alludes is the new American civilization emerging from the figurative frontier in the mythical West.

In *The Pathfinder*, genteel characters are on the whole conspicuous by their welcome absence. "The reader is to anticipate none of the appliances of people of condition in the description of the personal appearances of the group in question." [Instead, the reader is to anticipate increased attention to Leatherstocking, the figurative frontier in person.] At first sight, Mabel Dunham takes him for an Indian, and only later sees "that she was about to be addressed by one of her own colour, though his dress was so strange a mixture of the habits of the two races, that it required a near look to be certain of the fact." His face is sunburnt "bright red," we are several times told; morally, he is distinguished by "that stoicism which formed so large a part of his character, and which he had probably imbibed from long association with the Indians." Quartermaster Muir is not far wrong when he calls him " 'wild, half-savage, or of a frontier formation,' " though of course we must discover in these epithets implications other than the villainous quartermaster intends. " 'I may say,' " Pathfinder is always saying, " 'that my own feelings towards a Mingo' "—and toward everything else, he might have added— " 'are not much more than the gifts of a Delaware grafted on a Christian stock.' "

The supporting characters also show frontier formation. Mabel Dunham finds herself in an analogously mediate position, as perhaps she must if Leatherstocking is to take an interest in her: "She had lost the coarser and less refined habits and manners of one in her original position, without having quite reached a point that disqualified her for the situation in life that the accidents of birth and fortune would probably compel her to fill." Her awkward position seems to descend from her father, who occupies a "sort of neutral position" between officers and men. Mabel is also on the frontier, at this period of her life, in a more significant sense. "For the first time, Mabel felt the hold that the towns and civilization had gained on her habits sensibly weakened, and the warm-hearted girl began to think that a life passed amid objects, such as these around her, might be happy." Subsequently she informs Pathfinder, " 'One feels nearer to God, in such a spot, I think, than when the mind is distracted by the objects of the towns,' " and again, in the same conversation, " 'I find I'm fast getting to be a frontier girl, and am coming to love all this grand silence of the woods. The towns seem tame to me.' "

More than in the Tales of the 1820's, Cooper is eager to define discursively the nature of the mysterious Leatherstocking, paragon of probity, stability, self-discipline, simplicity, faith, energy, courage, integrity, prudence, sincerity, truthfulness, freshness of sensibility, and, over all, of a "beautiful and unerring sense of justice." He is America as America ought to be, and it is significant that as Cooper's sense of what America ought to be developed from the 1820's to the 1840's, he not only augmented and magnified Leatherstocking's virtues but gave them an increasingly aesthetic orientation. This development was to be completed only with *The Deerslayer* in the following year; at this penultimate stage, "the most surprising peculiarity about the man himself, was the entire indifference with which he regarded all distinctions that did not depend on personal merit." He also possesses "a natural discrimination, that appeared to set education at defiance"; that is, he constitutes a living proof that intelligence, imagination, and conscience, key to the other virtues, are rather innate than acquired. "In short, it was said of the Pathfinder . . . that he was a fair example of what a just-minded and pure man might be, while untempted by unruly or ambitious desires, and left to follow the bias of his feelings, amid the solitary grandeur and ennobling influences of a sublime nature; neither led aside by the inducements which influence all to do evil amid the incentives of civilization; nor forgetful of the Almighty Being, whose spirit pervades the wilderness as well as the towns." (Cooper was doubtless tempted to say "more than the towns.") Leatherstocking is a paradigm of the ideal democratic ethos in the Era of Good Feeling and Age of Jackson, the new man of the New World miraculously uncorrupted by (as it is ironically called) free enterprise.

Late in the novel, Pathfinder tells how he overcame three great temptations. Since the temptations are not great, and the morality used to circumvent them eccentric, the anecdote is primarily comic in effect. His real temptation is naturally Mabel Dunham, though it is not, strictly speaking, her rejection of him that, as Cooper says, "might be termed the most critical [instant] in our hero's life," but the possibility of her acceptance. This marital temptation is not at all comic, but in many ways painful, for surely being in love is the most improbable of all the improbable situations in which Leatherstocking is placed by his creator. Of course, there is no serious doubt of the outcome: Leatherstocking is a saint, with a vocation to celibacy. Throughout *The Pathfinder*, Cooper touches on Leatherstocking's limitations of personality, education, and background, which, superficially considered, might be thought to unfit him for domestic life with a beautiful young girl. He is also defined as a man preeminently susceptible to education of a more profound kind, and learn his lessons he assuredly does. Even before the final recognition scene, he has an uneasy sense that something has gone wrong with his life. To Mabel's question, " 'And our own Delaware, Pathfinder—the Big Serpent— why is he not with us, to-night?' " he replies: " 'Your question would have been more natural, had you said, why are *you* here, Pathfinder?—The Sarpent is in his place, while I am not in mine.' " Later he tells her: " 'I have indeed been on a false trail, since we met!' " Finally taking leave of Mabel and her lover Jasper Western, he says sadly: " 'I shall return to the wilderness and my Maker.' " In this way only can he be saved, for the path into the wilderness leads to the City of God which is his ultimate destination. Jasper and Mabel settle in New York, for there are, indeed, gifts and gifts. That Leatherstocking, possessor of the highest gifts within the compass of Cooper's imagination, is also provincial, superstitious, ignorant, and verbose, signifies Cooper's recognition of the obvious truth that even the highest gifts exist in, through, and sometimes despite, particular conditions.

As always in the Leatherstocking Tales, heroism is defined as transcendence; transcendence is perhaps most movingly displayed by one of Cooper's finest Indian characters, the Dew-of-June, who retains all the gifts of her people and at the same time passes beyond them. Like Leatherstocking, she is, in one sense, a limited being who instinctively (as it must seem) comports herself "with a delicacy that would have done honour to the highest civilization." Between her and Mabel Dunham exists what was evidently for Cooper an ideal relation: "As respects each other, there was perfect confidence; as regarded their respective people, entire fidelity." June explains to Mabel: " 'Don't only feel as Tuscarora—feel as girl—feel as squaw.' " In a passage eloquent with simple piety, and charged with animus toward the American people, Cooper sums her up: "Humble and degraded as she would have seemed in the eyes of the sophisticated and unreflecting, the image of God was on her soul, and it vindicated its divine origin by aspirations and feelings that would have surprised those who, feigning more, feel less."

Dew-of-June dies young, as do practically all Cooper's people who are too good for this world. To the general rule, Natty Bumppo is the notable exception; in an almost Freudian sense, he must die at his own time in his own way, not really so that Cooper can continue to write Leatherstocking Tales, as his resurrection after *The Prairie* might seem to imply, but so that this representative hero can atone for the sins of the civilization which rejects him even while he transcends it, and which continued to compound its sins even while Cooper was conducting the national examination of conscience. In all this endurance and transcendence, there is surely much of Cooper himself, as there is in the admirably suggestive Chingachgook, " 'a lone man in this world, and yet he stands true to his training and his gifts!' " Doubtless a devious meaning lurks behind Cooper's statement in the preface, that "the Indian character has so little variety, that it has been an object to avoid dwelling on it too much, on the present occasion." Nearly all the general descriptions of savage character apply equally to the author: " 'an Indian knows how to hold his tongue' "; "our heroine had often heard of the wonderful sagacity of the Indians, and of the surprising manner in which they noted all things, while they appeared to regard none"; "these children of the forests had many expedients that were unknown to civilization." The whites (Cooper's readers?) are notable for their complacent incompetence. " 'We Scots [says Corporal McNab] come from a naked region, and have no need, and less relish, for covers, and so ye'll be seeing, Mistress Dunham'——The corporal gave a spring into the air, fell forward on his face, and rolled over on his back." June defines the basic difficulty: " 'Yengeese too greedy—take away all hunting grounds—chase Six Nation from morning to night; wicked king—wicked people. Pale-face very bad.' " Mabel Dunham is compelled to admit that "there was much truth in this opinion"—"even in that distant day."

The Deerslayer; or, The First War-Path (1841) is much the most Romantic of the Tales. The civilized folk who dominated *The Pioneers*, and then lingered along the margins of the next three Tales, chiefly as military personnel, are gone. Cooper had apparently come to understand that the unifying conception of the frontier metaphor, with its mediating embrace of opposites, enabled him to comprehend in a single character both the civilized and the natural virtues. As he grows ever younger, Leatherstocking assimilates the better qualities of Judge Temple's civilization (foresight, prudence, responsibility), detached from implications of social, economic, or educational class. Leatherstocking now stands for nature *and* civilization *and* their dynamic interplay, which is greater than either alone. Cooper's progress was also a roundabout reversion in time from the alleged 1794 of *The Pioneers* to the alleged 1740 of *The Deerslayer*; as he retreated from contemporary civilization, he inevitably left behind the world of upper-class America and arrived in a simpler world where he could ignore such distinctions. Even more clearly than in *The Pioneers*, Cooper now saw that the real problem was not what American civilization might do with its Leatherstockings, but what American civilization might do with its Judge Temples. Cooper's best insight was that Judge Temples were expendable.

In the fresh purity of youth, Leatherstocking is surrounded by Indians good and evil, and by white frontiersmen conspicuously less admirable than the better Indians, or even, in certain respects, than the worst Indians. The central conception of *The Deerslayer* is the Double Frontiersman, represented by the opposition between Leatherstocking on the one hand, and Floating Tom Hutter and Hurry Harry March on the other. But the distinction between them must not be interpreted as primarily a distinction between ideal and real, for in that interpretation Leatherstocking's efficacy would be lost; and as the narrative carefully demonstrates, his enactment of the borderer's role, even before his initiation into the full horrors of border life, is quite as authoritative as March's and Hutter's. The proper distinctions are both aesthetic and ethical. The low frontiersmen, foils to the greater glory of Leatherstocking, are undeveloped human beings, even though they live in a setting singularly conducive to what Cooper regards as natural human development.

This apathy is disastrous, as we learn from the very different uses to which nature is put by Leatherstocking:

We have written much, but in vain, concerning this

extraordinary being, if the reader requires now to be told, that, untutored as he was in the learning of the world, and simple as he ever showed himself to be in all matters touching the subtleties of conventional taste, he was a man of strong, native, poetical feeling. He loved the woods for their freshness, their sublime solitudes, their vastness, and the impress that they everywhere bore of the divine hand of their creator. He seldom moved through them, without pausing to dwell on some peculiar beauty that gave him pleasure, though seldom attempting to investigate the causes; and never did a day pass without his communing in spirit, and this, too, without the aid of forms or language, with the infinite source of all he saw, felt, and beheld. Thus constituted, in a moral sense, and of a steadiness that no danger could appal, or any crisis disturb, it is not surprising that the hunter felt a pleasure at looking on the scene.

Leatherstocking is further characterized by "the freshness of his integrity, the poetry and truth of his feelings," and Chingachgook by "the poetry and truth of nature." The novel is full of natural beauties, usually called "holy," and the poetic characters' responses to them validate their credentials as true American heroes. "Most of the influence that such a scene is apt to produce on those who are properly constituted in a moral sense, was lost on Hutter and Hurry; but both the Delawares, though too much accustomed to witness the loveliness of morning-tide, to stop to analyze their feelings, were equally sensible of the beauties of the hour, though it was probably in a way unknown to themselves." As Cooper never tires of saying, "the whole was lost on the observers [Hutter and Hurry], who knew no feeling of poetry, had lost their sense of natural devotion in lives of obdurate and narrow selfishness, and had little other sympathy with nature, than that which originated with her lowest wants." *The Deerslayer* depends on the ethics of Emerson, which in turn depend on the aesthetics of Wordsworth; as in the later aesthetic ethics of Henry

James, Leatherstocking is *par excellence* the man on whom nothing is lost. His superiority appears to be a matter of election, for the aesthetic response plainly presupposes ethical awareness, and vice versa.

The more the issues of the novel are seen as ethical rather than as aesthetic, the more cleanly the image of the Double Frontiersman splits into polar opposites, until finally Tom Hutter is revealed as despicably insensible to Leatherstocking's captivity and probable death, "for while he knew how material his aid might be in a defence, the difference in their views on the morality of the woods, had not left much sympathy between them." Differences in moral view have been evident throughout. Leatherstocking spends his best energies in the avoidance of even necessary bloodshed, while Hutter and Hurry devote their worst talents to the pursuit of scalps. (In Cooper's view, they are clearly worse than the misguided Bushes.) For these "men who dreaded the approaches of civilization as a curtailment of their own lawless empire," Indians are fair game, and their extermination is legally justified by the scalp bounties the colony offers. Since the crime extends into the highest places, it is both colony and frontiersmen whose approaches Leatherstocking dreads. " 'I'm glad it has no name,' " he says of the lake, " 'or, at least, no pale-face name; for their christenings always foretell waste and destruction.' " Since practically all the action of *The Deerslayer* results from Indian-hating, whether regarded as regressive barbarism or as political policy, the fitting climax of the novel is the horrific vision of Tom Hutter: "The quivering and raw flesh, the bared veins and muscles, and all the other disgusting signs of mortality, as they are revealed by tearing away the skin, showed he had been scalped, though still living." So, in a manner of speaking, has America been scalped by Cooper; with some justice, he defends this savage act of poetic justice as one of the "decrees of a retributive Providence."

Significantly, the Double Frontiersman (Indian-hater and forest-philosopher) issues from a single situation. The novel is full of realistic details drawn from border life—house-raising, strange mixtures of furniture, love of sports and outdoor activities, freedom and familiarity of manners —and these realistic details compel us to attend to the fact of man's ability to choose between alternative modes of behavior within the same set of circumstances. Like Leatherstocking, Hurry Harry is a "creature equally of civilization and barbarism," but in nearly every other respect he is Leatherstocking's antithesis. Even the "physical restlessness that kept him so constantly on the move" is rather the opposite than the same kind of restlessness inspiring Deerslayer's geographical and spiritual mobility. There is a world of meaning in Leatherstocking's remark: " 'Never talk to Hurry about these things; he's only a borderer, at the best.' " His best is not good enough, for he is all too representative of a class. " 'Take 'em as a body, Judith, 'arth don't hold a set of men more given to theirselves, and less given to God and the law.' " Hurry Harry's clothing has "the usual signs of belonging to those who passed their time between the skirts of civilized society and the boundless forests," but he has learned nothing from either, or from their admixture. He is a frontiersman only in appearance, only, as it were, sartorially. He is a costumed adolescent, and the American woods are full of him.

Hurry Harry is as out of place as Duncan Heyward in this scene, which, as always, is the frontier, whether defined as "the whole region east of the Mississippi," for which Lake Glimmerglass and the surrounding forest are metonymous, or as the neutral ground (" 'a sort of common territory' ") between Mohicans and Mingos, Indians and Americans, human beings and animals, life and death, Heaven and Hell. Floating Tom's human nature " 'is not much like other men's human natur', but more like a muskrat's human natur'.' " He lives in Muskrat Castle, and is repeatedly said to burrow. He is not without potentially saving qualities—"directness of speech" and "decision in conduct" are two of them—and is finally, as all men are (though the prognosis for Hutter is less hopeful than for most), "of that fearful mixture of good and evil, that so generally enters into the moral composition of man." At the other ethical extreme, Hutter's feeble-minded daughter Hetty is (according to Hurry Harry) " 'what I call on the varge of ignorance, and sometimes she stumbles on one side of the line, and sometimes on t'other.' " As Deerslayer adds: " 'Them are beings that the Lord has in his 'special care. . . . The Redskins honour and respect them who are so gifted.' " The gifted girl shares many virtues with Deerslayer, most notably truthfulness, racial charity, ethical perspicacity, and natural piety. Her father says she has a settlements heart and a wilderness head; whatever more precise meaning this is intended to have, in general Cooper's phrase indicates that even in her feeble mental state she has everything worth having. Through her instincts, she approaches the animals; through her devotions, she approaches God, and in so doing is superior even to Deerslayer. Significantly, her religious ideas mingle Indian traditions and Christian doctrine, and she alone passes back and forth, literally and culturally, between the warring camps, until accidentally killed by their antagonism. "Thus died Hetty Hutter, one of those mysterious links between the material and immaterial world, which, while they appear to be deprived of so much that is esteemed and necessary for this state of being, draw so near to, and offer so beautiful an illustration of the truth, purity, and simplicity of another." In the course of his frontier novels, Cooper had all along been disengaging himself from American civilization, as understood by the world into which he was born, in order to create an American civilization worthier of the name, as he had also been disengaging the frontier metaphor from its literal origins, in order to apply it to more significantly ethical and religious situations. Now he transcends American civilization altogether. On the frontiers of Heaven, rather than on the Far Western plains where Leatherstocking dies, the Tales come to an end. Cooper had traveled a long way from Cooperstown, and clearly could go no further.[14]

At the heart of the Leatherstocking Tales is Cooper's vision of cultural relativism and pluralism, which in turn is sustained by a basic distinction between the reign of nature and the works of man; after all, for there to be an admixture, there must first have been a distinction. Nature is anterior, more stable, and thus more directly—or at least more simply—related to God; nature is the proximate, though not the ultimate, ground of being. In that sense— as the non-ethical, or the pre-ethical—nature is in contrast with the nightmare behavior of man; and as cyclical recurrence, nature is in contrast with the linear forms of human history, whether progressive or regressive. But since all men have available to them the same immediate access to nature, and through nature mediately to God, they may if they choose move back toward their single source and reaffirm an essential brotherhood. Paradoxically, nature, in itself neither good nor bad, is also the source of a spectrum of ethical behaviors, works of man, and civilizations.

Invaluable as they are, civilizations, or cultures, separate groups of men from each other. In Leatherstocking's conversation, the antithesis between "natur' " (as given) and "gifts" (as second nature, in traditions, mores, manners, styles) is almost never-ending. " 'I am too christianized to expect any thing so fanciful as hunting and fishing after death,' " he announces in *The Deerslayer*, discriminating his faith from the faith of his Indian friends, but not on that account diminishing his sympathy with them; " 'nor

[14] *The Oak Openings* (1848) suggests that Cooper later became uneasy at having gone so far. In this novel the Westward Movement is accepted and glorified as the spread of Protestant Christianity under the promptings of America's Providence. The problems raised by the Leatherstocking Tales are simply solved by converting the Indians. Or was it so simple? "Commenced on new part of *Openings*," Cooper admitted in his journal, "and wrote moderately, but not *con amore*. This book is not a labour of love, but a labour." *Correspondence of Cooper*, II, 734-735.

do I believe there is one Manitou for the red-skin, and another for a pale-face. You find different colours on 'arth, as any one may see . . . but only one natur'. . . . A natur' is the creatur' itself. . . . Now, gifts come of sarcum-stances.' " As he explains to Cap in *The Pathfinder*, in a still more catholic formulation: " 'With me, it is as on-creditable for a white man not to be a Christian, as it is for a red-skin not to believe in his happy hunting-grounds; indeed, after allowing for difference in traditions, and in some variations about the manner in which the spirit will be occupied after death, I hold that a good Delaware is a good Christian, though he never saw a Moravian; and a good Christian a good Delaware, so far as natur' is con-sarned.' " In the light of such remarks, the Double Indian and the Double Frontiersman split and realign themselves, and the deplorably disastrous relations in the United States between Indians and frontiersmen are replaced by the eter-nal warfare of opposing principles.

Increasingly insisting on Leatherstocking's conscience, Cooper's argument circles back to its beginnings, where everything comes together, for the sense of right and wrong is at once nature and the source of the highest civilization. The doctrine of cultural relativism was obviously en-couraged and sharpened by such American conditions as life in the woods and encounter with the Indian; it was, in fact, demanded by them, and by the sense of human decency, the necessity for self-respect, both for the times in which the Leatherstocking Tales were written and for posterity. The doctrine of cultural relativism was also an absolute religious principle, considerably antedating the birth of even the noblest concept of American civilization, and, con-ceivably, surviving its eventual decline or disappearance. In *The Deerslayer* we learn that it was the Moravians who first taught our hero " 'that all are to be judged according to their talents, or l'arning; the Indian, like an Indian; and the white man, like a white man.' " (Clearly, it was St. Paul who taught *them*.) As the dying Leatherstocking says to Hard-Heart: " 'There are many traditions concerning the place of Good Spirits. It is not for one like me, old and experienced though I am, to set up my opinions against a nation's. You believe in the blessed prairies, and I have faith in the sayings of my fathers. If both are true, our parting will be final; but if it should prove, that the same meaning is hid under different words, we shall yet stand together, Pawnee, before the face of your Wahcondah, who will then be no other than my God.' "

[With three of the Leatherstocking Tales behind him, Cooper wrote, curiously, in *Notions of the Americans*, that "all the attempts to blend history with romance in America, have been comparatively failures, (and perhaps fortunately,) since the subjects are too familiar to be treated with the freedom that the imagination absolutely requires. Some of the descriptions of the progress of society on the borders, have had a rather better success, since there is a positive, though no very poetical, novelty in the subject."[15] The preface he supplied for the entire series of Leatherstocking Tales in 1850 was more assured. "In a moral sense," he said, minimizing the tortuous development of his insight, "this man of the forest is purely a creation. The idea of delineating a character that possessed little of civilization but its highest principles . . . and all of savage life that is not incompatible with these great rules of conduct, is perhaps natural to the situation in which Natty was placed. He is too proud of his origin to sink into the condition of the wild Indian, and too much a man of the woods not to imbibe as much as was at all desirable, from his friends and companions. . . . Removed from nearly all the temptations of civilized life, placed in the best associations of that which is deemed savage, and favorably disposed by nature to improve such advantages, it appeared to the writer that his hero was a fit subject to represent the better qualities of both conditions, without pushing either to extremes."[16]

Cooper was an inventive genius, not a literary critic, and

[15] II, 111-112.
[16] Conveniently reprinted in *James Fenimore Cooper, Representative Selections*, ed. Robert Spiller (New York, 1936), pp. 306-307.

it is useless to demand more of him than this final recognition that Leatherstocking was purely and simply that new man, the generic American, the metaphor of the Western frontier fleshed out as a human being; whatever additional instruction we wish must be sought in the Tales themselves, and then in the literature they inspired. Cooper's achievement was perhaps limited by its being so intuitive, so much an affair of trial and error; certainly it was limited by hasty production, by novelistic conventions unworthy of his matter, and by a prose style only intermittently brilliant. Still, in the center of his rambling, disjointed narratives we can find, if we look for them, germs of a rich development. For all his shortcomings, Cooper's integrity and passion enabled him to nurture his basic figure until it grew beyond him—grew, in fact, to be nearly synonymous with early American literature. Thus he defined the age and became (insofar as any one man can be) the improbable founder of the national expression. The Leatherstocking Tales are not in any ordinary sense great art; but the rest of American writing through Whitman is a series of footnotes on them.

Nathaniel Hawthorne

1. SKETCHES OF WESTERN ADVENTURE

LIKE COOPER, Hawthorne was at heart a Western writer; and even more persistently than Cooper, he was determined to see himself in a Western light. As early as 1820 (age 15), he wrote his sister in Maine: "How often do I long for my gun and wish that I could again savagize with you. But I shall never again run wild in Raymond, and I shall never be so happy as when I did."[1] As late as 1853, he was still describing in idyllic terms those happy Leatherstocking years: "I ran quite wild, and would, I doubt not, have willingly run wild till this time, fishing all day long, or shooting with an old fowling-piece. . . . That part of the country was wild then, with only scattered clearings, and nine tenths of it primeval woods. . . . I would sometimes take refuge in a log cabin."[2] In 1833 or 1834, Hawthorne apparently made a real Western tour; if so, it was almost certainly for the purpose of refurbishing, consolidating, and

[1] Quoted in Manning Hawthorne, "Nathaniel Hawthorne Prepares for College," *New England Quarterly*, XI (1938), 72. See also *The American Notebooks*, ed. Randall Stewart (New Haven, 1932): "Oh that I could run wild!—that is, that I could put myself in a true relation with nature, and be on friendly terms with all congenial elements" (p. 169). The language is Emerson's, perhaps by way of Thoreau, with whom Hawthorne had recently been boating; the feeling was as much his as theirs.

[2] Quoted in Samuel T. Pickard, *Hawthorne's First Diary* (Cambridge, 1897), pp. 4-5. Later Hawthorne wrote his publisher: "I lived in Maine . . . like a bird of the air, so perfect was the freedom I enjoyed. But it was there I first got my cursed habits of solitude." Quoted in James T. Fields, *Yesterdays With Authors* (Cambridge, 1871), p. 113. See also Julian Hawthorne, *Hawthorne Reading* (Cleveland, 1902), p. 63.

confirming the kind of writing that issued from his dismal chamber during his literary apprenticeship.[3] The gist of the matter is that Hawthorne, like many another writer confined to the Atlantic seaboard, made what he could of what he was born with and what he was able to lay hands on. By a judicious use of the Romantic imagination, and sustained by precious little actual experience, he transformed New England into an available prototype of the West.

In his reminiscences, Howells tells us that even the Hawthorne of 1860 "was curious about the West, which he seemed to fancy much more purely American, and said he would like to see some part of the country on which the shadow (or, if I must be precise, the damned shadow) of Europe had not fallen."[4] At least on that occasion, our romancer's remarks on New England seem to have been fewer and less pleasant. Yet in a special way he might have spoken of both sections simultaneously. He was repeatedly drawn to unpopulous pockets of the East—such as the "rocky, woody, watery back settlement of New England" mentioned in "The Seven Vagabonds"—which he could reconceive as Western scenes. Alternatively, he was always following the trail of local history backward until it arrived at the wild West. Neither the literal place nor the literal time was in the final analysis controlling; but conjoined, New England and the past yielded an essential synthesis, the frontier, which, not very paradoxically, was also the American future. For Massachusetts, the past was the vanished West; the West was the surviving past. The laterally progressive nature of American historical development made these exchanges almost ridiculously simple. As James Hall said in a Western story: "It was such as all new towns in the west had once been; such, perhaps, as the hamlets were on the shores of the Atlantic."[5] And Sylvester Judd explained in a local novel: "The house where Mar-

[3] Randall Stewart, *Nathaniel Hawthorne: A Biography* (New Haven, 1948), pp. 42-43.
[4] *Literary Friends and Acquaintance* (New York, 1900), p. 53.
[5] "The Missionaries," in *Legends of the West* (Philadelphia, 1832), p. 96.

garet lived, of a type common in the early history of New England, and still seen in the regions of the West, was constructed of round logs."[6]

Hawthorne's close acquaintance with Western writing is perhaps best observed in the *American Magazine of Useful and Entertaining Knowledge*, which he edited from March through August 1836. For these six issues Hawthorne, slightly aided by his sister, provided nearly the entire copy, most of it excerpted or abstracted from articles and books he apparently found useful or entertaining or both. Entertainingly enough, the issues under Hawthorne's supervision are markedly more Western than those preceding or following. In the first number he included his own sketch, presumably autobiographical, "An Ontario Steam-Boat"; an account of "Captain Franklin's Expedition," emphasizing exploration, life in the wilderness, and Indians; a short sardonic squib called "Fashionable Wigs," about the New England frontiersman's custom (c. 1725) of wearing Indian scalps; generous excerpts from the "Letters" of Albert Pike, sketches of Arkansas about equally indebted to Cooper and Southwestern humor; "The Ohio," a short factual account of that beautiful river, copied from the *Cincinnati Luminary*; "Progress of Education in the West," from the *Western Advocate*; an article on "Climate," which inquires why American weather differs from European, and discusses the difference in terms of the inland idea of America; "Comparative Longevity," which also concerns the effects of climate on human life, and concludes with conjectures about "the situation of America, in a transition-state from a wild land to a cultivated one" (further talk of clearings in primeval forests, "the felling of the western woods and the miraculous growth of towns," the Erie Canal); "Religion in the West," from the *New York Evangelist*; a paragraph from Leonard Withington, *The Puritan* (1836), which argues that a nation's literature should reflect (like Lake Superior) "the scenery actually

[6] *Margaret. A Tale of the Real and Ideal* (Boston, 1845), p. 11.

around it"; and, finally, a long passage from Joseph Holt Ingraham, *The South-West* (1835), from which Hawthorne would excerpt again in April and once more in July.

Month after month, Hawthorne stuffed his pages with material from such books as Timothy Flint's *Recollections of the Last Ten Years* (1826) and Washington Irving's *A Tour on the Prairies* (1835), drawing much less often on other kinds of American sources. He printed perhaps a score of items about the Indian, which tended to be brief and superficial, unless they bore on ancient and gloomy wrongs perpetrated by Puritans. More than a dozen items concerned the backwoods, the prairies, the Northwest, the frontier, the social stages of history, or Western antiquities. Hawthorne notably came alive whenever it was a question of the shifting panoramas induced by America's "instantaneous" development, a favorite topic with all the Western writers. In a sketch called "Cincinnati," he quickly ran through the conventional series of social stages:

> Until the year 1788, the Indian or the hunter, standing on the circular line of hills, above the valley, of which we have described the outline, would have seen only the gigantic trees, and the river sundering the primeval forest with its tranquil breadth. Nearly twenty years later, from the same position, nothing was visible, save a rough backwoods settlement of five hundred people. But soon a marvellous change was to take place; in 1820, the once solitary vale had become populous with nearly ten thousand souls; and now, if the traveller take a view of Cincinnati from its wall of hills, he will behold busy streets, compact and massive edifices, the spires of churches, the smoke of manufactories, and all other characteristics of a city, containing thirty-five thousand inhabitants.

The accompanying engraving shows Cincinnati "now"; the rest was dreamed up by Hawthorne.

In "Habitations of Man," he described the frontier log house ("In our memory, there is a vivid picture of such an edifice, which we used to visit in our boyhood, while running wild on the borders of a forest-lake"), and the buffalo-skin lodges of the Kaskaia Indians "who roam through the Far West," while in "April Fools" he provincially ridiculed New England farmers migrating to the Mississippi Valley and Yankees enlisting for Texas. At the time Hawthorne lived with the aged poet Thomas Green Fessenden, who deliriously talked "about emigrating to Illinois, where he possessed a farm, and picturing a new life for both of us in that Western region";[7] doubtless he heard the same story later from Ellery Channing. But Hawthorne traveled primarily in imagination, and in imagination he escaped from the limitations of his region. Of all the Western entries in the *American Magazine*, the most fully developed fictionally is "The Duston Family," which is nearly as fine as a full-fledged Hawthorne story. The source is Cotton Mather. The moral feeling is anti-Mather, pro-Indian; and the setting is less Mather's New England than Hawthorne's Western frontier. From the same materials, Thoreau rendered a far more patriotic account in *A Week on the Concord and Merrimack Rivers.*

Almost from the beginning, Hawthorne was involved with the West. In "Sir William Phips" (1830) he hammers away at his subject's early conditioning "in a small frontier settlement." This early conditioning is further emphasized by a subsequent confrontation between the stately governor and a boyhood friend, "clad in a hunting-shirt and Indian stockings, and armed with a long gun. His feet have been wet with the waters of many an inland lake and stream; and the leaves and twigs of the tangled wilderness are intertwined with his garments." This man also wears the fashionable wig, or bloody trophy torn from the tangled wilderness of American political morality. There is even a group of Indians, "dull spectators of the strength that has swept away their race." The details of the sketch are sufficiently colonial, but their implications are supplied by

[7] All quotations of Hawthorne's tales and sketches are from *The Complete Works of Nathaniel Hawthorne*, ed. George P. Lathrop (Cambridge, 1883).

73

the literary climate of 1830, and the basic figures recur again and again in Hawthorne's writing. In "My Kinsman, Major Molineux" (1831), the hero is once more indirectly Western, a young savage come from his home in the woods to master the savageries of a more sophisticated society. The visual phenomena of civilization and nature exchange modalities, pillars to pines and back again, constraining our young kinsman to inquire: " 'Am I here, or there?' "— a somewhat useless question, since "here" and "there" refer to seasons of the soul. From time to time we see an allegorical character representing war and faction—perhaps suggested by the "Indians" at the Boston Tea Party—wearing a dualistic face, half red, half black, and followed by a personified nightmare of American history, "wild figures in the Indian dress . . . as if a dream had broken forth from some feverish brain."[8]

Whenever possible, Hawthorne elected a synthesis of time and place which constituted a creative enabling act for the entrance into his fiction of the ever-pressing Western idea. In "The Gentle Boy" (1831), the utility of historical removal is obvious: "The country having been settled but about thirty years, the tracts of original forest still bore no small proportion to the cultivated ground." In this completely American scene, Tobias Pearson, a Puritan settler from "a distant clime," heroically and dangerously lives detached from the community, in a house even closer than the others to the "western wilderness." Paradoxically, it is the other

---

[8] Among Hawthorne's tales and sketches not discussed in this section, the following contain further Western matter, usually marginal: "The Wives of the Dead" (frontier warfare), "The Canterbury Pilgrims" (Oregon expedition), "Alice Doane's Appeal" (traumatic Indian attack), "Fragments From the Journal of a Solitary Man" (Niagara, Western emigration), "The Prophetic Pictures" (paintings of Indians and scenes of frontier warfare), "The Threefold Destiny" (arrowheads), "A Virtuoso's Collection" (King Philip, Daniel Boone, Indian calumets), "The Procession of Life" (our "wondrous backwoodsman" as native Cicero), and "A Book of Autographs" (Thoreauvian observations on the Indian). See also Donald Clifford Gallup, "On Hawthorne's Authorship of 'The Battle-Omen,' " *New England Quarterly*, ix (1936), 690-699, and "Neutral Territory," below.

Puritans, and their enemies the Quakers, who are corrupted by too close and prolonged intercourse with the bedeviled forest, in the very act of carrying Westward the norms of culture: "savages were wandering everywhere among the settlers," we are at one point reminded. Yet at the quiet center of the story stands Ilbrahim, the sacred heart of ordinary decency, on every side badgered by human beastliness. From people like him and Pearson, Hawthorne seems to be saying, historically derives the development of an American civilization worthy of the name. The application of the tale is of course ethical and contemporary, the problematical nature of American civilization remaining in Hawthorne's day what it was in 1659, except that its crises, superficially considered, had moved and were moving farther and farther West. In 1831, New England visionaries were scheming to found a typical Puritan town in Oregon; in the same year, three Nez Percés and one Flathead Indian traveled from Oregon to St. Louis, according to evangelical publicists for the purpose of obtaining Bibles.[9]

"Roger Malvin's Burial" (1831) more sternly explores the disastrously exhilarating advance of civilization into the wilderness. The specific occasion is Lovewell's (or Lovell's) Fight (1725), "one of the few incidents of Indian warfare naturally susceptible of the moonlight of romance," as Hawthorne says in a sarcastic introductory paragraph. "Imagination, by casting certain circumstances judicially into the shade, may see much to admire." One of the circumstances cast judicially into the shade, but helpful for interpretation, is that the little band was after scalp bounties. Two survivors, Roger Malvin and his young friend Reuben Bourne ("limit," "boundary"), are first seen straggling home through the forest from this incursion into the heart of their own savagery. With " 'many and many a long mile of howling wilderness' " before them, Malvin, who is perhaps mortally wounded, decides to die where he is, and in effect tempts Reuben to abandon him; yet, "after

---

[9] Ray Allen Billington, *Westward Expansion: A History of the American Frontier*, 2nd ed. (New York, 1960), pp. 514-517.

all, it was a ghastly fate to be left expiring in the wilderness," for as Hawthorne blandly explains, "an almost superstitious regard, arising perhaps from the customs of the Indians, whose war was with the dead as well as the living, was paid by the frontier inhabitants to the rites of sepulture." Promising to return later and bury the bones, Bourne is "justified." Malvin's most devious argument is that he twenty years earlier abandoned a friend in circumstances he knows were dissimilar, and returned with a rescue party; " 'and he is now a hale and hearty man upon his own farm, far within the frontiers, while I lie wounded here in the depths of the wilderness.' " But as Bourne departs, he is visited by an extraordinarily revealing vision: "Death would come like the slow approach of a corpse, stealing gradually towards him through the forest, and showing its ghastly and motionless features from behind a nearer and yet a nearer tree." Death is an Indian slaughtered by the white man. But this is only one of his several disguises; Bourne returns to the settlements and some of the other masquerades.

With Malvin's daughter, who thinks her father dead and buried, he marries Malvin's frontier farm, but proves a "neglectful husbandman," and in proportion as the neighboring establishments improve—ironically from the cessation of Indian warfare following Lovewell's Fight, where Bourne was wounded in "defence of the frontiers"—his own deteriorates. Finally he accepts the ruined American's last recourse. "He was to throw sunlight into some deep recess of the forest, and seek subsistence from the virgin bosom of the wilderness." Hawthorne's tone is parodic to the point of cruelty, for this pioneering is no adventure but a compulsive Western return. "Oh, who, in the enthusiasm of a daydream, has not wished that he were a wanderer in a world of summer wilderness?" The "tangled and gloomy forest" through which the family wanders is equally natural and moral, and Bourne's "steps were imperceptibly led almost in a circle," eighteen years too late; standing by the rock where he abandoned Malvin, he shoots a "deer."

His wife prepares supper, singing a song about the frontier, hears the shot, and is proud of her son's prowess as a hunter. When he fails to appear, she searches for him, expecting to meet his face "from behind the trunk of every tree"— the same figure as Bourne's vision of evil. She finds only her husband, and the corpse of her son, who is the image of his father, a promising Indian-fighter who "was peculiarly qualified for, and already began to excel in, the wild accomplishments of frontier life," lying on the "grave" of Roger Malvin. The curse is expiated upon the dark and bloody ground where it was incurred.

"The Seven Vagabonds" (1832) represents a more cheerful aspect of Hawthorne's involvement with the literary West. First the story teller-narrator and then *seriatim* six popular entertainers, all of them alienated from the conventional patterns of American life, take refuge from a summer storm in a traveling show-wagon (actually called a "covered wagon") temporarily parked beneath a guidepost at the crossing of three roads. One leads to the sea (Old World), one to the forest (specifically Canada, but emblematically the wilderness), and one to the city (American civilization, the mediating term). The vagabonds propose to journey in company to " 'the camp-meeting at Stamford,' " evidently a sort of shorthand designation for a national literary debauch, perhaps along the lines of Kafka's Great Nature Theater of Oklahoma.

With two of the vagabonds, especially, the native artist must work out his personal salvation. One is a confidence-man, who shares with the comic Devil of popular fiction "a love of deception for its own sake, a shrewd eye and keen relish for human weakness and ridiculous infirmity, and the talent of petty fraud." Like the author of "Roger Malvin's Burial," he commands a great opportunity to "achieve such quantities of minor mischief" as are available to his "sneering spirit by his pretensions to prophetic knowledge," because "so far as he was concerned with the public, his little cunning had the upper hand of its united wisdom." His antithesis, and justification, is a Penobscot Indian, who

77

is ironically reduced to basket-weaving and archery, but who remains the representative modern hero and surrogate of the indigenous artist. When he enters, Hawthorne imagines "either that our wagon had rolled back two hundred years into past ages, or that the forest and its old inhabitants had sprung up around us by enchantment." The wagon stands at the crossroads, but Hawthorne is off to the past, the West. On native ground, Fate is summoning a parliament of free spirits, he tells us, among whom the dispossessed Indian is central: "Wandering down through the waste of ages, the woods had vanished around his path . . . but here, untamable to the routine of artificial life . . . here was the Indian still." This identification of the Indian with the American writer may sound like Thoreau, but in the year "The Seven Vagabonds" was published Thoreau was completing his college preparatory studies at Concord Academy.

"How came I among these wanderers?" the narrator inquires, and answers with a succinct account of America's youthful personality, as defined by the pioneering syndrome: the free mind, the open spirit, the restless impulse. "These were my claims to be of their society." He will become an itinerant novelist, a rather obvious trope for Hawthorne's conception of himself as somehow a Western writer.[10] The storm ceases; the vagrants sally forth from the wagon, only to learn from a traveling preacher (who proceeds Westward) that the camp-meeting is over. But for all his frustration, the newly-dedicated native artist now sees clearly his way among the several directions available to American

---

[10] "The Seven Vagabonds" probably belonged to an abortive series of tales tentatively called *The Story Teller*, in which various native fictions were to have been narrated within the framework of a Western tour. Such a project appears to be hinted by the story itself, and is further alluded to (as is "The Seven Vagabonds") in "Passages From a Relinquished Work" (1834), where Hawthorne fancifully discusses the projected framework in a decidedly nationalistic tone. See Nelson F. Adkins, "The Early Projected Works of Nathaniel Hawthorne," *Papers of the Bibliographical Society of America*, XXXIX (1945), 131-146, esp. 139-141.

men at the crossroads. In company with the local Indian, he sets out for the "distant city."

During 1835 Hawthorne published in the *New England Magazine* five more Western items: "My Visit to Niagara," "Old News," "Sketches From Memory," "The Ambitious Guest," and "Young Goodman Brown." The first of these is slight, almost certainly related to Hawthorne's 1833-1834 trip, and never collected by him. Possibly it was written in some sort of connection with *The Story Teller,* for although the narrator is not, so far as we learn, an itinerant novelist, he is evidently on the verge of "departure for the Far West." The visit to Niagara, where Hawthorne identifies himself, through his unaccountable apathy toward the national spectacle, with "Western traders," and where he buys a cane "curiously convoluted" (as in "Young Goodman Brown") from a Tuscarora Indian, is only a stage on a longer journey. As he departs on a lonely path, the "solitude of the old wilderness" appears to assert itself for his special benefit; the Great Falls was a standard emblem for the Western country, and Hawthorne is claiming to possess it more perfectly than anyone else.

"Old News" is a rather mechanical performance, but a magnificent example of Hawthorne rendering the wild West domestically available by moving backward in time, Eastward in space. From a purported reading of old newspapers, he conjures up New England life at regular intervals during the eighteenth century; the further back he goes, the nearer he approaches the West. The scene of the first sketch (the 1730's) is unmistakably the Atlantic frontier: "New England was then in a state incomparably more picturesque than at present . . . only a narrow strip of civilization along the edge of a vast forest, peopled with enough of its original race to contrast the savage life with the old customs of another world." Peopled also with "all sorts of expatriated vagabonds." The second scene ("The Old French War") is about twenty years later. Much is altered, much remains the same. By the time of the third sketch ("The Old Tory"), Hawthorne finds "fewer characteristic traits" than formerly. "Manners seem to have taken a modern cast," he says, visibly losing interest.

The "Sketches From Memory" are undoubtedly related to Hawthorne's Western travels. In the last one, he speaks of the "steamboat in which I was passenger for Detroit"; another, "The Canal Boat," is ostentatiously and realistically Western (Indians, forests, stumps, ague, boredom). At Rochester, he finds it "impossible to look at its worn pavements and conceive how lately the forest leaves have been swept away," a recurrent Hawthorne trope. And here he once again identifies himself with a vagrant Spirit of America, who "carried a rifle on his shoulder and a powderhorn across his breast, and appeared to stare about him with confused wonder, as if, while he was listening to the wind among the forest boughs, the hum and bustle of an instantaneous city had surrounded him." Wind among the forest boughs was another favorite Hawthorne metaphor, usually suggesting poetry or song.

In "Our Evening Party Among the Mountains," Hawthorne recounts a long conversation about Indian legends, particularly the Great Carbuncle ("few legends more poetical"), and declares himself willing and able to "frame a tale with a deep moral" on this theme. Unfortunately his companions the palefaces are unresponsive and unsympathetic; therefore, he goes on, "I was shut out from the most peculiar field of American fiction." Then he ironically blends with his audience, concluding with the improbable remark: "I do abhor an Indian story." How far Hawthorne was from abhorring an Indian story has already been made overwhelmingly plain in "The Notch of the White Mountains," where he develops one of his strangest and most powerful figures:

> In old times the settlers used to be astounded by the inroads of the northern Indians coming down upon them from this mountain rampart through some defile known only to themselves. It is, indeed, a wondrous path. A demon, it might be fancied, or one of the Titans, was

travelling up the valley, elbowing the heights carelessly aside as he passed, till at length a great mountain took its stand directly across his intended road. He tarries not for such an obstacle, but, rending it asunder a thousand feet from peak to base, discloses its treasures of hidden minerals, its sunless waters, all the secrets of the mountain's inmost heart, with a mighty fracture of rugged precipices on each side. This is the Notch of the White Hills. Shame on me that I have attempted to describe it by so mean an image—feeling, as I do, that it is one of those symbolic scenes which lead the mind to the sentiment, though not to the conception, of Omnipotence.

Somehow that unspeakable Notch involves Hawthorne's sense of his creative self at the deepest and most primitive level, identified with the gods, the processes of insemination and birth, the concupiscences and traumas of the New World.[11] But if life issues with a struggle from the Notch, so does death—ominously, and without warning. For this is the same Notch of "The Ambitious Guest," a parable of the native artist cut off from his potential audience by the spirit of the land he would gladly subdue to his own purposes for the common benefit. In "Sketches From Memory" the Notch is "the entrance, or, in the direction we were going, the extremity, of the romantic defile"; in the story it is also "a cold spot and a dangerous," where the wind whistles "like the choral strain of the spirits of the blast, who in old Indian times had their dwelling among these mountains, and made their heights and recesses a sacred region." Here the young aspirant, on his way to Burlington, " 'and far enough beyond,' " finds "poetry of native growth," a supper of bear's meat, and an unexpected landslide— presumably the kind referred to in the "Sketches" as "red pathways"—which kills him on the threshold of creation-destruction, or the Western frontier.

[11] The underlying figure is almost certainly obstetric, not to say vaginal, as in Melville's notorious "The Tartarus of Maids."

"The choral strain of the spirits of the blast" is like the sounds that ride Niagara, in the sketch of that name. "All that night," Hawthorne said of the Falls, "as there has been and will be for ages past and to come, a rushing sound was heard, as if a great tempest were sweeping through the air. It mingled with my dreams, and made them full of storm and whirlwind." This nightmare noise was also the ground bass for "Young Goodman Brown," in which "a confused and doubtful sound of voices" is intermittently heard, blending "the murmur of the old forest" (West) with the "familiar tones" of Salem village (East). Throughout the story, unconverted nature howls, roars, creaks, cries, and yells, "in homage to the prince of all," the prince being optionally the Devil and the genius of American history. Visual perceptions are perhaps even more conspicuously implicated in America's Western waywardness. The diabolical baptismal scene simultaneously derives from Hawthorne's eyewitness account of a fire on the banks of Lake Erie, which he thought "might have been transferred, almost unaltered, to a tale of the supernatural"—in "A Night Scene," "Sketches From Memory," Second Series—and from James Hall's account of a Western camp-meeting in "The Backwoodsman."[12] Hawthorne's inspiration typically

[12] "Nothing could exceed the solemn and beautiful effect of the meeting at night. The huts were all illuminated, and lights were fastened to the trunks of the trees, throwing a glare upon the overhanging canopy of leaves. . . . All around was the dark gloom of the forest, deepened to intense blackness by its contrast with the brilliant light of the camp." *Legends of the West*, p. 11. Hall's description, or even Hawthorne's, may equally derive from a comparable description of a Huron encampment in *The Last of the Mohicans* (Philadelphia, 1826): "A dozen blazing piles now shed their lurid brightness on the place, which resembled some unhallowed and supernatural arena, in which malicious demons had assembled to act their bloody and lawless rites" (II, 99); or, again: "The dying fires in the clearing, cast a dim and uncertain light on the dusky figures, that were silently stalking to and fro" (110). A variety of Notebook passages shows Hawthorne working hard with eye and mind to concretize and complicate his sensuous apprehension of standard Western symbols. See *The American Notebooks*, p. 31 (forest), p. 56 (cavern, brook, forest), and p. 159 (Hawthorne lost in a Concord forest, trying to walk from his house to Emerson's).

emerges from the fusion of direct perception and popular Western writing.

"Young Goodman Brown" is about American advance to the West, penetration into the dark forest of the unmapped future, which is also the buried past. As broadly hinted in the opening dialogue, the moral issue is bad faith in every conceivable sense, a failure of integrity sufficiently correlative with the American situation to justify the epithet "national." The hero will journey " 'forth and back' " between " 'now and sunrise' ": Brown's night journey is not merely psychological, but is also the temporal duration of the national movement through space to the Pacific Ocean, whose final significance is to be manifest at the end, if at all. With a nightmare mélange of hidden allusions to the American dream—doubled as the dream of his disturbed young wife, a sort of bosomy Columbia in a mobcap—and to the grim work of civilizing a virgin continent, the protagonist plunges darkly into the wilderness. Wherever he goes is a clearing, the trees magically opening and closing around his progress. At one point he sits on a stump, refusing to go farther; plainly, he is not the first pioneer passing this way. The farther he goes, the faster he goes, a phenomenon also characteristic of the Westward Movement, "until, quivering among the trees, he saw a red light before him, as when the felled trunks and branches of a clearing have been set on fire." This is not the sunrise of arrival, but a lurid Western landscape—aflame with the conflicting moral passions of actor and author—betokening a previous advance and an intermediate stage.

Brown's failure to keep faith is a failure not only of his own but of several generations. The Devil has helped his grandfather whip a Quaker woman, and encouraged his father to burn an Indian village during King Philip's War; and these are the same behaviors which generated the psychic wounds of "The Gentle Boy" and "Roger Malvin's Burial." Brown's refusal to believe in the sins of the past, or their present consequences, is evidently symptomatic of a representative American shortcoming, as in the disinclination (still widespread) to examine closely into the nature of the Westward Movement. " 'We are a people of prayer, and good works to boot,' " Brown declares, " 'and abide no such wickedness.' " His sudden swing to the opposite pole, his easy acceptance of the sins of the past, and his use of them to justify a continuing malefaction, may by certain carping critics be thought to hint an equally representative national inadequacy. Through the pages of "Young Goodman Brown," as through the annals of American history, runs the ethical absurdity of its always being too late to turn back. As a character in a contemporary novel happily informs us: " 'We have treated the Ingens so badly, that we cannot now live in peace, but are obliged to add insult to injury.' "[13] Brown enters the forest, thinking that Indians may lurk behind every tree; Indians he associates with the Devil; the minute he does so, the Devil is at his elbow. "Whither, then, could these holy men be journeying so deep into the heathen wilderness?" Into the depth of American humanity, which was also the blackness of darkness.

With one or two exceptions, the Western tales Hawthorne wrote during the next few years show a dwindling of intensity and commitment, a corresponding diminution of realism and artistry, and a faintly distressing habit of repeating old themes, images, and even phrases, with no fresh increment of meaning. "Old Ticonderoga: A Picture of the Past" (1836) was aptly titled; despite a considerable charm, it contained little new. "A Bell's Biography" (1837) is an obviously ironic historical sketch, in which social and cultural change is rendered through contrast with an enduring object; unfortunately, the bell has no reciprocal

---

[13] In James S. French, *Elkswatawa* (New York, 1836), I, 93. In the same volume is the following instructive colloquy (p. 143):

"And do you seriously think, Rolfe, that Heaven will hold us accountable for merely killing Ingens?"

"Perhaps not us, Earth, but when we shall sleep with our fathers, and our little republic become the first power upon earth, their fate may then rise up in judgment against it."

"How; what is to happen?"

organic relationship with the New World landscape in which Hawthorne was determined to embed it. "Endicott and the Red Cross" (1837) is hardly more novel, except in "looking forward" to *The Scarlet Letter*, not so much because the lady wears a red letter as because of the way Hawthorne was redesigning his scene (Endicott speaking): " 'The wolf and the bear meet us within halloo of our dwellings. . . . The stubborn roots of the trees break our ploughshares, when we would till the earth. Our children cry for bread, and we must dig in the sands of the sea-shore to satisfy them.' " Apparently Hawthorne already sensed the advantage of removing his frontier far enough backward and Eastward to avail himself of a neutral territory at the boundaries of forest and ocean. It was in the course of this enlargement and particularization that Hester Prynne left off being a "lost and desperate creature."

"The Great Carbuncle" (1836) is more impressive. Like the old Notch, " 'the gateway of this mountain region' " where it lurks, the Carbuncle is a secretive and compulsive symbol, however widely shared with other American writers and readers. In "A Virtuoso's Collection" (1842), Hawthorne spoke of it as "this mighty gem, which it had been one of the wild projects of my youth to discover. Possibly it might have looked brighter to me in those days than now." The story itself concludes with a similar confession: "[I] was lured, by the faith of poesy, to be the latest pilgrim of the GREAT CARBUNCLE." Whatever else it may be, the Carbuncle is Hawthorne's ambition to betray in fiction the ultimate secrets of the Great West. His fictive adventurers are first glimpsed in a typical bit of frontier behavior, temporarily laying aside their competitive animosities in order "to contribute a mutual aid in building a rude hut of branches," soon called a "wigwam." The pioneers have ascended—ascent in this story is the same as going West— to a "remote and solitary region," where "a vast extent of wilderness lay between them and the nearest settlement." The Amonoosuck River supplies the usual roaring noise, and there is also flickering, uncertain light. The Seeker is a mad Natty Bumppo, "a tall, lean, weather-beaten man, some sixty years of age . . . clad in the skins of wild animals." All the explorers are racked by Western fever. "They spoke of the innumerable attempts which had been made to reach the spot"—what spot, exactly?—"and of the singular fatality which had hitherto withheld success from all adventurers." According to Indian tradition, the Carbuncle is almost impossible of attainment, owing to a guardian spirit who repeatedly moves it "from peak to peak of the higher hills," or shrouds it in vapor. "But these tales"—predictably—"were deemed unworthy of credit."

Only humble domestic Hannah and Matthew—literally settlers, as the others are not—see the Carbuncle and survive. First Hannah tangles her hair in a bough, as nearly every one of Hawthorne's Western heroines is required to do. Then she and her husband rise from the forest into a barren landscape, conceivably suggestive of the Great Plains rising toward the Rocky Mountains; this stage of the Westward Movement always came as a shock to nineteenth-century Americans, who from the first were predisposed to envisage the West as a succession of green perspectives. Here they leave Nature for El Dorado, and finally arrive at a metaphysical frontier, climbing "as far and as high, between earth and heaven, as they could find foothold." Radiance breaks through the mist, and "one object after another started out of its impenetrable obscurity into sight, with precisely the effect of a new creation." But like nearly every other Western symbol in Hawthorne, the Carbuncle is as dangerous as enchanting. Wisely, the couple abandon the treasure and retreat to their ordinary lives; the Carbuncle's light begins to fade, and their tale meets an ever-diminishing credence.

In "The Great Carbuncle," the Seeker announces: " 'Having found it, I shall bear it to a certain cavern that I wot of, and there, grasping it in my arms, lie down and die, and keep it buried with me forever.' " Having seen it, he turns to marble. In "The Man of Adamant" (1836), Richard Digby's Carbuncle is his clear title to a religious revelation insuring salvation for himself and damnation for all besides. Determining to isolate himself from humanity in order to enjoy in unalloyed bliss his singular beatitude, Digby (naturally) "took an axe, to hew space enough for a tabernacle in the wilderness, and some few other necessaries, especially a sword and gun, to smite and slay any intruder upon his hallowed seclusion, and plunged into the dreariest depths of the forest." The farther West, the thicker the trees, the darker the scene, the better he likes it. The cave, or interiority of a ruined heart, is where he arrives and what he likes best. In a wilderness noisy with his monomaniacal laughter, Digby sees the spirit of Mary Goffe, an erstwhile disciple in England (actually dead), "wandering thus far into the forest, with her golden hair dishevelled by the boughs." She offers him "sympathy," in the form of a drink from the spring, or "gem of the wilderness," as Hawthorne called it in "A Rill From the Town Pump." But at the threshold of the cave, he dashes the chalice from her hand, his disease runs its course, and he turns to stone. A century later, "when the trackless forest of Richard Digby's day had long been interspersed with settlements," Digby and his cave are discovered by children, whose horrified parents dam the entrance with stones and dirt, obliterating all trace of the petrified man. Only a wild legend is left, in which belief once more gradually wanes.

Hawthorne's Western enthusiasm was likewise waning, and he wrote no more tales of the border for seven years. In "Earth's Holocaust" (1844), he somewhat halfheartedly removed to those Western prairies where in both fact and fiction mid-nineteenth-century America was always on fire; "as central a spot as any other on the globe," Hawthorne ambiguously calls it. Of course, there was good sense in locating so universal a conflagration, and so unrealistic a parable, in the vast spaces of the West—unless we begin to wonder where all the spectators come from; and thematically, the West doubtless recommended itself as the section most progressive, and in that respect, as in others, most American. But significantly Hawthorne stands on the sidelines, and the story's final implication is that none of the destruction will last, which is just as well, for in the holocaust much of the New World—including such achievements as Hawthorne's early fiction—is accidentally destroyed along with most of the Old.

For *Mosses From an Old Manse* (1846), Hawthorne wrote a charming preface purportedly describing the setting in which the contents were composed. Among them were Western items going back many years: "Roger Malvin's Burial," for instance, and "Young Goodman Brown." Perhaps the tone of "The Old Manse" is so Western because of what was being collected. On the other hand, some of the Western tone clearly derives from Hawthorne's encounters with Thoreau. A passage about abandoning "civilized life, cities, houses, and whatever moral or material enormities in addition to these the perverted ingenuity of our race has contrived," would seem to depend upon Hawthorne's inside knowledge of what was going on at Walden Pond. He also tells how he and Channing "delivered" themselves to the "free air, to live like the Indians," a behavior and sentiment their mutual friend must have endorsed, and probably suggested, though it also jibed with Hawthorne's sense of his own boyhood.[14] He is now concerned with ordinary facts about the local Indians, in whom he had earlier shown little detailed interest, and has even become an arrowhead fancier: "Thoreau, who has a strange faculty of finding what the Indians have left behind them, first set me on the search." Yet in the end, Hawthorne insists upon remaining Hawthorne. The long paragraph in which these Indian matters are discussed peremptorily concludes: "But

[14] In the same preface: "The painted Indian who paddled his canoe along the Assabeth three hundred years ago could hardly have seen a wilder gentleness displayed upon its banks [previously called "prairies"] and reflected in its bosom than we did. Nor could the same Indian have prepared his noontide meal with more simplicity. . . . The chief profit of those wild days to him [Channing] and me lay, not in any definite idea . . . but in the freedom which we thereby won from all custom and conventionalism and fettering influences of man on man."

this is nonsense. The Old Manse is better than a thousand wigwams."

Providence was already leading him, as he announced toward the end of this sketch, "from the Old Manse into a custom house." That was in Salem, where his deepest Western imaginings had previously arisen and would now arise once more, first in a story called "Main Street" (1849), of which he explained: "It has often occurred to me, that, if its growth from infancy upward, and the vicissitude of characteristic scenes that have passed along this thoroughfare during the more than two centuries of its existence, could be presented to the eye in a shifting panorama, it would be an exceedingly effective method of illustrating the march of time. Acting on this idea, I have contrived a certain pictorial exhibition." Salem was Cincinnati still. The first picture is "the ancient and primitive wood," where "the white man's axe has never smitten a single tree." Even so, "there is already a faintly traced path, running nearly east and west, as if a prophecy or foreboding of the future street had stolen into the heart of the solemn old wood." Crossed now and again by the "little streamlet" of *The Scarlet Letter*, the track is first made by Indians, of whom Hawthorne singles out the great Squaw Sachem, a preliminary type of Hester Prynne, a "majestic and queenly woman." Can it be, he rhetorically inquires, that a city shall exist here? "Must it not be a wilderness forever?" The first scene abruptly ends with an interruption from the audience. " 'The whole affair is a manifest catchpenny! . . . The trees look more like weeds in a garden than a primitive forest.' " But this was the necessary *habitus* of the Eastern American writer, the sensuous content of whose Western myth inevitably derived from the back yard. " 'Human art has its limits,' " Hawthorne says, passing to the second scene.

Now we have European settlers, and in great plenty axes, hunters, leather clothing, log cabins, clearings, stumps, pioneering zeal, spectatorial Indians, and all the other accoutrements of the Western mode. Dwellings rise instantaneously and miraculously; concurrently the forest track becomes

better defined, though still proceeding "from one clearing
to another" through light and shadow, "everywhere showing a decided line, along which human interests have begun
to hold their career." The Indians "perhaps are saddened
by a flitting presentiment that this heavy tread will find its
way over all the land; and that the wild woods, the wild
wolf, and the wild Indian will be alike trampled beneath
it. Even so shall it be." And even so would it be, in only
a few years, for that literary Indian, Nathaniel Hawthorne.
But now a ship arrives from England bearing another type
of Hester, "a rose of beauty from an English garden, now
to be transplanted to a fresher soil." Perhaps centuries later
"other flowers of the same race will appear in the same
soil, and gladden other generations with hereditary beauty.
Does not the vision haunt us yet?" More interpolated ob-
jections; but the author knows what he knows about Hester's daughter, who was also his own.

Item by item, the Puritan commonwealth takes shape,
preparing to conquer and be conquered by a continent.
Woods, wolves, Indians continue to recede before English
order; or is the natural disorder merely being transferred
to the people? Upon Major Hawthorne's warrant, Quakers
are once again whipped into the forest whence they came.
Then it is time for King Philip's War, in which Young
Goodman Brown's father fired an Indian village. But after
a brilliant scene concerning the witchcraft insanity, in which
Martha Carrier provides another broadly ironic analogue of
Hester, Hawthorne as always seems to lose interest; as well
he might, for the later townspeople can no longer imagine
that Salem was ever that imaginary West toward which
Hawthorne was once more traveling, and where he obviously
felt more was going on than in the nineteenth-century back-
water where he lived and wrote. Before Hawthorne can
come down to the present—"give a reflex of the very life
that is flitting past us"—his machine collapses and the pictures are over. For this mock catastrophe, the mock show-
man offers mock regrets, and his most captious critic, who

has not yet been shown *The Scarlet Letter*, but only its themes, cultural bearing, and national significance, demands his money back.

2. *THE SCARLET LETTER*

In 1846 Hawthorne wrote harshly of William Gilmore Simms's *Views and Reviews in American Literature, History and Fiction*, with special attention to "The Epochs and Events of American History, as Suited to the Purposes of Art in Fiction": "We cannot help feeling that the real treasures of his subject have escaped the author's notice. The themes suggested by him, viewed as he views them, would produce nothing but historical novels, cast in the same worn out mould that has been in use these thirty years, and which it is time to break up and fling away."[1] Hawthorne knew the tradition better than he knew how inescapably he was bound to accept and transform it. Years earlier he had excerpted for his magazine a long and suggestive passage about the Puritans from John Howard Hinton's *History and Topography of the United States,* which was in turn quoted at length from the *North American Review*: " 'Arrived at this outside of the world, as they termed it, they seemed to themselves to have found a place where the Governour of all things yet reigned alone. The solitude of their adopted land, so remote from the communities of kindred men that it appeared like another world,—a wild ocean before them, and an unexplored wilderness behind,—nourished the solemn deeptoned feeling. . . . If ever the character of men has been seen more than any where else in powerful action or development, and operated on by the force of peculiar and strongly moving causes, it was here. . . .' This is a powerful description, but the reality will be found much to exceed it."[2]

[1] Randall Stewart, "Hawthorne's Contributions to *The Salem Advertiser*," *American Literature*, v (1934), 331.

[2] Revised by Samuel Knapp (Boston, 1834), I, 39-40; *American Magazine of Useful and Entertaining Knowledge*, II (1836), 468.

The reality of *The Scarlet Letter* is born of an extraordinarily happy marriage between the time when it was written—a necessary component of the historical imagination, which Simms's and Hinton's formulations tended to overlook—and the time of which it presumes to speak. Hawthorne's sense of the two times rests on an accurate and imaginative perception of fundamental likeness, their common resemblance to the Western frontier, a mode of definition he had for twenty years been applying to cunningly selected aspects of the New England past. During her first exposure on the scaffold (or "point of view"), Hester Prynne's "preternaturally active" mind, anxious for relief from "the cruel weight and hardness of the reality," reverts to the English village of her youth, and the continental city of her early married life, before adjusting to the present facts of her infant in arms and badge of ignominy.[3] Her reality includes these, for they are cognate with it; but more broadly conceived, the reality is the setting, "this roughly hewn street of a little town, on the edge of the Western wilderness." ("Hewn" because chopped out of the forest with an axe.) The street is at once the "track along which she had been treading, since her happy infancy," and the course of empire to which Hawthorne devoted such copious attention in "Main Street."

The locale of *The Scarlet Letter* owes more to the Leatherstocking Tales than to any seventeenth-century view of the American situation. "What could they see," wrote William Bradford of the actual settlers, "but a hideous and desolate wilderness, full of wild beasts and wild men. . . . If they looked behind them, there was the mighty ocean which they had passed and was now as a main bar and gulf to separate them from all the civil parts of the world."[4] Bradford's community perches on the brink of the ocean;

[3] *The Scarlet Letter* quotations are from *The Centenary Edition of the Works of Nathaniel Hawthorne*, ed. William Charvat, Roy Harvey Pearce, Claude M. Simpson, Fredson Bowers, and Matthew J. Bruccoli (Columbus, Ohio, 1962-).

[4] *Of Plymouth Plantation, 1620-1647*, ed. Samuel Eliot Morison (New York, 1952), p. 62.

Hawthorne's crouches on the verge of the forest. For Bradford, the West is practically unimaginable; for Hawthorne,
the West is the meaning of America, and must necessarily
be imagined. Because of the time-space equations inherent
in the moving frontier, Hawthorne's setting engenders terrestrial, ideological, and temporal extensions which a man
in Bradford's position could not envisage. "East" is
Europe, Old World, the past; "West" is America, New
World, the future; and their topographical equivalents are
ocean and forest. Hawthorne concentrates on the point of
meeting between them, the moment of passage from old to
new, the frontier. In an America whose emergent newness—
which was also its fundamental definition—was always
looked for in the West, the imagined time about which
Hawthorne wrote essentially and metaphorically coincided
with the moving time in which he did the writing. In *The
Scarlet Letter* he brought the Puritans up to date by placing
them where they always were, but did not know they were.

The action of the novel oscillates between ocean and
forest. In chapter 14 Hester talks with Roger Chillingworth
by the sea, in chapter 17 with Mr. Dimmesdale in the
woods. The two men customarily walk together in one of
these places. (What other places are there?) When Hester
goes in search of Dimmesdale, she naturally seeks him
"along the shores of the peninsula, or on the wooded hills
of the neighbouring country." In fact, she finds him returning through the woods from a visit to "the Apostle Eliot,
among his Indian converts." Inevitably Hester lives where
the uncluttered natural scene is a perpetual reminder of the
historical processes underlying her passion, "on the outskirts of the town, within the verge of the peninsula, but
not in close vicinity to any other habitation," in a "small
thatched cottage"—Hawthorne's one concession to her English origins. Except that her situation is even more clearly
and comprehensively emblematic, she resembles Daniel
Boone, or Natty Bumppo, or, more likely, Henry Thoreau,
who had several years earlier lived at Walden Pond, writing
the first draft of his great book, and lecturing the citizens of

Concord on the meaning of his experiment in Western living. Hester's cottage "had been built by an earlier settler, and abandoned, because the soil about it was too sterile for cultivation, while its comparative remoteness put it out of the sphere of that social activity which already marked the habits of the emigrants. It stood on the shore, looking across a basin of the sea at the forest-covered hills, towards the west." From the vantage point of this highly significant residence, Hester Prynne looks over the bay, which is a little part of the ocean, at the forest, which is the beginning of the continent, and thus with one foreshortened glance takes in the whole scope of American development.

So too the final crowd scene is appropriately peopled by exemplary guests from ocean and wilderness, including frontiersmen from the "forest settlements," dressed in deer-skins. Pearl "ran and looked the wild Indian in the face; and he grew conscious of a nature wilder than his own. Thence, with native audacity . . . she flew into the midst of a group of mariners, the swarthy-cheeked wild men of the ocean, as the Indians were of the land." Hester also is identified with the Indians. Even before her first appearance in the novel, Hawthorne supposes that the spectators may have assembled to watch a "heterodox religionist . . . scourged out of the town," or a vagrant Indian "driven with stripes into the shadow of the forest"; the victim they get is a little of each, and in ways they fail to understand a better victim than they deserve. If Hester is close to the Indians, then by implication so is Hawthorne (as in "The Seven Vagabonds"). In the heroine's redeemed state, it is even reported that Indian arrows strike her breast and fall "harmless to the ground."

From forest climax to market-place denouement, Hester and her lover are suspended in the dilemma which has been insidiously affecting their destinies, and those of their wilfully unknowing neighbors, from the time the concept New World first got abroad in Europe.[5] Their "options" are

[5] Between 1503 and 1507, according to Edmundo O'Gorman, *The Invention of America* (Bloomington, Ind., 1961), pp. 113-124. See also Durand Echeverria, *Mirage in the West* (Princeton, 1957): "At

insistently spelled out by Hester: " 'Whither leads yonder forest-track? Backward to the settlement, thou sayest! Yes; but onward, too! Deeper it goes, and deeper, into the wilderness, less plainly to be seen at every step; until, some few miles hence, the yellow leaves will show no vestige of the white man's tread. There thou art free!' " Dimmesdale demurring, she tries the opposite direction: " 'Then there is the broad pathway of the sea! . . . It brought thee hither. If thou so choose, it will bear thee back again.' " Unfortunately, Hester's questions are only rhetorical, as she herself implies by introducing them within the framework of a broader query (to which the answer, for her, is "yes"): " 'Doth the universe lie within the compass of yonder town, which only a little time ago was but a leaf-strewn desert, as lonely as this around us?' " They are all, in one way or another, and Hawthorne with them, bound by a dark necessity, as Chillingworth acutely observes; the black flower of creative understanding blossoms as it must. Hester's reality—and the reality of the others, insofar as she imparts significance to them—is born on the frontier which, in this novel, and in the culture of which it is a typical illusion, has, like the act of love, or germ of evil, a consecration of its own.

The Scarlet Letter is naturally less concerned with the ocean of the past than with the forest of the future. Like the future, the forest is a free image, indeterminate and pluralistic, suggesting the widest range of personal and cultural possibilities. Without ruling out the obvious truth that propinquity to wild nature is bound to affect a man or culture—whatever they think—we may also infer that this effect will be qualified by what the man brings to nature. Inescapably, he humanizes the forest by projecting upon it his own desires, fears, and torments; filled with a false elation, Dimmesdale returns to the settlements after his secret interview with Hester, and "the pathway among the

---

an early date, probably in the sixteenth century, the semantic confusion inherent in the epithet *nouveau monde* had begun to cause the idea of a newly created world to overlap that of a newly discovered world" (p. 5).

woods seemed wilder, more uncouth with its rude natural obstacles, and less trodden by the foot of man, than he remembered it on his outward journey." The path is no wilder, but he is. So that wild witch Mistress Hibbins is forever accusing people of traveling into the forest to chaffer with the Devil. She is palpably attributing her own motives to the rest; she is also superstitiously distorting what can only be understood historically and aesthetically. To a degree, her particular form of insanity is shared by nearly everyone; by the scholarly Dimmesdale, "who had come from one of the great English universities, bringing all the learning of the age into our wild forest-land," and who is driven to wonder if he has made a pact with the Fiend; by "liberated" Hester, who asks if her first husband may be " 'like the Black Man that haunts the forest round about us' "; and by the childish imagination of Pearl, who in the forest associates Dimmesdale and the Black Man, the two personages about whom she is most curious.

The forest is delusive—visually and therefore metaphorically—and thus a natural source of confusion. Walking away from Hester, Dimmesdale wonders if their interview were a dream: "He threw a backward glance; half expecting that he should discover only some faintly traced features or outline of the mother and the child, slowly fading into the twilight of the woods." His doubt is partly occasioned by the well-known difficulty of seeing clearly in the dim light of a forest, through intervening trees and undergrowth, partly by the fact that he has never seen these two people very clearly. So Hester, back in the marketplace, finds it hard to imagine the forest as real. "Her spirit sank with the idea that all must have been a delusion." The forest is the mirror of a tricky memory, and of the modes of behavior which most bewilder it, the fading image of what could not, or should not, have happened. In a way, Hester is right, for the forest is the occasion and opportunity of sin, and in that sense unreal. Hester and Dimmesdale meet "in the dim wood" like "two spirits" after death, "coldly shuddering, in mutual dread." And when they decide to flee, it is like "breathing the wild, free atmosphere of an unredeemed, unchristianized, lawless region."

The wilderness is also the novel's action. " 'There is no path to guide us out of this dismal maze!' " (Hester to Chillingworth), as there is no simple interpretation to guide us out of *The Scarlet Letter*, nor out of the republic for which it stands. They are all, Hester reluctantly continues, " 'wandering together in this gloomy maze of evil, and stumbling, at every step, over the guilt wherewith we have strewn our path.' " More elaborately, Hawthorne describes the path into the forest, the deeds of his people, and the pattern of his fiction in interchangeable terms: "It was the point whither their pathway had so long been tending, and darkening ever, as it stole along. . . . The forest was obscure around them." The crucial interview between Hester and Dimmesdale begins: "Thus they went onward, not boldly, but step by step, into the themes that were brooding deepest in their hearts," until "their real thoughts" are "led across the threshold." The forest is within them and between them, as it is also around the clearing which men call Boston.

With the full weight of the American condition pressing them on, mother and daughter on a fateful day leave their cottage and cross the peninsula to the mainland. The footpath they take straggles "onward into the mystery of the primeval forest," more figurative at every step; more ambivalent, too, for "primeval" suggests both new and old. The forest "hemmed it in so narrowly, and stood so black and dense on either side, and disclosed such imperfect glimpses of the sky above, that, to Hester's mind, it imaged not amiss the moral wilderness in which she had so long been wandering." Yet there is always the "flitting cheerfulness" of sunlight "at the farther extremity of some long vista." So they arrive at the brook which Hawthorne had more than a decade earlier studied near the Notch,[6] and which he now identifies with Pearl—"the current of her life

[6] See *The American Notebooks*, ed. Randall Stewart (New Haven, 1932), p. 56.

gushed from a well-spring as mysterious." With "never-ceasing loquacity," the brook, like Hawthorne, whispers, or insinuates, "tales out of the heart of the old forest." Again like Hawthorne, it tells an "unintelligible secret of some very mournful mystery that had happened," or propheti-cally laments something still to happen, "within the verge of the dismal forest." As usual, Pearl stands on the "mar-gin" of it. " 'I have a strange fancy,' observed the sensitive minister, 'that this brook is the boundary between two worlds, and that thou canst never meet thy Pearl again.' " The brook is another image of the frontier; but the sensitive minister is wrong about Pearl and her mother—it is he who is cut off.

Pearl is at home in the forest, as even her mother is not, much less Dimmesdale or Chillingworth. Peace and gentle-ness flow from the "kindred wildness" to the little girl. She gathers wildflowers, and decorates herself with them, becom-ing "a nymph-child, or an infant dryad, or whatever else was in closest sympathy with the antique wood." This is not irony. Even more than her mother, yet through her mother, Pearl is a lay saint, and is most clearly seen, most vividly remembered, surrounded by the dark wilderness, but trans-figured with light: "It was strange, the way in which Pearl stood, looking so stedfastly at them through the dim medium of the forest-gloom; herself, meanwhile, all glorified with a ray of sunshine, that was attracted thitherward as by a certain sympathy." Pearl, it begins to dawn on us, is the Spirit of the West, the rising glory of America. *The Scarlet Letter* is not so much about actual, individual sin as about the interrelations of *original sin* (in several witty senses) and the birth of a nation. So much was strongly hinted in the opening chapter, where the rose-bush is said possibly to have "survived out of the stern old wilderness, so long after the fall of the gigantic pines and oaks that originally over-shadowed it."

"The founders of a new colony," Hawthorne acidly notes on the first page, "whatever Utopia of human virtue and happiness they might originally project, have invariably recognized it among their earliest practical necessities to allot a portion of the virgin soil as a cemetery, and another portion as the site of a prison." Cemetery and prison are especially appropriate to the Puritans, who envisaged no Utopia in the first place, and whose hearts were never especially stirred—as the nineteenth-century American heart so feverishly was—by metaphorical analogues of virgin soil. The prison already shows signs of age; the rusted "iron-work of its oaken door looked more antique than anything else in the new world." For all their rigid insensitivity, the Puritans are undergoing precisely the change which Frederick Jackson Turner (and Hawthorne, and many another) conceived as "Americanization," and attributed to the action of the frontier. The governor's mansion is planned "after the residences of gentlemen of fair estate in his native land" (which is not America), but perforce "with many variations, suggested by the nature of his building-materials, diversity of climate, and a different mode of social life." Likewise, "the exigencies of this new country had transformed Governor Bellingham into a soldier, as well as a statesman and ruler." But "in a hard soil and amid the close struggle for subsistence," he has been compelled to abandon "the native English taste for ornamental gardening." Still, John Wilson contends that pear, peach, and grape may yet be naturalized. All this is very human, and a trifle comic. In "The New England Holiday," Hawthorne implies that even in their festivities the Puritans are trying to maintain the customs of the Old World, and doing their usual bad job of it. Salvation lies elsewhere.

"Rooted almost at the threshold [of the Puritan prison], was a wild rose-bush," which Hawthorne finds "directly on the threshold" of his story. Out of the black interior issues the incomparably sexual Hester, "on the threshold of the prison-door" repelling the beadle: "and stepped into the open air, as if by her own free-will." (At the end, Dimmesdale instinctively repeats her gesture.) Slowly and painfully, American history begins, for the "threshold" over which Hester so dramatically steps from old to new, from confinement to liberation, and a keener suffering, is the domestic variant of the Western frontier.[7] Even during imprisonment she has been metamorphosed, so that the envious Puritan matrons are stunned to "perceive how her beauty shone out, and made a halo of the misfortune and ignominy in which she was enveloped." Hester has undergone "the new birth"—the doctrine which constitutes the central core of meaning in *The Scarlet Letter*.

The commanding image for the new birth is twofold, "transplanting" and "taking root." According to Chillingworth, Dimmesdale has failed to take a root in life. Hester is more tenacious. In a long, crucial passage, Hawthorne carefully explains her powerful "American" quality and the extra margin of reality which increasingly accrues to her:

> It may seem marvellous, that, with the world before her,—kept by no restrictive clause of her condemnation within the limits of the Puritan settlement, so remote and so obscure,—free to return to her birthplace, or to any other European land, and there hide her character and identity under a new exterior, as completely as if emerging into another state of being,—and having also the passes of the dark, inscrutable forest open to her,

[7] Among mid-nineteenth-century American writers, this was an almost platitudinous identification. As Charles Lanman explained, in *A Summer in the Wilderness* (New York, 1847): "The River Queen, as Saint Louis is sometimes called, is looked upon as the threshold leading to the wild and romantic region of the Upper Mississippi. . . . It is the point whence must start all distant expeditions to the North and West" (pp. 13-14). Cf. also Parkman, *The California and Oregon Trail* (New York, 1849): "Should any one of my readers ever be impelled to visit the prairies . . . I can assure him that he need not think to enter at once upon the paradise of his imagination. A dreary preliminary, protracted crossing of the threshold, awaits him before he finds himself fairly upon the verge of the 'great American desert'" (p. 42). Melville, of course, said it best (in *Pierre*, ed. Henry A. Murray, New York, 1949): "On the threshold of any wholly new and momentous devoted enterprise, the thousand ulterior intricacies and imperilings to which it must conduct; these, at the outset, are mostly withheld from sight; and so, through her ever-primeval wilderness Fortune's Knight rides on" (p. 206).

where the wildness of her nature might assimilate itself with a people whose customs and life were alien from the law that had condemned her,—it may seem marvellous, that this woman should still call that place her home, where, and where only, she must needs be the type of shame. But there is a fatality, a feeling so irresistible and inevitable that it has the force of doom, which almost invariably compels human beings to linger around and haunt, ghost-like, the spot where some great and marked event has given the color to their lifetime; and still the more irresistibly, the darker the tinge that saddens it. Her sin, her ignominy, were the roots which she had struck into the soil. It was as if a new birth, with stronger assimilations than the first, had converted the forest-land, still so uncongenial to every other pilgrim and wanderer, into Hester Prynne's wild and dreary, but life-long home. All other scenes of earth—even that village of rural England, where happy infancy and stainless maidenhood seemed yet to be in her mother's keeping, like garments put off long ago—were foreign to her, in comparison.

In order to maintain her reality, she must stay in the colony. The reality is not hers fortuitously nor by Providential dispensation, but organically and culturally, by virtue of superior adaptation. It is not merely Chillingworth's persistent persecution, nor Dimmesdale's change of heart and premature death, that prevents her permanent return to Europe. Through the metaphor which informs her, Hester Prynne is condemned to the neutral territory, thereupon to mediate, as best she may, the contradictions of the culture which gradually emerges through her personal anguish. Even at the end, when she so pathetically hopes to escape, "there was a sense within her,—too ill-defined to be made a thought, but weighing heavily on her mind,—that her whole orb of life, both before and after, was connected with this spot, as with the one point that gave it unity."[8]

[8] As in "The Custom-House" Hawthorne speaks of Salem as "the

Yet like the forest, the new birth is baffling. Hester almost misses her destiny, expecting a new life from her marriage with Chillingworth, "a new life, but feeding itself on time-worn materials, like a tuft of green moss on a crumbling wall." Nor does she receive new life directly from Dimmesdale, but from the suffering he causes her. He himself misses it entirely, except as we credit his Election Sermon with prophetic quality, and his dying confession with the attributes of grace. His anticipation of a "new life" abroad with Hester is as absurd as her effort to undo the past. The new birth is always characterized by indirection and uncertainty of effect. According to Dimmesdale's theology—fictionally correct—the child redeems Hester, but not himself, as a later generation redeems an earlier, or as Hawthorne in *The Scarlet Letter* redeems his own ancestry. Then what are we to make of Chillingworth bequeathing "a very considerable amount of property, both here and in England" to Pearl, so that she becomes "the richest heiress of her day, in the New World"? Chillingworth's bequest is the freest act of charity in the novel. Has he of all men participated secretly in the new birth? We can hardly conclude against him.

This principle is so vital to the novel that even Hester's abortive and sometimes naïve strivings in the direction of free-thinking are accommodated to it and dignified. Eschewing the passion which her situation prevents, she becomes a Renaissance bluestocking; she is also responding to a local situation, the American frontier, with its concomitant intellectual overtones for the Eastern writer:

> Standing alone in the world . . . she cast away the fragments of a broken chain. The world's law was no law for her mind. It was an age in which the human intellect,

---

inevitable centre of the universe" for himself. In the novel, the point of unity is literally the scaffold, culturally the frontier, anagogically the Cross. At the outset, Hester and Pearl are compared with the Blessed Virgin and Christ. "But only by contrast," Hawthorne is quick to add. Too quick to add.

newly emancipated, had taken a more active and a wider range than for many centuries before. . . . [Men had overthrown and rearranged] the whole system of ancient prejudice, wherewith was linked much of ancient principle. Hester Prynne imbibed this spirit. She assumed a freedom of speculation, then common enough on the other side of the Atlantic, but which our forefathers, had they known of it, would have held to be a deadlier crime than that stigmatized by the scarlet letter. In her lonesome cottage, by the sea-shore, thoughts visited her, such as dared to enter no other dwelling in New England.

Her emancipation is part of a wider movement of mind, originally stimulated and intermittently sustained by the impact upon the Old World of the existence and potentiality of the New. Like Crèvecœur's American, she enters the passes of the dark, inscrutable forest—the West of the human heart—temporarily and magnificently free of ancient principle.

To poor Hester, Hawthorne imputes concern for a number of reforms agitated by the "movement party" of his own day. Like a premonition of Margaret Fuller, she occupies herself with "the Woman Question." "Hester Prynne, whose heart had lost its regular and healthy throb, wandered without a clew in the dark labyrinth of mind. . . . There was wild and ghastly scenery all around her, and a home and comfort nowhere." Again, in reaction from authoritarian obduracy, Hester makes a brief foray into progressive education, achieving the usual results. But at least her intentions are kindly, as were those of the faintly ridiculous Bronson Alcott—alluded to in "The Custom-House" as the kind of man from whom one occasionally needs relief—who in 1830 published *Observations on the Principles and Methods of Infant Instruction*, and in 1836-1837 *Conversations With Children on the Gospels*. Hester is no more successful in her attempt to converse with Pearl on "those truths which the human spirit, at whatever stage of immaturity, imbibes with such eager interest." She is finally compelled to recognize that no woman "stained with sin" may prophesy the new order. Yet even at the end, she comforts women afflicted by passion and male tyranny, and continues to predict the revelation of a "new truth," establishing "the whole relation between man and woman on a surer ground of mutual happiness." Hawthorne nervously interjects: "when the world should have grown ripe for it."

His response to the West was always both powerful and uneasy; he was hardly reassured by now having on his hands a formidable and formidably erotic female perpetually coalescing in image with the forest and the Indian, and then again with women who hold professional Conversations:

> She had wandered, without rule or guidance, in a moral wilderness; as vast, as intricate and shadowy, as the untamed forest, amid the gloom of which they were now holding a colloquy that was to decide their fate. Her intellect and heart had their home, as it were, in desert places, where she roamed as freely as the wild Indian in his woods. For years past she had looked from this estranged point of view at human institutions, and whatever priests or legislators had established; criticizing all with hardly more reverence than the Indian would feel for the clerical band, the judicial robe, the pillory, the gallows, the fireside, or the church. The tendency of her fate and fortunes had been to set her free. The scarlet letter was her passport into regions where other women dared not tread. Shame, Despair, Solitude! These had been her teachers,—stern and wild ones,—and they had made her strong, but taught her much amiss.

Hester is the wilderness, Dimmesdale the settlements. If he is too tame, she is too wild. (How does she manage to include both gallows and fireside on her single, subversive list?) The truth must lie between the lovers, or in their reciprocity. Specifically, their daughter is the "material union" and "spiritual idea" in whom they meet.

For all her small size and simplicity of line, Pearl bewilders everyone in the book. " 'What, in Heaven's name, is she?' " asks Chillingworth. " 'Is the imp altogether evil? Hath she affections? Hath she any discoverable principle of being?' " The meaning of *The Scarlet Letter* turns on this question, to which no one but Hawthorne has the answer. Dimmesdale feebly replies: " 'None,—save the freedom of a broken law. . . . Whether capable of good, I know not.' " This first-born native child is America in person, "dark and wild," yet "worthy to have been brought forth in Eden"; possessed of "native grace," and with a nimbus or "absolute circle of radiance around her"; charming the beholder by "a spell of infinite variety; in this one child there were many children." She defies definition and category. Apparently her nature lacks "reference and adaptation to the world into which she was born," but it is the Puritans, not Pearl, who lack reference and adaptation. Like the burgeoning native culture of which she is so magnificent a specimen, her personality is compounded of elements "all in disorder; or with an order peculiar to themselves, amidst which the point of variety and arrangement was difficult or impossible to be discovered." So long as we think of her as the disordered product of sin, she remains enigmatic. But this point of view we are expressly forbidden to espouse. "A lovely and immortal flower, out of the rank luxuriance of a guilty passion," she is the wild rose who remains when the black forest is cleared away, related to her origins but not reducible to them.

Her anxious, sympathetic mother is almost as distraught as the rest, feeling "like one who has evoked a spirit, but, by some irregularity in the process of conjuration, has failed to win the master-word that should control this new and incomprehensible intelligence." The master-words—to suggest a few of the associated terms implied by the age's sense of its mission and meaning—are "the New World," "America," "the West," "the Frontier," "the Future," and, most of all, perhaps, for Hawthorne and his contemporaries, "the Poet," upon whose definitive *mimesis* the other master-words attended. As with any poet, "the spell of life went forth from her ever creative spirit, and communicated itself to a thousand objects." As with Hawthorne himself, "the pine-trees, aged, black, and solemn, and flinging groans and other melancholy utterances on the breeze, needed little transformation to figure as Puritan elders; the ugliest weeds of the garden were their children, whom Pearl smote down and uprooted, most unmercifully." In passage after passage, Pearl prefigures Young America. Her "never-failing vivacity of spirits" is almost certainly acquired in the West, in 1850 (as earlier) a region, idea, or form of behavior, about equally notable for "new and untransmitted vigor" and for "a doubtful charm."

The scarlet letter is the first object she notices. Later she pelts it with flowers. Pearl, the wild rose, is the flower; the flower is the letter; the letter is Pearl. "It was the scarlet letter in another form; the scarlet letter endowed with life!" In the forest, Hester flings the letter away; Pearl compels her to put it back. She is always her mother's cultural conscience. By the ocean, she makes of eelgrass, and places on her bosom, a "freshly green" A. Characteristically, she acts "as if the one only thing for which she had been sent into the world was to make out its hidden import." Hester tells her " 'the green letter, and on thy childish bosom, has no purport.' " The purport is that green is an even better color for the new birth than red, more suggestive of growth; it also anticipates the forest of the next chapter. In this scene on the beach, Pearl's principle of being is increasingly manifest. "In the little chaos of Pearl's character, there might be seen emerging—and could have been, from the very first—the stedfast principles of an unflinching courage,—an uncontrollable will,—a sturdy pride, which might be disciplined into self-respect,—and a bitter scorn of many things, which, when examined, might be found to have the taint of falsehood in them." It sounds like a (slightly skeptical) view of American foreign policy; or like an idealized frontiersman; or like Thoreau.

A means Adultery, Able, and so on. More inclusively and

more pointedly, A is for America. That is why in "The Custom-House" a mystic meaning streams from it, "subtly communicating itself to my sensibilities," as Hawthorne says, "but evading the analysis of my mind." That is why the letter and Pearl are interchangeable emblems. That is why the letter "enspheres" Hester from society, ensphering also Hester and Pearl together, and then again from each other. That is why the American eagle hovers over the entrance to "The Custom-House," which is the entrance to *The Scarlet Letter*, and why Hawthorne introduces his novel with a discussion of practical American politics.[9] In "The Minister's Vigil," a meteor lights the sky, and Dimmesdale thinks it takes the shape of A. "Nothing was more common, in those days," Hawthorne observes, "than to interpret all meteoric appearances, and other [irregular] natural phenomena . . . as so many revelations from a supernatural source. . . . It was, indeed, a majestic idea, that the destiny of nations should be revealed, in these awful hieroglyphics, on the cope of heaven. A scroll so wide might not be deemed too expansive for Providence to write a people's doom upon. . . . But what shall we say, when an individual discovers a revelation, addressed to himself alone, on the same vast sheet of record!" We shall say that Dimmesdale is wrong, but the novel right. The A in the sky is no sign of adultery, but of the coming republic, by the author displayed to the whole people. Next day the sexton tells Dimmesdale that in honor of Governor Winthrop's death, the portent is interpreted to mean "Angel." The Puritans are seldom good interpreters. In the final scene, when everyone is still staring at Hester's letter, attracted and repelled, only the Indians are able to imagine that "the

[9] In "The Custom-House," Hawthorne also speaks of Salem (now a rotting seaport) as not so long ago a "wild and forest-bordered settlement"; of the aged Collector (General James F. Miller) as "the stalwart soldier of the Niagara frontier," and as the governor "over a wild Western territory" (Arkansas); of "those wild, free days on the Assabeth," and of conversations with Thoreau "about pine-trees and Indian relics, in his hermitage at Walden" (as in "The Old Manse"); and, most topically, of the California Gold Rush.

wearer of this brilliantly embroidered badge must needs be a personage of high dignity among her people." So, by extension, must needs be the man who embroidered the novel of which this badge is emblematic.

No element in the fantastic pattern of *The Scarlet Letter* is easy to isolate for examination; perhaps none is less so than Chillingworth. Yet we can hardly afford to dismiss as villain this man who arrives on the scene in the cast-off clothes of Natty Bumppo, and immediately takes a stand on the periphery of the marginal Puritan world. Hester first sees him from the scaffold, "on the outskirts of the crowd," in company with an Indian, and "clad in a strange disarray of civilized and savage costume." There is no question about his being damaged by his raw encounter with the virgin land. If nothing ever seems quite his fault, still Chillingworth represents a distorted response to the West, and is in that sense clearly inferior to Hester and Pearl. On the other hand, his experiences lie in the right direction; like Hester, he has tried to learn; and this guarantees him a relevance superior to Dimmesdale's, even though the Indians, and Hester too, have taught him much amiss. " 'I have learned many new secrets in the wilderness,' " he pathetically tells her. He is desperately concerned with the crucial American synthesis, the experience of the frontier, which for him invariably fails, either because the elements are wrong—as an amateur physician he tries to combine Indian lore and Old World alchemy—or because he makes a wrong use of them, or, more simply, because he is too old, seeking his New World too late. Still using his basic metaphor, Hawthorne tells us that after Dimmesdale's death, Chillingworth withers "like an uprooted weed," having lost the "principle of his life."

He is neither Old World nor New but a confused relationship between them. In connection with Hester alone, he is suggestive of the Old World's mistaken effort to possess, constrain, and judge the New. He is irresistibly drawn to her: " 'Up to that epoch of my life, I had lived in vain' "; she gives herself to him, insisting to the end: " 'I felt no love, nor feigned any' "; everything turns out badly. Yet Chillingworth accepts the initial responsibility: " 'Mine was the first wrong, when I betrayed thy budding youth into a false and unnatural relation with my decay.' " But if the New World would have remained forever unknown except for discoverers from the Old, then neither world can blame their interconnection or their inevitable separation on the other or on itself; Chillingworth's wrong, as well as Hester's, must finally be referred to the nature of things rather than to sin. Their relationship is abnormal; what should have been parental has become marital; propriety is restored only when Chillingworth finally relinquishes his claim on Hester and transfers his devotion to her—and, in a sense, his—daughter. The confusions of world history, and the reciprocity of hemispheres, are resolved through a commonplace realism in the workings of time; in the course of the processes, Hester is saved from Dimmesdale, Dimmesdale from Chillingworth, and Chillingworth from himself.

But not until he has solved the problem of isolation, which he shares with all the other major characters. Early in the novel, he is identified as a nomad or wanderer—the first term suggesting a reprehensible looseness, according to the social-stages-of-history theory, the second a meritorious freedom, according to Hawthorne's view of the native artist: " 'Here, on this wild outskirt of the earth, I shall pitch my tent; for, elsewhere a wanderer, and isolated from human interests, I find here a woman, a man, a child, amongst whom and myself there exist the closest ligaments.' " But from the beginning, something is wrong: he "bent his eyes on Hester Prynne . . . like a man chiefly accustomed to look inward, and to whom external matters are of little value and import, unless they bear relation to something within his mind." In this, and a number of comparable shortcomings, he is Dimmesdale's double. Like Wakefield, Chillingworth decides "to withdraw his name [Prynne] from the roll of mankind." For the rest of the novel, he parodies the new birth.

By means of her ignominy, her letter, her special habitation, and her new birth, Hester is as isolated as Chilling-worth. Alienation is the source of her developing reality, but also the source of her errors and emotional debilitation. Hawthorne's characteristic imagery repeatedly enforces the truth that the letter has "the effect of a spell, taking her out of the ordinary relations with humanity, and inclosing her in a sphere by herself." Part of her personality eventually finds a public role to play, but "in all her intercourse with society . . . there was nothing that made her feel as if she belonged to it." She never really escapes that "magic circle" which is "a forcible type of the moral solitude in which the scarlet letter enveloped its fated wearer."

The Scarlet Letter is a tragedy of privation and dis-continuity. If the act of love lies entirely outside its limits, that is not primarily because Hawthorne dared bring it no nearer, but because his theme demanded the exclusion. Through participation in historical processes beyond their understanding, each of the persons in *The Scarlet Letter* is grievously wounded, and only Hester and Pearl in any way recover. Wives have no husbands, children no fathers, fathers no daughters. The family is not a family, or, rather, is two grotesquely overlapping families. Yet time and again, family feeling flares up, usually bringing with it erotic long-ing: in the Governor's mansion, on the midnight scaffold, and in the forest, where the parents behold their child "with a feeling which neither of them had ever before experi-enced." At such moments, we realize what is missing from all the other pages. For the most part, it is the young hus-band and father who is most conspicuously absent from the group portrait, the most alienated of all the novel's people, the most irresponsible and guilty contributor to its action. Despite the sympathy with sinners that warms his pulpit eloquence, he has the air of "a being who felt himself quite astray and at a loss in the pathway of human existence, and could only be at ease in some seclusion of his own."

Hester's reality steadily augments, but it is Dimmesdale's "unspeakable misery" to lose "the pith and substance out of whatever realities there are around us, and which were meant by Heaven to be the spirit's joy and nutriment. To the untrue man, the whole universe is false,—it is impalpable, —it shrinks to nothing within his grasp. And he himself, in so far as he shows himself in a false light, becomes a shadow, or, indeed, ceases to exist." Such is Dimmesdale's progress, recurrently called to his attention by the aggravating remarks of young Pearl. Halfway through the book, he makes a halfway successful effort to reverse this progress: "The minister felt for the child's other hand, and took it. The moment that he did so, there came what seemed a tumultuous rush of new life, other life than his own, pouring like a torrent into his heart, and hurrying through all his veins, as if the mother and the child were communicating their vital warmth to his half-torpid system. The three formed an electric chain." According to Hawthorne's isolation-communion ambivalence, the new birth, or new life, may be figured either by the spreading roots of self-reliance or by the closed circuit of human solidarity. Even so, Dimmesdale's electrical connections are loose. Pearl asks him when he will stand with her and her mother in public. The professional theologian replies, " 'At the great judgment day!' " Pearl laughs.

All this is preparatory for the final scene, the minister's public confession, "partly supported by Hester Prynne, and holding one hand of little Pearl's." She too has had much difficulty opening an intercourse with the world. Sometimes she is alone with her mother "in the same circle of seclusion." Sometimes she is "entirely out of the sphere of sympathy or human contact," partaking of the universal loneliness, or withdrawn to the enigmatic ground of her own special predicament. Happily, her destiny is to move in a better direction; as she begins to do so, Hawthorne quietly avails himself of the traditional metaphor for happy American destinies: "She took her mother's hand in both her own, and gazed into her eyes with an earnestness that was seldom seen in her wild and capricious character. The thought occurred to Hester, that the child might really be seeking to approach her with childlike confidence, and doing what she could . . . to establish a meeting-point of sympathy." The frontier is the isolated person's instinctive motion toward a common humanity. That eloquent passage which constitutes the novel's emotional climax is thus indirectly substantiated by the national rhetoric, and especially by the underlying concept of "neutral ground," but with the characteristic nuances of Hawthorne's particular brand of hopefulness and sorrow. (The look on Dimmesdale's face is both "triumphant" and "ghastly.") All that is and will be, and all that might have been, coalesce at the heart of probability. Pearl kisses her father, and everything is fulfilled. Hawthorne's ironies have run their course. Pearl is humanized, and her future secured; the agonies of the new birth are temporarily over.

Thirty years later Henry James said that *The Scarlet Letter* "was the finest piece of imaginative writing yet put forth in the country," and "the best of it was that the thing was absolutely American."[10] With exemplary indirection, Hawthorne appears to intimate a comparable opinion. Returning from the forest, Dimmesdale throws away a half-finished draft of his Election Sermon and starts afresh. At sunrise, "there he was, with the pen still between his fingers, and a vast, immeasurable tract of written space behind him!" In view of what this Election Sermon portends, Dimmesdale is not altogether unlike Hawthorne approaching his climax; neither is he unlike the American people writing their collective destiny over vast immeasurable tracts of free land. Two days later, as if possessed, the minister delivers his surprisingly political address, which, if a good enough imitation of Puritan preaching, bears also a curious resemblance to the demagogic oratory of Hawthorne's day, or, for that matter, to the secret insinuations of *The Scarlet Letter*. To Hester, the whole sermon communicates a meaning of passion and sorrow, "entirely apart from its indistinguishable words"; and so it may to us. Now perhaps understanding the A-for-America which shone in the midnight skies, Dimmesdale explores "the relation be-

[10] *Nathaniel Hawthorne* (New York, 1880), p. 108.

tween the Deity and the communities of mankind." He has assimilated Hawthorne's major metaphor, his subject having "special reference to the New England which they were here planting in the wilderness. And, as he drew towards the close, a spirit as of prophecy had come upon him, constraining him to its purpose as mightily as the old prophets of Israel were constrained; only with this difference, that, whereas the Jewish seers had denounced judgments and ruin on their country, it was his mission to foretell a high and glorious destiny for the newly gathered people of the Lord." Yet through the discourse runs "a certain deep, sad undertone of pathos." The Election Sermon is the type, implied meaning, and summary of the novel. Through it, Dimmesdale seems reborn at the point of death; he totters like an infant.

The Scarlet Letter has more conclusions than the American West has meanings. As in Charles Brockden Brown's *Wieland*, the international aspect of the plot finds a double issue. The surviving characters recoil upon Europe, Pearl, like Clara Wieland, remaining there, while Hester returns to resume the national talisman "of her own free will." Like Brown's Carwin, her salvation requires native soil; in it, she roots down.[11] Our last glimpse of her is at the threshold of the hut, now as weathered and worn as the prison. In another way, Hawthorne resolves his theme, and his dual response to American history, with a brilliant speculation on the subject "whether hatred and love be not the same thing at bottom." Deciding that they are both the same and opposite, he at least temporarily reconciles "in the spiritual world" the medieval minister and the modern physician, with all their conflicting and overlapping ambiguities, thereby somewhat reconciling the Old World and the New, and his perpetual uneasiness toward both. In still another connection, he declares: "We have thrown all the light we could acquire upon the portent," ostensibly the letter on

[11] Why, then, does Pearl ("the Spirit of the West, the rising glory of America") remain in Europe? Perhaps because, as the completely native and fully defined American, she is now free to go where she likes. See below, "Hawthorne's Last Stand."

Dimmesdale's chest, but perhaps more pertinently the heavenly manifestation of America. We would gladly, he continues, as if confessing how deeply he had suffered personally from that letter, "erase its deep print out of our own brain; where long meditation has fixed it in very undesirable distinctness." Hawthorne's meditation on the American West and the Western frontier had been going on about twenty years. Now in middle age he began to take leave of it, bequeathing to Hester and Dimmesdale a dark tombstone containing on its face only a simple A, "as the curious investigator may still discern, and perplex himself with the purport." Philosophically or formally considered, the Western frontier was always a reconciliation of opposites; so in the end there are two graves—"with a space between"—and one stone.

3. NEUTRAL TERRITORY

The best of Hawthorne is located within the same tradition of cultural understanding which informs the Leatherstocking Tales, a tradition not merely of substance, as in "the matter of the West," but also of metaphor and its correspondent narrative and discursive forms. "The Maypole of Merry Mount," for example, is both a story about the West and a formal imitation of the Western frontier. In a headnote citing historical authority for this particular "philosophic romance," Hawthorne says that "the facts, recorded on the grave pages of our New England annalists, have wrought themselves, almost spontaneously, into a sort of allegory."[1] Very likely they did, for the poetic space spontaneously occupied by Hawthorne's tale is simply the magnificent but only vaguely geographical ground down the middle of which the American people ran an imaginary metonymous line—"that admixture of civilization, and of the forest"—in order to give their burgeoning sense of national purpose and destiny a perceptible definition.

[1] Quotations in this section are from *The Complete Works of Nathaniel Hawthorne*, ed. George P. Lathrop (Cambridge, 1883), except for *The Scarlet Letter*, which is quoted from *The Centenary Edition of the Works of Nathaniel Hawthorne*, ed. William Charvat,

"Two hundred years ago, and more, the old world and its inhabitants became mutually weary of each other. Men voyaged by thousands to the West," as in 1835 they were voyaging still. Hawthorne's story concerns the long weary process through which Old World culture was transported to, and modified by, the existentially stricter environments of the New, where two representative and antithetical groups, both oriented toward the American frontier, especially command his interest. "It could not be," says Hawthorne of the Merry Mounters (almost as if he wished it were), "that the fauns and nymphs, when driven from their classic groves and homes of ancient fable, had sought refuge, as all the persecuted did, in the fresh woods of the West." Watching the scenes of revelry, the more solidly established Puritans compare their masqued rivals to "those devils and ruined souls with whom their superstition peopled the black wilderness." Here the Puritans are making themselves at home—black wildernesses being second nature with them—as the Merry Mounters are not.

It is thus at first glance surprising that Hawthorne declines to award the Puritans a clear-cut victory, as both common sense and his historical sources must have tempted him to do. The anomaly confirms what the headnote hints: Hawthorne's controlling source is no New England annalist but the typical American conception of the Western frontier, which divided only to unite, and which robbed all unseemly contradictions of their pain. Hawthorne resolves the issue— that "jollity and gloom were contending for an empire," an issue formulated, as usual, only to *be* resolved—by providing as the central focus of his story a pair of young lovers who share the best traits of both sides, as Leatherstocking and Henry Thoreau, to name only two of the age's representative heroes, comprehended the virtues of white civilization and Indian liberty. Hawthorne's allegorical action sets the terms of "life as it is"; but "life as it is" necessarily

---

Roy Harvey Pearce, Claude M. Simpson, Fredson Bowers, and Matthew J. Bruccoli (Columbus, Ohio, 1962-   ), and *Doctor Grimshawe's Secret*, which is quoted from the modern edition by Edward H. Davidson (Cambridge, 1954).

depends upon a sense of American civilization which turns out to be practically equivalent to a definition of the Western frontier. More subtly, the story also reveals the terms of American writing as it is, or as, in Hawthorne's heyday, it was coming to be: neither jollity (imagination) nor gloom (realism) wins the New World, but a blend of the two.

This general pattern of thought repeats itself in "The Maypole of Merry Mount" through a variety of perspectives. The revelers are deliberately located at a point of meeting between the animal and the human; they are "the crew of Comus, some already transformed to brutes, some midway between man and beast, and the others rioting in the flow of tipsy jollity that foreran the change." One youth emblematically wears stag head and antlers, another the "grim visage" of a wolf, the third the beard and horns of a goat. A fourth is disguised as a bear, except that he wears pink silk stockings; and he is mentioned together with a "real bear of the dark forest," who conveniently wanders along, so that his "inferior nature" may ritualistically rise "half way, to meet his companions as they stooped." This mimic metamorphosis also includes a "Salvage Man . . . girdled with green leaves," and "by his side, a noble figure, but still a counterfeit . . . an Indian hunter, with feathery crest and wampum belt." For all the jollity, there is an uneasy air of savagery erupting into civilized conditions, the basic ambiguity of American culture. Civilization in the New World is seen as frail and uncertain, relatively defenseless against raids from either the barbaric wilderness or the befuddled heart of man (in certain of Hawthorne's moods, synonymous). Yet together with disaster a saving realism rushes at sunset "from the black surrounding woods," not only in the persons of Puritans ("black shadows have rushed forth in human shape") but in the actual shadows, which seem to mean, in the following order, death, awareness of death, and a consequent adjustment of wish-fulfillment to fact, as when "waking thoughts start up amid the scattered fantasies of a dream."

Even the Anglican priest is figured according to the frontier formula, in token of a further dualism related to the reversion-to-savagery theme, "canonically dressed, yet decked with flowers, in heathen fashion, and wearing a chaplet of the native vine leaves." Some of the Maypole flowers are "from English seed," while others are "blossoms of the wilderness." The lovers are fixed at the exact moment of transition from one state of being to another, and in this lies their redemption: "There they stood, in the first hour of wedlock, while the idle pleasures, of which their companions were the emblems, had given place to the sternest cares of life, personified by the dark Puritans. But never had their youthful beauty seemed so pure and high as when its glow was chastened by adversity." Hawthorne's imagination is so colored by the American notion of the frontier as a reconciliation of opposites that situation after situation appears to him in that guise.

So it was in the beginning. A quarter-century later, at the effective end of Hawthorne's career, precisely the same animal-human antithesis-and-reconciliation turns up in *The Marble Faun* (1860), where jollity and gloom contend for an even larger empire. "A Faun, copied from that of Praxiteles, and another who seems to be dancing, are exceedingly pleasant to look at. I like these strange, sweet, playful, rustic creatures, almost entirely human as they are, yet linked so prettily, without monstrosity, to the lower tribes. . . . Their character has never, that I know of, been brought out in literature; and something very good, funny, and philosophical, as well as poetic, might very likely be educed from them. . . . The faun [is] a natural and delightful link betwixt human and brute life, and with something of a divine character intermingled."[2] So Hawthorne

[2] The correct reading of this passage was supplied by Norman Holmes Pearson, from his forthcoming edition of Nathaniel Hawthorne, *The French and Italian Notebooks*. The passage includes this curious remark: "In my mind, they connect themselves with that ugly, bearded woman, who was lately exhibited in England, and by some supposed to have been engendered betwixt a human mother and an orang-outang; but she was a wretched monster."

wrote in his Notebooks, after a visit to the Villa Borghese. The ultimate germs of his idea were still the conventional Western frontier, and the literary Indian ("link betwixt human and brute life," "lower tribes," and so on), with whom he had identified his youthful literary fortunes in "The Seven Vagabonds." Now these tropes are debased and almost totally disencumbered of geographical, historical, or cultural meaning; yet for all the pretty posturing, and the many peripheral matters into which Hawthorne was eventually led, the diction and rhythm of the novel repeatedly point to the original source: "The characteristics of the brute creation meet and combine with those of humanity in this strange yet true and natural conception of antique poetry and art. . . . Neither man nor animal, and yet no monster, but a being in whom both races meet on friendly ground. The idea grows coarse as we handle it, and hardens in our grasp."

This most nebulous of Hawthorne's novels is shot through with allusions to "tribes" and "wilderness," and naturally so, for the Faun's narrative progress is from Innocence to Civilization through Savagery. But Donatello, or the idea of him, never really hardens or grows sufficiently coarse; at the end he is still "this anomalous creature between the Real and the Fantastic." As Hawthorne says about one of his typical settings, where the main point is the interaction of man and nature: "The result is an ideal landscape, a woodland scene that seems to have been projected out of the poet's mind." A few pages later, he is even more revealing: "It was as if they had strayed across the limits of Arcadia, and come under a civil polity where young men might avow their passion with as little restraint as a bird." It was of course "like a bird in the air" that Hawthorne lived as a boy in the wilderness of Maine, where he first got his "cursed habits of solitude."

Of Donatello, Miriam remarks: " 'He is not supernatural, but just on the verge of nature, and yet within it. What is the nameless charm of this idea, Hilda?' " Hilda does not care to know, and Hawthorne seems to have forgotten—

though a creature on the verge of nature, and yet within it, like a pioneer happily hovering on the hither edge of free land, would appear to be identified, however confusingly, with the Western frontier. " 'There is something very touching and impressive in this statue of the Faun,' " Kenyon replies. " 'In some long-past age, he must really have existed. Nature needed, and still needs, this beautiful creature; standing betwixt man and animal, sympathizing with each, comprehending the speech of either race, and interpreting the whole existence of one to the other. What a pity that he has forever vanished from the hard and dusty paths of life.' " Hawthorne's language is the language of a passing era; in almost the same words, Thoreau argued that mankind needed the Indian, and Brownson argued that mankind needed Christ. In more than one sense, Hawthorne is wandering between two worlds, for whether he knew it or not the frontier had disappeared sometime between the writing of *The Scarlet Letter* and *The Marble Faun*. This perhaps explains his puzzled sense of anachronism. The curious resemblance between Kenyon's description of the statue and the American Indian, or an Indian trader, may be susceptible of the same explanation.

By the 1840's and 1850's, the process of doubling the metaphorical frontier had become almost automatic with American writers, major and minor. Pathfinders like Cooper and Hawthorne had discovered the trick earlier. In "The Haunted Mind" (1834), Hawthorne may already be seen self-consciously attempting to define a pseudo-metaphysical state of being by compelling the frontier metaphor to transfer from one context to another its all-too-predictable implications. Except for a rhetorical genius like Poe or Thoreau—and Hawthorne was only rarely a rhetorical genius, besides having no talent for metaphysics—this manner of speaking was seldom impressive. At best, the relation between the Western frontier and ambiguously Romantic mental conditions was only a loose analogy; at worst, the analogy might conceal serious contradiction, or the writer be tempted to say what he would not otherwise care to have said.

"The Haunted Mind" opens with description of that "singular moment" (pun) midway between waking and sleep. "You find yourself, for a single instant, wide awake in that realm of illusions, whither sleep has been the passport." Hawthorne is evidently trying to formulate something about arrested time, whatever that might be, and is meanwhile drifting toward a geographical trope. "Passport" suggests going to Europe, but the realm of illusions soon begins to take shape closer to home. "Yesterday has already vanished among the shadows of the past; to-morrow has not yet emerged from the future. You have found an intermediate space, where the business of life does not intrude; where the passing moment lingers, and becomes truly the present." The realm of illusions is the moving Western frontier displaced onto a pure time model: vanished (or vanquished) past to the East of the line, emergent future to the West of the line, and the present (the only reality) *upon* the line, or, as in Crèvecœur, *within* the intermediate space. But for this occasion the metaphor is wrong, or, more accurately, Hawthorne's motive is inappropriate to the standard metaphor. The frontier fails to specify the intensest cultural reality, the most concentrated meaning, as it was supposed to do; instead, it suggests Hawthorne's irresponsible abdication from them. (As he never tired of saying, the present is nonexistent.) Along with other self-indulgences which he elsewhere found so contemptible because he was so prone to them, this intermediate space between sleep and waking is welcomed as an amiably lazy retreat from reality in favor of "the sluggish ecstasy of inaction." Inaction suggests death (and some Poe-like details concerning shrouds, coffins, and burials), and death calls forth a train of young Hawthorne's ever-ready allegorical creatures. Then he suddenly reverts to a tepid adolescent erotic fantasy, whose initial image reveals the dreamer sinking "in a flowery spot, on the borders of sleep and wakefulness." The flowery spot is evidently a Western prairie, unlocated but presumably in the general neighborhood of the frontier—which could never be located either, but only poetically evoked through the language of grounds and limits, borders and confines, boundaries and verges, intermediate spaces and neutral territories. The vagueness eminently suits the theme, which is finally only what even Hawthorne admits is "a doubtful parallel" between waking from "the wilderness of sleep" and from death.[3]

Still, "The Haunted Mind" is an invaluable locus for the kind of doubled frontier metaphor with which Hawthorne's writing was embellished from first to last, and which, in his happiest moments, was the informing principle of his fiction (as in *The Scarlet Letter*) and of his theory of fiction (as in "The Custom-House"). In these second-stage metaphors, the original figure of the frontier—civilization, nature, and the neutral territory—was applied to generally comparable situations (such as known, unknown, and the neutral territory) with results sometimes commanding and sometimes calamitous. Especially when too detached from their Western source, the doubled metaphors were often perfunctory or implicit, and it is difficult to estimate what kind or degree of vitality lay behind them, or even whether the author knew they were there. Most of them involve the typically Romantic obsession with boundaries of time, sanity, or existence—situations probably impossible of conception without some kind of spatial language. The more significant fact is that the spatial language regularly chosen by Hawthorne and his American contemporaries was derived from their sense of the Western frontier. In "A Select

[3] Despite the calamities of "The Haunted Mind," Hawthorne continued to entertain this impossible theme in private. "We sometimes congratulate ourselves at the moment of waking from a troubled dream: it may be so the moment after death." *Works*, IX, 33. "An essay on various kinds of death, together with the just-before and just-after." *The American Notebooks*, ed. Randall Stewart (New Haven, 1932), p. 99. In *Doctor Grimshawe's Secret* a character says: " 'It may be, this is the way that the dead feel, when they awake in another state of being, with a dim pleasure, after passing through the brief darkness of death. It is very pleasant' " (p. 235).

Party," the Man of Fancy calls a castle in the air " 'a sort of no man's land, where Posterity may make acquaintance with us on equal terms.' " Here the frontier is the literary imagination, or point of meeting between present and future, pragma and prophecy. Conversely, in *The House of the Seven Gables*, "there is sad confusion, indeed, when the spirit thus flits away into the past, or into the more awful future, or, in any manner, steps across the spaceless boundary betwixt its own region and the actual world." This metaphor is sadly confused: on the one hand the neutral territory, or spaceless boundary, is the danger zone between the soul's possession and the impinging world, and, on the other hand it is the present, defined as the moment of transition between future and past. The boundary is paradoxically "spaceless" because the American frontier was; nobody knew whether it was a line or an area. In such passages as these, the topics and treatments vary, while the metaphor remains fundamentally the same. Its explicit Western content is almost always zero; yet its very existence depends upon the prior existence of the American frontier. In "P's Correspondence," it would be comical "if, after missing his object [literary fame] while seeking it by the light of reason, he should prove to have stumbled upon it in his misty excursions beyond the limits of sanity." Hester Prynne recognizes that Dimmesdale stands "on the verge of lunacy, if he had not already stepped across it." The English nobleman in *Doctor Grimshawe's Secret*, according to Hawthorne's plan, "shall walk on the verge of lunacy, and at last step over."

It sounds like the world of Poe, yet Hawthorne was past master of this particular mannerism before Poe began to publish his tales. In "A Gentle Boy," Ilbrahim "led her by the hand, in his quiet progress over the borders of eternity, [and] Dorothy almost imagined that she could discern the near, though dim, delightfulness of the home he was about to reach." Hester's badge of ignominy throws a "gleam, in the sufferer's hard extremity, across the verge of time. It had shown him where to set his foot, while the light of earth was fast becoming dim, and ere the light of futurity could reach him." Hawthorne's metaphorical frontiers are more appealing when more social and realistic. In "Main Street" he judges the Thursday Lecture an institution worth retaining "as bearing relations to both the spiritual and ordinary life, and bringing each acquainted with the other." The Lecture is neutral territory between spiritual and temporal, imbued with the qualities of both, and thereby empowered to reconcile them. In the local newspaper, Hawthorne wrote how American social conditions offered the rude and the refined "a common ground of courtesy and kindliness to meet upon."[4] More explicitly, in the Palazzo Barbarini he noted that the servants of cardinal, prince, and duke used a single domestic hall for "a common territory and meeting-ground." Thus closely do we approach the original frontier whence all the fanciful borders arose.

The largest concentration of such metaphors is probably in *The Blithedale Romance* (1852), which also contains a host of unintegrated references to the American West. (See "Hawthorne's Last Stand.") Zenobia is "just on the hither verge of her richest maturity," while Priscilla is "on the outer limit of girlhood." According to Coverdale, "Hollingsworth would have gone with me to the hither verge of life, and have sent his friendly and hopeful accents far over on the other side, while I should be treading the unknown path." The modern mesmerist, "even if he profess to tread a step or two across the boundaries of the spiritual world, yet carries with him the laws of our actual life, and extends them over his preternatural conquests," as if he were administering one of America's Western territories; and the rattle of soil on a coffin is "that final sound, which mortality awakens on the utmost verge of sense, as if in the vain hope of bringing an echo from the spiritual world." Here Hawthorne seems temporarily under the spell of Poe. More reasonably, Coverdale imagines phantoms "that invariably haunt the mind, on the eve of adventurous enterprises, to

[4] Randall Stewart, "Hawthorne's Contributions to *The Salem Advertiser*," *American Literature*, V (1934), 335-336.

warn us back within the boundaries of ordinary life," and speaks of "the sense of vast, undefined space, pressing from the outside against the black panes": both of these metaphors accurately and movingly reflect the fundamental American experience, whether of crossing the frontier in the Westward direction or merely of thinking about it at home.

Most centrally of all, as Coverdale says: "My hope was, that, between theory and practice, a true and available mode of life might be struck out." Unfortunately, in view of the fact that Blithedale is an obvious paradigm for American civilization, and Coverdale an obvious surrogate for the American writer, "the clods of earth, which we so constantly belabored and turned over and over, were never etherealized into thought. Our thoughts, on the contrary, were fast becoming cloddish. Our labor symbolized nothing."[5] The prosaic world contends with the poetic imagination, not yet entirely at ease in the new environment; the conflict between them was Hawthorne's perpetual problem, as his Notebooks show; or as a character in *Doctor Grimshawe's Secret* puts it: " 'How strangely everything evades me! . . . There is no medium in my life between the most vulgar realities, and the most vaporous fiction, too thin to breathe.' " Understandably, Hawthorne's most desperately brilliant appropriations of the major American figure (*The Scarlet Letter*, again, excepted) were in the realm of aesthetics.

The innermost chamber of "The Custom-House" is the passage where Hawthorne fancifully pretends to describe the psychology of his composition. The aesthetic background is the ever-portentous dualism of fact and fiction, as illustrated, for example, in Cooper's 1847 preface to *The Crater*: "Truth is not absolutely necessary to the illustration of a principle, the imaginary sometimes doing that office quite as effectually as the actual." The solution is through the

[5] Cf. Margaret Fuller in *Summer on the Lakes* (1844): "Every fact is impure, but every fact contains in it the juices of life. Every fact is a clod, from which may grow an amaranth or a palm." *The Writings of Margaret Fuller*, ed. Mason Wade (New York, 1941), p. 68.

agency of moonlight, or Romantic imagination.[6] Native re-
finements are furnished by the metaphorical frontier, since
the 1820's moving farther and farther from the Eastern
writer and perhaps on that account more and more freeing
itself from geographical actualities. "Moonlight, in a
familiar room, falling so white upon the carpet, and showing
all its figures so distinctly,—making every object so minutely visible, yet so unlike a morning or noontide visibility,
—is a medium the most suitable for a romance-writer to get
acquainted with his illusive guests." Hawthorne lists some
objects in the moonlit room, and proceeds: "All these details, so completely seen, are so spiritualized by the unusual
light, that they seem to lose their actual substance, and become things of intellect." Precisely what happens to the
Western frontier. "Thus, therefore, the floor of our familiar
room has become a neutral territory, somewhere between the
real world and fairy-land, where the Actual and the Imaginary may meet, and each imbue itself with the nature
of the other."[7] Hawthorne continues to refer to wall, ceiling,
furniture, but we are already deep in the magic forest where
Hester Prynne from time to time resorts. The neutral territory is the meeting point between the facts of American
history and the painfully growing American mind. From
that conjunction the metaphor of the Western frontier once
more arises to effect a significant restatement of imported

[6] In "My Kinsman, Major Molineux": "The moon, creating, like
the imaginative power, a beautiful strangeness in familiar objects,
gave something of romance to a scene that might not have possessed
it in the light of day."

[7] The source of Hawthorne's description—but with no implications
for the poetic imagination—is in *The American Notebooks*, pp. 124-
125 (October 13, 1848). Neither does the frontier metaphor appear
in it. The Notebooks passage is dominated by Hawthorne's feeling
of compositional frustration, and in that context the national trope
was useless. Probably it came to mind when he had successfully
completed *The Scarlet Letter*, and was casting about for a figure to
express problems solved. Of course, the frontier metaphor was also
at the heart of the novel, and according to my analysis the ground
of Hawthorne's triumph; that would be an additional, and perhaps
sufficient, point of entry for the Notebooks passage into "The
Custom-House."

European thought. Was it evoked by Hawthorne's awareness that the novel to follow was in essence a novel about the West?

Probably. But perhaps Hawthorne had additional motives for modifying the Wordsworthian formula—"to throw over them [incidents and situations from common life] a certain colouring of imagination, whereby ordinary things should be presented to the mind in an unusual aspect." Wordsworth concentrates on the imagination. Hawthorne's shift to the frontier metaphor, and to the aesthetics of Coleridge, enables him to concentrate on the intractability of experience, an intractability poor Hawthorne had good reason to know about. In the Coleridgean view, if the imagination colors the facts, the facts in their turn color the imagination. And Hawthorne's imagination is the perfect case in point, for the modes of apprehension which he imposed on all the dualistic categories susceptible of the imposition—and these were manifold, since he characteristically thought in dualistic terms—were in the first instance derived from the American sense of the Western frontier as somehow a metaphor resolving the inescapable American dualism, Manifest Destiny vs. inferiority complex. Indeed, as we look backward over the tortuous development of our early literature, it seems impossible to determine whether the American mind was primarily formed by the basic facts of American experience or whether these basic facts were primarily formed by the American mind. All we can be sure of is their reciprocity, a reciprocity precisely analogous to the historical situation, as it existed in the imaginations of men, and from which the metaphor of the frontier was born, nature in the neutral territory changing civilization while at the same time being changed by it. "What then is the American, this new man?" Crèvecœur's troublesome question was answerable only by reference to where the new man lived and what he lived for. Hawthorne's articulation of an aesthetic so closely revealing the literary situation of his country, and embodied in the central metaphor of the national dilemma, was significant for more than Hawthorne; it was, in fact, the moment of full and self-conscious maturity for American literature, when the promise of Cooper was redeemed. What is it but a theory of realism, or imaginative truth, magnificently congruent with the actual conditions of American life?

Finally this scene, this neutral territory, where the Actual and the Imaginary meet and imbue themselves with each other, and where the meeting is warmed into life by light from the fireplace—i.e., by the indispensable American virtue of "sympathy"—this neutral territory is reflected in a mirror (form? aesthetic distance?). "Glancing at the looking-glass, we behold—deep within its haunted verge—the smouldering glow of the half-extinguished anthracite, the white moonbeams on the floor, and a repetition of all the gleam and shadow of the picture, with one remove farther from the actual, and nearer to the imaginative. Then, at such an hour, and with this scene before him, if a man, sitting all alone, cannot dream strange things, and make them look like truth, he need never try to write romances." In speaking of the mirror's haunted verge—standard talk for the American forest—Hawthorne has managed to insinuate one more reference to the figurative West, into which he is preparing a few pages later to propel Hester. So too his removes from the actual toward the imaginative may well be read in two senses, the obvious aesthetic meaning overlaid by, or looming out of, the quasi-ideological, quasi-geographical motions of American civilization actualizing Westward from the known to the unknown, from origins to choice.

In the preface to *Twice-Told Tales* (1851), the frontier metaphor is even more deeply submerged, and still the argument rests upon its presence through the whole as analogical structure. To a want of encouragement in his early years, characteristically melodramatized, Hawthorne attributes the slightness of his production. He deliberately ignores the tales and sketches written in those years and passed over in collecting the *Tales*, but included in *Mosses From an Old Manse*; six months hence, he would gather more of this early work in *The Snow-Image*. "They have the pale tint of flowers that blossomed in too retired a shade," Hawthorne goes on, in a passage often quoted, and often misunderstood, "the coolness of a meditative habit, which diffuses itself through the feeling and observation of every sketch. . . . Whether from lack of power, or an unconquerable reserve, the Author's touches have often an effect of tameness." Some of this is true, much false; the Author is gently pulling our leg. In his prefatory essay to the *Mosses*, he concluded with the same ironic self-deprecation and the same sentimental-sarcastic flower imagery: "these idle weeds and withering blossoms," he called his recent productions; earlier ones were "old, faded things, reminding me of flowers pressed between the leaves of a book."

So in the *Twice-Told Tales* preface he advances from mock apologies to open praise. Pretending merely to give his pale blossoms their due, Hawthorne lavishes backhand commendation on them. "They have none of the abstruseness of idea, or obscurity of expression, which mark the written communications of a solitary mind with itself. They never need translation. It is, in fact, the style of a man of society. Every sentence, so far as it embodies thought or sensibility, may be understood and felt by anybody who will give himself the trouble to read it, and will take up the book in a proper mood." What could be better? But as we know, Hawthorne was in 1830 writing almost as well as he ever would. "The Gentle Boy" and "Roger Malvin's Burial" were in a publisher's possession by January of that year, and were certainly written earlier.[8] In this belated preface, Hawthorne is writing still another piece of fiction, a story about himself as the typical young American writer, initially divided by the crucial Transcendental antithesis between subject and object, the common starting point of native intellectuals and fiction-mongers. These early tales are marked by a radical split between content (pale) and style (worldly). What, then, can they be, whence came they, and what is their principle of being? The American answer was

[8] Julian Hawthorne, *Nathaniel Hawthorne and His Wife: A Biography* (Boston, 1884), I, 131-132.

naturally the metaphorical frontier, with all its attendant overtones.

Hawthorne defines *Twice-Told Tales* as the result of just such a paradoxical interpenetration and creative transcendence, carefully calling attention to the structure of his metaphor, while with equal care he keeps all but the structure out of sight: "This statement of apparently opposite peculiarities leads us to a perception of what the sketches truly are. They are not the talk of a secluded man with his own mind and heart . . . but his attempts, and very imperfectly successful ones, to open an intercourse with the world."[9] He began to tip his hand as early as the burlesque preface to "Rappaccini's Daughter" (1844), in which he offered the gentle reader a half-true, half-false, ironic self-portrait: "As a writer, he seems to occupy an unfortunate position between the Transcendentalists . . . and the great body of pen-and-ink men who address the intellect and sympathies of the multitude. If not too refined, at all events too remote, too shadowy, and unsubstantial in his modes of development to suit the taste of the latter class, and yet too popular to satisfy the spiritual or metaphysical requisitions of the former, he must necessarily find himself without an audience." His position was of course anything but unfortunate, for what he described was once again the neutral territory, the figurative frontier which guaranteed his relevance.

But that relevance was soon lost, for if the ostensible content of the prefaces remains fairly steady, their implications and tone do not. Through the preface to *The House*

---

[9] The phrase was common currency, and is also found, for example, in Captain Adam Seaborn, pseud., *Symzonia* (New York, 1820): "I was about to reach the goal of all my wishes; to open an intercourse with a new world and with an unknown people" (p. 96); and in Poe's 1836 review of *Astoria*: "[Mackenzie] suggested the policy of opening an intercourse between the Atlantic and Pacific Oceans," where Poe is quoting Irving (ch. 3) word for word. See also Orestes Brownson: "The human race has contrived, some way or other, to open relations with the objective world." "Synthetic Philosophy," *Democratic Review*, XI (1842), 570.

of the Seven Gables, dated only sixteen days after *Twice-Told Tales*, we find a rising curve of self-assurance, and then a falling away. At first glance, the preface to *The Blithedale Romance*, that novel containing all the painfully peripheral frontier metaphors, looks like familiar ground. He remembered Brook Farm, Hawthorne says, as "the most romantic episode of his own life,—essentially a day-dream, and yet a fact,—and thus offering an available foothold between fiction and reality." From this formulation the frontier metaphor is gone, and with it all suggestion of harmonious reconciliation, replaced by a figure (foothold) that in this context (which is not the context of "The Great Carbuncle") hints of wilfulness, insecurity, and potential disaster. The poles of Hawthorne's basic antithesis have drifted too far apart: "fact" and "day-dream" constitute a more repellent pair than "Actual" and "Imaginary," and "fiction" vs. "reality" is still more ominous. By the time of *The Marble Faun*, where the novel itself reveals the failure of the figurative frontier to mean what it once meant, Hawthorne's preface sounds tired and querulous. "Italy, as the site of his Romance, was chiefly valuable to him as affording a sort of poetic or fairy precinct, where actualities would not be so terribly insisted upon as they are, and must needs be, in America. No author, without a trial, can conceive of the difficulty of writing a romance about a country where there is no shadow, no antiquity, no mystery, no picturesque and gloomy wrong, nor anything but a commonplace prosperity, in broad and simple daylight."

His imagination, which once throve on the perpetual battle between the world and the self, had simply given up, as the dedicatory preface to *Our Old Home* nakedly revealed:

> These and other sketches, with which in a somewhat rougher form than I have given them here, my journal was copiously filled, were intended for the side-scenes and backgrounds and exterior adornment of a work of fiction of which the plan had imperfectly developed

itself in my mind, and into which I ambitiously proposed to convey more of various modes of truth than
I could have grasped by a direct effort. Of course, I
should not mention this abortive project, only that it
has been utterly thrown aside and will never now be
accomplished. The Present, the Immediate, the Actual,
has proved too potent for me. It takes away not only
my scanty faculty, but even my desire for imaginative
composition, and leaves me sadly content to scatter a
thousand peaceful fantasies upon the hurricane that is
sweeping us all along with it, possibly, into a Limbo
where our nation and its polity may be as literally the
fragments of a shattered dream as my unwritten
Romance.

So he confessed himself to ex-President Pierce, who had
once tried to smile the hurricane from its course. In fact,
Hawthorne had come to this pass well before 1863. Except
in the earliest years, and then again at the time of writing
The Scarlet Letter, the balance he held between private
sensibility and public truth was almost unbelievably pre-
carious. In the late twenties and early thirties, Hawthorne
was in large part formed and for a while sustained by his
magnificently ironic vision of the horrors and glories being
enacted on that ever-receding frontier where the newest
nation was likewise articulating its uniquely millennial spirit
and applying that spirit to the rapid solution of humanity's
age-old problems. Then in the early fifties the frontier
vanished. At about the same time, Hawthorne commenced
a long personal withdrawal which was destined to end only
when the nation—and, with it, American philosophy and
American literature—fell apart. During a decade and a
half of increasing national agony, he slowly faded like the
Cheshire Cat.

Edgar Allan Poe

1. SOUTH AND WEST

"MANY OF THESE POEMS ARE OLD FRIENDS," Poe wrote in a review of William D. Gallagher's *Erato, Number I* (1835), a modestly regional volume dedicated to Timothy Flint, "in whose communion we have been cheered with bright hopes for the Literature of the West."[1] This was not platitude. No important American writer was more realistically concerned with, and more accurately informed about, that literature of the West which in the mid-1830's flooded the country.[2] At the *Southern Literary Messenger*, Western poems, sketches, and fictions poured over Poe's desk.[3] In his first issue as editor (December 1835), Poe reviewed James Hall's *Sketches of History, Life, and Manners, in the West*;

[1] Quotations in this section are from *The Complete Works of Edgar Allan Poe*, ed. James A. Harrison (New York, 1902), and *The Letters of Edgar Allan Poe*, ed. John W. Ostrom (Cambridge, 1948). Letters *to* Poe are in *Works*, XVII. Gallagher edited a variety of Western periodicals, and in 1841 compiled *Selections from the Poetical Literature of the West*. One of the selections prompted an Eastern reviewer to inquire how long it would be "before some trans-Alleghanian reviewer will entertain his readers, even as we are now doing, with quotations from a volume of 'Selections from the Poetical Literature of West of the Rocky Mountains.'" "The Poetry of the West," *Democratic Review*, IX (1841), 36.

[2] Perhaps in part occasioned by extra-literary causes; cf. Caroline Kirkland in *Western Clearings* (New York, 1845): "The years 1835 and 1836 will long be remembered by the Western settler—and perhaps by some few people at the East, too—as the period when the madness of speculation in lands had reached a point to which no historian of the time will ever be able to do justice. . . . The 'man of one idea' was every where: no man had two" (p. 4).

[3] Both before and during Poe's tenure as editor, the *Messenger*'s policy was pro-Western.

Clinton Bradshaw, a first novel by Frederick W. Thomas, who was soon to be widely identified as a Western writer;[4] and *Legends of a Log Cabin. By a Western Man* (Chandler R. Gilman), dedicated to the author's friend Charles Fenno Hoffman, who had just written *A Winter in the West. By a New-Yorker*. And in connection with Theodore S. Fay's *Norman Leslie*, as un-Western a performance as can be imagined, Poe ridiculed a feeble detail by mock-heroic invocation of Southwestern humor: "Alas! Mr. Davy Crockett,—Mr. Davy Crockett, alas!—thou art beaten hollow—thou art defunct, and undone! thou hast indeed succeeded in grinning a squirrel from a tree, but it surpassed even thine extraordinary abilities to smile a lady into a fainting fit!" It was a good month's work, and not without an appropriate reward; among the quoted puffs in the *Messenger*'s next number were included words of commendation from the *Boon's Lick Democrat*.

From the beginning, Poe tended to intensify and exploit that widespread identification (or confusion) of South and West which permitted Hoffman, for example, to speak of emigrants from New England to Ohio as "eastern," but of emigrants from Virginia to Kentucky as "western."[5] By

---

[4] Thomas later became Poe's favorite correspondent and probably his best friend. In "Autography" (1841), Poe spoke with guarded approval of his novel *East and West*, and even said that Thomas' long poem, *The Emigrant; or, Reflections While Descending the Ohio*, "will be read with pleasure by every person of taste." A few months earlier, Thomas wrote Poe of a projected novel (apparently unconsummated): "I shall take my hero, through various adventures in the south east and west." In between these two occasions, Thomas sent Poe a long letter showing how "Western" he was. Typically, it was to Thomas that Poe wrote, less than a year before his death: "I shall be a *littérateur*, at least, all my life; nor would I abandon the hopes which still lead me on for all the gold in California."

[5] *A Winter in the West* (New York, 1835), II, 139-140. In *The South-West. By a Yankee* (New York, 1835), Joseph Holt Ingraham used each of the following nouns, adjectives, and compounds, in an attempt to locate Louisiana and Mississippi: "south and west" (II, 33), "south or west" (38), "western" (50), "southern" (57), and "south-west" (68). On p. 48 of the same volume, he placed Natchez among "border settlements" of the "newly settled south and west." In 1845 Simms inaugurated the *Southern and Western Monthly*

selection, emphasis, and ambiguity, Poe could make such a book as A. B. Longstreet's *Georgia Scenes* (1835) sound far more Western than it really was. Longstreet was "a very Theophrastus in duodecimo," with respect to "that class of southwestern mammalia who come under the generic appellation of 'savagerous wild cats.' "[6] One story told of "the oddities of a backwood reel," while another was "an admirable picture of school-boy democracy in the woods." Wherever the woods were, there was the West. Poe also spoke with a knowing air of "forcible, accurate and original generic delineations of real existences to be found sparsely in Georgia, Mississippi and Louisiana, and very plentifully in our more remote settlements and territories"—the ambiguous pronoun "our" meaning equally Southern, American, and, of course, Western. "The Gander Pulling" he explained by reference to an "unprincipled barbarity not infrequently practised in the South and West," and "The Shooting Match" he praised for its "portraiture of the manners of our South-Western peasantry." *Georgia Scenes*, as a whole, was "a sure omen of better days for the literature of the South"; but the literature of the South was to all intents and purposes the literature of the West—and thereby the literature of America—under Southern auspices.

Perhaps because it connoted hard practicality and humble origins, Poe applied to this literature of the South (West) criteria infrequently emphasized in his other criticisms; he pointedly admired the pragmatically realistic and deplored the ambitiously "literary." Despite an *"over-abundant"* style, even a *History of Texas*, doubling as an emigrants' guide, won his respect on utilitarian grounds: "a valuable addition to our very small amount of accurate knowledge in regard to Texas." He was much less favorably disposed

---

Magazine and Review, which a year later briefly merged with the *Messenger* under the improbable title, *Southern and Western Literary Messenger and Review*.

[6] During Poe's brief stay at the University of Virginia, the faculty expelled a student from Kentucky for biting. *Letters*, I, 6.

toward such items as Ingraham's Romantic fiction *Lafitte: The Pirate of the Gulf. By the Author of the South-West.* In the same issue, he fairly decimated an emigrant-and-Indian novel, *Elkswatawa; or, The Prophet of the West. A Tale of the Frontier,* by James S. French, "the author, we believe, of '*Eccentricities of David Crockett*,' a book of which we know nothing beyond the fact of its publication." (Such performances were by Poe's contemporaries called "scalping" or "tomahawking"; in general, Poe was regarded as a "savage" critic.) It was the novelistic defects that Poe objected to—the slovenly construction, the tepid imitation of Scott; the Indian parts were somewhat better, he thought, but only as "forming a portion of our Indian history." Dealing with the Western productions of men he admired on other grounds, Poe was sometimes less critical. Nathaniel Beverley Tucker's novel *George Balcombe*, a story about both Virginia and Missouri (where Tucker once lived), was simply "*the best* American novel."[7] Bryant's poem "The Prairie" possessed "descriptive beauty . . . of a high order," and was "as a local painting" wholly "excellent."[8] Still, Poe pointedly refused to admire, or even to understand, the following lines of "The Disinterred Warrior":

[7] The hero is conceivably a prototype of Poe's Dupin; see, especially, his mysterious powers of deduction in the opening chapter. Balcombe attributes his ratiocinative abilities to Western conditions: " 'You see how curiosity whets observation, and how that is whetted by a residence in this remote country.' " In his review, Poe described this character as "frank, ardent, philosophical, chivalrous, sagacious—and, above all, glorying in the exercise of his sagacity."

[8] Among early American poets, Bryant poetized more about the West than did any one else before Whitman. He especially liked to dwell on the Indian (melancholy and departing), and on the pioneer (self-reliant and arriving), setting them against grandiose backdrops of forest and prairie. In the late 1820's and early 1830's, Bryant also wrote a number of Western tales, which are generally in the mode of James Hall or Hawthorne. In 1832, and several times thereafter, he visited the West, whence resulted the more realistic but duller prose of "Illinois Fifty Years Ago," and sizeable portions of *Letters of a Traveller* (New York, 1850). Like other minor writers of the age, Bryant was rarely able to fuse his facts with his fancies, and seems especially bifurcated on the subject of the West.

For he was fresher from the hand
  That formed of earth the human face,
And to the elements did stand
  In nearer kindred than our race.

For all his interest in "our Indian history," and in the unprincipled barbarities with which the American back-woodsman imitated the native savage, Poe was not Thoreau. "The theorizers on Government," he argued later, "who pretend always to 'begin with the beginning,' commence with Man in what they call his *natural* state—the savage. What right have they to suppose this his natural state? Man's chief idiosyncrasy being reason, it follows that his savage condition—his condition of action *without* reason—is his *un*natural state."

In 1838 he wrote a letter regretfully declining an editor's invitation to review Irving, claiming to have "read nothing of his since I was a boy, save his 'Granada.' " And yet, he went on: "It is a theme upon which I would like very much to write, for there is a vast deal to be said upon it. Irving is much overrated, and a nice distinction might be drawn between his just and his surreptitious and adventitious reputation—between what is due to the pioneer solely, and what to the writer." Perhaps it was his entire neglect to draw such a nice distinction that induced Poe to forget one of the longest reviews he ever wrote—published in the previous year—of Irving's *Astoria; or, Anecdotes of an Enterprise Beyond the Rocky Mountains.*[9] More likely, his oversight was occasioned by the recent publication in book

[9] In addition to *Astoria*, that great entrepreneurial epic in honor of John Jacob Astor (partly written in Astor's house), Irving gave the public two other book-length Western narratives: *A Tour on the Prairies* (1835), a thin mixture of description, sentiment, comedy, and legend; and *The Rocky Mountains; or, Scenes, Incidents, and Adventures in the Far West; Digested From the Journal of Capt. B. L. E. Bonneville . . . And Illustrated From Various Other Sources* (1837), of which the title sufficiently reveals the provenance. There were also shorter Western items in *The Sketch Book* (1819-1820) and subsequent collections.

form of his own *Narrative of A. Gordon Pym*. Some of *Pym*'s connections with *Astoria* would not bear looking into.

Poe's review of *Astoria* is surprisingly factual and detailed, most of it close paraphrase or summary from Irving; some is verbatim quotation, with or without quotation marks. At the outset, he effectively bypasses the author, and the issues with which his reviews were usually concerned: "The work has been accomplished in a masterly manner— the modesty of the title affording no indication of the fulness, comprehensiveness, and beauty, with which a long and entangled series of detail, collected, necessarily, from a mass of vague and imperfect data, has been wrought into completeness and unity." Few of Poe's aesthetic judgments are less accurate, and the only possible explanation is that he is more interested in the material than in Irving. He speaks excitedly of "the thrilling details of this catastrophe" —the explosion of the *Tonquin*, which reappears, slightly disguised, and transported from West to "South," in *Pym*. Or he explains how one group of Irving's settlers "now found themselves in a perilous situation, a mere handful of men, on a savage coast, and surrounded by barbarous enemies." Describing an equally nerve-racking land expedition, he first apologizes and then apostrophizes: "We do not intend, of course, to proceed with our travellers throughout the vast series of adventure encountered in their passage through the wilderness. To the curious in these particulars we recommend the book itself. No details more intensely exciting are to be found in any work of travels within our knowledge." All in all, Irving's labyrinthine tale of gigantic ambition and unexampled disaster was right down Poe's alley; and perhaps it went without saying that its details would be more exciting still if found in a novel, which, as it happened, Poe was in the process of writing, the first installment of *Pym* appearing in the same issue of the *Messenger* as his review of *Astoria*. However genuine his delight in such a Western narrative as *Astoria*, Poe's fundamental inclinations were inevitably to compel him in the direction of fiction, of art. Whether superficially con-

sidered (in terms of literary theft), or more deeply considered (in terms of response and motivation), the literature
of the West was grist for his own creative mill, and any
Western book which came to his attention must, until proven
innocent, be regarded as a source.

Living in the alien North—he moved to Philadelphia in
1838, and in 1844 to New York—Poe sharpened the attitudes toward Western writing which he had developed in
the South. In a review of Simms's *Damsel of Darien*, he pro-
tested the conventional ease with which American writers
permitted the universe to underwrite their requirements for
cultural innovation: " 'And how natural, in an age so
fanciful [Simms was saying], to believe that the stars and
starry groups beheld in the new world, for the first time by
the native of the old, were especially assigned for its government and protection!' Now if by the old world be meant
the East, and by the new world the West, we are quite at
a loss to know what *are* the stars seen in the one, which
cannot be equally seen in the other." He mercilessly as-
saulted Seba Smith's pretentious *Powhatan; A Metrical
Romance, In Seven Cantos*, on the grounds that Smith
understood no essential difference between retailing the epic
facts of American history and writing a poem. In "Never
Bet the Devil Your Head," a story published two months
later, he alluded to *Powhatan* as the kind of poem to which
overzealous modern critics were fond of attributing arcane
(nonexistent) significance.

Later in 1841, Poe wrote his second series of papers on
"Autography." Here for the third time is Seba Smith, author
of *Powhatan* ("which we do not very particularly admire");
Smith writes "such a MS. [i.e., prose style] as David
Crockett wrote." Yet here again is also Poe's respect for the
minor man of American letters one way or another connected
with the practical affairs of Southern or Western literary
culture. William D. Gallagher "has the true spirit, and will
rise into a just distinction hereafter." John Tomlin has contributed to *Graham's* from Jackson, Tennessee, *and* "to
several of the Southern and Western Journals." Mr. J.

Beauchamp Jones (of Baltimore) "is the author of a series of papers of high merit now in course of publication . . . and entitled 'Wild Western Scenes.'" (Jones's papers eventually became one of the trashiest novels of the day, reaching in fifteen years a fortieth edition.) G. G. Foster, Esq. (editor of a journal in St. Louis) "has acquired much reputation, especially in the South and West, by his poetical contributions to the literature of the day." Mr. Richard Penn Smith has written a "pseudo-auto-biography called 'Colonel Crocket's Tour in Texas.'"

This generosity toward the lowly was partly an act of compensation for Poe's growing annoyance with the great names of American literature, all of whom happened to be New Yorkers or New Englanders. In connection with *The Damsel of Darien*, he had strenuously objected to South-westerner Simms's dedication to Paulding, ostensibly on grammatical grounds; but it is a fair guess that what really riled him was Simms's addressing Paulding as "one of the earliest pioneers in the fields of American letters."[10] Poe was more and more obsessed with the question of "originality," with the distinction between what is due the pioneer, and what the writer. "Among all the *pioneers* of American literature, whether prose or poetical," he wrote in a review of Brainard's poems, "there is *not one* whose productions have not been much overrated by his countrymen." The chief culprits were those Northerners who stood in his way, first Irving, then others: "Is there any one so blind as not to see that Mr. Cooper, for example, owes much, and that Mr. Paulding owes *all* of his reputation as a novelist, to his early occupation of the field?" (Paulding's most recent novel was *Westward, Ho!*—a psychological romance of Western adventure, somewhat in the mode of *Pym*, which Poe wrote at Paulding's suggestion.) With a triumphant air, Poe added the final outrageous insult: "We might, at

---

[10] This was a common convention, as in the opening lines of Fitz-Green Halleck's "Red Jacket":

COOPER, whose name is with his country's woven,
First in her files, her PIONEER of mind—

any moment, have as many Mr. Coopers as we please."
Present competitors, of any serious pretensions, were likely
to fare even worse. In the same issue of *Graham's* in which
he dealt with the adventitious reputations of Cooper and
Paulding, Poe found a place for Cornelius Mathews, their
most ambitious heir apparent in Knickerbocker exploitation
of the literary West, and especially for *Wakondah; The
Master of Life. A Poem*: "this trumpery declamation, this
maudlin sentiment, this metaphor run-mad, this twaddling
verbiage, this halting and doggrel rhythm, this unintelligible
rant and cant!" Perhaps still oversensitive to the facts of
his own indebtedness, he pointed out that the design of the
poem "seems to be based upon a passage in Mr. Irving's
'Astoria.'" But most of the poem consisted of speeches, "the
queerest, and the most rhetorical, not to say the most miscellaneous orations we ever remember to have listened to
outside of an Arkansas House of Delegates." This was a
standard mode of abuse.

The chief pioneer was naturally Cooper, to whom Poe
turned again in 1843, with a relatively gentle review of
Wyandotté. None of the Leatherstocking Tales was ever
reviewed by Poe, though he several times alluded to them,
and the five volumes in that series are all listed in the headnote; Poe began his review by saying that "in its general
features" *Wyandotté* was "precisely similar to the novels
enumerated in the title." He went on to demonstrate his
thorough familiarity with the ground rules for Western
romance, speaking, for instance, of the time-space equations
enabling Cooper to construct his forest narratives close to
home. *Wyandotté* takes place in "a region of which the
novelist has already frequently written [Western New
York], and the whole of which, with a trivial exception,
was a wilderness before the Revolution."

As was his wont, Poe insisted on calling attention to a
number of stylistic errors, chiefly in the form of syntactical
ambiguity; but perhaps his own prose was not wholly free
of the same fault. "In saying that the interest depends,
first, upon the nature of the theme, we mean to suggest that

this theme—life in the Wilderness—is one of intrinsic and universal interest, appealing to the heart of man in all phases." It seems finally impossible to determine whether "in all phases" modifies "the heart of man" (all men, in whatever mood, are intrigued by this theme), or "this theme" (men are intrigued by this theme, whatever form it assumes). Poe's continuing discussion does little to resolve the puzzle. The wilderness is "a theme, like that of life upon the ocean"—a loaded subject for himself, as for Melville, and with neither of them wholly separable from the West—"so unfailingly omniprevalent in its power of arresting and absorbing attention, that while success or popularity is, with such a subject, expected as a matter of course, a failure might be properly regarded as conclusive evidence of imbecility on the part of the author. The two theses in question have been handled *usque ad nauseam*—and this through the instinctive perception of the universal interest which appertains to them. . . . A man of genius will rarely, and should never, undertake either." Probably he meant to say, among other things, that the wilderness was susceptible of treatment under many guises, and that Cooper might better explore it in less obvious contexts.[11] (Perhaps he was also musing on his own recent wreck in *The Journal of Julius Rodman*.) In 1836, he had welcomed Ingraham's *South-West* according to familiar criteria: "It is, indeed, a matter for wonder that a similar object has never been carried into execution before. The South-West, embracing an extensive and highly interesting portion of the United States, is completely *caviare* to the multitude. Very little information, upon whose accuracy reliance may be placed, has been

[11] A very curious passage in *Pym*, where the protagonist attempts to fit together three pieces of torn paper, may conceivably be a further reference to the Leatherstocking Tales, of which three had been published by 1838. The torn paper carries a message which must be reconstructed with great difficulty; which is finally found on the "under side" (suggestive of Poe's usual language for allegory); which is in several senses admonitory; and which when reconstructed concludes: " '*I have scrawled this with blood—your life depends upon lying close.*' "

hitherto made public concerning these regions of Eldorado." But then he withdrew at least half the praise: "The Professor is indebted, generally, for his success, more to the innate interest of his subject matter, than to his manner of handling it."[12] So Bryant's poem, "The Hunter of the Prairies," was "a vivid picture of the life of a hunter in the desert. The poet, however, is here greatly indebted to his subject."

Despite such obvious crotchets, Poe was in the main both knowing and discriminating about the literature of the West. He continued to assault the melodramatic writing of, for example, Henry B. Hirst, in *The Coming of the Mammoth, The Funeral of Time, and Other Poems*, the first item of which was another interminable Indian legend, "the most preposterous of all the preposterous poems ever deliberately printed by a gentleman arrived at the years of discretion." On the other hand—though conceivably for reasons of literary politics—he more than made amends to Cornelius Mathews. The underlying purpose of *Big Abel, And the Little Manhattan*, he wrote, was "contrasting, apart from conventionality, the true values of the savage and civilized state"; and so it was "an ingenious, an original, and altogether, an excellent book—a book especially well adapted to a series which is distinctively American." The series was Wiley and Putnam's Library of American Books, which also included *Journal of an African Cruiser*, ed. Hawthorne, Poe's *Tales* and *The Raven and Other Poems, Western Clearings* by "Mary Clavers" (Caroline Kirkland), and which promised as future titles *The Forest and the Prairie* (finally published as *The Wilderness and the War Path*) by James Hall, and "a new volume" (*Mosses From an Old Manse*) by Hawthorne.[13] In the same series were four titles by Simms. *The Wigwam and the Cabin* Poe called (only a few weeks before similarly honoring

[12] *Southern Literary Messenger*, II (1836), 122-123.

[13] See facsimile advertisement facing p. xv in Thomas O. Mabbott's introduction to *The Raven and Other Poems* (New York, 1942). Melville's *Typee* later appeared in this series.

Mathews) "decidedly the most American of the American books" in Wiley and Putnam's Library, quoting with evident approval Simms's claim to have represented truthfully " 'the border history of the South. I can speak with confidence of the general truthfulness of its treatment. The life of the planter, the squatter, the Indian and the negro—the bold and hardy pioneer and the vigorous yeomen—these are the subjects.' "

In "The Literati of New York City" (1846), Poe noticed George H. Colton, author of *Tecumseh*, a poetical equivalent of *Elkswatawa*, and accurately described it as "insufferably tedious"; he discussed also William Kirkland, author of a famous essay, both informational and promotional, "The West, the Paradise of the Poor," and Margaret Fuller, whose Western narrative, *Summer on the Lakes*, he called "a remarkable assemblage of sketches." From it Poe quoted, and obviously admired, a rather Poesque passage wherein the effect of Niagara is ominously likened to the premonitions of death, and especially to the sense of naked savages about to strike from behind. Once again Irving, Cooper, Paulding, Bryant, and Halleck are set down, to their considerable diminution, as "our literary pioneers." But Charles Fenno Hoffman's *A Winter in the West*, at whose title Poe had previously jeered, is said to convey "the *natural* enthusiasm of a true *idealist*, in the proper phrenological sense, of one sensitively alive to beauty in every development. Its scenic descriptions are vivid, because fresh, genuine, unforced." This sounds more like *Julius Rodman* as it was supposed to be than *A Winter in the West*. Even so, Poe raised his eyebrows, by means of quotation marks, at Hoffman's presuming to write about the " 'far West.' " Yet in this particular sketch, Poe was so mellow as to allow merit to one of Hoffman's Indian poems, except for its being first-person narrative, so that the "hero is made to discourse very much after the manner of Rousseau."

But of all the Western Literati, Caroline Kirkland (wife of William) bore away the prize. Without impugning Poe's critical acumen—very likely she *was* the best of the lot—it is perhaps worth mentioning that she never influenced nor was influenced by him; neither was she a leading figure in the literary politics of sectionalism. On the positive side, her books were realistic and modest. She described one of them as "a veracious history of actual occurrences, an unvarnished transcript of real characters, and an impartial record of every-day forms of speech,"[14] which was a justifiable claim, and in connection with another promised: "No wild adventures,—no blood-curdling hazards,—no romantic incidents."[15] However different from Poe's peculiar bent, this was the kind of Western writing he was always disposed to welcome. *A New Home* was an "undoubted sensation," not from adventitious circumstances, but by virtue of *"truth and novelty*. The west at the time was a field comparatively untrodden by the sketcher or the novelist. In certain works, to be sure, we had obtained brief glimpses of character strange to us sojourners in the civilized east, but to Mrs. Kirkland alone we were indebted for our acquaintance with the *home* and home-life of the backwoodsman. With a fidelity and vigor that prove her pictures to be taken from the very life, she has represented 'scenes' that could have occurred only *as* and *where* she has described them. She has placed before us the veritable settlers of the forest, with all their peculiarities, national and individual." *Forest Life* was possibly even better: "It gives us, perhaps, more of the philosophy of Western life, but has the same freshness, freedom, piquancy. Of course, a truthful picture of pioneer habits could never be given in any grave history or essay so well as in the form of narration, where each character is permitted to develop itself." Aside from her realism, Poe was doubtless responding to her wit and good sense, her sophisticated prose style, her anecdotal competence, and her incisive social commentary, virtues for the most part absent from Western writing of the 1830's and 1840's.

Her third book, *Western Clearings*, was best of all. As in

[14] *A New Home—Who'll Follow? or, Glimpses of Western Life* (New York, 1839), pp. 7-8.
[15] *Forest Life* (New York, 1842), I, 10.

his treatment of *Georgia Scenes*, which *Western Clearings* somewhat resembles, Poe dwelt on its contents fondly and with the air of a true connoisseur, indulging himself in such imaginative flights as: "Only those who have had the fortune to visit or live in the 'back settlements' can enjoy such pictures to the full." Still, if he had not been West in fact— rumors that Poe once made a Western trip remain unconfirmed—he had visited there often enough in fancy and fiction to conclude, with a sufficient show of authority: "Unquestionably, she is one of our best writers, has a province of her own, and in that province has few equals. Her most noticeable trait is a certain *freshness* of style, seemingly drawn, as her subjects in general, from the west." An unknown enthusiast expressed the same sentiments more floridly: "Her voice comes to us out of the far unknown wilderness from which she sends it forth, like the clear ringing song of a bird, issuing from the heart of a wood."[16]

But Poe's response to the literary West must in the last analysis be interpreted within the context of a deeply personal, or even neurotic, identification of his own troubled destiny, and the destiny of his section, with the Western myth. Paradoxically, this neurotic involvement was at the same time a matter of intense practical moment with him, and is therefore best observed in those portions of his correspondence dealing with attempts to found a literary journal. As early as 1840, he wrote about the *Penn Magazine* to Frederick W. Thomas: "Your own experience and friendship will suggest the modes by which you may serve me in St Louis." Thomas answered with a letter full of specific information, literary and commercial, about that Western emporium. Two years later, Poe wrote Thomas Holley Chivers in Georgia (still about the *Penn Magazine*): "I believe I have many warm friends, especially in the South and West, and were the journal fairly before the public I have no doubt of ultimate success." Poe must have written so more than once to Chivers, for two years later Chivers used almost the same language in a letter to Poe:

[16] *Democratic Review*, XI (1842), 217.

"You have friends in the South and West, who will support you in the undertaking."

Meanwhile Poe was dispatching the same or similar letters to others; to Charles Anthon, for example, in 1844: "I knew from personal experience that lying *perdus* among the innumerable plantations in our vast Southern & Western Countries were a host of well-educated ⟨& but little prejudiced⟩ men si[n]gularly devoid of prejudice who would gladly le[n]d their influence to a really vigorous journal."[17] In point of fact, what Poe knew was that he wanted to edit and, ideally, own a journal as much like the *Southern Literary Messenger* as possible, but even more explicitly than the *Messenger* devoted to the literature of the West. In 1843, John Tomlin wrote from Tennessee about the now abandoned *Penn*: "I had caused to be noticed in various newspapers of the South and West, your project. . . . Could you have once started, your success would have been complete."[18] There was little or no exaggeration in Poe's claim (in "Boston and the Bostonians") : "As we very confidently expected, our friends in the Southern and Western country (*true* friends, and *tried,*) are taking up arms in our cause— and more especially in the cause of a national as distinguished from a sectional literature. They cannot see (it appears) any farther necessity for being ridden to death by New-England." To clinch his point, Poe quoted two laudatory notices, one emanating from Charleston, and the other from St. Louis.

Poe never gave up, and never changed his tune. To George Eveleth he wrote in 1848: "My plan [the illusory journal was now called the *Stylus*] is to go through the South & West & endeavor to interest my friends." A few weeks later, to N. P. Willis: "I must get a list of, at least, five hundred subscribers to begin with:—nearly two hundred I have already. I propose, however, to go South and

[17] Angle brackets indicate cancelled words.

[18] In 1845, Poe told Chivers about Tomlin, in support of his contention that " 'I have many strong friends in the South and West.' " *Chivers' Life of Poe*, ed. Richard Beale Davis (New York, 1952), p. 44.

West, among my personal and literary friends—old college and West Point acquaintances—and see what I can do." Only six months before his death, he was busily corresponding with a prospective backer in Illinois, who had suggested to Poe the idea of a journal with "duplicate publication, East & West," and still projecting a brilliant future along the same plausible but impractical lines: "My plan, in getting up such a work as I propose, would be to take a tour through the principal States—especially West & South."

As early as the review of *Georgia Scenes*, Poe had closely associated South and West, but in no such obsessive fashion as this. He must have increasingly come to feel, or have been made to feel, that the South, as a literary region, was of insufficient weight to hurl crushingly upon the despised tyrannical North. Searching for an ally, he naturally seized upon the West, which traditionally belonged to the whole nation, and was therefore especially useful to a man arguing himself on the side of a national literature. Of course, Poe's "plan" failed to materialize; he took no trip to the West, but went to Richmond and Baltimore, where he found neither patron nor journal, but only death. This was the end of his own bright hopes for the literature of the West, yet it would be erroneous to conclude that the Western dreams died with the man. Much more excitingly than in his book reviews, Poe's private West is in his fiction and in his aesthetics, where it has influenced generations of readers without their being aware of it; to these exciting and mysterious regions of El Dorado his Western criticisms point the way.

2. NARRATIVES OF EXPLORATION AND DISCOVERY

The terror, Poe wrote in his preface to *Tales of the Grotesque and Arabesque* (1840), "is not of Germany, but of the soul," leaving us still to inquire how it got there. The most reasonable conjecture is that so much of the terror as was cultural rather than personal—if indeed there exists such a thing as a personal trauma unrelated to culture—came from the savage West.[1] Lured by "a kind of nervous restlessness," the narrator of "MS. Found in a Bottle" (1833) is precipitated through a series of bizarre adventures into a "world of ocean," and thence driven due South.[2] Symbolically, due South is the "unknown," the "absolute," or "death"; allegorically, it is a displaced West. The storm which drives the story strikes with a "wilderness of foam"—Cooper's novels are full of comparable phrasings—soon carrying us "farther to the southward than any previous navigators." Like Crèvecœur's (and everybody else's) representative American, the protagonist is metamorphosed: "A feeling, for which I have no name, has taken possession of my soul—a sensation which will admit of no analysis, to which the lessons of by-gone times are inadequate, and for which I fear futurity itself will offer me no key. . . . Yet it is not wonderful that these conceptions are indefinite, since they have their origin in sources so utterly novel. A new sense—a new entity is added to my soul."

[1] Sadistic performances like "Hop-Frog" are perhaps as easily accounted for in terms of American history as in terms of Poesque psychology. "A drunken trapper might, as happened once, douse the hair of a sleeping companion with alcohol, then turn his victim into a human torch with a brand from the camp-fire." Ray Allen Billington, *The Far Western Frontier, 1830-1860* (New York, 1956), p. 47. In *American Humor* (New York, 1931), Constance Rourke relates Poe to the more callous aspects of the Southwestern comic mode (pp. 179-186). The following tales and sketches (not discussed in the text) contain marginal Western matter, usually in the form of passing allusions: "The Man That Was Used Up" (Indian-fighting), "The Colloquy of Monos and Una" (unexplored primeval forests), "The Thousand-and-Second Tale of Scheherazade" (natural wonders in the West), "Von Kempelin and His Discovery" (California Gold Rush), and "X-ing a Paragrab": "The only occasion on which he [Mr. Touch-and-go Bullet-head] did not prove infallible, was when, abandoning that legitimate home for all wise men, the East, he migrated to the city of Alexander-the-Great-o-nopolis, or some place of a similar title, out West."

[2] Unless otherwise specified, quotations in this section are from *The Complete Works of Edgar Allan Poe*, ed. James A. Harrison (New York, 1902).

"Unwittingly," the narrator daubs a folded sail with a tar-brush. "The studding-sail is now bent upon the ship, and the thoughtless touches of the brush are spread out into the word DISCOVERY." As if poised on the ever-moving, never-changing frontier, the ship seems "doomed to hover continually upon the brink of Eternity, without taking a final plunge into the abyss." But then quickly an irresistible current carries the ship to the vortex, the narrator, in spirit, assisting: "A curiosity to penetrate the mysteries of these awful regions, predominates even over my despair, and will reconcile me to the most hideous aspect of death. It is evident that we are hurrying onwards to some exciting knowledge— some never-to-be-imparted secret, whose attainment is destruction. Perhaps this current leads us to the southern pole itself." Desire, disaster—the desire of disaster, the disaster of desire—these are the fundamental elements in Poe's parable of American exploration. The equally demonic "Silence—A Fable" (1837) takes place near a river, on what may be a prairie, at the "boundary of the dark, horrible, lofty forest," full of "low underwood" and "tall primeval trees," over which "the gray clouds rush westwardly forever." Later the scene is called a "wilderness," and "the vast illimitable desert."

Poe's only completed novel, *The Narrative of Arthur Gordon Pym of Nantucket* (1838), again comprehends simultaneously the themes of life in the wilderness and life upon the ocean. From "MS. Found in a Bottle," phrases persist—"a perfect wilderness of foam," for example—as well as details of broader implication, such as the compulsive quest for absolute South, and the consequent disappearance into the void. "We were still hurrying on to the southward, under the influence of a powerful current. And now, indeed, it would seem reasonable that we should experience some alarm at the turn events were taking—but we felt none." Then once more the abrupt and mysterious end: "The darkness had materially increased, relieved only by the glare of the water thrown back from the white curtain before us. . . . And now we rushed into the embraces of the cataract, where a chasm threw itself open to receive us. But there arose in our pathway a shrouded human figure, very far larger in its proportions than any dweller among men. And the hue of the skin of the figure was of the perfect whiteness of the snow." As in *Moby-Dick*, the whiteness is doubtless both ethnological and Lockean; as in *The Prairie*, the figure is doubtless Terminus.

Pym is another tale of Western adventure and exploration, again cast in the guise of a voyage to the South Pole. "These are the principal attempts which have been made at penetrating to a high southern latitude," Poe wrote, after listing earlier expeditions—as in the *Astoria* review, following Irving, he listed previous explorations of the Far West, and would do so again in the introductory chapter of *Julius Rodman*—"and it will now be seen that there remained, previous to the voyage of the Jane, nearly three hundred degrees of longitude in which the Antarctic circle had not been crossed at all. Of course a wide field lay before us for discovery." In the elaboration of these "Southern" adventures, Poe drew heavily on *Astoria* for a whole series of mishaps (storm, shipwreck, famine, cannibalism, betrayal, losing the way, slaughter of or by natives), and perhaps even for formal elements; the abrupt, sometimes inexplicable shifts from sequence to sequence in *Pym* curiously resemble the gaping fissures and cleavages of Irving's sprawling narrative, more conspicuous than ever in Poe's redaction of it. Even a South Seas source like Jeremiah N. Reynolds, Poe managed to Westernize, as when, in support of Reynolds' projected expedition to "the great Pacific and Southern oceans," he argued in the *Messenger*, five months before he began to serialize *Pym* there: "Our pride as a vigorous commercial empire, should stimulate us to become our own pioneers in that vast island-studded ocean, destined, it may be, to become, not only the chief theatre of our traffic, but the arena of our future naval conflicts. Who can say, viewing the present rapid growth of our population, that the Rocky Mountains shall forever constitute the western boundary of our republic, or that it shall not stretch its dominion from sea to sea. This may not be desirable, but signs of the times render it an event by no means without the pale of possibility." If national policy were thus practically identical with private ambition, and if the South Seas were fated to yield up their watery secrets to "our own pioneers," then for the American writer even the Pacific Ocean must become (as in *Moby-Dick*) still another West, by associative transfer among such ambiguous overlapping terms as "the South-west" and "the South Seas."[3] (In the preface, A. G. Pym promises an "extraordinary series of adventure in the South Seas and elsewhere." Later he speaks of sailing "between the south and west" to "the debated ground.")

Therefore our narrator is at the outset of his strange voyage furnished with an account of "the expedition of Lewis and Clarke to the mouth of the Columbia"; their solid, respectable presence reminds us that even the most fantastic, and apparently ungeographical, adventures of a Poe are ultimately related to historical actuality. Therefore on the island of Tsalal, Pym and his comrades sport knives "somewhat resembling the Bowie knife now so much used throughout our western and southern country." Therefore Poe includes, under the pretext of describing the "rookeries" of albatrosses and penguins, an elaborate burlesque of Western settlement. Therefore, especially, he concentrates on a "hybrid" or "half-breed Indian," the "line-manager, who went by the name of Dirk Peters. This man was the son of an Indian woman of the tribe of Upsarokas, who live among the fastnesses of the Black Hills near the source of the Missouri. His father was a fur-trader, I believe, or at least connected in some manner with the Indian trading-posts on Lewis river." Peters has an "indentation on the crown (like

---

[3] According to Melville (a real expert), " 'South Seas' is simply an equivalent term for 'Pacific Ocean' "; text reconstructed by Merton M. Sealts, Jr., in *Melville as Lecturer* (Cambridge, 1957), p. 156. One newspaper report said that the lecturer called the same water "the whole Western ocean"; quoted in Merrell R. Davis, "Melville's Midwestern Lecture Tour, 1859," *Philological Quarterly*, xx (1941), 48.

that on the head of most negroes)," wears a bearskin wig, adding "no little to the natural ferocity of his countenance, which betook of the Upsaroka character," and his "ruling expression never varied under the influence of any emotion whatever." The black Indians at the end of the story—in whose caves arrowheads are found—represent an obvious fusion of at least two of "The Three Races in the United States" (title of a major chapter in Tocqueville's *Democracy in America*) ; through Poe's somewhat mechanical red-black-white symbolism, we are never for more than a few pages allowed to forget the three races. Peters is one way or another related to all, and thus appropriately the true hero of the novel, Pym being only its protagonist. "I have been thus particular in speaking of Dirk Peters," Poe-Pym explains, "because, ferocious as he appeared, he proved the main instrument in preserving the life of Augustus, and because I shall have frequent occasion to mention him hereafter in the course of my narrative—a narrative, let me here say, which, in its latter portions, will be found to include incidents of a nature so entirely out of the range of human experience, and for this reason so far beyond the limits of human credulity, that I proceed in utter hopelessness of obtaining credence for all that I shall tell, yet confidently trusting in time and progressing science to verify some of the most important and most improbable of my statements." In the concluding "Note," Peters is said to be still alive, as Pym is not, "and a resident of Illinois." He may be heard from yet.

The novel is almost entirely motivated by what can be readily enough identified as Western fever. Pym, in many respects the consciousness of Peters, as well as a sort of proto-Ishmael, is driven by an "ardent longing for the wild adventures incident to the life of a navigator." Stories of the sea—equivalent to forest, plains, or desert, as South is to West—inflame his "enthusiastic temperament, and somewhat gloomy, although glowing imagination." His imagination, being in some respects Poe's, is rather one-sided: "My visions were of shipwreck and famine; of death or captivity among barbarian hordes; of a lifetime dragged out in sorrow and tears, upon some gray and desolate rock, in an ocean unapproachable and unknown. Such visions or desires—for they amounted to desires—are common, I have since been assured, to the whole numerous race of the melancholy among men—at the time of which I speak I regarded them only as prophetic glimpses of a destiny which I felt myself in a measure bound to fulfill." As William Carlos Williams was to say about Poe: "His greatness is in that he turned his back and faced inland, to originality, with the identical gesture of a "Boone."[4] Facing inland—in Williams' sense—was never easy, painless, or safe. But Poe's genius rarely shines forth with more splendor than in this revelation that Pym's desires were "common" and "melancholy," not to say masochistic. It is an indispensable piece of information about the national past.

Pym's visions are also upon occasion identifiable as fusions of Southern and Western landscapes; in the following passage, for example, the infernal deserts are also bayous: "Then deserts, limitless, and of the most forlorn and awe-inspiring character, spread themselves out before me. Immensely tall trunks of trees, gray and leafless, rose up in endless succession as far as the eye could reach. Their roots were concealed in wide-spreading morasses, whose dreary water lay intensely black, still, and altogether terrible, beneath. And the strange trees seemed endowed with a human vitality, and, waving to and fro their skeleton arms, were crying to the silent waters for mercy, in the shrill and piercing accents of the most acute agony and despair." Perhaps these are the same waters of "The City in the Sea," where destruction, despair, damnation, and the throne of Death are all located "Far down within the dim West."[5] Or else Pym's visions of the West are almost magical; penetrating the interior of the savage island, "at every step we took inland the conviction forced itself upon us that we were in a country differing essentially from any hitherto

[4] "Poe," *In the American Grain* (Norfolk, Conn., 1925), p. 226.
[5] *The Poems of Edgar Allan Poe*, ed. Killis Campbell (Boston, 1917), p. 59.

visited by civilised men." The trees and rocks are strange.
So is the fabulous striped water which "formed the first
definite link in that vast chain of apparent miracles with
which I was destined to be at length encircled." The water
is neither colorless nor of any uniform color. "We perceived
that the whole mass of liquid was made up of a number of
distinct veins, each of a distinct hue; that these veins did
not commingle; and that their cohesion was perfect in regard
to their own particles among themselves, and imperfect in
regard to neighboring veins." As Tocqueville was observing, a few years earlier: "The danger of a conflict between
the white and the black inhabitants of the Southern states
of the Union (a danger which, however remote it may be,
is inevitable) perpetually haunts the imagination of the
Americans, like a painful dream."[6] So did the memory of
conflict with the Indian. Poe is obsessed with both painful
dreams, alternatively exploiting their horrors and attempting to exorcise them. Years later, in "Marginalia," he supported the notion of calling the United States "Appalachia"
on the grounds that we might thus "do honor to the Aborigines, whom, hitherto, we have at all points unmercifully
despoiled, assassinated and dishonored." In *Pym*—with the
notable exception of Dirk Peters—the dark races are dishonored and assassinated with the most reckless abandon;
but this is not necessarily Poe's animus.

Certainly we must understand that black Indians (with
Polynesian overtones) are by no means the only savages in
the book. So far as deception, treachery, and pointless butch-
ery are concerned, the white man is in every respect their
equal. Pym is sanctimoniously voluble about the "barbarous,
subtle, and bloodthirsty" behavior of the islanders, and glad
to see them violently repaid. It is the Americans, however,
who mutiny—clearly a greater sin than betraying an obvious
enemy—and who engage in cannibalism, an episode evidently suggested by *Astoria*, or by Owen Chase's tale of the

[6] *Democracy in America*, trans. Henry Reeve (1835 and 1840),
revised by Francis Bowen (1862), corrected and ed. Phillips Bradley
(New York, 1945), I, 376.

Essex, which also contributed to *Moby-Dick*. For pure sadism, the mutiny transcends the savage imagination. (No wonder they fear anything white.) In the final chapter, Peters and Pym press beyond savagery into the Absolute Unknown, and end in either illlumination or calamity, or both; the figure who receives, or blocks them, is perfectly white; possibly the white man has achieved another of his dubious victories. But the transcribed hieroglyphic shapes of the caves in the mountains are traced to verbal roots meaning: "To be shady" and "To be white" and "The region of the south," and these three roots are inexorably connected. The South is as ever the American West, and Poe, Lord of his own creation, has as usual the last ambiguous word: *"I have graven it within the hills, and my vengeance upon the dust within the rock."* The hieroglyphics apparently have their origin in the Piasa Rocks near Alton, Illinois, about which Poe might have read in Edmund Flagg, *The Far West* (1838); according to Flagg, Piasa was an Indian name for *"The bird that devours men,"* and indeed Poe offers us a recognizable "birdman" in the picture which poses as Figure 4 in chapter 23.

Two years later, Poe's second "novel," *The Journal of Julius Rodman, Being an Account of the First Passage Across the Rocky Mountains of North America Ever Achieved by Civilized Man*, came to disaster. Loudly advertising his hero as an explorer into the unknown, Poe was in a geographical sense at least theoretically well-equipped. Rodman's goal, "an exceedingly wide tract which is still marked upon all our maps as *unexplored*, and which, until this day [1840, that is, when Poe was publishing *Rodman*, not 1791-1792, when the adventures were supposedly taking place], has always been so considered," was evidently Alaska;[7] *"and the most interesting particulars of the narrative now published have reference to his adventures and discoveries therein"* (Poe's italics, as usual). Not content

[7] "This tract lies within the 60th parallel on the south, the Arctic Ocean on the north, the Rocky Mountains on the west, and the possessions of Russia on the east." Poe apparently interchanged "west" and "east," an easy error; the whole point of Rodman's expedition is to *pass* the Rocky Mountains.

with envisaging a single triumph, he was also tempted to claim for his hero a passage through the Rocky Mountains antedating Lewis and Clark's. Thus he tied himself to an actual route (Lewis and Clark's)—at least for the beginning, which was all he ever wrote—and mired himself in sources and documents. Like Irving before him, Poe was forced to rely on secondhand materials (thirdhand, by the time he had taken them from Irving); no matter how often he transferred them to his page, or proclaimed their thrilling interest, these brute facts of the Westward Movement remained for him intractable. *Julius Rodman* exudes precisely that "luke-warm and statistical air which pervades most records of this kind," and which, especially after thus insulting other people's Western narratives, it most behooved Poe to avoid.

There were other difficulties. Because the only structural design organic to an American exploratory expedition was continuous physical motion Westward, Poe's materials almost automatically prevented the possibility of a significant action, and especially of an end. (This problem he had circumvented with considerable ingenuity in "MS. Found in a Bottle" and in *Pym.*) Either the adventurer must finally arrive at a particular locality and send home his report—never, in the nature of things, world-shaking—or he must return in person, in either case condemning the story to anticlimax. Later, Poe rebuked the folly of Richard Adams Locke (of moon-hoax fame) in attempting to give "the *finale* of the adventures of Mungo Park in Africa—the writer pretending to have come into possession by some accident of the lost MSS. of the traveler. No one, however, seemed to be deceived . . . and the adventures were never brought to an end." According to Poe's introduction of his own "manuscript," Rodman came home from the great unknown in 1794, settled in Virginia, married, and fathered three children. It seems a tepid conclusion for so unusual a man.

Poe was equally trapped in the self-defeating contradictions of "originality." "The Journal which follows," he exulted, prematurely, and repeatedly, "not only embodies a relation of *the first* successful attempt to cross the gigantic barriers of that immense chain of mountains which stretches from the Polar Sea in the north, to the Isthmus of Darien in the south . . . but, what is of still greater importance, gives the particulars of a tour, beyond these mountains, through an immense extent of territory which, *at this day*, is looked upon as totally untravelled and unknown, and which, in every map of the country to which we can obtain access, is marked as '*an unexplored region.*' It is, moreover, the *only* unexplored region within the limits of the continent of North America." This was of course the best of all possible reasons for exploring it, and by no mere coincidence exactly analogous to the reasons regularly urged by Poe on behalf of his other literary experiments.

But as he wrote later in a review of Hawthorne: "There is clearly a point at which even novelty itself would cease to produce the legitimate originality, if we judge this originality, as we should, by the effect designed; this point is that at which *novelty becomes nothing novel.*" Elsewhere he had written that in every beautiful thing

> strangeness—in other words *novelty*—will be found a principal element; and so universal is this law that it has no exception even in the case of this principal element itself. Nothing, unless it be novel—*not even novelty itself*—will be the source of very intense excitement among men. Thus the *ennuyé* who travels in the hope of dissipating his *ennui* by the perpetual succession of novelties, will invariably be disappointed in the end. He receives the impression of novelty so continuously that it is at length no novelty to receive it. And the man, in general, of the nineteenth century—more especially of our own particular epoch of it—is very much in the predicament of the traveller in question.

This was more than he knew in 1840, although five years earlier he could have read in the *Southern Literary Messenger* the following analysis of Irving's *Tour on the Prairies*:

"In spite of an agreeable and highly descriptive style, the mind becomes wearied with the monotony of a journey through the solitudes of the Western Prairies, and after we have once formed a tolerably distinct idea of a buffalo hunt, and the lasoing of the wild horse, we become tired of the repetition of adventures, which possess so little variety."[8] Boredom was an inevitable ingredient of the ordinary Western narrative, and the same strictures might be urged against hundreds of them. Yet the idea that the West was intrinsically interesting died hard; in the same year, Charles Fenno Hoffman was claiming: "There is an ever saliant [sic] freshness in the theme of 'The Far West,' which prevents its becoming trite or tiresome."[9]

Ironically, it was Flagg's *The Far West: or, A Tour Beyond the Mountains*, from which Poe probably borrowed for *Pym*, and from whose subtitle (to mention nothing more) he was evidently filching once again, that had only recently elicited in the *Knickerbocker* another complaint Poe might have heeded: "The 'West' has, within the last two or three years, been a favorite subject with many writers. IRVING, HOFFMAN, HALL, and other well known authors, have delineated its scenery, and dilated upon nearly all that could interest us in the manners and customs of the settlers and the Indians, until the subject seemed to be entirely exhausted of interest, and nothing of importance remained to be added to our stock of knowledge. Still, the 'West' continues to furnish food for native writers, and the present work carries us pleasantly over the same ground, which we have so often travelled with the author's literary predecessors."[10] Whether for want of money, or from irresistible attraction, Poe undertook the tritest theme of all, a curious ineptitude in the man who valued originality above everything, and a further irony in view of the fact that the West was the standard American symbol for the new. The more Poe in *Julius Rodman* emphasized the novel, the more

[8] I (1835), 456.
[9] *A Winter in the West* (New York, 1835), I, iii.
[10] XIII (1839), 81.

he implicated himself in the platitudes of the day; fitfully proclaiming the unique worth of the unique, he wearily plodded the best-travelled road. Originality was the basic idea of his culture. Unfortunately, he was also treading close on the heels of such recent revelations as Samuel Parker's *Journal of an Exploring Tour Beyond the Rocky Mountains . . . Containing a Description of the Geography, Geology, Climate, and Productions; And the Number, Manners, and Customs of the Natives. With a Map of Oregon Territory* (1838), and John K. Townsend's *Narrative of a Journey Across the Rocky Mountains, to The Columbia River* (1839). These volumes constitute two more of the many reasons why Poe found it desirable to cast his narrative back to 1791-1792.

Aside from this evasive manipulation of time, all he could do was supply a narrator as little *ennuyé* as possible, and keep him moving, even though the motion were no more than a stale progression through successive Western landscapes, each featuring another round of imitative description. According to Poe, Rodman is hypochondriacal, and writes "with a vast deal of romantic fervor." He is "possessed with a burning love of Nature; and worshipped her, perhaps, more in her dreary and savage aspects, than in her manifestations of placidity and joy. He stalked through that immense and often terrible wilderness with an evident rapture at his heart which we envy him as we read. He was, indeed, *the man* to journey amid all that solemn desolation which he, plainly, so loved to depict."[11] *The Journal of Julius Rodman* is, among other things (hack work, hoax, and perhaps parody), secret autobiography of a loose and general kind, and the Poe of the introductory chapter scarcely worth discriminating from the fictional narrator, either explorer being activated, and readily identified, by a moody passion for making unique and daring raids upon the terrible unknown. That some sort of surreptitious, or

[11] At this point, Rodman seems a curious blend of Reynolds (see *Works*, IX, 314) and Poe. It will be remembered that Poe, on his deathbed, repeatedly called for Reynolds, no one knowing why.

perhaps unconscious, transference of motive is afoot is strikingly suggested by Poe's ascription of a parallel transference to Rodman. "The hunting and trapping designs, of which he speaks himself," Poe tells us, "were, as far as we can perceive, but excuses made to his own reason, for the audacity and novelty of his attempt. There can be no doubt, we think, (and our readers will think with us,) that he was urged solely by a desire to seek, in the bosom of the wilderness, that peace which his peculiar disposition would not suffer him to enjoy among men. He fled to the desert as to a friend."

For Poe, unfortunately, the desert declined to bloom. With a great show of learning, he discourses on the habits of beavers, the various tribes of Indians, the changes in vegetation and topography, only occasionally possessed of a suitable afflatus, as in Rodman's response to the Missouri River:

> As I looked up the stream (which here stretched away to the westward, until the waters apparently met the sky in the great distance) and reflected on the immensity of territory through which those waters had probably passed, a territory as yet altogether unknown to white people, and perhaps abounding in the magnificent works of God, I felt an excitement of soul such as I had never before experienced, and secretly resolved that it should be no slight obstacle which should prevent my pushing up this noble river farther than any previous adventurer had done. At that moment I seemed possessed of an energy more than human; and my animal spirits rose to so high a degree that I could with difficulty content myself in the narrow limits of the boat. I longed to be with the Greelys [conventional Kentuckians] on the bank, that I might give full vent to the feelings which inspired me, by leaping and running in the prairie.

Where the waters meet the sky, where earth meets Heaven, an emergent frontier metaphor helps release a spate of Romantic feeling which, however conventional, is also personal. It is Poe, and no mere Rodman, who is possessed "of an energy more than human," or wishes he were. Writing realistically about the West, however, Poe has simply nothing to say, and quickly collapses into the trivial and inane, as in the ridiculous picture of himself, or his factotum Rodman, cavorting in the prairie. Several more details of the like nature, and Poe is content to scramble back to safety among his paltry facts. In the next paragraph he is full of news about a cave "sixteen or seventeen feet high, and at least fifty feet in width," to which information he appends a footnote insisting on Rodman's scrupulosity in matters of measurement, but granting, only to turn round and defend it, his habit of "exaggeration" so far as *effects* are concerned.

After this curious excursion, the narrative resumes its mechanical course until chapter 5 (Poe resumes his mechanical course in *Burton's Gentleman's Magazine* until May 1840).[12] "As we proceeded on our journey," Rodman obligingly informs us, "I found myself less and less interested in the main business of the expedition, and more and more willing to turn aside in pursuit of idle amusement—if indeed I am right in calling by so feeble a name as amusement that deep and most intense excitement with which I surveyed the wonders and majestic beauties of the wilderness. No sooner had I examined one region than I was possessed with an irresistible desire to push forward and explore another." Under the guise of Western adventure, Poe describes, or asserts, his private personality, which is

[12] Along the way, Poe indulged some very unwise self-puffery. In another periodical he reviewed his progress, writing on January 29: "The Journal of Julius Rodman is continued, and a vivid description given of the persons and equipments of the travellers, who proceed up the Missouri as far as the mouth of the Platte. We prophecy that this will prove an intensely interesting narrative." Clarence S. Brigham, "Edgar Allan Poe's Contributions to *Alexander's Weekly Messenger*," *Proceedings of the American Antiquarian Society*, LII, N.S. (1942), 70. Again on April 1 (perhaps to be read with caution): "The 'Journal of Julius Rodman' progresses beautifully. The travellers are far on their way, and will soon enter a tract of country hitherto undescribed" (108).

surprisingly congruent with and doubtless formed by the prevailing sentiments of his compatriots toward Westward expansion. ("This may not be desirable, but signs of the times render it an event by no means without the pale of possibility.") "As yet, however, I felt as if in too close proximity to the settlements [the real world, or other works about the West?] for the full enjoyment of my burning love of Nature, and of *the unknown*." In the next sentences, we move even further into the West of Poe's aesthetic. "I could not help being aware that *some* civilized footsteps, although few, had preceded me in my journey—that *some* eyes before mine own had been enraptured with the scenes around me. . . . I was anxious to *go on*; to get, if possible, beyond the extreme bounds of civilization." Poe wanted to be, in short, a pioneer (though not of the Irving-Paulding-Cooper breed). But he also knew that he was failing. He wrote one more installment and quit. Somewhere, he had taken a wrong turning. The idea of exploration, one of the few genuine impulses behind his writing, gave itself up to him only when detached from the geographical, literary, or popular West, and subsumed under some other ostensible matter.

Henceforth he would be more subtle. A year later, he was ready with "A Descent Into the Maelström," a parable of discovery at the limits of horrified endurance and miraculous return. In this story Poe triumphantly risked an identification of his archetypal voyage with exploration of the American West which in its availability to the reader lies about halfway between the devious concealment of *Pym* and the naked exposure of *Julius Rodman*. Although he purportedly describes the coastal waters of Norway, his exposition is crowded with Western references. The auditor and the old man look from a cliff upon a "wilderness of surge," and hear the sea as "the moaning of a vast herd of buffaloes upon an American Prairie." Even more amazing, it is a duality in the sea, a point of meeting between opposed forces or impulses, which sets this world at odds with itself. At the same time the buffaloes are heard, the current which has (apparently) been running West turns East, and "in five minutes the whole sea, as far as Vurrgh, was lashed into ungovernable fury." (As Mrs. Hale remarked in a story called "The Emigrant": "In the autumn of 1818 . . . the tide of emigration rolled so rapidly from the Eastern States to the West, as almost to cause a returning current."[13] In the first chapter of *The Prairie*, Cooper spoke of the vortex attending the tide of Western emigration. In the third chapter of *The Pathfinder*, published the year before "A Descent Into the Maelström," he associated Western waterfalls, the Maelström, Niagara, and whirlpools.) Poe's Maelström sends forth "an appalling voice, half shriek, half roar, such as not even the mighty cataract of Niagara ever lifts up in its agony to Heaven"; Niagara is specified not only because it was a standard Western reference, but because there was in fact a famous whirlpool a few miles from the Great Falls.[14] No "ordinary accounts of this vortex" can convey "the faintest conception either of the magnificence, or of the horror of the scene—or of the wild bewildering sense of *the novel* which confounds the beholder." The West was apparently a mid-nineteenth-century name for the abyss (physical or metaphysical); with courage and intelligence, it could sometimes be dominated. " 'I suppose it was despair that strung my nerves.' "

"A Descent Into the Maelström" implies a deeper and better balanced, if not necessarily a more complicated, attitude about the fate of the nation than is found in any of Poe's previous confrontations of the American West. "The Island of the Fay," published a month later, is still more

---

[13] *The Token for 1829* (Boston, 1828), p. 328. So Margaret Fuller in 1844 imagined Chicago and Buffalo "the two correspondent valves that open and shut all the time, as the life-blood rushes from east to west and back again from west to east." *The Writings of Margaret Fuller*, ed. Mason Wade (New York, 1941), p. 23.

[14] Standard Western reference as in Joseph Rodman Drake's poem, "Fragment. Tuscara," quoted by Poe in a review:

> To couch upon the grass and hear
> Niagara's everlasting voice
> Far in the deep blue West away . . .

(*Works*, XI, 21-22, n. 2)

philosophical. "Nullus enim locus genio est." The locus is a rivulet and island "amid a far-distant region of mountain locked within mountain." On three sides, the river is surrounded by forest; it appears to have no exit, "but to be absorbed by the deep green foliage of the trees to the east," while in the open or Western direction "there poured down noiselessly and continuously into the valley, a rich golden and crimson water-fall from the sunset fountains of the sky." The West is the source of light and movement for "us sojourners in the civilized east."

> So blended bank and shadow there,
> That each seemed pendulous in air—

For the new context, Poe adapts a couplet from "The City in the Sea," and thus further establishes the island within the dim West.

"My position enabled me to include in a single view both the eastern and western extremities of the islet; and I observed a singularly-marked difference in their aspects." Despite the setting sun, the West suggests youth, love, and the future: "There seemed a deep sense of life and joy about all." But "the other or eastern end of the isle was whelmed in the blackest shade." The point of interpenetration, or frontier, is significantly located at the funereal Eastern end of the island, where "the shade of the trees fell heavily upon the water, and seemed to bury itself therein, impregnating the depths of the element with darkness." At the moment of union between conception and mortality, where directions reverse and identities interchange, the source of light ambiguously casts death upon the receptive East, and the process seems perpetual: "I fancied that each shadow, as the sun descended lower and lower, separated itself sullenly from the trunk that gave it birth, and thus became absorbed by the stream; while other shadows issued momently from the trees, taking the place of their predecessors thus entombed." If the West is originative, the home of the new, by definition it moves toward completion in the past, the old, the interred.

164

Then to Poe appears the Fay, the Spirit of the West, strangely suggesting the Indian maiden of early American poetry. (Indeed, Poe's entire sketch somewhat resembles James Hall's poem, "The Isle of the Yellow Sands.") She makes her way "slowly into the darkness from out the light at the western end of the island. She stood erect, in a singularly fragile canoe, and urged it with the mere phantom of an oar. While within the influence of the lingering sunbeams, her attitude seemed indicative of joy—but sorrow deformed it as she passed within the shade. Slowly she glided along, and at length rounded the islet and re-entered the region of light." But now she seems a year older, and in that degree less light. The East-West axis of the island lies along and within the stream of time, at one end of which the sun goes down. For all the cyclical, reciprocal pattern of Western influence and Eastern assimilation, the entire process is subject to change. The West will be won, America will age. So the story ends: "But at length, when the sun had utterly departed, the Fay, now the mere ghost of her former self, went disconsolately with her boat into the region of the ebony flood,—and that she issued thence at all I cannot say,—for darkness fell over all things, and I beheld her magical figure no more." Of course, we know the sun also rises; but that will be a new day, and another period in American history. Insofar as the genius of the place is also a genius of the times, there will be a different Fay.

"The Masque of the Red Death. A Fantasy" (1842) is an even subtler, and incomparably less reassuring, parable of American history.[15] In the same issue of *Graham's* which

[15] "The Masque of the Red Death" evidently owes something to Poe's general awareness of William D. Gallagher as a Western writer, coupled with his knowledge of a particular Gallagher poem, "The Revelers," which recounts party banter between a disguised intruder and a Bacchanal, who in the last stanza forces the issue:

> He struck—and the stranger's guise fell off,
>   And a phantom form stood there,
> A grinning, and ghastly, and horrible thing,
>   With rotten and mildewed hair:

carried the story, Poe was reviewing Hawthorne's *Twice-Told Tales*, and noting with admiration that "a strong under-current of *suggestion* runs continuously beneath the upper stream of the tranquil thesis. In short, these effusions of Mr. Hawthorne are the product of a truly imaginative intellect."[16] So were Poe's effusions; but his under-currents ran deeper than Hawthorne's, and his thesis is consequently much more difficult to read. "The Masque of the Red Death," which is in several details indebted to "Howe's Masquerade," is perhaps not impossible to fathom, however, once we begin to suspect that Prince Prospero is a typically ironic allegorical name for the United States, and the "Red Death" a somewhat more complicated emblematic equivalent for the Indian—or for American maltreatment of the Indian, together with Indian reprisal—and thus for one crucial aspect of the West. Prince Prospero's plans, it is said, "were bold and fiery, and his conceptions glowed with barbaric lustre. There are some who would have thought him mad. His followers felt that he was not." His followers feel what they wish to feel, but the story declines to sustain their confidence. Certainly their situation is unpropitious. "The 'Red Death' had long devastated [or "depopulated"] the country. No pestilence had ever been so fatal, or so hideous. Blood was its Avatar and its seal—the redness and

---

And they struggled awhile, till the stranger blew
    A blast of his withering breath;
And the Bacchanal fell at the Phantom's feet,
    And his conqueror was—DEATH!

This poem is in *Erato, Number I*, the volume in whose communion Poe was cheered with hopes for the Literature of the West; the connection with "The Masque of the Red Death" is noticed in Ralph L. Rusk, *The Literature of the Middle Western Frontier* (New York, 1925), I, 339-340.

[16] Most of Poe's better-known, disparaging comments about allegory were made later, most notoriously in his second (1847) review of Hawthorne. (Yet in 1846, at the end of "The Philosophy of Composition," he spoke favorably of the "under-current of meaning" in "The Raven.") Three of his early tales carry subtitles suggesting a more relaxed attitude in the 1830's: "King Pest the First. A Tale Containing an Allegory," "Shadow. A Fable," and "Siope—A Fable" (later, "Silence—A Fable").

the horror of blood." Meanwhile Prince Prospero ("happy and dauntless and sagacious") retires with a thousand select courtiers to a well-provisioned and impregnable abbey. "With such precautions the courtiers might bid defiance to contagion. The external world could take care of itself. In the meantime it was folly to grieve, or to think. The prince had provided all the appliances of pleasure." After six months in this truly American situation, Prince Prospero undertakes to give a masked ball.

The core of the story is Poe's description of the setting in which this masquerade is enacted. There are seven rooms, "so irregularly disposed," according to the Prince's eccentric taste, "that the vision embraced but little more than one at a time." Conceivably Poe implies that the nature of American history, in 1842 consisting almost entirely of political revolution and geographical expansion, enforces a certain discontinuity of perception. "There was a sharp turn at every twenty or thirty yards, and at each turn a novel effect." The rooms are—as one likes—the stages of society, or the various Americas lying progressively Westward. Each is a different color. "That at the eastern extremity was hung, for example, in blue"—the aristocratic color?— and then purple, green, orange, white, violet, in that order, the stained glass windows matching the hangings. But the seventh room (at the Western extremity) is different, "closely shrouded in black" but "in this chamber only, the color of the windows failed to correspond with the decorations. The panes here were scarlet—a deep blood color." The color scheme is the same as in Hawthorne's "My Kinsman, Major Molineux," and so is the air of ominous foreboding. (One remembers, also, the Prynne-Dimmesdale escutcheon at Boston: "ON A FIELD, SABLE, THE LETTER A, GULES.") "In the western or black chamber the effect of the fire-light that streamed upon the dark hangings through the blood-tinted panes, was ghastly in the extreme, and produced so wild a look upon the countenances of those who entered, that there were few of the company bold enough to set foot within its precincts at all." Against the Western

wall of this Westernmost apartment stands a huge clock—
like the setting sun in "The Island of the Fay"—hourly
striking a note of doom ("exceedingly musical") that temporarily interrupts the festivities.

Through these chambers writhe a thousand dreams; no
need inquiring what nationality. "But to the chamber which
lies most westwardly of the seven, there are now none of
the maskers who venture; for the night is waning away; and
there flows a ruddier light through the blood-colored panes;
and the blackness of the sable drapery appals; and to him
whose foot falls upon the sable carpet, there comes from
the near clock of ebony a muffled peal more solemnly em-
phatic than any which reaches *their* ears who indulge in the
more remote gaieties of the other apartments." At the stroke
of midnight, in the fulness of time, the ultimate horror of
the American frontier—the West as Annihilation, the
Indian as Retribution—suddenly erupts into the party, as,
in "Roger Malvin's Burial," Death like the corpse of an
Indian warrior stalked the forest. Even the rumor of this
feared, hated, inescapable presence is sufficient to elicit
from the polite company a "murmur, expressive of dis-
approbation and surprise—then, finally, of terror, of horror,
and of disgust." The new masquer is dressed as a "stiffened
corpse," and more specifically as "the type of the Red
Death." Clearly he has "gone beyond the bound of even
the prince's indefinite decorum." Like Pym in the counter-
mutiny scene, or Madeline Usher bursting from the coffin,
"his vesture was dabbled in *blood*." Standing in "the eastern
or blue chamber," the outraged Prospero defies him. But the
intruder passes "within a yard of the prince's person," and
calmly retraces his steps from East to West as far as the
violet (next to last) room. Prospero gives chase, dagger—
or Bowie knife?—in hand. At the "extremity of the velvet
apartment," that is, upon the final frontier, the intruder
turns and fronts him. ("There arose in our pathway a
shrouded human figure . . . of the perfect whiteness of the
snow.") Prospero falls dead. The revelers frantically hurl
themselves upon the unwelcome guest, only to gasp "in

unutterable horror" at finding his costume "untenanted by any tangible form." He is only the shape of the American conscience.

Poe's response to the literary West exhibits a surprising range of attitude and tone, and, considering the depth and intensity of his personal involvement with it, a surprising control. Never did he write a Western tale more savage in its attack on American moral complacency than "The Masque of the Red Death"; never did he write a Western idyl more serenely ironic than "Morning on the Wissahiccon," sometimes known as "The Elk" (1844).[17] This sketch opens quietly with a general view of American landscape, especially as represented by British travelers to the European imagination, and thus indirectly, and the more powerfully, to the American. Poe complains of the travelers' incorrigible concentration upon the East Coast. "They say little, because they have seen less, of the gorgeous interior scenery of some of our western and southern districts—of the vast valley of Louisiana, for example,—a realization of the wildest dreams of paradise."

But "the real Edens of the land lie far away from the track of our own most deliberate tourists," in exemplification of which broad truth Poe offers us the Wissahiccon, "about six miles westward of Philadelphia." By means of this cunningly calculated exposition—a maneuver not different in kind from the sleight of hand practiced by Hawthorne at Salem or Thoreau at Concord—this nearby brook becomes as Western as the Mississippi. A restrained and objective description of the river follows, but the heart of the performance is in the concluding allegory. Floating with the current in a skiff, Poe tells how he "sank into a half slumber, during which my imagination revelled in visions of the Wissahiccon of ancient days . . . when the red man trod alone, with the elk." A few sentences later, the elk is made even more explicitly metonymous for the Indian: "I saw, or dreamed that I saw, standing upon the extreme verge of

[17] The source of this sketch is almost certainly "The Wissahiccon," authorship unknown, *Southern Literary Messenger*, II (1835), 24-27.

the precipice, with neck outstretched, with ears erect, and the whole attitude indicative of profound and melancholy inquisitiveness, one of the oldest and boldest of those identical elks which had been coupled with the red men of my vision."

With the greatest delicacy, the sketch then opens to us the vistas of native fantasy, and assesses their availability. "During this interval my whole soul was bound up in intense sympathy alone. I fancied the elk repining, not less than wondering, at the manifest alterations for the worse, wrought upon the brook and its vicinage, even within the last few years, by the stern hand of the utilitarian." But then the animal stirs; the dreamer awakens; a whisper is heard from the bushes, whence a servant emerges to lure and capture the wild spirit. "Thus ended my romance of the elk. It was a *pet* of great age and very domestic habits, and belonged to an English family occupying a villa in the vicinity." With the final sentence, the sketch subtly returns to its considerations of European, and especially British, tyranny over the American literary scene. The elk who is the Indian is also, not unimaginably, the too impressionable, the too easily tamed native writer.

Of course, there were writers and writers. " 'Let us suppose only,' " says the doctor in "A Tale of the Ragged Mountains" (1844), " 'that the soul of the man of to-day is upon the verge of some stupendous psychal discoveries.' " Perhaps in part because of his inability to master the West directly, Poe in the 1840's became deeply concerned with what can only be understood as a psychological—or, in the literal sense, metaphysical—equivalent of the American frontier. The hero of this "Tale of the Ragged Mountains" is in several respects a metamorphosed or resurrected Julius Rodman, melancholy, neurotic, "in the highest degree, sensitive, excitable, enthusiastic. His imagination was singularly vigorous and creative." Alone, or with a dog, he regularly explores "the chain of wild and dreary hills that lie westward and southward of Charlottesville," where Poe went to college.

One extraordinary morning the protagonist enters the mountains and undergoes a "singular" experience. For all its singularity, this experience depends on the direction his exploration takes and upon his preliminary response to what he sees. " 'The scenery which presented itself on all sides, although scarcely entitled to be called grand, had about it an indescribable, and to me, a delicious aspect of dreary desolation. The solitude seemed absolutely virgin. I could not help believing that the green sods and the gray rocks upon which I trod, had been trodden never before by the foot of a human being. So entirely secluded, and in fact inaccessible, except through a series of accidents, is the entrance of the ravine, that it is by no means impossible that I was indeed the first adventurer—the very first and sole adventurer who had ever penetrated its recesses.' " He might as well be in Alaska. In this situation, and under the influence of morphine, by some species of hallucination (subsequently hypothesized as mesmeric, and explained as medical) he finds himself in Benares, in the thick of an anti-British insurrection, and, a few minutes later, "dead." He has temporarily exchanged identities with another old friend of the doctor's—between whom and himself exists "a very distinct and strongly marked *rapport*, or magnetic relation"—who was in fact killed years before in a comparable uprising.

Such a story is not to be taken literally; neither is it to be dismissed as fantastic. The important consideration is that Poe has placed his protagonist in a sort of limbo between life and death (in striking parallel with Hawthorne's performance in "The Haunted Mind" and elsewhere) which constitutes a border situation metaphorically comparable to the American sense and definition of the Western frontier. It is no mere coincidence that the experience in question befalls him in the mountains "that lie westward and southward of"—no matter where. Neither is it inconsequential that in this daring attempt to translate the generic cultural experience of the actual Westward Movement into parallel psychological and individual terms, Poe should instinctively return to the scene where his youthful literary ambitions, and with them his richest fantasy-life ("the gorgeous interior scenery of some of our western and southern districts"), almost certainly proliferated most hugely. In "Marginalia" (1846), he strongly implied that his prevailing literary ambition was to realize verbally "a class of fancies, of exquisite delicacy, which are *not* thoughts, and to which, *as yet*, I have found it absolutely impossible to adapt language. . . . They seem to me rather psychal than intellectual. They arise in the soul (alas, how rarely!) only at its epochs of most intense tranquility—when the bodily and mental health are in perfection—and at those mere points of time where [*not* when] the confines of the waking world blend with those of the world of dreams." Two opposed, contiguous worlds, blending at the point of interpenetration, where antithesis fades and creation becomes possible: the ultimate source of Poe's ambition is still the American frontier.

These "fancies," or "visions," afford "a glimpse of the spirit's outer world." From the meeting point between waking and dreaming, Poe climbs by analogy, and by way of Western values and tonalities (as documented in "MS. Found in a Bottle," *Narrative of Arthur Gordon Pym*, *Journal of Julius Rodman*, and other tales), to the point of meeting between life and eternity: "and I arrive at this conclusion—if this term is at all applicable to instantaneous intuition—by a perception that the delight experienced has, as its element, but *the absoluteness of novelty*. . . . It is as if the five senses were supplanted by five myriad others alien to mortality." In view of the fact that he is not consciously concerned with the West in this passage, Poe's inability to keep the frontier out of it is even more remarkable. "I have proceeded so far . . . as to prevent the lapse from *the point* of which I speak—the point of blending between wakefulness and sleep—as to prevent at will, I say, the lapse from this border-ground into the dominion of sleep." How important all this was to Poe is unmistakably announced at the end of the note: "Nothing can be more certain than that even a partial record of the impressions would startle the universal intellect of mankind, by the *supremeness of the novelty* of the material employed, and of its consequent suggestions. In a word—should I ever write a paper on this topic, the world will be compelled to acknowledge that, at last, I have done an original thing."

Poe had already written a few original papers on this topic. In "Instinct Vs Reason—A Black Cat" (1840), he said that "the line which demarcates the instinct of the brute creation from the boasted reason of man, is, beyond doubt, of the most shadowy and unsatisfactory character— a boundary line far more difficult to settle than even the North-Eastern or the Oregon."[18] In "The Colloquy of Monos and Una" (1841), he charted in outrageous detail the vaguer and more significantly American borderland of "annihilation" between death and rebirth, whereupon was enacted "the first obvious and certain step of the intemporal soul upon the threshold of the temporal Eternity." More outrageously still, "The Premature Burial" (1844) depends upon an insoluble problem, defined and perhaps even proposed by the geographical conditions of American history: "To be buried while alive, is, beyond question, the most terrific of these extremes which has ever fallen to the lot of mere mortality. That it has frequently, very frequently, so fallen, will scarcely be denied by those who think. The boundaries which divide Life from Death, are at best shadowy and vague. Who shall say where the one ends, and where the other begins?"

Who shall say precisely where the Western frontier was in 1844? It is not so much Poe who is bizarre as we who have read him without understanding. In his restless patrol along the lines between the senses, between waking and sleep, between sanity and insanity, between order and disorder, between normality and abnormality, between sentience and insentience, between the organic and the inorganic, between life and death, between good and evil,

[18] Quoted by Brigham in "Poe's Contributions to *Alexander's Weekly Messenger*," p. 71.

between Heaven and earth, he was the typical American of his age, eccentric primarily in the boldness and determination with which he carried forward his investigations. *Ceteris paribus*, that applies even to "The Facts in the Case of M. Valdemar" (1845).[19] The most grotesque horrors in Poe's writing—mesmerisms, catalepsies, premature burials, forays into madness—are attempts to explore the neutral territory between categories of being, the debatable ground of the soul's possession. The terror, as well as the poetic sentiment, is identical with the figurative structure of the Western frontier.

[19] According to the narrator of this story, "My attention, for the last three years, had been repeatedly drawn to the subject of Mesmerism; and, about nine months ago, it occurred to me, quite suddenly, that in the series of experiments made hitherto, there had been a very remarkable and most unaccountable omission:—no person had as yet been mesmerized *in articulo mortis*." See also the conclusion of "Mesmeric Revelation," in the previous year: "Had the sleep-waker, indeed, during the latter portion of his discourse, been addressing me from out the region of the shadows?"—with which cf. *The Letters of Edgar Allan Poe*, ed. John W. Ostrom (Cambridge, 1948), I, 257.

Henry David Thoreau

1. THE ESSENTIAL WEST

IN *A Week on the Concord and Merrimack Rivers* (1849), Thoreau said of Sir Walter Raleigh's prose: "There is a natural emphasis in his style, like a man's tread, and a breathing space between the sentences. . . . His chapters are like English parks, or say rather like a Western forest, where the larger growth keeps down the underwood, and one may ride on horseback through the openings."[1] The final sentence, especially, suggests Thoreau's idealized conception of the West—spacious and free from clutter—almost as if he had in the back of his mind his prospective isolation in Concord. For the most part, his metaphors were even more obviously internalized, or, as the psychoanalysts like to say, introjected. After all, one common meaning of the West was "inland" or "the interior." So Thoreau admonished himself: "Let us migrate interiorly without intermission, and pitch our tent each day nearer the western horizon. The really fertile soils and luxuriant prairies lie on this side the

[1] Quotations in this section are from *The Writings of Henry David Thoreau* (Boston, 1906), supplemented by *The Making of Walden, With the Text of the First Version*, ed. J. Lyndon Shanley (Chicago, 1957); *The Journal of Henry D. Thoreau*, ed. Bradford Torrey and Francis H. Allen (Boston, 1906), supplemented by *Consciousness in Concord; the Text of Thoreau's Hitherto "Lost Journal," (1840-1841)*, ed. Perry Miller (Boston, 1958); *The Correspondence of Henry David Thoreau*, ed. Walter Harding and Carl Bode (New York, 1958), which also contains letters *to* Thoreau; and *Collected Poems of Henry Thoreau*, ed. Carl Bode, enlarged edition (Baltimore, 1964).

Alleghanies."[2] (But which side the Alleghanies is "this side"?) So he admonished the public:

It is easier to discover another such a new world as Columbus did, than to go within one fold of this which we appear to know so well; the land is lost sight of, the compass varies, and mankind mutiny; and still history accumulates like rubbish before the portals of nature. But there is only necessary a moment's sanity and sound senses, to teach us that there is a nature behind the ordinary, in which we have only some vague preëmption [i.e., squatter's] right and western reserve as yet.

And though, once again, the metaphor wobbles, between ideas of "within" (West as interior) and "behind" (West as trans-Alleghany), its basis in the national passion is sufficiently clear.

The West, the frontier, were so deeply internalized in Thoreau that they issued from his pen sounding like second nature, even when they also sounded like other writers. "Such early morning thoughts as I speak of occupy a debatable ground between dreams and waking thoughts. They

[2] *Journal*, I, 131. Like the good New Englander that he was, Thoreau cultivated a strong distaste for richness of all sorts, and this provincial asceticism clearly conditioned his attitude toward the actual West. "They [local ponds] are all the more interesting to me for the lean & sandy soil that surrounds them. Heaven is not one [of] your fertile Ohio bottoms, you may depend on it." *Correspondence*, p. 431. In the same vein, Timothy Flint had written about the country West of Wheeling: "There is something . . . to me almost appalling in this prodigious power of vegetation. For there is with me, in some manner, an association of this thing with the idea of sickness." *Recollections of the Last Ten Years* (Boston, 1826), p. 28. See also "Early Records of the Concord Lyceum," in Kenneth Walter Cameron, *Transcendental Climate* (Hartford, Conn., 1963): "Nov. 21st. 1832 . . . This question was then discussed V.I.Z. *Is a fertile soil best calculated to call forth the energy of a people?* . . . Decided in the negative" (III, 668). There are also entertaining entries for April 17, 1833 ("*Ought New England to encourage emigration to the West?*"), and for January 17, 1838 ("*Are the rigor of the climate and the stubborn[n]ess of the Soil in New England favorable to the developement of character?*") (III, 670, 687).

are a sort of permanent dream in my mind." The seashore
was "a sort of neutral ground, a most advantageous point
from which to contemplate this world." Pond foam was
"the debatable ground between two oceans [water and air],
the earth, or shore, being only the point of resistance, where
they are held to mingle." Birds in general were "but
borderers upon the earth . . . which seem to flit between us
and the unexplored," and the wood thrush in particular was
the "mediator between barbarism and civilization."[3]

The underlying ground of comparison was made amply
clear in the *Week*: "The wilderness is near as well as dear
to every man. Even the oldest villages are indebted to the
border of wild wood which surrounds them, more than to
the gardens of men. There is something indescribably inspiriting and beautiful in the aspect of the forest skirting
and occasionally jutting into the midst of new towns. . . .
Our lives need the relief of such a background, where the
pine flourishes and the jay still screams." The West that
Thoreau had in mind was prophetic, religious, aesthetic—
the fountain of being, the source of renewal, the spring of
art. Mountains on the Western horizon he called "the un-
disputed territory between earth and heaven." In a more
elaborately figurative formulation, he said: "It is not the
fringed foreground of the desert nor the intermediate oases
that detain the eye and the imagination, but the infinite,
level, and roomy horizon, where the sky meets the sand, and
heavens and earth, the ideal and actual, are coincident,
the background into which leads the path of the pilgrim."[4]

Pilgrim and pathfinder, Thoreau was forever playing with
the words frontier and front, trying to detach them from
literality. In his so-called lost journal he observed: "There
are two sides to every sentence; the one is contiguous to me,
but the other faces the gods, and no man ever fronted it."
Even more to the point, in *The Maine Woods*: "Here, then,

[3] These frontier metaphors are in *Journal*, x, 141; *Writings*, iv,
186 (*Cape Cod*); *Journal*, xiv, 63; *Consciousness in Concord*, p.
161; *Journal*, v, 293.
[4] *Journal*, v, 141; i, 473-474.

one could no longer accuse institutions and society, but must front the true source of evil." In the *Week*, he wrote of Concord, N.H.: "We found that the frontiers were not this way any longer. This generation has come into the world fatally late for some enterprises." Ignoring the main facts about the actual Western frontier—that it had never been anywhere in particular, and that it was always on the move—Thoreau argued that if the frontiers had left New England they no longer existed. The excluded middle of his crazy syllogism reads: "It is unthinkable to leave home." Therefore the frontiers were to be stripped of all connotation of place, redeemed for contemplation and poetry:

> The frontiers are not east or west, north or south; but wherever a man *fronts* a fact, though that fact be his neighbor, there is an unsettled wilderness between him and Canada, between him and the setting sun, or, farther still, between him and *it*. Let him build himself a log house with the bark on where he is, *fronting* IT, and wage there an Old French war for seven or seventy years, with Indians and Rangers, or whatever else may come between him and the reality, and save his scalp if he can.

"IT" was the inexpressible, or, to the heroic poet, the not yet expressed.

Understandably, a man holding such views might occasionally write with scant regard for the facts. In his youth, Thoreau perpetrated a number of bad poems on the subject of America's cardinal points; one went:

> The needles of the pine,
> All to the west incline.

Another hinted a paradoxical truth which always made him uncomfortable:

> In the East fames are won,
> In the West deeds are done.

In a third, he was wilfully capricious, perhaps seduced by the rhyme:

Dong, sounds the brass in the east,
As if to a funeral feast,
But I like that sound the best
Out of the fluttering west.[5]

And as late as 1860, he was still exploding in a personal
letter: "Look at mankind. No great difference between two,
apparently; perhaps the same height and breadth and
weight; and yet to the man who sits most E. this life is a
weariness, routine, dust and ashes, and he drowns his imaginary cares (!) (a sort of friction among his vital organs),
in a bowl. But to the man who sits most W., his *contemporary* (!) it is a field for all noble endeavors, an elysium,
the dwelling place of heroes & knights."[6] To his 1840-1841
Journal he confided: "In the sunrise I see an eastern city
with its spires, in the sunset a western forest." Or as he wrote
in the *Week*: "It may be that the forenoon is brighter than
the afternoon, not only because of the greater transparency
of its atmosphere, but because we naturally look most into
the west, as forward into the day, and so in the forenoon

[5] "The needles of the pine" was finally used as epigraph for "A
Walk to Wachusett," which is full of Western symbolism; it also
appears in the *Journal* under the title of "Westward, Ho!" (I, 259).
Later, Thoreau read in his favorite Alexander Henry and confirmed
by his own observation (*Journal*, IV, 136-137) that pine needles in-
cline "East" rather than "West," but he wrote no further on the
subject. "In the East fames are won" appeared in "Thomas Carlyle
and His Works" (1847), introduced by the usual sentimental complaint: "Literature speaks how much still to the past, how little
to the future, how much to the East, how little to the West." See
also the inept poem, "With frontier strength ye stand your ground,"
used both in "A Walk to Wachusett" and the *Week*. Rejecting this
poem for the *Dial*, Margaret Fuller urged the young aspirant: "Say
not so confidently All places, all occasions are alike." *Correspondence*, pp. 56-57.

[6] And again, somewhat more calmly, in *The Maine Woods*: "You
carried so much topography in your mind always,—and sometimes
it seemed to make a considerable difference whether you sat or lay
nearer the settlements, or farther off, than your companions,—were
the rear or frontier man of the camp. But there is really the same
difference between our positions wherever we may be camped, and
some are nearer the frontiers on feather-beds in the towns than others
on fir twigs in the backwoods." *Writings*, III, 221-222.

see the sunny side of things, but in the afternoon the shadow of every tree."

"Westward is heaven, or rather heavenward is the west," he wrote in his *Journal*, making a flimsy analogy between the sun's apparent course and man's. "The way to heaven is from east to west round the earth. The sun leads and shows it. The stars, too, light it." One of Thoreau's hardest lessons was learning that statements which are literally untrue are also figuratively untrue, unless the two meanings stand in the relation of irony. But "Westward the course of empire" sentiments would almost always fetch him— so long as he refused to think about them closely—even, in *Cape Cod*, to an affectionate regard for California: "It was a poetic recreation to watch those distant sails steering for half-fabulous ports, whose very names are a mysterious music to our ears . . . bound to the famous Bay of San Francisco, and the golden streams of Sacramento and San Joaquin, to Feather River and the American Fork, where Sutter's Fort presides, and inland stands the City de los Angelos." (The gross geographical error is illuminating.) In another chapter, Thoreau faced the beaches of Europe, together with the fables of Atlantis and the Hesperides, and engendered an amazing rhetoric on the text "heaven is found to be farther west now":

A little south of east was Palos, where Columbus weighed anchor, and farther yet the pillars which Hercules set up; concerning which when we inquired at the top of our voices what was written on them,—for we had the morning sun in our faces, and could not see distinctly,—the inhabitants shouted *Ne plus ultra* (no more beyond), but the wind bore to us the truth only, *plus ultra* (more beyond), and over the Bay westward was echoed *ultra* (beyond). We spoke to them through the surf about the Far West, the true Hesperia, ἕω πέρας or end of the day, the This Side Sundown, where the sun was extinguished in the *Pacific*, and we advised them to pull up stakes and plant those pillars of theirs on the shore of California, whither all our folks were gone,—the only *ne* plus ultra now.

"Whither all our folks were gone"—only rarely did Thoreau permit himself public response to such unpalatable facts. For the most part, in *Cape Cod*, "West" means "Heaven," or perhaps "death."

In "Walking" (c. 1851-1852), which contains what is probably the longest sustained meditation on the West in American literature, Thoreau was at his most unreasonably and unrealistically reckless. "I wish to speak a word for Nature, for absolute freedom and wildness, as contrasted with a freedom and culture merely civil. . . . I wish to make an extreme statement." The essay was once called "The Wild," and in it we learn that "the West of which I speak is but another name for the Wild."[7] Actually, "Walking" is one long tissue of clichés. "We go eastward to realize history and study the works of art and literature, retracing the steps of the race; we go westward as into the future, with a spirit of enterprise and adventure." As frequently in early American writing, the sunset—an obvious image for old age or death—is compelled into the service of a facile progressivism: "Every sunset which I witness inspires me with the desire to go to a West as distant and as fair as that into which the sun goes down. He appears to migrate westward daily, and tempt us to follow him. He is the Great Western Pioneer whom the nations follow."[8] Not surprisingly, "Columbus felt the westward tendency more strongly than any before," and the Western world he discovered was fabulously fertile. From this "western impulse" of European discovery "sprang the commerce and enterprise of modern times." Some of these observations are true, or partly true, if not very original; but it is a

[7] In his *Journal*, Thoreau was writing: "I see a white pine dimly in the horizon . . . while at the same time I hear a robin sing. Each enhances the other. That tree seems the emblem of my life; it stands for the west, the wild. . . . The pine tree that stands on the verge of the clearing, whose boughs point westward" (III, 452-453).

[8] "All fair action in man is the product of enthusiasm—There is enthusiasm in the sunset." *Consciousness in Concord*, p. 164.

dubious rhetoric, indeed, which permits a man of Thoreau's talents to argue that the superior American climate and geography will make "our understanding more comprehensive and broader, like our plains,—our intellect generally on a grander scale."[9] Neither is it particularly intelligent, or even amusing, to say that a true patriot should be ashamed to admit "that Adam in paradise was more favorably situated on the whole than the backwoodsman in this country." Approaching downright falsehood, Thoreau further alleges that "our sympathies in Massachusetts are not confined to New England; though we may be estranged from the South, we sympathize with the West. There is the home of the younger sons." Not, however, of *this* younger son, for obviously Thoreau, and indeed most New Englanders, sternly disapproved the process of transferring New England's population to the West. He was only paying lip service to the platitudes: that the West would one day (somehow) reconcile North and South,[10] and that ambitious young men should go West and grow up with the country. It is an ironic fact that Horace Greeley was Thoreau's unofficial literary agent.

"We would fain take that walk, never yet taken by us through this actual world, which is perfectly symbolical of the path which we love to travel in the interior and ideal

[9] For standard statements of the standard doctrine, see such standard spokesmen as Daniel Drake, in *Discourse on the History, Character, and Prospects of the West* (1834), ed. Perry Miller (Gainesville, Florida, 1955): "The extended limits of the West, and the broad navigable rivers which traverse it in every direction, exert on the mind that expanding influence, which comes from the contemplation of vast natural objects" (p. 8); or James Hall, in "The Emigrants," *Legends of the West* (Philadelphia, 1832): "Accustomed to the contemplation of great mountains, long rivers, and boundless plains, the majestic features of their country swelled their ideas" (p. 171).

[10] At Harvard in 1837 Thoreau was already writing in an assigned essay: "How much mischief have those magical words, North, South, East, and West occasioned! Could we not rest satisfied with one mighty, all-embracing West, leaving the other three cardinal points to the Old World?—methinks we should not have cause for so much apprehension about the preservation of the Union." Quoted in Franklin B. Sanborn, *The Life of Henry David Thoreau* (Boston, 1917), p. 156.

world." Nature's "subtle magnetism" inevitably leads this walker Southwest, or between West and South-Southwest. (Thoreau in Concord sat N.N.E. with respect to the nation.) "The outline which would bound my walks would be, not a circle, but a parabola, or rather like one of those cometary orbits which have been thought to be non-returning curves, in this case opening westward, in which my house occupies the place of the sun." ("All things are up and down, east and west, to *me*," he wrote in his *Journal*.) One scarcely knows whether to laugh or cry. Thoreau's house is the sun, and the Westward-moving American people only a non-returning line orbiting around it. He does not really walk to the West, but only in that direction, and then straight home again; he need not walk in that direction at all, the metaphor slily assures us, because whatever is worthy in America approaches and then speeds away from him, where he sits most W.

"Let me live where I will, on this side is the city, on that the wilderness, and ever I am leaving the city more and more, and withdrawing into the wilderness. I should not lay so much stress on this fact," he continues, admitting how widely shared his preferences really were, though of course they were also perfectly symbolical, "if I did not believe that something like this is the prevailing tendency of my countrymen. I must walk toward Oregon, and not toward Europe. And that way the nation is moving, and I may say that mankind progress from east to west."[11] He had frequently said it, and so had thousands of other men, for several decades. He continues to say it. The settlement of Australia is a "retrograde movement," simply because it is a movement East instead of West. The Tartars think there is nothing West of Tibet. "It is unmitigated East where they live," is Thoreau's contemptuous rejoinder.

[11] "I know not how significant it is, or how far it is an evidence of singularity, that an individual should thus consent in his pettiest walk with the general movement of the race." This observation, like many in "Walking," is plainly disingenuous.

Apparently he forgot what he had said in the *Week*: "Farthest west is but the farthest east."

Such is the gist of "Walking"; only when he approached religious parody did Thoreau manage to make impressive prose out of what he was supposed to feel, but obviously could never feel, about the actual West. "What I have been preparing to say is, that in Wildness is the preservation of the World"; or "I believe in the forest, and in the meadow, and in the night in which the corn grows." These were primarily aesthetic propositions. How detached Thoreau was from the Westward Movement is sufficiently indicated by another of his frontier metaphors: "I feel that with regard to Nature I live a sort of border life, on the confines of a world into which I make occasional and transient forays only." He was a frontiersman, a pioneer, but only in a manner of speaking, that is, indirectly, for the West he fronted was always in the end a name for something else, or for an altogether nameless "IT." There is the source of Thoreau's superficial weakness, and his terrifying power.

For Thoreau, there were two Wests: an ideal West, which he adored, and a real West, which he feared and hated. This problem was not his alone. According to the Transcendental lecturers: "At the Mississippi your Western romance fades into a reality of some grimness" (Emerson).[12] "At home again and thankful for its privileges and opportunities, all the more pleasurable after the privations and discomforts of loafing about that slovenly West" (Alcott).[13] In Thoreau's mind, there seems to have been an absolute hiatus between the sentiments of the poems quoted earlier (and *Cape Cod* and "Walking") and those expressed but not published in the following scrap of verse:

> —The cowards hope the brave man's way,
> And distant promise of a day—
> While the late risen world goes west
> I'll daily bend my steps to east.

[12] Quoted in James Elliot Cabot, *A Memoir of Ralph Waldo Emerson* (Boston, 1887), II, 754.
[13] *Journals*, ed. Odell Shepard (Boston, 1938), p. 313.

He might have been thinking of Oriental philosophy. Still, it is impossible to overlook an air of resentment and perversity which was never entirely absent from Thoreau's response to the actual West. Like Poe, he had a bad case of pioneer egotism. For all the idealistic palaver of "Walking," it was precisely the prevailing tendency of his countrymen to walk toward Oregon which convinced him of the desirability of heading the other way. (He would not have missed the ridiculous aspect of so many people fleeing to the same place to get away from each other.)

Not unexpectedly, the California Gold Rush drew his contempt more often than it drew his admiration. In a moral way, there was much to be said against it, and Thoreau bated none of the opportunities for invective. In "Life Without Principle" (c. 1854), he delved into the ethics of the case for several pages, with his usual zeal and single-mindedness. In an early draft of *Walden*, he wrote in disgust: "To show how little men have considered what is the true end of life—or the nature of this living which they have to get—I need only remind you how many have within the last month started for California with the muck rake on their shoulders." Thoreau strongly disapproved a number of the leading characteristics of American civilization in his time. Naturally it was unpleasant to watch these characteristics overspread the last continent and fatten themselves for posterity, especially when the most venal and destructive behaviors—land speculation, anti-intellectualism, hypocrisy—were tacitly defended on the ground of their utility in winning the West. "The Anglo-American can indeed cut down, and grub up all this waving forest," he wrote in *The Maine Woods*, "and make a stump speech, and vote for Buchanan on its ruins, but he cannot converse with the spirit of the tree he fells, he cannot read the poetry and mythology which retire as he advances." So much was irrefutable. On the other hand, men being what they are, according to Thoreau's austere critique, how could they conceivably go West for proper reasons? Or, from the standpoint of the Transcendental doctrine of the irrelevance of place, originally designed to protect the Easterner from his inferiority complex toward Europe, why should they go West at all?

At times, he was disposed to be generous. John Brown attended "the great university of the West, where he sedulously pursued the study of Liberty"; perhaps it helped that Brown was "by descent and birth a New England farmer." There is simply no consistency in Thoreau's attitudes toward the West (though there is an easy explanation of the inconsistency); he is sweetly sentimental on one page and sourly realistic on the next. On the one hand, there is "Walking," with all its windy affirmation; on the other hand, there is a personal letter, of the same period, with its blunt candor:

> The whole enterprise of this nation which is not an upward, but a westward one, toward Oregon California, Japan &c, is totally devoid of interest to me, whether performed on foot or by a Pacific railroad. It is not illustrated by a thought it is not warmed by a sentiment, there is nothing in it which one should lay down his life for, nor even his gloves, hardly which one should take up a newspaper for. It is perfectly heathenish—a flibustiering [*sic*] *toward* heaven by the great western route. No, they may go their way to their manifest destiny which I trust is not mine. May my 76 dollars whenever I get them help to carry me in the other direction.

As there were two Wests, so there were two Thoreaus.

"At length, like Rasselas and other inhabitants of happy valleys," he wrote in the *Week*, "we had resolved to scale the blue wall which bounded the western horizon, though not without misgivings that thereafter no visible fairyland would exist for us." By means of his extraordinary verbal ingenuity, he extracted from experience an internal or essential meaning by virtue of which he was enabled, or even enjoined, to disregard the actual content of experience in favor of a higher law. All too often, Thoreau's invocations of higher law had as their purpose provincial patriotism or personal aggrandizement. In his furtive, Transcendental

186

way, he was always trying to insinuate one or both of the following closely-connected doctrines: (1) New England was more West than the West, and (2) by remaining in New England he was more a pioneer than the pioneers. "This fair homestead has fallen to us, and how little have we done to improve it, how little have we cleared and hedged and ditched! We are too inclined to go hence to a 'better land,' without lifting a finger, as our farmers are moving to the Ohio soil; but would it not be more heroic and faithful to till and redeem this New England soil of the world?" So much for "Paradise (To Be) Regained" (1843). New England was his own rocky reality, not the irresponsible evasions permitted by the rich Ohio soil. But Thoreau sometimes practiced precisely what he preached against, the evasion of reality; the true merits of the two sections, for the actual pursuit of agriculture, were evidently far from his mind.

He was pitifully eager to show how West New England was. In "A Walk to Wachusett" (1843), he told how, "passing through Sterling, we reached the banks of the Stillwater, in the western part of the town. . . . We fancied that there was already a certain western look about this place, a smell of pines and roar of water." Obviously he was piqued by those invidious comparisons between the wonderful West and the insipid East which the American nationalistic myth made practically obligatory, even for himself on those occasions when he courted popularity, as in "Walking." He believed in the West, the Wild; very well, then, here they were: "The botanist refers you, for wild [ness] and we presume wild plants, further inland or westward to so many miles from Boston, as if Nature or the Indians had any such preferences. Perchance the ocean seemed wilder to them than the woods. As if there were primarily and essentially any more wildness in a western acre than an eastern one!"[14]

The argument from botany was quite as effective with men. "It is a solitary and adventurous life, and comes nearest to that of the trapper of the West, perhaps," he said of

[14] *Journal*, IX, 55-56.

timber prospectors in *The Maine Woods*. "They work ever with a gun as well as an axe, let their beards grow, and live without neighbors, not on an open plain, but far within a wilderness." A few pages later he made clear which set of pioneers he regarded as the more genuine:

> I was interested to see how a pioneer lived on this side of the country. His life is in some respects more adventurous than that of his brother in the West; for he contends with winter as well as the wilderness, and there is a greater interval of time at least [i.e., if not of distance] between him and the army which is to follow. Here immigration is a tide which may ebb when it has swept away the pines; there it is not a tide, but an inundation, and roads and other improvements come steadily rushing after.

Then with what can only seem a strangely premeditated perversity, Thoreau took the final step and arrived at his real point: his neighbors were more estimable than the pioneers. (Obviously, he was more estimable than they.) "The retirement in which Green has lived for nearly eighty years in Carlisle is a retirement very different from and much greater than that in which the pioneer dwells at the West; for the latter dwells within sound of the surf of those billows of migration which are breaking on the shores around him, or near him, of the West, but those billows have long since swept over the spot which Green inhabits, and left him in the calm sea."[15] Significantly, Green's "calm sea" is not an image of peace but of meaningless isolation and lonely pathos.

In order to preserve his sense of essential rectitude from the disquieting intrusions of actuality, Thoreau cultivated in his strenuous idealistic way an almost hysterical passion for staying at home. As he wrote Harrison Blake: "Where is the 'Unexplored land' but in our own untried enterprises? To an adventurous spirit any place,—London New York, Worcester, or his own yard, is 'unexplored land,' to seek

[15] *Journal*, III, 9-10.

which Freemont & Kane travel so far. To a sluggish & defeated spirit even the Great Basin & the Polaris are trivial places. If they ever get there (& indeed they are there now) they will want to sleep & give it up, just as they always do. These are the regions of the Known & of the Unknown." The West was not a place or a direction, but an idea, a metaphor, or even a word; whatever it was, it was *his* West. As he wrote to Thomas Cholmondeley: "The *great west* and *north west* stretching on infinitely far and grand and wild, qualifying all our thoughts. That is the only America I know. I prize this western reserve chiefly for its intellectual value. That is the road to new life and freedom . . . and knowing this, one need not travel it. That great northwest where several of our shrubs, fruitless here, retain and mature their fruits properly." In the light of that idea, Thoreau proposed to live his life, and harvest his literary crops. He intended nothing so vulgar as moving to the West, or even visiting it; mere knowledge, he never tired of saying, was not the game he chased. He hunted beasts of the spirit, and those, his instinct correctly assured him, abounded in New England.

He was always the most partisan of regionalists, and indeed made the West itself contribute to his conviction of the absolute centrality of the place where he happened to find himself. "I am glad if your western experience has made you the more a New Englander," he wrote to a relative in 1857, as he had once written a disconsolate exile in Buffalo (who had written him: "We look to the east for our guiding star for there our sun did rise"): "It is curious that while you are sighing for New England the scene of our fairest dreams should lie in the west—it confirms me in the opinion that places are well nigh indifferent." This was an article of faith with Thoreau, but applied to actual places only. To the ideas of place he was preternaturally sensitive.

"Nature is as far from me as God," he wistfully noted in 1850, "and sometimes I have thought to go West after her." In 1838 he had written his brother John, proposing that they "start in company for the West," perhaps Ohio or Kentucky, to found or teach in a school. "Go *I* must at all events," he added. But he did not go; looking over his life as a whole, we see how impossible it was that he should. After *Walden*, when he was a little famous, he several times considered the possibility of a lecture tour in the West— *"if they shall want me,"* he pathetically wrote to a friend, underscoring the words. They didn't. Only at the very end, on doctor's orders, in an attempt to restore his health and save his life, did he finally penetrate that interior he had so much brooded over. From the trip his friends sentimentally expected a literary bonanza. One man wrote from Chicago: "I hope you will have a pleasant time get heartily well and write a book about the great West that will be to us what your other books are." In Concord, during Thoreau's absence, Bronson Alcott indulged a similar line of reflection:

> The West opens a new field for his observations; and to one whose everyday walk was an expedition into some unexplored region of Concord in search of novelties, though his track had been taken but yesterday, that wilderness must have surprising attractions. . . . I know not to whom that wild country belongs if not to this old explorer, and think it has waited with an Amazonian patience for his arrival. . . . His visit must have been predestined from the beginning, and this lassitude of these late months only the intimation of his having exhausted these old fields and farms of Concord of the significance they had for him.[16]

Alcott understood his neighbor no better than the man in Chicago. The wild country belonging to this old explorer had no particular connection with the actual West, except by way of initial suggestion and subsequent reaction. All of which was amply proved in the event: Minnesota and Henry Thoreau, standing face to face, found nothing to say to one another. Thoreau had predicted as much for years, using the names of various Western states. Naturally,

[16] *Journals of Alcott*, p. 340.

he kept a journal ("Notes on the Journey West"); dutifully he observed whatever he encountered, entered a number of facts about Indian customs, past and present, and constructed his usual detailed lists of distances, costs, trees, flowers, and birds.[17] Or perhaps what he really discovered on the verge of death was a final justification for his decision not to follow the sun, that Great Western Pioneer, and all his impetuous, mindless countrymen, but to stay in Concord and think. Oddly enough, he was right. It was his vocation to be right. Had he gone to Ohio or Kentucky, he would never have written *Walden*.

2. *WALDEN*: THE PIONEER

Thoreau was at first inclined to think that "we must look to the West for the growth of a new literature, manners, architecture, etc. Already there is more language there, which is the growth of the soil, than here; good Greekish words there are in abundance,—good because necessary and expressive; 'diggings,' for instance."[1] This was not novel. For years, the insistent call for a native literature, free of European taint, or shadow, had been conventionally phrased in terms of the section Americans knew least about, but relied on to provide answers for their problems. And like many Americans, Thoreau apparently began by thinking the mere fact of unsettled land was inherently appropriate to, and therefore automatically productive of, poets. Thus in "Thomas Carlyle and his Works" he accounted for Carlyle's *not* being a poet: "The condition of England demands a hero, not a poet. Other things demand a poet; the poet answers other demands. . . . He [Carlyle] lives in Chelsea, not

---

[17] The "Notes" are in *Thoreau's Minnesota Journey: Two Documents*, ed. Walter Harding, Thoreau Society Booklet No. Sixteen (Geneseo, New York, 1962), pp. 1-44.

[1] *The First and Last Journeys of Thoreau*, ed. Franklin B. Sanborn (Boston, 1905), 1, 85. Also in "Walking": "The West is preparing to add its fables to those of the East." But Thoreau's amplification of that remark is embittered by political disillusion, and muddied by the common confusion of American West and Western Hemisphere.

on the plains of Hindostan, nor on the prairies of the West, where settlers are scarce, and a man must at least go *whistling* to himself." But that simplistic view is far from Thoreau's best thought on the relation of geography, or external circumstances, to poetry.

Like every other literary light of his generation, Thoreau was determined to participate in this new expression which was somehow to issue from the Great West. But how could he see himself, as see himself he must, in the role of Western writer, if he was equally determined never to leave his New England home? Long before he wrote *Walden; or, Life in the Woods* (1854), he was approaching a *modus operandi*.[2] His relationship with the West would be metaphorical. "Our brave forefathers have exterminated all the Indians," begins a typical meditation in *A Week on the Concord and Merrimack Rivers*, "and their degenerate children no longer dwell in garrisoned houses nor hear any warwhoop in their path." But then the argument takes a radical turn. "We have need to be as sturdy pioneers still," he continues, making his usual easy progress from fact to fancy, and from fancy to symbol. "We are to follow on another trail, it is true, but one as convenient for ambushes. What if the Indians are exterminated, are not savages as grim prowling about the clearings to-day?"[3] *Walden* would show

[2] I find anticipations of the stay-at-home-pioneer principle as early as "Natural History of Massachusetts" (1842): "There are trappers in our midst still, as well as on the streams of the far West, who night and morning go the round of their traps, without fear of the Indian." The same year an anonymous reviewer was saying in the *Boston Miscellany of Literature*: "The great charm of [Caroline Kirkland's] 'A New Home' and of a 'Forest Life' is, that they tell us 'just what we want to know' of that wonderful country to which half of us mean to go, while the other half, in resolving to stay at home, think of, and talk of it almost as much as the emigrants themselves" (II, 92).

[3] *The Writings of Henry David Thoreau* (Boston, 1906), I, 124. This crucial passage has at least two previous existences, in *First and Last Journeys*, I, 9 (according to Sanborn the diary of Thoreau's trip up the Concord and Merrimack rivers), and in *Consciousness in Concord; the Text of Thoreau's Hitherto "Lost Journal," (1840-1841)*, ed. Perry Miller (Boston, 1958), p. 145. The note of positive

that there were. It would primarily show Henry Thoreau as the essential pioneer, or true poet. That equation also he laid down in the *Week*: "The poet is no tender slip of fairy stock, who requires peculiar institutions [or places either, he was probably thinking] and edicts for his defense, but the toughest son of earth and of Heaven." Sliding off that implicit frontier metaphor, Thoreau falls to his matter: "It is the worshippers of beauty, after all, who have done the real pioneer work of the world."[4]

Of course, a connection between the Westward Movement and American poetry existed—what American looking to the West for his new literature could doubt it?—but it was more realistic, and therefore more stimulating, to think of pioneer and poet as in one sense analogous and in another sense cause and effect. In that view, or views, as finally expressed in *The Maine Woods*, there was ample room for reservation, when necessary, on the relative value of the two roles, or even for a reversal of cause and effect:

> The poet's, commonly, is not a logger's path, but a woodman's. The logger and pioneer have preceded him, like John the Baptist; eaten the wild honey, it may be, but the locusts also; banished decaying wood and the spongy mosses which feed on it, and built hearths and humanized Nature for him. . . . [Yet] not only for strength, but for beauty, the poet must, from time to time, travel the logger's path and the Indian's trail, to drink at some new and more bracing fountain of the Muses, far in the recesses of the wilderness.

What Thoreau concedes by statement, he retrieves by metaphor; if he came into the world fatally late to be John the

consolation, of which I make so much, is absent from the Sanborn version.

[4] In "Natural History of Massachusetts," Thoreau describes science "breaking ground like a pioneer for the array of arts that follow in her train"; in the same essay he calls the compiler of the report he is ostensibly reviewing a "pioneer." In another review— "Paradise (To Be) Regained"—he says that Etzler is "not one of the enlightened practical men, the pioneers of the actual."

Baptist, he was still in time to be Christ. The pioneer is the forerunner of the poet, by whose authoritative word his partial promise is fulfilled; his chief purpose is to provide the poet materials of language, to pave the way for him. Yet their relation, in nineteenth-century parlance, is also the relation of matter and spirit, action and contemplation: the essential poet is the final cause of the manifestation, pioneer.

This flexible, imaginative, and fundamentally sound conception was obviously motivated by Thoreau's paradoxical response to the universal expectation of a Western literature. Specifically, he argued the literary necessity of abjuring the actual West in order more profitably to possess the essential West. If he was unable to rest easy in that posture, it was possibly because the two Wests lay so far asunder in his mind, but also because he knew he could prove his case only by performance, by making the West, and the Western pioneer, into metaphors more significant than the things themselves. Considering how highly his countrymen valued these things, Thoreau put his literary career in great jeopardy with this decision to be more Western by staying home; yet precisely this artistic challenge was the primary stimulus of *Walden*. Several years after the event, Thoreau was still nervously defending himself:

> The poet has made the best roots in his native soil of any man, and is the hardest to transplant. The man who is often thinking that it is better to be somewhere else than where he is excommunicates himself. If a man is rich and strong anywhere, it must be on his native soil. Here I have been these forty years learning the language of these fields that I may the better express myself. If I should travel to the prairies, I should much less understand them, and my past life would serve me but ill to describe them. Many a weed here stands for more of life to me than the big trees of California would if I should go there.[5]

[5] *The Journal of Henry D. Thoreau*, ed. Bradford Torrey and Francis H. Allen (Boston, 1906), x, 190-191. More heatedly, and

He fails to do himself justice, for in *Walden* he not only made Concord weeds stand for more of life than the big trees of California, but made them stand for the same kind of life. When Thoreau was through with them, all weeds were Western. Even so, he was unable to maintain much serenity of tone; in another *Journal* passage we see him almost helplessly descending into the old irascibility, still using his contempt for the American West as an emblem of personal inviolability:

> If you would really take a position outside the street and daily life of men, you must have deliberately planned your course, you must have business which is not your neighbors' business, which they cannot understand. For only absorbing employment prevails, succeeds, takes up space, occupies territory, determines the future of individuals and states, drives Kansas out of your head, and actually and permanently occupies the only desirable and free Kansas against all border ruffians.[6]

And yet—and finally—despite the truculence, despite the false reasoning, from neither of which he was ever entirely emancipated, Thoreau had available to him in this identification of poet and pioneer a basic resemblance which, when he thought about it honestly and hard enough, was both legitimate and rewarding. "If you have ever done any work with these finest tools, the imagination and fancy and reason, it is a new creation, independent on the world, and a possession forever. . . . You have to that extent cleared the wilderness."[7] So he could always say; so he could sometimes do.

---

less specifically: "Think of the consummate folly of attempting to go away from *here*! When the constant endeavor should be to get nearer and nearer *here*. . . . How many things can you go away from? They see the comet from the northwest coast just as plainly as we do, and the same stars through its tail. Take the shortest way round and stay at home. . . . *Here*, of course, is all that you love, all that you expect, all that you are. Here is your bride elect, as close to you as she can be got. . . . Foolish people imagine that what they imagine is somewhere else" (xi, 275).

[6] *Journal*, ix, 36. [7] *Journal*, ix, 350.

Thoreau's new creation was a character derived from the Western pioneer, and from popular literature about him, but differing from both in realism, seriousness, integrity, intelligence of purpose. That is why other pioneers, factual and fictive, so often sound like parodies of Thoreau. In "The Backwoodsman," James Hall sententiously defined the type, allegedly from firsthand observation:

> The quiet courage of his glance, the self possession and calm vigilance of his manner, together with a certain carelessness and independence of mien, would have pointed him out as a genuine pioneer, who loved the woods, and was most happy when roaming in pursuit of game, or reclining in his solitary retreat, with no companion but his faithful dog. Nor was this fondness for the silence of the wilderness the result of unsocial feelings: the hunter loved his friend, and enjoyed the endearments of his own fireside; but he forsook them in the same spirit in which the philosopher retires to the seclusion of his closet,—to enjoy unmolested the train of his own reflections, and to follow without interruption a pursuit congenial with his nature. Though unacquainted with books, he had perused certain parts of the great volume of nature with diligent attention. The changes of the seasons, the atmospherical phenomena, the growth of plants, and the habits of animals, had for years engaged his observing powers; and without having any knowledge of the philosophy of schools, he had formed for himself a system which had the merit of being often true, and always original.[8]

Thoreau improved upon the conventional pattern by having some knowledge and a decent prose style; but from the outset he modeled his life and art, his motives and manners, on the standard American protagonist.

[8] *Legends of the West* (Philadelphia, 1832), p. 23. Most of Thoreau's basic attitudes, but never so well expressed, can be found in such popular classics as Irving's *A Tour on the Prairies*, Parkman's *California and Oregon Trail*, and most particularly—because here the closest verbal echoes are heard—in the writings of Caroline Kirkland.

In playing the role of pioneer in his own back yard, or Emerson's (he frequently refers to himself as a "squatter"), and finding in that role the best analogue with the literary experience, Thoreau somewhat resembles Poe, though he carried the process of identification to a degree of intensity and specification altogether beyond Poe's capacities or needs. The difference is perhaps best understood in terms of Thoreau's incomparably closer relation with a particular and appropriate landscape (not to mention his incomparably greater gift for landscape in general). Thoreau's situation at Walden was not only more "like" the pioneer's—woods and lakes and solitude—but the image of the pond was in his mind from the beginning. "24 years ago I was brought from the city to this very pond—through this very [bean-]field," he began to say in an early draft of *Walden*, sadly enfeebled by revision. "It is one of the most ancient scenes stamped on the tablets of my memory. That woodland vision for a long time occupied my dreams. The country then was the world—the city only a gate to it."[9]

City and country are ostensibly local references, yet with an obviously organic equivalence to East and West respectively. ("Ever I am leaving the city more and more. . . . I must walk toward Oregon.") Then this quasi-geographical duality is superimposed on another, the duality of the self and the world—always a standard consideration with the Romantic writer—so that moving from city to country, from East to West, is equivalent to moving from the privacies of immaturity toward full contact with life beyond one's self. Thoreau's special twist, as it was the pioneer's, is to envisage the life without as equally unpeopled. Walden Pond was for Thoreau the outside world, by communion with which he defined and expressed his inner being; Walden Pond, at the same time, was his Western fetish. In the

[9] Quotations of the early draft are from *The Making of Walden, With the Text of the First Version*, ed. J. Lyndon Shanley (Chicago, 1957), quotations of *Walden* from *Writings*, II. This particular passage variously appears in *Making of Walden*, p. 177; *Writings*, II, 172; and, in its fullest and loveliest form, *Journal*, I, 380-381.

Week, he told how the brothers, after their initial shock at discovering the frontiers were not this way any longer, "at length crossed on prostrate trees over the Amonoosuck, and breathed the free air of Unappropriated Land," a metaphor suggesting that Thoreau was already aware, or nearly aware, of the feasibility of depicting his personal situation in terms of free land in the West. His full maturity may undoubtedly be dated from the day when he first realized that his true Unappropriated Land lay by the shores of Walden Pond; when he realized that the phrase Unappropriated Land might be understood in several senses; and when, having noted all this, he proceeded to appropriate those several meanings, first for life, and then, more permanently, for letters.

The opening paragraph of *Walden* clearly establishes the fundamental comparison between the Western pioneer and the fictional narrator upon which the work is constructed:

> When I wrote the following pages, or rather the bulk of them, I lived alone, in the woods, a mile from any neighbor, in a house which I had built myself, on the shore of Walden Pond, in Concord, Massachusetts, and earned my living by the labor of my hands only. I lived there two years and two months. At present I am a sojourner in civilized life again.

The wit is like Mark Twain's at the end of *Huckleberry Finn*, especially the way the ironic flash of "sojourner" suddenly transforms "civilized life" from a condition to a place—the reverse of the process by which the West was universalized—while at the same time defining that "place" as peripheral rather than central. Thoreau's little joke says that he resembles the pioneers—and more especially, perhaps, the Mountain Men—in love of nature, but differs from them in the ability to regard conditions as freely as the actual pioneers regarded places. (We know how much mobility Thoreau possessed with respect to actual places.) In a way, he is the son of the pioneer; but he carries on the family tradition in his own style. The substance of his remarks, without the humor, turns up regularly in Western travels; in *Commerce of the Prairies* (1844), Josiah Gregg bewails, lugubriously and for several pages, his loss of freedom upon returning to "civilized life in the United States."[10] Irving's Captain Bonneville says the same.

Thoreau emphasizes woods more than water: in the American imagination woods were a sign of the West in a way which the pond could hardly be (except for Hawthorne's lakes, "gems of the wilderness," or Thoreau's White Pond, "the gem of the woods"). He insists on the fact that he lived a mile from any neighbor: a place of low population density was one of two, and only two, possible definitions of the Western frontier, the other being metaphorical, the meeting point between civilization and nature, which is also implied in this first paragraph and often mentioned thereafter. He tells us he lived alone, in the "wilderness": loneliness and isolation were the most obvious social aspects of the pioneer's life. (In fact Thoreau was much less alone than he suggests.) He lived in a house built by himself, and in what he elsewhere calls a "clearing": on the frontier nearly every one lived in such a house, whereas in Concord Thoreau's self-sufficiency was ostentatious and didactic. In connection with each of these details, what was natural under pioneer conditions becomes in Concord highly dramatic, by Thoreau's simple switch of cultural contexts. In the midst of civilization, he lives like a backwoodsman, or like some Leatherstocking encircled by Judge Temple's civilization. He has brought the West, and some of the realism of pioneer life, to the edge of the village, for purposes of contrast and criticism. From the pond, or "Squaw Walden," Thoreau visits the villagers ("prairie-dogs"), "like a friendly Indian." Concord, Massachusetts is directly specified, to enforce the point that the frontier is wherever you are.

He went to the woods to play pioneer. He left the woods, as he tells us in the "Conclusion," for as good a reason; in

[10] *Early Western Travels, 1748-1846*, ed. Reuben G. Thwaites (Cleveland, 1904-1907), XX, 219-221.

fact, for the same reason. Like the pioneer he imitated, but in no such trivial sense, Thoreau moved on when novelty palled. Probably he recognized that to persist unduly in the role of pioneer was ironically to betray its essential freshness, which would have been doubly ironic in view of the fact that the role was popularly defined in terms of freshness. ("Perhaps it seemed to me that I had several more lives to live.") He was far more perceptive than poor Poe in this respect: "It is remarkable how easily and insensibly we fall into a particular route, and make a beaten track for ourselves. I had not lived there a week before my feet wore a path from my door to the pond-side." Even the pioneer virtue of originality could evidently become through constant repetition its own deadliest stereotype.[11]

Thus at the beginning and end of *Walden* Thoreau asserts his major comparison. It should not be assumed that this comparison is only an enveloping flourish, abeyant through the rest of the book. On the contrary, Thoreau's sense of himself as pioneer is all but constant. It explains, for example, his addiction to local history, here as in the *Week*. His purpose is precisely that of the historical romancers—Cooper, Hawthorne, Hall, Bird, Kennedy, Simms —who regularly equipped themselves with Western settings by returning to earlier days. With respect to the confrontation of civilized man and savage nature, seventeenth-century Massachusetts represents the same stage of development as mid-nineteenth-century Minnesota. Especially for such a man as Thoreau, it was far more agreeable to step backward in time, while remaining in the same place, than to move, even fictively, to a region less well known and less well liked. The seventeenth-century historians enable Thoreau to include the Western perspective; they tell of the place where he is when it was *the* frontier, and thus

[11] The word pioneer was for Thoreau more verb than noun, and implied behavior rather than person. In an early poem, he even coined an atrocious word, "pioneer*er*" (his italics), apparently in order to enforce the point that pioneering was an activity possible to all. *Collected Poems of Henry Thoreau*, ed. Carl Bode, enlarged edition (Baltimore, 1964), p. 88.

furnish firsthand accounts of the pioneer effort of an older time. This attraction is plain in the way he introduces his excerpts, as well as in the kinds of passage he usually selects: "Gookin, who was superintendent of the Indians subject to the Massachusetts Colony"; "Old Johnson, in his 'Wonder-Working Providence,' speaking of the first settlers of this town, with whom he was contemporary"; "when Winslow, afterward governor of the Plymouth Colony, went with a companion on a visit of ceremony to Massasoit on foot through the woods."

No other American writer approaches Thoreau's ability to persuade us that wherever he finds himself is West. *Walden* rests firmly on the outrageous proposition that a man can live "at the West" or "on the frontier" without going near either. Thereby Thoreau is both apart from and a part of the central national experience: apart from it, because in the popular mind the geography was anything but insignificant, and it was the literal moving ("progress") to the West which set off the train of wonders, while to Thoreau the mere geography, compared with the state of mind, was contemptible enough; yet a part of the national experience, too, for without the existence of the lonely and adventurous pioneer, Thoreau would have lacked a model of behavior to imitate and quarrel with. In fact, he would have lacked a subject; on nearly every other topic, as his minor works show, he was an indifferent writer.

Unquestionably Thoreau was aware how closely the West affected his best writing, though it also seems likely that he was sometimes willing to cover his tracks. He knew there was rough correspondence, but with a difference that to him meant everything, between his actions at Walden Pond and the restless behavior of his compatriots. We surprise him in the act of exploiting this correspondence in the following passage from the first version, which he excluded from the final text: "Sometimes there would come half a dozen men to my house at once—healthy and sturdy working men. . . . One a handsome younger man a sailor-like—Greek-like man —says to me to-day—'Sir, I like your notions—I think I shall live so myself. Only I should like a wilder country, where there is more game. I have been among the Indians near Apallachicola. I have lived with them. I like your kind of life. Good-day, I wish you success and happiness.' "[12] Thoreau must have relished these compliments only for a while; in the long run he would have been aghast at his admirer's failure to understand the metaphorical nature of where he lived and what he lived for, a failure of comprehension especially exasperating because Thoreau developed these particular ideas in order to justify his not going West. Had he retained the passage, there must needs have been added an astringent remark or two, touching on the sailor-like man's reductive interpretation of the meaning of Walden. But it is to be suspected that Thoreau's main reason for omitting this incident, which another writer might have turned into high comedy, was its too naked revelation of the secret connections between his own performance and the national infatuation.

In *Walden*, comparisons and contrasts between the hero and his pioneer model are manifold. The major contrast resides in their antithetical attitude toward geographical movement. Another resides in the fact that Thoreau's private Westward Movement makes no compromise with the more conspicuous forms of cultural regression accompanying frontier conditions in nineteenth-century America, but boldly intends the opposite result: to make room for the life of the mind by clearing the ground of trivial considerations, including those which exercised the pioneer. *Walden* is no guidebook for emigrants, but a manual for poor students; much of its excellence depends upon the energetic intelligence with which Thoreau attacked the problem of a higher culture for himself and his contemporaries. It is easy enough to see that on any actual frontier, Thoreau would have been wretched, not from physical hardship, but for want of those intellectual, moral, and cultural civilities which were more nearly necessities with him than with most

[12] Substantially the same passage appears earlier in *Journal*, I, 366.

Americans. Concord Lyceum, the *Dial*, intimate association with men like Emerson, Hawthorne, Alcott, Channing: would he have found those in Iowa? The actual Westward Movement was not a quest for literary culture, nor conducive to it, except in the minds and imaginations of writers in the rear.

A third important contrast between Thoreau and his pioneer counterpart—closely related to the last one—lies in their radically divergent attitudes toward work and material possessions. For Thoreau, labor was valuable as discipline and as a source of tropes, and then additionally as it permitted him to enter upon, and find time for the life of the spirit. The pioneer notoriously alternated between an indolence less creditably motivated and a feverish activity devoted to the acquisition of the encumbrances Thoreau was anxious to shed. The average American went West (when he had the money) in the hope of improving his economic status. Thoreau went to Walden, his personal West, to embrace voluntary poverty. The actual Western farmer, on the so-called agricultural frontier, was a ludicrous copy of Thoreau's Concord neighbors: more ludicrous than they, because living in a situation which might have taught him better. Was not Thoreau, taking his cue from the frontier that might have been, spending his life in Concord instructing by example his village friends who were now too far behind the frontier to read its lessons at all? Thoreau worked in order that he might think, as he believed all men should; and the challenge of the frontier might show them how to work and think more inventively, with more relevance. Most of his compatriots in Concord and Kansas worked (or quarreled) in order to postpone the possibility of thought. As Thoreau readily perceived, such evasions might be managed as easily in the West as at home; or perhaps more easily, for in the West men might still invoke the pressures of necessity with some show of plausibility. "For more than five years I maintained myself thus solely by the labor of my hands," he tells us in "Economy," scoring one of his central points off his ambiguous relation to pioneer and villager, "and I found that, by working about six weeks in a year, I could meet all the expenses of living. The whole of my winters, as well as most of my summers, I had free and clear for study." No wonder people were disturbed.

These genuine and fundamental disagreements between the pioneer and the narrative *persona* constitute one obvious source of *Walden*'s richly, but intermittently, ironic tone. The lyric tone has among other sources the feelings flowing from Thoreau's personal enaction of those qualities in the pioneer's life with which he was most deeply sympathetic. "Nature" was the most rewarding common ground between pioneer and poet, though as a Transcendental poet Thoreau often defines this ground as the tension between society and solitude. Like the other Transcendentalists, Thoreau customarily elects solitude; in making this election, he was also —as perhaps the others were, too, less consciously—once again transfiguring and appropriating to his own uses the pattern of choices popularly associated with the heroic frontiersman. Not only are the similarities between the two roles amazingly exact, but Thoreau directly alludes to the privacy of his situation in the most explicitly Western way. "There is commonly sufficient space about us," he begins to say in "Solitude," already claiming for his own situation one of the values regularly attributed to the frontier; "Our horizon is never quite at our elbows." Then he continues, much more particularly, to speak once more of his Walden life in terms of population density: "My nearest neighbor is a mile distant, and no house is visible from any place but the hilltops within half a mile of my own." It sounds, as undoubtedly it was intended to sound, more like Daniel Boone than a young poet. Thoreau immediately proceeds to the analogy which perpetually energized his thought: "For the most part it is as solitary where I live as on the prairies."[13]

---

[13] This question of population density turns up frequently in the *Journal*. "I can easily walk ten, fifteen, twenty, any number of miles, commencing at my own door, without going by any house. . . . Concord is the oldest inland town in New England, perhaps in the States, and the walker is peculiarly favored here. There are square miles in my vicinity which have no inhabitant" (II, 52). "My in-

Thoreau's passion for solitude was stimulated by the need for a decent leisure and privacy in support of his studies and writing. It was also—perhaps more importantly—an end in itself. Like many a frontier squatter, or like the hunters and trappers who preceded him, Thoreau often gives the appearance (but who can say with what deliberation?) of fleeing society with an almost paranoid panic: "Wherever a man goes, men will pursue and paw him with their dirty institutions, and, if they can, constrain him to belong to their desperate odd-fellow society." Of course, he specifically refers to a commonwealth which enforces the Fugitive-Slave Law; but it is hard to avoid feeling that if the enormity were not this one, it would be another. Thoreau's sensitivity to pain was as acute as the pioneer's; in either case, the luxury of withdrawal, symbolic or actual, depended on the existence of those sparsely populated, and only nominally administered, territories in the West.

He could even proclaim the all-sufficing "gregariousness" of nature. "I experienced sometimes that the most sweet and tender, the most innocent and encouraging society may be found in any natural object, even for the poor misanthrope and most melancholy man." As he goes on to describe his intuitions, doubts, and convictions in greater detail, we see more clearly how he and the pioneer alike were caught in a paradox which caused them to swing to and fro, between a conception of pure solitude and a conception emphasizing

---

heritance is not narrow. Here is no other this evening. Those resorts which I most love and frequent, numerous and vast as they are, are as it were given up to me, as much as if I were an autocrat or owner of the world, and by my edicts excluded men from my territories. Perchance there is some advantage here not enjoyed in older countries. There are said to be two thousand inhabitants in Concord, and yet I find such ample space and verge, even miles of walking every day in which I do not meet nor see a human being, and often not very recent traces of them. So much of man as there is in your mind, there will be in your eye. Methinks that for a great part of the time, as much as it is possible, I walk as one possessing the advantages of human culture, fresh from society of men, but turned loose into the woods, the only man in nature, walking and meditating to a great extent as if man and his customs and institutions were not" (437).

the reciprocal relations of society and solitude. If Thoreau seems primarily bent on preserving the purity of his contact with nature by maintaining a proper distance from other people, he is equally obliged to express his lonely sympathy in social metaphors. The wavering and confusion is typical of American thought about the West, for a man thinking of the West might conceive himself as altogether beyond the frontier (and thus in a state of absolute solitude, or nature) or on it (and thus in a state of qualified solitude, where civilization and nature interact). In the following sentences, Thoreau tries to avoid this confusion by disentangling himself from the one Western idea (frontier) in favor of the other (state of nature); but as he evidently feels called upon to justify his choice by embodying the state of nature in imagery suggestive of multitudes of other people, he effectually creates precisely that meeting point and interplay between nature and society which he is presumably rejecting:

> I have never felt lonesome, or in the least oppressed by a sense of solitude, but once, and that was a few weeks after I came to the woods, when, for an hour, I doubted if the near neighborhood of man was not essential to a serene and healthy life. To be alone was something unpleasant. But I was at the same time conscious of a slight insanity in my mood, and seemed to foresee my recovery. In the midst of a gentle rain while these thoughts prevailed, I was suddenly sensible of such sweet and beneficent society in Nature, in the very pattering of the drops, and in every sound and sight around my house, an infinite and unaccountable friendliness all at once like an atmosphere sustaining me, as made the fancied advantages of human neighborhood insignificant, and I have never thought of them since.[14]

So he labored to prepare an answer—a remarkably full answer, even if not, from the nature of the case, entirely clear—to the question, whether he was lonely in his hut in

[14] The passage is further complicated by the fact that "an infinite and unaccountable friendliness" undoubtedly refers to God.

the woods. It was the first question people asked the pioneer.

For Thoreau, Nature was always sufficient compensation for any presumed deficiencies attaching to the loss of social contact. Nature was freedom, and freedom was one of America's favorite words. To live "in nature," or near it, was to "go free." ("Eastward I go only by force; but westward I go free," was Thoreau's pun in "Walking.") That was the philosophical, or as we should say sentimental, background of pioneering. "This is a delicious evening, when the whole body is one sense, and imbibes delight through every pore. I go and come with a strange liberty in Nature, a part of herself." He is forever asking, "What do we want most to dwell near to?"—another of the basic questions arising from the possibilities of pioneer life—to which he returns the basic pioneer answer, only slightly sweetened with Transcendental overtones: "Not to many men surely, the depot, the post-office, the bar-room, the meeting-house, the school-house, the grocery, Beacon Hill, or the Five Points, where men most congregate, but to the perennial source of our life" —which was in the West, and not in the West. Or more pointedly: "It would be better if there were but one inhabitant to a square mile, as where I live. The value of a man is not in his skin, that we should touch him." Every time Thoreau recurs to this matter of population density, he makes another connection between his lonely life in the woods, with all its Transcendental ups and downs, and the lonely life of the backwoodsman, who was, we might say, only a lower development of the same type, and whose motives and actions were by Thoreau purified and intensified and elevated to the articulate coherence of poetry.

Like the pioneer, Thoreau arranged his life on the basis of "unfenced nature reaching up to your very sills," and "no path to the civilized world." Perhaps his lost hound, bay horse, and turtle-dove—Thoreau's famous symbols of Romantic longing—were what the other Americans were also looking for, pushing restlessly across the enormous continent in search of something more than, though obviously including, free land and economic improvement. Thoreau was one of the few men in his day to achieve a working language for the universal hunger. In the nature of things, his language was oblique. As Constance Rourke says of the hound-horse-dove passage: "This beautiful and cryptic poetry was cast into Thoreau's discourse a little awry: he suddenly stopped, as if unable to pursue further the theme or its implications."[15] But he stopped only on the last frontiers of meaning. On the hither edge, he commanded an uncanny ability to ascertain and express his feelings, which were at bottom common to the entire society. This is why *Walden* moves us as it does; no statement of Thoreau's personal preferences, however brilliant, could possibly carry such authority. Despite its nonconformity, which is superficial, *Walden* speaks with the power of a whole people.

Aside from "Solitude," the subject upon which Thoreau touches his pioneer model most closely, though not always most profitably, is economy. Again, his thought springs from organic analogy with—sometimes it seems an almost literal imitation of—frontier life at the West. The flowers are different, the roots are the same. More precisely, Thoreau is an exotic flower growing from a graft on the gnarled stock of the pioneer type. The pioneer stock bore no flowers of its own; it bloomed only in this strange man of Concord, this stay-at-home pioneer who was always adopting the real pioneer's habits, his manners, his very modes of existence. What else is Thoreau doing—though here the imitation is sterile enough, and productive of no very lovely results—when he declares that it is "cheaper . . . to select a fresh spot [of land] from time to time than to manure the old"? That ruinous agricultural practice was thoroughly characteristic of the Westward Movement; was, in fact, one of its contributory causes, whose effects are not yet erased from the American land or the American mind.

Thoreau's whole conception of economy, excepting such parts of it as derive from the frontier metaphor, which never intrigued the Western settler as it did the Eastern writer, remarkably resembles the credo of the agricultural

15 *American Humor* (New York, 1931), p. 168.

pioneer: "If one would live simply and eat only the crop which he raised, and raise no more than he ate, and not exchange it for . . . luxurious and expensive things, he would need to cultivate only a few rods of ground." The economic gist of *Walden* can be stated in three propositions:

1. Perfect self-sufficiency is the preferable social organization (anarchism, the model of the small land-holder).
2. The least commerce with others is the best (isolation, distrust of specialization).
3. Consumption should equal production (reciprocity and wholeness within the local unit).

As his best economic critic says, "Thoreau's ideal economic unit—the single homestead based on subsistence agriculture and handicrafts—belongs in the context of the movement to settle the frontier."[16] At Walden Pond, Thoreau may have come close to realizing such an ideal, but for the most part he worked as a surveyor, or he and his family manufactured pencils, which they exchanged for more basic commodities. Perhaps he also tended to forget that his ideal economic conditions were not quite what the typical pioneer sought, but what the remoteness and crudity of his situation compelled him to accept. The pioneer never wanted what Thoreau wanted him to want. But in his running fight with Eastern materialism, Thoreau made of Western necessities moral desiderata.

Simplify, simplify, simplify! Thoreau was led to that all-encompassing imperative by his experience of economic and moral independence in the woods. However indirectly, he was led to the independence by the pioneer. Locally and personally, he enacted a sort of ideal paradigm of the process of deculturation necessarily—but reluctantly, so far as creature comforts were concerned—repeated by the pioneer on every successively Westward frontier of American civilization. Thoreau's real quest was for an authentic self,

[16] Leo Stoller, *After Walden: Thoreau's Changing Views on Economic Man* (Stanford, 1957), p. 28.

whence a new, and truer, civilization might burgeon. Yet he also resembled his countrymen in paradoxically looking to the West as the source of the new, and finding there primarily a sanction for an older, simpler, more natural life. In reaction against the increasing complexity of American urban and industrial development, he clung desperately to the fundamentals of an earlier period—still available for contemporary contemplation at the West—hoping to assimilate permanently for himself and his nation the lessons of the frontier before it should vanish forever.

Although in *Walden* he sedulously avoids any appearance of recommending his way of life to all, in his heart of hearts Thoreau idealized the exigencies of the frontier to the point where he tended to see in them absolute (though not literal) models for every one, at any time, in any place. Returning to the subject in *The Maine Woods*, he praised the life of the hunter almost without qualification: "But the former [the hunter] is comparatively an independent and successful man, getting his living in a way that he likes, without disturbing his human neighbors. How much more respectable also is the life of the solitary pioneer or settler in these, or any woods,—having real difficulties, not of his own creation, drawing his subsistence directly from nature,—than that of the helpless multitudes in the towns."[17] The pioneering situation made for a necessary relation to reality which was practically the definition of the instrumental wisdom Thoreau sought. "I think that I could spend a year in the woods," he wrote, again in *The Maine Woods*, "fishing and hunting just enough to sustain myself, with satisfaction. This would be next to living like a philosopher on the fruits of the earth which you had raised, which also attracts me." Of course, he had already lived a little of each of these lives in the woods at the pond; just enough to appropriate them as possibilities for art, but not too much to interfere seriously with his practice of that art. This reciprocal play between the economics of subsistence and the philosophy of

[17] This passage is immediately preceded by remarks on population density in Maine.

composition is one of the chief glories of *Walden*. Deliberately and self-consciously, Thoreau placed himself in the position of the pioneer, and voluntarily educated himself in the hardships of that position, in order to ask on behalf of his people the fundamental questions, questions which were inescapably (one would think) forced upon the pioneer, but to which, in Thoreau's opinion, he was returning incorrect answers, or no answers at all. What does man want first? How does he get it? What does he want next? What is the relation between the worth of the thing and the expenditure of life required to procure it? In secular terms, Thoreau worked out for his culture what he must have thought of as an economic, and inexpensive, plan of salvation.

Perhaps his chief glory is that he was forever dissatisfied with the either-or exclusions of the actual frontier: raising crops vs. cultivating the arts. His own passion—as it was the passion of Cooper, Hawthorne, Poe—was for both-and solutions; in desiring to encompass these, he was led, like the others, to the figurative frontier, and to the broadest questions of all. For it was the frontier itself, or at least the Americans' anxious and uncertain sense of it, always somewhere ahead of them, that proposed the basic terms of that endless nineteenth-century discussion about the ambiguous interaction between American civilization, as thus far developed from European germs, and the virgin land, silent and empty, inviting, threatening, coercing, creating, but in precisely what ways could not yet be altogether ascertained— except that it involved the fresh future of a redeemed humanity, in whose Westernmost van one always found the archetypal pioneer, the American, this new man. From the time of Crèvecœur, the edge of the wilderness prompted the exiled European to ask the bewildering questions. Thoreau could answer them because he was, in fact as in fiction, the essential pioneer. In *A Yankee in Canada*, he tells us that every New England house "stands on the highway of nations, and the road which runs by it comes from the Old World and goes to the far West." New England was the neutral ground, or frontier, after all, and Thoreau, in his great moments, lived at the center of that great metaphor.

3. *WALDEN*: THE FRONTIER

After a few designedly introductory and diagnostic pages —ten pages, in the standard edition—Thoreau's argument takes a sudden upswing. "It would be some advantage to live a primitive and frontier life," he informs us, with a studied casualness of tone that has perhaps induced us to overlook the centrality of the allusion, "though in the midst of an outward civilization, if only to learn what are the gross necessaries of life and what methods have been taken to obtain them."[1] Thoreau's "primitive and frontier life," surrounded by "outward civilization"—a very ambiguous term—suggests a wilderness fortress, or frontier stockade, with this curious inversion, that it is the savage who defends the fort; the image of rear-guard action perhaps represents Thoreau, rather late in the day, defending the essential frontier. In the earliest surviving manuscript of *Walden* he wrote the following tentative but enthusiastic passage: "Why not live always a rude and frontier life—full of adventures and hard work—learn much—travel much—though it be only through these woods & fields! There is no other country than this—here is the field and the man.—The daily boundaries of life are expanded & dispersed and I see in what field I stand." Readers with a good command of the text will see at once how this passage was later dismantled, and its various components scattered through the book, several of them developing into memorable sentences: "I have travelled a good deal in Concord," "We need to witness our own limits transgressed, and some life pasturing freely where we never wander," or, for that matter, "It would be some advantage to live a primitive and frontier life."[2]

[1] Quotations of *Walden* are from *The Writings of Henry David Thoreau* (Boston, 1906), II; quotations of the early draft are from *The Making of Walden, With the Text of the First Version*, ed. J. Lyndon Shanley (Chicago, 1957).

[2] The remnants of this passage appear to be in "Baker Farm," *Writings*, II, 230.

Thoreau's social and economic thought, although closely resembling the fundamental principles of the agricultural pioneer, was also profoundly affected by the frontier metaphor. He is not especially original, but squarely within the strongest tradition of American letters, when he asks (rhetorically, for the answer was familiar): "Is it impossible to combine the hardiness of these savages with the intellectualness of the civilized man?" Of course it is not impossible, but invigorating and recreative, as *Walden* undertakes to show. The important word is "combine," which carries for this passage suggestions of the standard motive of the frontier metaphor (inclusive harmony) as well as of its typical form (reconciliation of opposites); with such a metaphor, a man might play one value (savagery, for instance) against its opposite (civilization) as long as he liked, and emerge with a new value (ambiguity) somehow comprehending both.

As Thoreau considers this question of subsistence, which occupies much of his attention in *Walden*, images of the West flit in and out of his mind. On the previous page, defining the phrase *"necessary of life,"* he was saying: "To many creatures there is in this sense but one necessary of life, Food. To the bison of the prairie it is a few inches of palatable grass, with water to drink." Throughout "Economy" especially, Thoreau is constantly comparing "civilized" housing, furniture, clothing, and the like—"possessions," in general—with their savage, and specifically with their Indian, counterparts. Such comparison is inevitably to the detriment of American materialism, and insofar as we rest our understanding here, without looking more closely into its practical bearings, we are likely to conclude that Thoreau uses savage custom (nearly equivalent to "nature") as a criterion. But this is to take entirely too superficial, or introductory, a view of the matter. Every good reader knows that Thoreau recommends no return to nature, nor to savage conditions, but only a move in that direction, which, as it must obviously start from "civilization," means a move in the direction of function and simplicity, not at all primitive but very highly civilized. (*That* is the advantage of living a primitive and frontier life.) Savage life affords him, then, not only a mode of criticism, but an indispensable term equal and opposite to (false) civilization, or conventionality; the antithesis between these two terms provides him exactly the structure requisite for defining the truest civility, by means of the frontier metaphor, as reconciliation at the meeting point between nature (as possibility) and civilization (as understood and practiced in the United States of the 1850's). The frontier metaphor enables Thoreau to entertain capacious and flexible, if also caustic, views of the subject, and especially to preserve whatever he likes from either conception. It is the time-honored Leatherstocking arrangement.

Without it, Thoreau's social criticism might have been comparatively trifling and dogmatic, for there was in his time hardly another conception of American society worth the writer's serious attention. As it stands, his analysis of the social scene is characterized by an admirable poise and delicacy. Within the pattern of traditional ideas associated with the American conception of the frontier, Thoreau found sufficient scope for Veblenesque commentary ("the childish and savage taste of men and women for new patterns" in clothing); for an attack on property ownership, or rather non-ownership ("In the savage state every family owns a shelter as good as the best, and sufficient for its coarser and simpler wants. . . . In modern civilized society not more than one half the families own a shelter"); for a devastating analysis of modern society's extraordinary inability to distribute its accumulating wealth on a basis of practical justice ("Would the savage have been wise to exchange his wigwam for a palace on these terms?" considering that "the cost of a thing is the amount of what I will call life which is required to be exchanged for it"); for a lament on modern loss of mobility and the failing sense of nature ("In our climate, in the summer, it [the house] was formerly almost solely a covering at night. In the Indian gazettes a wigwam was the symbol of a day's march"); for a moral assault

on the nineteenth century's obsession with material progress
at the expense of intellectual and spiritual culture (*"If the
civilized man's pursuits are no worthier than the savage's
. . . why should he have a better dwelling"*?); and for a
radical indictment of class inequality ("But how do the poor
minority fare? Perhaps it will be found that just in proportion as some have been placed in outward circumstances
above the savage, others have been degraded below him").
The condition of the poor in America, England, and Ireland,
he adds, with a final twist—two twists—of the knife, is
worse than that of "the North American Indian, or the
South Sea Islander, or any other savage race before it was
degraded by contact with the civilized man."

For all their impressive range and variety, these amazing
observations issue from a single metaphorical matrix, the
standard literary figuration of the Western frontier, which
almost automatically compelled the writer at least occasionally to revert to the central facts of American experience,
at the same time inviting him to understand those facts in
the light of whatever other ideas he might happen to entertain—so long as those ideas took the shape of opposition
and were susceptible of resolution. It was the ideal *mimesis*
for the mid-nineteenth-century American literary problem,
an almost perfect instrument for blending the most realistic
native materials with the most far-reaching social criticism,
moral commentary, or philosophical speculation. The frontier metaphor also enabled Thoreau to keep his several kinds
of criticism related and intelligible within a single pattern,
with the assurance that this pattern would turn out affirmatively. "But I wish to show at what a sacrifice this advantage [no matter what advantage] is at present obtained, and
to suggest that we may possibly so live as to secure all the
advantage without suffering any of the disadvantage." (He
is of course speaking of civilized and savage life.) Thoreau
was no man to give up advantages easily; he merely wanted
"more," or, in fact, "all." Ideally, "the civilized man is a
more experienced and wiser savage."

At least in *Walden*, Thoreau met handsomely Arnold's

demand—the sternest, if vaguest, a critic ever made—that the writer see life steadily and see it whole; inevitably he did so by seeing it within the American context, where civilization was always in dangerous and exhilarating touch with nature, and nature was only another name for the unknown. This was another beneficent consequence of the frontier metaphor, that it continually prompted the American writer to bridge the gap between what he knew (which was not much, he and the country being so recent) and what he most needed to learn about himself and his rapidly accelerating civilization. In this sense, too, the frontier metaphor was the central *mimesis* of the age, whose widespread literary articulation not only profoundly affected, but was practically equivalent to the development of the American mind. Nature was the not yet known; village life was metonymous for the life already understood and mastered, i.e., civilization. "Our village life would stagnate if it were not for the unexplored forests and meadows which surround it. We need the tonic of wildness. . . . At the same time that we are earnest to explore and learn all things, we require that all things be mysterious and unexplorable, that land and sea be infinitely wild, unsurveyed and unfathomed by us because unfathomable. We can never have enough of nature." Because he understood that American civilization must be defined in terms of forced contact with nature—in other words, that a new nation, with everything yet to learn, and the future before it, has no choice but to be humble— Thoreau, and writers like him, molded the national consciousness more than free land ever did. Free land disappeared, but *Walden* remains. Driven by the neurotic necessity to explain and justify his own refusal to participate directly in the Westward Movement, Thoreau discovered the essential truth which Frederick Jackson Turner was never entirely to comprehend: that the national transformation (or "new birth") was taking place, and could only take place, within the minds and hearts of men, and that their being physically on the frontier had no very magical effect upon them. If he knew what he sought, the new man might perhaps find it, and himself too, as easily in Concord as elsewhere; but if he failed to imagine what he ought to seek, he might look for it endlessly over the empty continent, as well as in his own empty head, and find at last the same old platitude.

In *Walden,* Thoreau continued to indulge his etymological puns, not so trivially as in the *Week,* where he rather aimlessly envisaged man *"fronting* it," but equally for the purpose of freeing his major term from a constraining literality. "The low shrub oak plateau to which the opposite shore arose stretched away toward the prairies of the West and the steppes of Tartary, affording ample room for all the roving families of men." (Free access to the West, or nature; Thoreau's position defined as transitional between East and West, the midpoint of man's Westward migrations.) "Both place and time were changed, and I dwelt nearer to those parts of the universe and to those eras in history which had most attracted me." (Transcendental India, Homeric Greece, Confucian China.) But in view of its ultimate result, this irruption of regard for the Old World must be considered largely diversionary: "I discovered that my house actually had its site in such a withdrawn, but forever new and unprofaned, part of the universe." (Pioneer analogy, completely divorced from literal context.) Then still another point of reference, in praise of the morning: "There was something cosmical about it; a standing advertisement, till forbidden, of the everlasting vigor and fertility of the world." (Free land as fertility; sun as Great Western Pioneer.) And so to the famous paragraph:

> I went to the woods because I wished to live deliberately, to front only the essential facts of life, and see if I could not learn what it had to teach, and not, when I came to die, discover that I had not lived. I did not wish to live what was not life, living is so dear; nor did I wish to practise resignation, unless it was quite necessary. I wanted to live deep and suck out all the marrow of life, to live so sturdily and Spartan-like as to put

to rout all that was not life, to cut a broad swath and shave close, to drive life into a corner, and reduce it to its lowest terms, and, if it proved to be mean, why then to get the whole and genuine meanness of it, and publish its meanness to the world; or if it were sublime, to know it by experience, and be able to give a true account of it in my next excursion [i.e., my next book after the *Week*].

The whole passage constitutes another of Thoreau's general imitations of the pioneer, and, with the abundant imagery drawn from a variety of human interests and activities (agriculture, commerce, eating, education, history, hunting, mathematics, publishing, warfare), it plainly intends a total statement. The totality depends on the starting point (to front the essential facts of life), and the starting point is the frontier metaphor compressed in a single word.

The ultimate intention of the passage, and thus of *Walden*, is epistemological-aesthetic, and involves the usual metaphorical comparison of four terms. Thoreau speaks of what we might call the frontier between subject and object. As nature and civilization meet and interpenetrate—either in a general way or in the specific encounters between the pioneer and his new environments—losing their ostensible antithesis in a new unity, so the "I" of the passage and the "facts of life" meet and interpenetrate for an equally creative and transcendent end. In either case, the process is reciprocal and involves both reconciliation and progress. The "I" not only confronts, but is confronted, with the obvious consequence that both are finally subsumed in a new synthesis, the work of art, *Walden*. Thus "front," normally a transitive verb, under the impact of American conditions quietly turns into a copulative. With such an aesthetic understanding, freely available to him in the country's literary culture —minus the metaphor of the frontier, he would have found much the same thing in Coleridge's *Biographia Literaria*— Thoreau binds as best he can the two divergent or even antagonistic tendencies of his expression, the one toward introspection or groundless fancy, the other toward accurate but unilluminated observation of nature. When the two tendencies coincide, or meet upon the neutral ground of the Romantic conception of imagination—especially as redefined, or refigured, under the metaphor of the frontier, by Hawthorne in "The Custom-House"—Thoreau is a poet. When one or the other preponderates, he is an idle talker or a string collector.

Thoreau reconciles all his antitheses but one upon that imaginary neutral ground proposed by the metaphor of the frontier. The exception of course is the antithesis between one's self and other people's selves. Yet we must not too hastily attribute this lapse to the single cause of temperamental inadequacy, no matter how tempting such an explanation may be, but consider also the literary pressures. As we have seen, the conception of pure solitude sometimes associated with the Western pioneer was not wholly compatible with the conventional mediation of solitude and society encouraged by the frontier metaphor; thus a second explanation of Thoreau's prickly independence lies in the possibility that the frontier metaphor simply had to give way at this one point to the overpowering force of the pioneer model. According to the habit of thought which formed, and was formed by, the frontier metaphor—and to which Thoreau happily submits on nearly every other occasion—he ought to have taken his stand at the meeting point between solitude and society, as his mentor Emerson was doing, in both theory and practice. Thoreau goes so far as to juxtapose successive chapters on "Solitude" and "Visitors," but this gesture in the direction of fair play is not very impressive, partly because "Visitors" is not. To all intents and purposes, *Walden* is a hymn to solitude.

"Individuals, like nations, must have suitable broad and natural boundaries, even a considerable neutral ground, between them." The context of this remark is amiability itself, but the frontier metaphor is full of animus. Persons, like nations, according to the most cynical view of international relations, require broad and suitable boundaries to

keep them from each other's throats. It scarcely needs arguing that such connotations are entirely at odds with the
expected implications of the traditional image of the neutral
ground. Thoreau's meeting point is no meeting point at all,
but an empty space, useful for the prevention of hostilities.
Either his temperament, or his commitment to the pioneer
value of well-guarded isolation, has kept the image from resolving the problem. The problem he shared with Hawthorne, and others; Hawthorne, in particular, must have
deplored his solution of it. But Hawthorne would have
smiled (a smile of recognition) upon Thoreau's way of defining the present moment as the juncture between equal
opposites: "In any weather, at any hour of the day or night,
I have been anxious to improve the nick of time, and notch
it on my stick too; to stand on the meeting of two eternities,
the past and future, which is precisely the present moment;
to toe that line." Some of these images are uniquely Thoreau's (especially the stick-notching); but the temporal-
spatial line he toes, where eternities meet, is part of his
literary inheritance, the shared traditional metaphor of the
Western frontier.

Under the steady persuasion of Thoreau's favorite figure,
nearly every object in *Walden* assumes qualities associated
with the frontier. His beloved bean-field becomes "as it were,
the connecting link between wild and cultivated fields; as
some states are civilized, and others half-civilized, and others
savage or barbarous, so my field was, though not in a bad
sense, a half-cultivated field." Not in a bad sense, and not
in a literal sense, either. The bean-field is Thoreau's frontier
between the civil and the natural (or savage) conditions.
Surely we are to think of those beans as beans; but we are
also expected to move rather quickly from the perception of
beans to the far more important consideration of Thoreau's
real field of activity, with the results of that activity upon
the real state of his soul. (Such words as "state" and "field"
easily provoke metaphorical extension; ghosts of all the dead
metaphors—"state of nature," "state of society," "field of
endeavor," "field of vision"—hover around this passage.)

Of course, we are expected to find them admirable; yet Thoreau asks for our admiration on no personal grounds, but rather on the grounds of the vigor and energy with which in his own life he is prosecuting, in an essential way, the national *mythos*. His bean-field, with all its attendant implications for the culture of the soul, is the meeting point between civilization and nature; in a word—the word Thoreau knows better than to use directly—the frontier.

So with his even better-beloved pond. Though it could hardly be thought of as a frontier in the primary sense of a neutral territory between civilization and nature, yet Thoreau found it easily amenable to a looser, and ultimately more important, figurative construction. As Flint's Pond is "our greatest lake and inland sea," so Walden Pond is his personal frontier between earth and Heaven, between natural and divine. "Walden is blue at one time and green at another," Thoreau tells us, as if he were making a physical observation merely, but with the Transcendentalist's careful eye for perspective, "even from the same point of view." But the next sentence clearly invites a wider speculation: "Lying between the earth and the heavens, it partakes of the color of both." Obviously, it is through the ambiguous word "heavens" that Thoreau opens his literal description to supranatural considerations. So far, he had on his hands only another of those tiresome Transcendental puns, with which the lesser members of the movement were always trying to assure themselves of a faith not really held. Even this lovely passage is perhaps a little marred by that characteristic failing. But Thoreau's metaphor depends for its genuine effect far less on his substitution of the sentimental "heavens" for the ordinary word "sky" than on the legitimate ambiguity (in this situation) of the word "color." Walden is green like the earth, blue like the sky. Its water partakes of —takes from, shares in—the color of both. Thoreau's image is perfectly justified as realistic observation. Yet in this context, and as we allow the image to work on us, the word "color" comes to lie between grammatical categories. Although technically a noun, it has also the general force of a transitive verb ("to change the color of, dye, tint, stain, imbue with color, etc."); and as a verb it readily becomes part of an unstated figure expressive of any kind of action whose effect is analogous to coloring (such as Heaven's nearly imperceptible effect on earth, and vice versa). "Color" acquires further support for its status as a verb and as a tacit figure from the suggestions of easy blending furnished by the literal image; for what are the colors involved in this comparison but green and blue, continuous on the scale of light, and therefore indistinguishable at their meeting point? Consistent with American thinking about the Western frontier, Thoreau's metaphysical boundary is not a line that divides but a line that joins.

Finally, "color" may also suggest the much needed (by this particular conceit) implication of speciousness, misrepresentation. Thus Thoreau allows the snake of criticism (only a little snake) to enter his metaphorical paradise. We begin with sentimentality and end with skepticism; in between, at the center of the figure, earth and sky indubitably color the pond, prompting our question whether this world and Heaven may not likewise meet and interpenetrate at a scarcely imaginable but equally lovely point. (The scarcely imaginable point might be conceived as lying within the sensibilities of poets who in their imagery keep on good terms with both nature and God.) The success of such writing, which is in the best sense poetic rather than doctrinal, depends partly on the way Thoreau's terms insist upon retaining their literal integrity, while metaphorical interpretations unobtrusively arise from them—we see the pond as both natural and divine, "even from the same point of view"—and partly on the incredible skill with which he permits one of those unobtrusive interpretations ("color" as misrepresentation) to subject the entire metaphorical process to internal criticism. Thoreau is most winning when he sticks close to his images and lets them do most, but not all, of the talking. In his dealings with the pond, he characteristically elects the delicate approach.

He possessed a truly miraculous gift for breathing fresh

meaning into moribund metaphors (witness his resurrection of "castles in the air"); and by the mid-fifties—if we may trust the evidence of Hawthorne and Melville—the frontier metaphor was beginning to fail for everyone but Thoreau. His reclamation of the frontier metaphor is nowhere more brilliant than in connection with the pond; his connection with the pond is nowhere more obviously devout than in the following sentences: "A field of water betrays the spirit that is in the air. It is continually receiving new life and motion from above. It is intermediate in its nature between land and sky."[3] There are figures here almost past counting, but the one which contributes most richly is "spirit," whose ascending meanings of breath, flow of air, life principle, and God are all germane to the argument, which attempts through nature to reconcile man and deity. In Thoreau's manipulation of these various meanings, the crisis plainly occurs at the phrase "spirit that is in the air." Thoreau skillfully contains his major predication (that God, as the life principle, is immanent in—*in*—the air, or natural world) within the double significance of "spirit" as both God and motion of air. This major predication he then further protects by placing it in a dependent (and restrictive) phrase, where its truth must be assumed; the grammar places it beyond examination. The revelation of the ambiguous meaning of "spirit" is "betrayed" by water, not by

---

[3] In an earlier version, the middle sentence reads: "It has new life and motion." *The Journal of Henry D. Thoreau*, ed. Bradford Torrey and Francis H. Allen (Boston, 1906), II, 57. Thoreau's understanding of the metaphysical possibilities in this particular image evidently came later, but he was always inordinately fond of this kind of figure: "There it [Walden Pond] lies all the year reflecting the sky—and from its surface there seems to go up a pillar of ether, which bridges over the space between earth and heaven. Water seems a middle element between earth and air." *Consciousness in Concord; the Text of Thoreau's Hitherto "Lost Journal," (1840-1841)*, ed. Perry Miller (Boston, 1958), p. 186. "It seems natural that rocks which have lain under the heavens so long should be gray, as it were an intermediate color between the heavens and the earth." *Journal*, IV, 134. "We had our first, but a partial view of Ktaadn, its summit veiled in clouds, like a dark isthmus in that quarter, connecting the heavens with the earth." *Writings*, III, 36.

the writer, and thus we receive it at a remove, as we are also put off guard by at first thinking Thoreau alludes only to the effect of wind on water. Finally, we receive the revelation from a natural agent who offers it reluctantly, with the persuasive power customarily attributed to understatement, and with an air of utter objectivity. What does the water care whether God exists or not?

But if God and the life principle are truly in the air—and Thoreau's mastery of pun and figure and syntax not only insists for the moment on the identity of their physical and spiritual presence but prevents our refutation of either the presence or the identity—then we are more than half ready to think that this immanence in nature may well receive new life and motion from above—at which point the argument quietly shifts from God as immanent to God as transcendent. This readinesss of belief is naturally reinforced by our awareness that water does in fact receive the appearance of life (i.e., motion) from the air, as the air which moves the surface of the pond is in turn moved by the upper air. What we accept, then, is the argument that if spirit (breath-air-life-God) is a plausible trope of the relations between physical existence and the eternal principles which at once inform and transcend that existence, we may with equal propriety transfer this degree of assurance to the possibility of there really existing a correspondence between the progression from water to air to upper air and the progression from nature to immanent deity to transcendent deity. The passage finds its basic structure in the frontier metaphor, which is implied by the sentence, "It is intermediate in its nature between land and sky," and which provides the requisite form of mediation (immanent deity) between apparently irreconcilable conceptions (nature as nature, God as God). "Field of water" brings another dead metaphor to life, mainly for the purpose of doubling our perception of how things lie between. By virtue of the metaphor in "field," the pond is intermediate between land and water, as well as between land and sky. But by virtue of the same metaphor, the land also begins to liquefy; which lovely metamorphosis, as with "color" in the previous passage, may well be thought to provide the fluidity of tone best suited to the entertainment of this sort of speculation, neither too grudging nor too credulous, but pleasantly open, like water and air, to the slightest stir of suggestion. And who can, in the last analysis, be grudging toward a man who writes like that? Has he not proved that his pond is in fact a meeting point between the various antitheses upon which his perceptions (as instructed by the spirit of the age) are patterned? Has he not lured back the nearly dead metaphor from the shades of platitude to the sparkling light of real life?

Whatever the issue, Thoreau pivots at the point of equilibrium between opposing values; characteristically he elects not one nor the other (nor neither) but both. "I found in myself, and still find, an instinct toward a higher, or, as it is named, spiritual life, as do most men, and another toward a primitive rank and savage one, and I reverence them both. I love the wild not less than the good." As his personal imitation of the pioneer role induced him to take the frontier metaphor more seriously than any of his contemporaries, so the metaphor of the frontier—strongly implied in that last passage, which for the hundredth time seeks to establish a situation propitious to creative resolution at the juncture of nature and civilization, the "wild" and the "good"—simultaneously led to the complementary conception of himself as the essential pioneer. Only a few sentences after "I love the wild not less than the good," we find him once more alluding to hunters on the prairie, trappers on the Missouri and Columbia Rivers, and so forth. "There is a period in the history of the individual, as of the race, when the hunters are the 'best men,' as the Algonquins called them." Except in those cases where it seems likely that his determination to be more a pioneer than any mere Westerner encouraged him to think of his locale in terms of the frontier metaphor, it seems impossible to determine which of the two—imitation of the pioneer or emphasis on the frontier—is cause, and which effect. ("If you stand right fronting and face to face to a fact, you will see the sun glimmer on both its surfaces, as if it were a cimeter.") Paradoxically, this almost perfect equivalence and reciprocity between the metaphor of the frontier—that marvellous synecdoche of the West which had yielded so many and such various meanings and structures to Cooper, Hawthorne, Poe, and now to Thoreau—and the relatively direct confrontation of the West (not so much Thoreau's incessant talk about it as his much more impressive creation of *Walden* in the form of analogy between pioneer and poet), marks the crucial turning-point in the history of the West upon the American mind. In only three years, Melville was to envisage them as entirely antagonistic principles, drawing on the frontier metaphor for wonderfully sardonic effects, and thus in an altogether different kind of balance— a more amusing reciprocity, and perhaps truer to life, but marking the end of development. So fragile and transitory, apparently, is the moment of finest flowering, when the essential meaning of a nation's history is met by the answer- ing mind of the poet who can render it most adequately. The balance of positive force between the West as metaphor and the West as substance (waiving the question how sub- stantial it all was) is found only in Thoreau—which is in itself almost unbelievable, when we remember by what an unpromising road he came to it—and only successfully in *Walden*. Never again was the frontier to shed such beneficent influences upon an American work of imagination.

That so happy a balance should appear in Thoreau is perhaps to be explained both by the historical moment and by the intensity of his personal involvement; both aspects of the literary West were necessary to him, and necessarily correlative. In passage after passage, he frames his motive, and defines his being in terms of the Western pioneer; in passage after passage (many of them the same), he sees the world in terms of American preoccupation with the frontier. Without the model of the pioneer, he would have lacked both vocation, in the overserious, Transcendental sense, and per- sonal identity (he might never have eluded Emerson);

without the frontier metaphor, he would have split down the middle and fallen open in two halves. Though it may sometimes look like it in the lesser works, his involvement with the West was by no means "literary," in any superficial sense, and no mere trick of rhetoric. His appropriations of the pioneer and the frontier are after all viable only as we are convinced of the integrity of his personal commitment to such values as exploration, mobility, experiment; values traditionally, and in a way correctly, attributed to the Western experience (even bearing in mind Thoreau's strict critique of the actual quality of that experience), and thence to the national character at large (or "ideally"). A man cannot merely say he loves the wild, but must (if he be a poet) give evidence of it, as he must, with perhaps even greater difficulty, give evidence of his love for the good. Significantly, Thoreau's statement that he loves the wild not less than the good follows and takes its authority from his confession that he was once tempted to seize a woodchuck and eat him raw. Insofar as we believe him, *Walden* passes over from rhetoric to poetry. At most points in *Walden*, we are surely entitled to believe him, with fewest reservations, or none.

Lingering over the many excellences of it, we are thus compelled to admit that for all his peculiarities and perversities, Thoreau's relation to the West was in nearly every respect more positively rewarding than that of any of his contemporaries (though *The Scarlet Letter*, *Moby-Dick*, and *The Confidence-Man* are almost as Western), and that insofar as we agree to define the age in terms of its imaginative response to the West and to the frontier, Thoreau belongs at or near the center of the definition. What is particularly pleasant to linger over is the way his usual vices and follies have in *Walden* been metamorphosed by the technical mastery we call poetic genius—which is no facile skill with language but a control of consciousness, a discipline of life—into art of a rare maturity. Where a certain element in his attitude toward the West had tempted him (and would tempt him again) into childish superciliousness and aggression, he is instead magnanimously secure, imperturbably right: "We are in great haste to construct a magnetic telegraph from Maine to Texas; but Maine and Texas, it may be, have nothing important to communicate." Such improvement can scarcely be accounted for by Thoreau's increased ability to entertain the possibility of Maine being as "barbarous" (i.e., as Western) as Texas, though perhaps that is part of it. The more fundamental change lies in the seriousness and precision of language, the propriety and realism of the image, the authority of tone, the truth of the wit. Thoreau's antagonism to the West remains, as we may sufficiently verify in some laconic remarks toward the end of his "Conclusion," the famous passage where he decides "not to live in this restless, nervous, bustling, trivial Nineteenth Century, but stand or sit thoughtfully while it goes by," and by doing so guarantees his survival beyond the Nineteenth Century and all its so-called "internal improvements." The approach to that statement is by way of a list of current attractions he does not intend to seek out; of these attractions, four are places; of the four, two are American. They are California and Texas.

Such places formed no part of Henry Thoreau's West, though without them he would have had no West to speak of. His special West was Concord, and, even more, his own soul. His personal frontier was his relation with reality (nature, language, God). When that relation was true, his art was true, in the only way art can be; when that relation was false, his art suffered the necessary consequences. Even in *Walden*, then, he must struggle and struggle to keep the relation right; with most of the book already behind him, he continues to meditate at length:

> What does Africa,—what does the West stand for? Is not our own interior white on the chart? black though it may prove, like the coast, when discovered. Is it the source of the Nile, or the Niger, or the Mississippi, or a Northwest Passage around this continent, that we would find? Are these the problems which most concern

mankind? . . . Be rather the Mungo Park, the Lewis and Clark and Frobisher, of your own streams and oceans; explore your own higher latitudes. . . . Nay, be a Columbus to whole new continents and worlds within you, opening new channels, not of trade, but of thought. . . . What was the meaning of that South-Sea Exploring Expedition, with all its parade and expense, but an indirect recognition of the fact that there are continents and seas in the moral world to which every man is an isthmus or an inlet, yet unexplored by him . . .[4]

This passage has often been taken to be a deliberate imitation of a famous sentence in Sir Thomas Browne's *Religio Medici*: "We carry with us the wonders we seek without us: there is all Africa and her prodigies in us; we are that bold and adventurous piece of Nature, which he that studies wisely learns in a *compendium* what others labour at in a divided piece and endless volume."[5] But that famous sentence, so impressive in other respects, is altogether less specifically (or desperately) committed than Thoreau's elaboration on it. For Browne, Africa is only an illustrative image, the traditionally likely place for "prodigies"; for Thoreau, what the West stands for is the question of questions. In broadest and deepest terms, what the West stands for is the interior and the future of the American continent, and then by analogous transfer to the American, this new man, the innermost being and destiny of those who have been called to the discovery and expression of what humanity has discovered to express in the New World. The West is the soul of the American writer. "Explore thyself. Herein are demanded the eye and the nerve."

Consequently we must always insist that the effect of

[4] The paragraph ends with one of Thoreau's most haunting sentences: "Start now on that farthest western way, which does not pause at the Mississippi or the Pacific, nor conduct toward a worn-out China or Japan, but leads on direct, a tangent to this sphere, summer and winter, day and night, sun down, moon down, and at last earth down too."

[5] *The Works of Sir Thomas Browne*, ed. Geoffrey Keynes (London, 1928-1931), I, 21.

the West upon the American mind was not literal or mechanical (as how could it have been?), nor so trivial in its
bearings as our intellectual historians have led us to suppose, but imaginative, aesthetic, formal, stylistic. For this
reason, final comment on *Walden* can only be stylistic. It is
the happiest propriety of all—but not very surprising—that
Thoreau should himself phrase his stylistic ambitions in
imagery derived from his lifelong contemplation of the
Western frontier. As usual, he leads up to his major point
with a considerable compositional subtlety: "I learned this,
at least, by my experiment; that if one advances confidently
in the direction of his dreams, and endeavors to live the life
which he has imagined, he will meet with a success
unexpected in common hours. He will put some things behind, will pass an invisible boundary." What can that confident advancing be but the Westward Movement? Did
not the American dream lie in that direction? What is the
life he imagined and lived but the life of the pioneer? Did
he not meet uncommon success in the role? What else is the
invisible boundary but the imaginary Western frontier?
Thoreau's only inadvertence in this passage is the implication that he can *pass* the boundary, whereas salvation required him to *toe that line*. This contradiction he would
never resolve.

He finally arrives at his best formulation of the style of
Walden, a style in every true sense one with its substance,
taut but inclusive, direct but flexible, realistic but venture-
some, traditional but new:

> It is a ridiculous demand which England and America
> make, that you shall speak so that they can understand
> you. . . . I fear chiefly lest my expression may not be
> *extra-vagant* enough, may not wander far enough be-
> yond the narrow limits of my daily experience, so as to
> be adequate to the truth of which I have been convinced.
> *Extra vagance!* it depends on how you are yarded. The
> migrating buffalo, which seeks new pastures in another
> latitude, is not extravagant like the cow which kicks

over the pail, leaps the cowyard fence, and runs after her calf, in milking time. I desire to speak somewhere *without* bounds; like a man in a waking moment, to men in their waking moments; for I am convinced that I cannot exaggerate enough even to lay the foundation of a true expression. . . . In view of the future or possible, we should live quite laxly and undefined in front, our outlines dim and misty on that side.

To the end, Thoreau seems undetermined whether he means to be on the frontier or beyond. But surely that unseemly cow is the essentially Eastern or derivative writer, whether in his docile or hysterical mood, and the migrating buffalo (seeking another latitude) the poet of the West, the Wild, Henry David Thoreau.

"For the growth of a new literature," I have quoted him as saying, "we must look to the West." So Thoreau, remaining in the East, looked to the West, and from the looking learned to conceive and then bring to completion the most representative masterpiece of the new literature. With some show of logic, after all; a man can hardly look to the West, if the West is where he is. No writer who lived in the West found much to say about it; and indeed, except as it came to exist in men's minds and imaginations, there was little to say. Granted that Thoreau, and the other major figures of the mid-century, lacked firsthand knowledge of the West; at least they had the advantage of a long perspective, and that advantage they capitalized on for all it was worth, and sometimes more. So the modern reader who wishes to recover some sense of how the new American literature came out of the West to make the American mind must look and look closely to such books as *Walden* through the long perspective of time, and see if he cannot still learn something of what they have to teach. What he learns will depend on how he is yarded.

Herman Melville

1. EARLY WESTERN TRAVELS

"AND I AM SPECIALLY DELIGHTED AT THE THOUGHT, that those strange, congenial feelings, with which after my first voyage, I for the first time read 'Two Years Before the Mast,' and while so engaged was, as it were, tied & welded to you by a sort of Siamese link of affectionate sympathy— that these feelings should be reciprocated by you, in your turn, and be called out by any White Jackets or Redburns of mine—this is indeed delightful to me."[1] So Melville, in a style anticipatory of his passionate epistles to Hawthorne, unburdened himself to Richard Henry Dana, Jr., in 1850. No wonder it was to Dana that Melville felt tied and welded, for almost certainly it was Dana's book more than any other that enabled him to realize, through *Moby-Dick*, the richest motif of his literary production, implicit identification of the Western Ocean and the American West. *Two Years Before the Mast* was at once a story of life upon the ocean and a story of life in the wilderness (unspoiled landscape, Indians, traders, hunters, trappers, settlers); it was the first great emigrants' guide for young men—and prospective beachcombers—going to California by sea instead of overland. When Melville read it (evidently on its publication in 1840), he was himself between ocean voyages, and had just returned from an inland trip to Illinois,[2]

---

[1] *The Letters of Herman Melville*, ed. Merrell R. Davis and William H. Gilman (New Haven, 1960), p. 106.

[2] For beachcombers, sailors, and pioneers, see "The South Seas,"

where he had unsuccessfully sought employment or fortune in or about the famous Galena lead mines, and had amused himself reading Cooper's *The Red Rover*, a piratical-patriotic novel which turns up in Dana's introduction, and a new edition of which Melville reviewed only six weeks before he wrote the letter to Dana. It was an odd conjunction of circumstances, of which the first result was apparently to send Melville to the South Seas as if he were once again traveling to the West—as Poe, only recently, had envisaged Reynolds, and then himself, doing. The second result was *Moby-Dick*.

Melville's dominant imaginative structure, the voyage, was thus given to him in experience years before he commenced writing, and then neatly reinforced by literary example. And fortunately it was given to him, both in fact and in fiction, in a curiously doubled form. Ocean voyages and exotic islands were all very well in their way, but without Western implications how could they have been brought home to American businesses and bosoms? Up to *Pierre*, Melville's literary adventures all took place outside the continental limits of the United States, four of them to the West of California and Oregon. He was to this extent, and for at least these few years, an indefinite number of jumps ahead of the ever-more-rapidly-moving frontier. And the Pacific-West connection furnished him also these further advantages, that whereas the sea was in his writing almost automatically Americanized, and made available for novels aspiring to centrality within the somewhat hysterically nationalistic literary conventions of America, the thematic West was immeasurably enhanced by association with such oceanic ideas as flux, inscrutability, death, and the uncon-

---

in Merton M. Sealts, Jr., *Melville as Lecturer* (Cambridge, 1957), pp. 162 and 176. The primary evidence for the Western trip is in "Sketch of Major Thomas Melville Junior by a Nephew" (Gansevoort-Lansing Collection, New York Public Library): "In 1841 [*sic*] I visited my now venerable kinsman in his western home."

scious.[3] As Melville said in *Mardi*: "Though America be discovered, the Cathays of the deep are unknown."[4]

From the beginning, Melville's fiction was also to make use of the more traditional American pattern of the figurative frontier. According to one of Frederick Jackson Turner's several definitions, "the frontier is the outer edge of the wave"—a metaphor Melville would have liked, at least until he thought about it—"the meeting point between savagery and civilization."[5] In that sense, or senses, Melville's first three novels were about the frontier, for the Marquesas, Tahiti, and "Mardi" with which he courted the reading public were all conceived as lying either on or beyond the point of meeting between white civilization (European, American, Melvillean) and a deeper-toned savagery (Polynesian, Western, Melvillean). Even in the seagoing and for the most part Easterly-traveling novels, *Redburn* and *White-Jacket*, the fundamental dialectic of civilization-savagery is never far from mind; and in all five books we are repeatedly and pointedly reminded, by language, or by allusion, or by allegory, of the American West.

In *Typee: A Peep at Polynesian Life* (1846), Melville persistently calls the Marquesans "savages"—about one hundred and thirty-five times, by informal count—when he might easily have restricted himself to the neutral language of "native" or "islander," which he also uses, though much less often. For Melville's audience, the word savage carried powerful and relatively precise meanings, both ennobling (Rousseauistic) and pejorative (suggestive of infantilism, superstition, intractability, hostility, treachery); either way,

[3] Like Thoreau, Melville was given to acid remarks about the actual West, especially as it impinged upon his literary business. In 1846 he loftily wrote John Murray: "You would be greatly diverted to read some of the comments [on *Typee*] of our Western Editors and log-cabin critics" (*Letters*, p. 38). Five years later he repeated the charge to Richard Bentley: "This country & nearly all its affairs are governed by sturdy backwoodsmen—noble fellows enough, but not at all literary" (p. 134).

[4] Unless otherwise specified, quotations in this section are from *The Works of Herman Melville* (London, 1922-1924).

[5] *The Frontier in American History* (New York, 1920), p. 3.

it immediately conjured up that arch savage, the American Indian.[6] And insofar as the Indian becomes implicated in these early narratives, Polynesia recedes in favor of the Great West. Occasionally Melville contrasts Polynesian and Indian, for example in their treatment of women. More often he lists their virtues in parallel, as offsets to civilized inadequacy: "the courage of the North American Indian, and the faithful friendships of some of the Polynesian nations." Elsewhere, and nearly always as part of a major attack on American-European arrogance, he sees Polynesian and Indian as interchangeable or even identical emblems. In the course of one great blast, Melville deliberately refers to the Marquesan as "the voluptuous Indian," as if the Indian were the commanding image for all the magnificence of the easygoing life. In another primitivistic context, where Melville is supposed to be thinking of South Sea islanders, he speaks instead of "the luxurious Indian."

Cooper and a host of other writers were equally vague about specific differences among primitive peoples, and frequently spoke of Polynesians as Indians, but somehow their remarks seemed "safe" in a way that Melville's did not. As his fury mounts against the sins of the white man, Melville strikes closer and closer home: "The Anglo-Saxon hive have extirpated Paganism from the greater part of the North American continent; but with it they have likewise extirpated the greater portion of the Red race." The virulence of contemporary conventional response to *Typee* suggests that Melville's Polynesian-Indian analogy was not entirely lost on patriotic readers. "The book abounds in

[6] Most of the time Melville simply allows the connotations of "savage" to breed their own ambiguities. Occasionally he interpolates such remarks as "How often is the term 'savages' incorrectly applied!" (ch. 4), or "The term 'savage' is, I conceive, often misapplied" (ch. 17). Melville's identification of Polynesian and Indian was doubtless helped along by widespread contemporary speculation about the Oceanic origin of the American aborigines. See the book by his friend Alexander W. Bradford, *American Antiquities and Researches Into the Origin and History of the Red Race* (New York, 1841), p. 434.

praises of the life of nature, *alias* savageism," complained
an evangelical type, "and in slurs and flings against missionaries and civilization. . . . We are sorry that such a
volume should have been allowed a place in the 'Library of
American Books.' "⁷ The better reviewers, however, took the
opposite tack, and one of them showed rare perception:
"Since Dana's 'Two Years Before the Mast,' we have had
nothing to compare with it in point of fresh and natural
interest."⁸

The freshness was still within a recognizable tradition.
Such popular Western historians as John A. McClung
regularly glorified such an actual adventurer as Colonel
James Smith by calling him "the first anglo-American who
penetrated into the interior of the Western country—at
least the first who has given us an account of his adventures.
. . . His adventures will be found particularly interesting,
as affording more ample specimens of savage manners and
character, than almost any other account now in existence."⁹
So Tommo and Toby are "pioneers," who hack their way
through a forest of cane (as if Nukuheva were Kentucky),
encounter Niagaras of waterfalls, and are shaken with ague,
for their invasion of the happy valley is by simple correspondence and obvious geographical extension the archetypal American behavior epitomized. "The whole landscape
seemed one unbroken solitude, the interior of the island
having apparently been untenanted since the morning of
the Creation; and as we advanced through this wilderness,
our voices sounded strangely in our ears, as though human
accents had never before disturbed the fearful silence of the
place." Even after learning that the place is tenanted by
the loquacious Typees, Tommo continues to insist that "we

---

⁷ Quoted in Jay Leyda, *The Melville Log* (New York, 1951), I,
211—in which see also pp. 224, 246, 250, and 259. Years later, a
newspaper reviewer, understandably confused, wrote of Fayaway:
"There are few who do not have sentimental recollections of the
fair, lithe, graceful Indian girl." Quoted in Sealts, *Melville as Lecturer*, p. 44.
⁸ Quoted in *The Melville Log*, I, 210.
⁹ *Sketches of Western Adventure* (Maysville, Ky., 1832), pp. 13-14.

were the first white men who ever penetrated thus far back into their territories." Later, the Typees' main highway seems "as difficult to travel as the recesses of a wilderness." The pioneers finally arrive at a state of nature, idyllic, deceptive, and ultimately wearisome, where one of them must languish in a condition not remarkably different from that of the representative victim in a captivity narrative. The rest of the book is devoted to Tommo's captors, the children of nature, and their savage customs. It ends with an anguished and violent—not to say savage—escape into civilized life again.

Such is the general pattern of *Typee*, whose incidental imagery is even more suggestive of the frontier, or interpenetration between Western civilization and unspoiled nature. In a vivid tableau, the ugly French fleet intrudes an unwelcome presence upon one of Melville's loveliest landscapes; or, stated in more specifically human terms: "The next moment they stood side by side, these two extremes of the social scale—the polished, splendid Frenchman, and the poor tattooed savage. . . . At what an immeasurable distance, thought I, are these two beings removed from each other. . . . 'Yet, after all,' quoth I to myself, 'insensible as he is to a thousand wants, and removed from harassing cares, may not the savage be the happier man of the two?' " Theoretically, Melville is *beyond* the frontier (that's why he jumped ship), reveling in uncontaminated nature and native girls. Actually, he prefers to think of himself as *on* the frontier, where he can indulge his penchant for comparison and contrast, and talk endlessly about (for example) syphilis. Introduced by Christian zeal and spread by pagan license, the disease splendidly illustrates his already sardonic view of civilized-savage reciprocities. Melville, of course, remains uncommitted. Rejecting alike an uncritical acceptance of the purely savage (specifically cannibalism, but more comprehensively the mindless existence) and an uncritical insistence that all cultures conform to one dull standard, he concludes: "Truth, who loves to be centrally located, is again found between the two extremes," as of course in America it was always supposed to be. With this embryonic frontier metaphor, Melville established the central line he would follow in book after book, a line falling between European civilization, as played at by the Americans, and reversion to barbarism, another New World pastime. Like all the major writers in the tradition of Cooper, he had somehow to discover a neutral ground including the best of each and transcending both. But in *Typee*, the results of his quest were ultimately negative; and generally they were to be so for Melville, except as his aesthetic achievement may be thought to encompass and surpass the basic cultural contradictions of his milieu. Despite the manifold attractions of the Typees, the novel's typifying figure is the King of Oahu, who "has lost the noble traits of the barbarian, without acquiring the redeeming graces of a civilized being."

Of *Omoo: A Narrative of Adventures in the South Seas* (1847), Melville wrote his English publisher: "I think you will find it a fitting successor to 'Typee'; inasmuch as the latter book delineates Polynisian Life in its primitive state—while the new work, represents it, as affected by intercourse with the whites."[10] However inaccurately, this blurb sufficiently conveys the amateur anthropologist's renewed determination to come to the point. Again we find savagery (in each of Melville's books, there is something left over from the one before), and "pioneers" (if only in the persons of a few foolish missionaries). Again we find the degrading and arrested frontier (Cooper's Leatherstocking formula turned inside out), its victims "years ago brought to a stand, where all that is corrupt in barbarism and civilization unite, to the exclusion of the virtues of either state; like other

[10] *Letters*, p. 53. Cf. Timothy Flint: "At the time, when this history commences, they [the Shoshonee Indians] might still have been considered a simple, unchanged and unsophisticated people. This narrative contemplates them at the point of the first palpable influence of the introduction of money, and what we call civilization. It cannot fail to present a spectacle of great moral interest." *The Shoshonee Valley* (Cincinnati, 1830), I, 24-25. In *Typee* (ch. 17), Melville summed up Polynesian felicity "in one word—no Money!"

uncivilized beings brought into contact with Europeans, they must here remain stationary until utterly extinct." Again we find explicit contrast, implicit comparison, of South Sea islanders and American Indians. "How different from the volatile Polynesian in this, as in all other respects, is our grave and decorous North American Indian. While the former bestows a name in accordance with some humorous or ignoble trait, the latter seizes upon what is deemed the most exalted or warlike." The planters Zeke ("born in the backwoods of Maine") and Shorty live in a "wilderness of woodland," and more specifically in a "cleared tract . . . level as a prairie," where "the nature of virgin soils in general" is a perpetual problem and topic of conversation. Tahitians ride horses "like Pawnee-Loups," and girdle trees—"sad monuments of the fate which befell the inhabitants of the valley." The protagonist introduces himself as "a sailor before the mast" who has previously wandered "in the interior" of Nukuheva, and was "detained" in "captivity" by "a primitive tribe of savages." He sails from the Marquesas to Tahiti through "the immense blank of the Western Pacific," an ambiguous term Melville was on the verge of learning to exploit, "considerable portions" of which "still remain wholly unexplored." In the Society Islands he makes himself sandals "from a bullock's hide, such as are worn by the Indians in California," and, retreating in imagination to a much earlier frontier, tries to prove Doctor Long Ghost an American by "throwing out a hint concerning Kentucky, as a land of tall men." As if transported from Dana's book to Hawaii, "Spanish hunters, men regularly trained to their calling upon the plains of California . . . mounted upon trained Indian mares" hunt cattle and traffic in hides. (Details very like these also appear in Francis A. Olmsted, *Incidents of a Whaling Voyage*, and Charles Wilkes, *Narrative of the U.S. Exploring Expedition*.) The more Melville thought of himself as an American writer—which inevitably involved both an ideological and an imagistic commitment to the West—the more he drew out the Western associations of his early travels, enhancing them, as always, with judicious raids on appropriate books.[11]

"Romance, as well as empire, it seems must travel westward," wrote a reviewer, breathlessly keeping up with Melville's course. "There is indeed no end to the illusions with which an active fancy may invest that vast Continent of Islands that lies outstretched in the great Pacific Ocean."[12] With *Mardi: And a Voyage Thither* (1849), Melville made a notable leap toward Westernizing the entire ocean, all it contained, and everything it could be made to stand for. Over and above the new spate of allusions, *Mardi* contains two overlapping allegories, both of which are concerned to explicate Melville's increasingly personal and aesthetic identification with the Great West. The mere presence of so much allegory indicates a major shift of vision. Whereas the first two books concentrated on savage life from a highly civilized point of view, *Mardi* is devoted to an examination of civilized life from a presumed native point of view. The character of Marbonna, in *Omoo*, affords us an almost perfect introduction to this new point of view: "a philosopher of nature—a wild heathen, moralizing upon the vices and follies of the Christian court of Tahiti—a savage, scorning the degeneracy of the people among whom fortune had thrown him." Marbonna is Herman Melville practicing a role—"White Taji, a sort of half-and-half deity"—which he would play, off and on, the rest of his days. Consequently the best Mardians, Media and Babbalanja, are idealized frontiersmen consummately comprehending the civilized virtues in a primitive context, and with a decidedly savage flair.

[11] Yet except for Dana, Parkman, and Hall, there is surprisingly little external evidence for Melville's appropriation of Western materials from published sources. Merton M. Sealts, Jr., "Melville's Reading"—*Harvard Library Bulletin*, II (1948), 141-163, and subsequent issues—necessarily concentrates on Melville's book holdings in the later years, when the West of his youth was a thing of the past. For information about Melville's relation to Cooper, see *Letters*, pp. 144-145, and his reviews of *The Sea Lions* and *The Red Rover* in the *Literary World*, IV (April 28, 1849), 370, and VI (March 16, 1850), 277.

[12] *Sartain's Union Magazine*, V (1849), 126.

In the famous passage about the poet Lombardo, Melville revealingly elaborates his own literary passions: "He did not build himself in with plans; he wrote right on; and so doing, got deeper and deeper into himself; and like a resolute traveller, plunging through baffling woods, at last was rewarded for his toils. 'In good time,' saith he, in his autobiography, 'I came out into a serene, sunny, ravishing region; full of sweet scents, singing birds, wild plaints, roguish laughs, prophetic voices. Here we are at last, then,' he cried; 'I have created the creative.' And now the whole boundless landscape stretched away. Lombardo panted; the sweat was on his brow; he off mantle; braced himself; sat within view of the ocean." If "the whole doctrine of symbolism is in these words,"[13] as it may well be, the whole doctrine of American symbolism is realized in a paradigmatic historical action, struggling through the forest in order to reach, first the prairie, and then the West Coast. Arriving in these places is the same as creating the creative because both achievements were inextricably involved with the national ambition to invent a new literature in terms of the new West. A typical Western novel often began with a comparable figurative action: "At length, issuing from the wood, I entered a prairie, more beautiful than any I had yet seen."[14] Melville, moreover, getting deeper and deeper into himself, is as much the West as Lombardo (assuming that as usual the Mississippi is the West as unifier): "And as the great Mississippi musters his watery nations: Ohio, with all his leagued streams; Missouri, bringing down in torrents the clans from the highlands; Arkansas, his Tartar rivers from the plain;—so, with all the past and present pouring in me, I roll down my billow from afar." In another passage the consciousness of genius is said to be " 'an empire boundless as the West.' " If the achievements of the poet are as much national as personal, they are also as much private

[13] Charles Feidelson, Jr., *Symbolism and American Literature* (Chicago, 1953), p. 173.
[14] Nathaniel Beverley Tucker, *George Balcombe* (New York, 1836).

as public. In *Omoo*, Melville alluded to "green solitudes inland," conceivably meaning the soul.

The general allegory of *Mardi* is relatively simple. The protagonist is engaged in a Thoreauvian quest for an absolute or essential West—reality, truth, God. Unfortunately, the geographical and spiritual implications of this quest are in almost total contradiction, and Melville is thereby driven to immolate his hero (and doubtless himself) upon a theory of eternal and inherently meaningless "progress," or process. It is no use arguing that Melville is really headed "westward, out of the West," into the East.[15] Despite all the decorative Orientalism, Melville not only makes it abundantly plain that Taji means to voyage West perpetually—penetrating "farther and farther into the watery wilderness"—but also that the East (or home of Christ) is the last place in the world he wants to be. In order to escape this dilemma, Melville was apparently willing to sail West out of the real world altogether, or even out of his imagined fictional world: a solution perhaps inevitable, given the inconvenient roundness of the globe, but unpromising for art.[16] Ignoring these obvious considerations, Melville from the opening pages launches his hero on "this western voyage," "cut off from all hope of returning," in company with the sun (Thoreau's Great Western Pioneer), whose demi-deity Taji purports to be. "It was," he somewhat too easily remarks, "our easiest course." "Westward," he has told us

[15] James Baird, *Ishmael* (Baltimore, 1956), p. 85.

[16] By the time of *Moby-Dick*, Melville knew better: "Round the world! There is much in that sound to inspire proud feelings; but whereto does all that circumnavigation conduct? Only through numberless perils to the very point whence we started" (ch. 52). Later still, he revealed what may have lain behind the general allegory: "While our visionaries have been looking to the South Seas as a sort of Elysium, the Polynesians themselves have not been without their dream, their ideal, their Utopia in the West. As Ponce de Leon hoped to find in Florida the fountain of perpetual youth, so the mystic Kamapiikai left the western shore of the island of Hawaii, where he suffered with his restless philosophy, hoping to find the joy-giving fountain and the people like to the gods." Quoted in Sealts, *Melville as Lecturer*, p. 172.

earlier, "lay numerous groups of islands, loosely laid down upon the charts, and invested with all the charms of dreamland"; and again: "Due west, though distant a thousand miles, stretched north and south an almost endless Archipelago, here and there inhabited, but little known; and mostly unfrequented, even by whalemen, who go almost everywhere." So Taji continues his "passage to the westward" until he arrives at Mardi, where his course fortunately takes a different shape (circular). But when Mardi is exhausted, Taji can only begin again, and on the last page he is still going, direction unspecified but not very difficult to guess. *Mardi* is nearly as irresponsibly picaresque as *Omoo*, and its general allegory is part-&-parcel unworkable.

With some propriety, *Mardi* contains Melville's most overblown apostrophes to the Western spirit. "Oh, reader, list! I've chartless voyaged. With compass and the lead, we had not found these Mardian isles. . . . And if it harder be than e'er before to find new climes, when now our seas have oft been circled by ten thousand prows,—much more the glory! But this new world here sought is stranger far than his, who stretched his vans from Palos. It is the world of mind. . . . In bold quest thereof, better to sink in boundless deeps, than float on vulgar shoals; and give me, ye gods, an utter wreck, if wreck I do." Such prayers are always granted in the terms of the asking. "Dreams! dreams! golden dreams," another bathetic passage runs, "endless, and golden, as the flowery prairies that stretch away from the Rio Sacramento, in whose waters Danae's shower was woven;— prairies like rounded eternities: jonquil leaves beaten out; and my dreams herd like buffaloes, browsing on to the horizon, and browsing on round the world; and among them, I dash with my lance, to spear one, ere they all flee." But there is still worse:

West, West! West, West! Whitherward point Hope and prophet-fingers; whitherward, at sunset, kneel all worshippers of fire; whitherward in mid-ocean, the great whales turn to die; whitherward face all the Moslem dead in Persia; whitherward lie Heaven and Hell!—West, West! Whitherward mankind and empires—flocks, caravans, armies, navies; worlds, suns, and stars all wend!—West, West!—Oh boundless boundary! Eternal goal! Whitherward rush, in thousand worlds, ten thousand thousand keels! Beacon, by which the universe is steered!—Like the north star, attracting all needles! Unattainable forever; but forever leading to great things this side thyself!—Hive of all sunsets!—Gabriel's pinions may not overtake thee!

Melville moves from his general to his specific allegory through ambiguities inherent in the term New World. On their circular tour, the voyagers visit Vivenza (the United States), "a fine country in the western part of Mardi," the fundamental part of Kolumbo (the Western Hemisphere) —" 'last sought, last found . . . pray Oro, it be not squandered foolishly,' " the prevailing sentiment and moral of the Leatherstocking Tales. Here if anywhere the sentimental poet looks to find Yillah, America's bleached Beatrice; the skeptical philosopher wonders; the pragmatic historian seems to think it less likely she dwells " 'in the wild wilderness of Vivenza, than in the old vineyards of Porpheero,' " or Europe. In the specific as distinguished from the general allegory, Melville often makes sense, if not very original sense. Did not Vivenza's bards, he inquires, leaving the questionable question unanswered, pronounce its people "a fresh start in the Mardian species; requiring a new world for their full development?"

In this comparatively realistic context, issues which prove insoluble in the perversely anti-historical general allegory are at least definable. Even Melville's wilder demographic predictions lie within the confines of possibility: " ' 'Tis the old law:—the East peoples the West, the West the East; flux and reflux. And time may come, after the rise and fall of nations yet unborn, that, risen from its future ashes [predicated on the revolutionary violence of 1848], Porpheero shall be the promised land, and from her surplus hordes Kolumbo people it.' " Time is always on the American side, together with space, the American correlative of time. The Temple of Freedom (or Federal Constitution) is upheld by thirty pillars of palm, "four quite green; as if recently added; and beyond these, an almost interminable vacancy, as if all the palms in Mardi were, at some future time, to aid in upholding that fabric." The green palms are Texas, Florida, Iowa, and Wisconsin; Mardi (the whole world) may or may not be a slip of the pen for Vivenza.

The young Melville's more explicit views of the Vivenzan West are largely conventional. He subscribes to the safety valve theory, which was at least as old as Franklin, finding in the " 'wild western waste,' " temporary insurance against the age-old horrors of Europe. American liberty was fathered by the Pilgrims, he tells us, and nursed in the woods. These are the clichés of the schoolroom. But Melville is sometimes capable of diving for less superficial truth. If the democratic virtues are nurtured by the wild woods, and the woods are disappearing, then inevitably " 'the recoil must come,' " as Frederick Jackson Turner was dramatically to observe several decades after the event.[17] Already there is ample evidence of human ability to misconstrue the freedom of the wild woods. The silliest man in Vivenza is Alanno of Hio-Hio, a chieftain from "a distant western valley" (Senator William Allen of Ohio, chairman of the Foreign Affairs Committee, a notorious loudmouth and warmonger, especially on the Oregon Question). Unfortunately, he is all too typical of the new West, for whose actual inhabitants the best Melville can say is that "they were a fine young tribe, nevertheless. Like strong new wine they worked violently in becoming clear. Time, perhaps, would make them all right." Their worst vice is political rapacity, several times

---

[17] Others had made the same observation long before Melville. In *Recollections of The Last Ten Years* (Boston, 1826), Timothy Flint wisely wrote: "Alas! for the moving generation of the day, when the tide of advancing backwoodsmen shall have met the surge of the Pacific. They may then set them down and weep for other worlds" (p. 203).

mentioned in the context of Manifest Destiny—a doctrine to which young Melville was not always immune—and conclusively demonstrated in terms of Indian despoliation. "Not yet wholly extinct in Vivenza were its aboriginal people, a race of wild Nimrods and hunters, who year by year were driven farther and farther into remoteness, till, as one of their sad warriors said, after continual removes along the log, his race was on the point of being remorselessly pushed off the end." Is it Melville's amateurish inconsistency, or the hint of a deeper meaning, that in the same allegory the Americans themselves appear as Indians? Perhaps another clue lurks in Melville's prophetic disgust over the California Gold Rush, whitherward all good Americans were soon to be so feverishly wending, according to the forty-niners in the poet's vision, to "die in golden graves." Surely this vision is strikingly at odds with the endless golden dreams browsing around the Rio Sacramento.

But on the whole, Melville was now on target. Some of his readers perhaps were not. George W. Curtis spoke warmly of *Mardi* as "essentially American . . . although not singing Niagara or the Indians."[18] It is hard to know what more he wanted. Both within and without the two allegories, Western allusions in *Mardi* are all but innumerable. Many of these references concern Indians, to whom Melville was beginning to attach a far wider variety of meanings than the simple ambivalences of *Typee*. Leaving his avenging pursuers in the rear, Taji direly remarks: "Let the Oregon Indian through brush, bramble, and brier, hunt his enemy's trail, far over the mountains and down in the vales; comes he to the water, he snuffs idly in air." Volcanic Mardian islands emit smoke "as from Indian wigwams in the hazy harvest-moon," a comparison simultaneously soothing and smoldering. Near Taji's native dwelling, old Jarl settles down "in a little wigwam in the grove," and later the peripatetic talkers send up smoke as from "a Michigan wigwam." Teeth in the world of Mardi are valued "very much as belts of wampum among the Winnebagoes of the North."

[18] *Nile Notes of a Howadji* (New York, 1851), p. 201.

A self-exiled Tapparian is "like poor Logan the last of his tribe." Not only Montezuma and Powhattan, but "the Red Man's Great Spirit gave suppers." Melville's references to the Indian run the whole range of emotion from the pleasures of eating and drinking to the terrors of annihilation. In the best American literary tradition (Hawthorne, Poe, *et al.*), Death is a wild Indian driving us (bison, people) " 'into his treacherous fold.' "[19]

Despite their ubiquity, most of Melville's early Western references are incidental, and not worth troubling about except as they prepare an appreciation of similar aspects in the later masterpieces. In *Mardi*, the references are likely to turn up in catalogs (e.g., the Illinois mounds were not reared in a day, nor Kentucky's Mammoth Cave dug), or in the interminable Mardian similes (a sword from a swordfish is "inflexible as Crocket's rifle tube; no doubt, as deadly"). It is of some interest, on the other hand, that Melville's Western references are preponderantly farther West than his predecessors'. His Indians are more often than theirs Plains Indians. He is fascinated with bison. (At one point, savages are bison; at another point, bison are worlds.) And he is positively in love with the prairies, which he is beginning to identify with the sea: "It's famous botanizing, they say, in Arkansas' boundless prairies; I commend the student of Ichthyology to an open boat, and the ocean moors of the Pacific." The force of that remark is about equally to discriminate and to join the two topographies. Elsewhere, Melville comes even nearer a complete fusion, yet still maintains a rhetorical distinction: "Over that tideless sea we sailed; and landed right, and landed left. . . . As, after wandering round and round some purple dell, deep in a boundless prairie's heart, the baffled hunter plunges in; then, despairing, turns once more to gain the open plain; even so we seekers now curved round our keels; and from that inland sea emerged. The universe again before us; our quest, as

[19] See also Melville to Hawthorne (*Letters*, p. 132), where the Indian is an obvious—though here obviously playful—symbol for death and destruction.

wide." This passage is in the chapter opening "West, West!"

Finally, in *Mardi* we find for the first time in Melville's writing a notable efflorescence of frontier metaphors, chiefly but not exclusively philosophical in nature. Unlike Ireland, Scotland gives England no trouble, " 'for, geographically one, the two populations insensibly blend at the point of junction,' " a mild figurative echo of the old miscegenation problem at home, and a good example of the American frontier figure being reapplied to analogous situations abroad. But Melville's frontiers are only rarely innocuous. In a calm, "the two gray firmaments of sky and water seemed collapsed into a vague ellipsis. . . . And this inert blending and brooding of all things seemed gray chaos in conception." (In *Omoo*, also, there was a "grayish image of chaos in a sort of sliding fluidity.") Describing a previous calm, Melville offers an even more striking model of the American frontier, equally expressive of horrified dismay: it seems as if the ship must have "drifted into the outer confines of creation, the region of the everlasting lull, introductory to a positive vacuity." By no casuistry can this figure be reconciled with the Western dithyrambs of *Mardi*, for if the "outer confines of creation" are by literary origin the farthermost advances of American civilization, what are the "everlasting lull" and the "positive vacuity"? What but the fabulous frontier, the wondrous West? Something in Melville does not love them, despite his growing fascination with "things infinite in the finite; and dualities in unities."

Between novels—if indeed the harried young author ever was—Melville kept his hand in with book reviewing, of which the most significant instance (not counting "Hawthorne and His Mosses" as a review) was his examination of Francis Parkman's *The California and Oregon Trail* (1849).[20] Melville begins by objecting to the pretentious and misleading title, and then passes to a far more serious charge: Indian-hating. He takes particular umbrage at Park-

[20] The *Literary World*, IV (March 31, 1849), 291-293. That Melville later regretted having attacked Parkman (*Letters*, p. 96) hardly means that he changed his mind about the moral issue involved.

man's saying "that it is difficult for any white man, after a domestication among the Indians, to hold them much better than brutes," and at Parkman's further insinuation that "the slaughter of an Indian is indifferent as the slaughter of a buffalo."[21] On the contrary, as Melville argues with a new-found eloquence: "We are all of us—Anglo-Saxons, Dyaks, and Indians—sprung from one head, and made in one image. And if we regret this brotherhood now, we shall be forced to join hands hereafter." But the rest of the book Melville praises without stint, mostly by paraphrase and extended quotation, incidentally dwelling on some of his own favorite images (Indians as smokers, prairie as ocean). "He who desires to throw himself unreservedly into all the perilous charms of prairie life," he exclaims, "in short, he who desires to quit Broadway and the Bowery—though only in fancy—for the region of wampum and calumet, the land of beavers and buffaloes, birch canoes and 'smoked buckskin shirts,' will do well to read Mr. Parkman's book." Melville had obviously read Mr. Parkman's book with care and relish. It apparently confirmed in him an already long-standing commitment to the literary West, and supplied a few topics for further meditation.

In *Redburn: His First Voyage* (1849), Melville most nearly approached Dana. The protagonist is a Western innocent of sorts, some of whose supercilious manner may well be parodic of Parkman, and the novel's main point is the impact of sea and civilization (naturally "savage") upon his "roving disposition" and "young inland imagination." Aboard the *Highlander*, the veteran sailors incessantly bait this landlubberly youth, "advising me as soon as ever I got home to pin my ears back, so as not to hold the wind, and sail straight away into the interior of the country, and never stop until deep in the bush, far off from the least running brook . . . and out of sight of even the smallest

[21] I am quoting Melville, of course. Examples of the kind of thing that annoyed him most may be examined in *The California and Oregon Trail* (New York, 1849), pp. 202, 316-317.

puddle of rainwater."²² Returning to the United States, Redburn imagines that the ship "ploughed the watery prairie," the metaphor dramatically sustained by the fact that the lonely adolescent can almost smell home: "Even from that desert of sand-hillocks [Cape Cod]—methought I could almost distinguish the fragrance of the rose-bush my sisters and I had planted, in our far inland garden at home. Delicious odors are those of our mother earth; which like a flower-pot set with a thousand shrubs, greets the eager voyager from afar." Even "mother earth," tritest of clichés, freshens a little in this context, for of course it is his own mother Redburn has in mind. The very nails were drawn from the boat when the song of the West was properly sung; it requires an act of will to remember that Redburn does not live on the prairie at all, but in upstate New York.

If *Redburn*'s fictional world is affected by the literary West, there will naturally be Indians in it. The improvident greenhorn himself appears as an aboriginal infant, sleeping without mattress on the bare boards of a pitching bunk, "like an Indian baby tied to a plank, and hung up against a tree like a crucifix." Later, at a rural church near Liverpool, the local populace stares at him: "No Indian, red as a deer, could have startled the simple people more." The evil sailor Jackson is a different kind of savage (bad Indian), though the language through which he comes to us is suspiciously tainted by Wellingborough Redburn's Sunday School background: "He was a horrid desperado; and like a wild Indian, whom he resembled in his tawny skin and high cheek-bones, he seemed to run amuck at heaven and earth. He was a Cain afloat." Redburn's imagination is inland *and* bromidic, and the two qualities seem to be loosely related. "We talk of the Turks, and abhor the cannibals; but may not some of *them* go to heaven before some of

²² Cf. *Two Years Before the Mast* (New York, 1840): " 'Go away, salt water!' says Tom. 'As soon as I get both legs ashore, I'm going to shoe my heels, and button my ears behind me, and start off into the bush, a straight course, and not stop till I'm out of the sight of salt water!' " (p. 450).

us? We may have civilized bodies and yet barbarous souls."

In the course of his talkative ramble, Redburn compares his sea outfit with the Texas rangers' (shirt collar and spurs); speaks knowingly of Iowa fever and boarding-houses, concluding that "they are very ill-bred and un-polished in the western country"; imagines the Gulf Stream "a sort of Mississippi of hot water flowing through the ocean"; pointedly prefers his precious *Picture of Liverpool* to "the brief, pert, and unclerkly handbooks to Niagara and Buffalo of the present day"; likens interlocking Liver-pool docks to "the great American chain of lakes"; indulges in the usual Melvillean references to Kentucky (tall men), prairies (flowery or burning), and buffalo; tells English acquaintances about the Ohio River and Illinois (where he has never been, but Melville has); and vacuously rhapso-dizes on German immigrants, Wisconsin crops, and Amer-ica's imperial potentialities: "On this Western Hemisphere all tribes and people are forming into one federated whole; and there is a future which shall see the estranged children of Adam restored as to the old hearthstone in Eden. The other world beyond this, which was longed for by the de-vout before Columbus' time, was found in the New; and the deep-sea lead, that first struck these soundings, brought up the soil of Earth's Paradise." Even the vague symbolical West of *Mardi* reappears in Redburn's youthful meditation on the compass: "I wondered how it was that it pointed north, rather than south or west; for I do not know that any reason can be given why it points in the precise direc-tion it does. One would think, too, that, as since the begin-ning of the world almost, the tide of emigration has been setting west, the needle would point that way; whereas, it is forever pointing its fixed forefinger toward the Pole."

Minor characters help fill out the inland idea. Redburn's aristocratic friend Harry Bolton is resolved "to precipitate himself upon the New World, and there carve out a fresh fortune," for even so far from his customary haunts as Liverpool, he is "as much in a foreign land, as if he were already on the shores of Lake Erie." Apparently he thinks "that we Yankees lived in wigwams and wore bear-skins," and, upon arriving in New York, exults: " 'Let's see something of these United States of yours. I'm ready to pace from Maine to Florida; ford the Great Lakes; and jump the River Ohio, if it comes in the way.' " On the passage out, Larry and *Gun-Deck* debate the relative merits of savagery and "snivelization," *Gun-Deck* in particular providing a vehicle for Melville's continuing assault on Parkmanism.[23] "He had served in the armed steamers during the Seminole War in Florida, and had a good deal to say about sailing up the rivers there, through the everglades, and popping off Indians on the banks. . . . It was a rat-killing war, he said." Melville would return to this subject.

Meanwhile his nationalistic harangue continued in *White-Jacket; or, The World in a Man-of-War* (1850). "God has predestinated, mankind expects, great things from our race; and great things we feel in our souls. . . . We are the pioneers of the world; the advance-guard, sent on through the wilderness of untried things, to break a new path in the New World that is ours. In our youth is our strength; in our inexperience, our wisdom." This was high-water mark for Melville's jingoistic Westernism, and the tide was already turning. As White-Jacket has previously told us, "We [sailors] expatriate ourselves to nationalize with the universe." Concurrently, Melville's ambivalent fury at both civilized and savage inhumanity intensified. Abating somewhat his former pleasure in cultural disparity as a means of puncturing the pretensions of all, he now desired to dwell on a shared capacity for disaster and nihilating, or in other words that passionate sense of Innate Depravity and Original Sin which he was soon to visit upon poor Hawthorne. "But as the whole matter of war is a thing that smites common sense and Christianity in the face; so everything connected with it is utterly foolish, unchristian, barbarous,

[23] *Gun-Deck* may equally derive from the sailor in J. Ross Browne's *Etchings of a Whaling Cruise* (London, 1846), who "entered the navy of the United States, and went to Florida on an Indian-hunting expedition" (p. 184). Melville reviewed this book for the *Literary World*, March 6, 1847.

brutal, and savouring of the Feejee Islands, cannibalism, saltpetre, and the devil." A few pages later, even that slight whiff of comedy has blown away: "War almost makes blasphemers of the best of men, and brings them all down to the Feejee standard of humanity."

The *White-Jacket* Indians are as various as those in *Redburn*. Their cheerful council-fire is an aboriginal equivalent of the metropolitan club; and Indian sachems circulating the pipe suggest "peace, charity, and goodwill, friendly feelings, and sympathizing souls." The Commodore is as "mysterious and voiceless in his authority as the Great Spirit of the Five Nations." In another passage, the sailors tear "the tough hide from their pork, as if they were Indians scalping Christians." Conversely, but less comically, a braggart marine private (native-born American) tells "a surprising tale of his hand-to-hand encounter with Osceola, the Indian chief, whom he fought [in the Florida everglades] one morning from daybreak till breakfast-time." But the most memorable Indian passage in *White-Jacket*—or perhaps in all Melville's writing—is the allegedly remembered impression of "a scene once witnessed in a pioneer village on the western bank of the Mississippi. . . . One florid crimson evening in July, when the red-hot sun was going down in a blaze, and I was leaning against a corner in my huntsman's frock, lo! there came stalking out of the crimson west a gigantic redman, erect as a pine, with his glittering tomahawk, big as a broad-axe, folded in martial repose across his chest. Moodily wrapped in his blanket, and striding like a king on the stage, he promenaded up and down the rustic streets, exhibiting on the back of his blanket a crowd of human hands, rudely delineated in red; one of them seemed recently drawn." According to a moccasined pioneer bystander, this man is " 'the *Red-Hot Coal*,' " and each hand represents a victim; he has just come from the local sign-painter's shop with a new ornament. Doing the Indian the justice of applying to him the same ethical standards he would apply to himself, Melville moralizes on this outrageous savagery, and then equates it with more complex modes of barbarism, ending with the familiar question: "Are there no Moravians in the Moon, that not a missionary has yet visited this poor pagan planet of ours, to civilize civilization and christianize Christendom?" The savage is unquestionably threatening, theatrical, bizarre; his tomahawk is too big; he stalks; the entire performance, on the part of both nature and man (red-hot sun, *Red-Hot Coal*), is florid and rhetorical. The very terms of Melville's question make plain that this is neither a realistic picture of the Indian nor primarily a criticism of him, but a generalized portrait of mankind, especially in his North American phase. Significantly, the tomahawk looks like a broad-axe.

Quite apart from these darkening ethical tones, and a little at odds with them, the old parade of comparatively superficial Western allusions continues unchecked. In a rare moment of nautical skylarking, *"Kentucky bites* were given, and the *Indian hug* exchanged"; the narrator imagines swinging his hammock "on a high bluff of the Mississippi," and declares martial law as cruel and untameable as Missouri grizzly bears. According to Jack Chase, at the battle of Navarino " 'the bay was covered with masts and yards, as I have seen a raft of snags in the Arkansas River' "; Greece, from the depredations of Turkey, is "that tomahawked state"; a happy fool named Landless walks the deck "as if it were broad as a prairie." The purser's steward (incipient confidence-man) has "been a clerk in a steamer on the Mississippi River; an auctioneer in Ohio." Melville predicts the Panama Canal, foresees travelers boarding trains at Cape Cod for Astoria, and envisages Oregon's beau monde vacationing in the Spice Islands. "Such must be our national progress." Melville's continental imagination is still in the ascendant, and his island imagination has almost sunk below the horizon. "With this huge Lake Ontario [water in the hold] in us, the mighty *Neversink* [Melville's ship the *United States* and Melville's country the United States] might be said to resemble the united continent of the Eastern Hemisphere—floating in a vast ocean herself, and having a Mediterranean floating in her." Untangling that com-

254

plicated image, we find the Great Lakes identified with the Mediterranean, so that the Midwest becomes the corresponding birthplace of New World civilization. One night White-Jacket and his saturnine friend Nord (he who stalks off into the woods at the end of the voyage) "scoured all the prairies of reading," but another time Jack Chase (who was English) argued that " 'there never was a very great man yet who spent all his life inland. A snuff of the sea, my boy, is inspiration.' " Yet finally, "far inland, in that blessed clime whitherward our frigate now glides, the last wrong in our frigate will be remembered no more," inland now being Heaven. There seems to be a dialogue going on in Melville's heart between inland and ocean, toward both of which he yearned but which he was unable at the moment entirely to reconcile.

Even Staten Land, metaphysically considered (and rhetorically inflated), is at several analogous removes Western. Seen from the sea its "far inland pinnacles loomed up, like the border of some other world. Flashing walls and crystal battlements, like the diamond watch-towers along heaven's furthest frontier." Cape Horn is "this extremity of both the inhabitable and uninhabitable world," a description simultaneously suggesting the limits of American settlement —especially when preceded by references to buffalo-robe shirts, mooseskin drawers, and wigwams—and the limits of existence. The novel's climax occurs at the hither edge of the latter extremity, when White-Jacket plummets from a yardarm. "Next moment the force of my fall was expended; and there I hung, vibrating in the mid-deep. What wild sounds then rang in my ear! One was a soft moaning, as of low waves on the beach; the other wild and heartlessly jubilant, as of the sea in the height of a tempest. Oh soul! thou then heardest life and death: as he who stands upon the Corinthian shore hears both the Ionian and Aegean waves. The life-and-death poise soon passed; and then I found myself slowly ascending, and caught a dim glimmering of light."

Melville's finest prose to date may serve to mark the

end of his early Western travels, which was also the end of his literary apprenticeship. In real life, and then in retrospective imagination, he had voyaged inland and overseas, and everywhere he went was in one way or another the West; but he had not, except occasionally, really journeyed very far into the depths of American civilization, or of himself, though he had spoken of doing both. When he wrote Dana the letter about his "White Jackets or Redburns," he also made the first surviving reference to his new book, "the 'whaling voyage,'" and nothing in his remarks suggests a book substantially different from his previous books. In hindsight, however, it is easy to see that practically all the elements of *Moby-Dick* were now at hand —all, that is, except the aesthetic authority required to transfigure elements into major form. Between *White-Jacket* and *Moby-Dick*, Melville himself may be said to have hung in mid-deep. Surely for him too there were moments of wild jubilation, and more moments of soft dismay. Surely for him too there was a feeling of ascending, slowly, and of catching a dim, or perhaps not so dim, glimmering of the light. We have scripture for it.

2. *MOBY-DICK*

Six months into the first draft of his major novel, Melville met Hawthorne, and began to read him closely; from that moment, their careers intertwined. Aside from the altered character of *Moby-Dick; or, The Whale* (1851), finally dedicated to Hawthorne, "in Token of my admiration for his genius," the first fruit was a brilliantly provocative critical essay, wherein Melville committed himself more than ever to a tragic view of life, and to an extravagant though not unintelligent literary nationalism. In the beginning he spoke of "the enchanting landscape in the soul of this Hawthorne," and later this landscape was unmistakably identified for the American reader: "Your own broad prairies are in his soul; and if you travel away inland into his deep and noble nature, you will hear the far roar of his Niagara."[1] Hawthorne's interior was the interior of the continent; in that, his Americanism consisted; and if it was also true, as the same paragraph concluded, that "genius, all over the world, stands hand in hand, and one shock of recognition runs the whole circle round," then Melville too was galvanically interior, Western, and American. Arguing that Shakespeare was by no means unapproachable, but had in fact recently been approached, Melville paid Hawthorne a more than handsome compliment and welcomed himself to the same inland company. "Men, not very much inferior to Shakespeare, are this day being born on the banks of the Ohio"; born of water, apparently, and of the Western spirit. Melville may secretly have alluded to the conception of a new masterpiece, as magnificent as *The Scarlet Letter*—recently published but only barely mentioned in this essay—or even more magnificent. If so, his great democratic God was surely to bear him out in it.

Behind the inscrutable richness of feature, behind the manifold complications of development and suggestion, *Moby-Dick* is reasonably simple, and even, given the nature of American civilization halfway through the nineteenth century, predictable. Basically, this is a hunting story. Not only does the novel as a whole take that shape, but many parts of it do ("The First Lowering," "Stubb Kills a Whale," "Stubb & Flask kill a Right Whale," "The Pequod meets the Virgin," "The Grand Armada," and so forth to the end); the ongoing action is timed by preliminary, intermittent actions metonymous of the overarching design; aside from their relatively harmless conclusions, each of these actions is the novel in miniature. And an American hunting story, regardless of ostensible locale, was inevitably a story about the West. As Washington Irving remarked in

---

[1] "Hawthorne and His Mosses" appeared in the *Literary World* for August 17 and 24, 1850, and is best edited in Willard Thorp, *Herman Melville, Representative Selections* (New York, 1938). Other quotations in this section are from *Moby-Dick; or, The Whale*, ed. Luther S. Mansfield and Howard P. Vincent (New York, 1952), or, in the case of *Israel Potter* and *Mardi*, from *The Works of Herman Melville* (London, 1922-1924).

Astoria (1836): "A western trapper is like a sailor; past hazards only stimulate him to further risks. The vast prairie is to the one what the ocean is to the other, a boundless field of enterprise and exploit. However he may have suffered in his last cruise, he is always ready to join a new expedition; and the more adventurous its nature, the more attractive is it to his vagrant spirit." Ishmael opens the book by announcing his assumed name, preparatory to joining the greatest expedition of all, and then says of himself: "I am tormented with an everlasting itch for things remote. I love to sail forbidden seas, and land on barbarous coasts." Over and beyond the name's Biblical associations ("He will be a wild man"),[2] Ishmael (The Wanderer, Mr. Omoo) immediately involves us with a representative man from the lowest rung of the ladder in the social-stages-of-history theory—even if we are not specifically reminded of the famous ne'er-do-well frontiersman in Cooper's *Prairie*. Thus in the very first sentence Melville avails himself of the long-standing American ambivalence toward this hero-scapegoat figure to furnish a "low" hero for a story designed to subvert the entire theory: "I abominate all honorable respectable toils, trials, and tribulations of every kind whatsoever." In *Moby-Dick*, as so frequently in early American writing, the nomadic stage is not only the earliest form of society (or no-society), but clearly the best. "Normal" social roles are thereby reversed, savages becoming models for heroic emulation and shipowners subjects of ridicule. Ultimately, the reversal depends on Melville's identification of himself with the hunter, so that his own intellectual quests and feats appear as instances of the wider, or narrower, behavior of tracking and killing animals.

A further clue to essential meaning resides in the almost continuous Western references. Without adequate explanation of their presence in such profusion, this plethora of allusion may well strike an honest and sensitive reader as

---

[2] Parkman had quoted part of the Biblical tag (Genesis, xvi, 11-12) in connection with "fierce savages" (i.e., "bad Indians"), in *The California and Oregon Trail* (New York, 1849), p. 354.

gratuitous, puzzling, or even indecorous. For example, Melville evokes the barrenness of Nantucket ("no Illinois") by saying that three blades of grass in a day's walk constitute a "prairie," and tells us that the Nantucketer "lives on the sea, as prairie cocks in the prairie." ("Let America add Mexico to Texas, and pile Cuba upon Canada . . . two thirds of this terraqueous globe are the Nantucketer's.") Ahab's diabolical crew send their whaleboat along the water "like a horizontal burst boiler out of a Mississippi steamer." A few pages later, Flask falls to "rearing and plunging in the boat's stern like a crazed colt from the prairie." Then a squall at sea is said to "roar," "fork," and "crackle" around the ship "like a white fire upon the prairie," and even a legless London whaleman beggar's stump is joked about in terms of a stump in "the western clearings." The sailors sit on their boats' gunwales "like Ontario Indians," and Stubb's crew, watching him dig for ambergris, look "as anxious as gold-hunters." During "The Chase—Second Day" the crew's fears are routed by Ahab "as timid prairie hares that scatter before the bounding bison," and the same day, on viewing Moby Dick, they shout with "buckskin lungs." It is little help to be told that Texas is only a Fast-Fish "to that apostolic lancer, Brother Jonathan," or that Egyptian mummies measure less than "a modern Kentuckian in his socks." To be sure, Melville is here as always inordinately allusive, inordinately eclectic; but in *Moby-Dick* there are more references to the American West than to Polynesia (or England; or the ancient world; or the Near East; or the history of philosophy; or anything else); and all these references appear to head in one direction, as if arranging themselves along lines of force in a pre-existing magnetic field. There are almost more allusions to the West than to whaling; and the whales themselves, we quickly learn, are as often as not buffaloes.[8]

[8] Melville was undoubtedly piqued by Parkman's assertion that "except an elephant, I have seen no animal that can surpass a buffalo bull in size and strength. . . . At first sight of him every feeling of sympathy vanishes" (p. 401). On a very superficial level,

Ishmael, of course, is a rather indifferent and desultory kind of hunter, except as he speaks for that hunter of hunters —or hunter *after* hunters—the author. Midway between them, and central to the action, stands Captain Ahab, pivoting on his peg, bloody and unbowed, literally and figuratively a man of the chase whose time is running out. Still, he eradicates evil like a reformer, and nature like a pioneer. As if he had once undergone Indian torture, "he looked like a man cut away from the stake, when the fire has overrunningly wasted all the limbs without consuming them." Appropriately, his doom, which Ishmael and Melville barely avoid, is prophesied by an old Gay Head squaw, for in nearly every conceivable way Ahab moves and has his being beyond the frontier, an "alien" to Christendom. "He lived in the world, as the last of the Grisly Bears lived in settled Missouri. And as when Spring and Summer had departed, that wild Logan of the woods, burying himself in the hollow of a tree, lived out the winter there, sucking his own paws; so, in his inclement, howling old age, Ahab's soul, shut up in the caved trunk of his body, there fed upon the sullen paws of its gloom!" Ahab is simultaneously hunter and hunted—he hunts himself—and therefore as isolated as the game disappearing just ahead of the Indian who hunted it until driven from the scene by encroachments of the white man's frontier. In *Moby-Dick*, Melville's Western epic similes are likely to be thus concatenated, one significant action cunningly growing out of another. The "wild eyes" of the crew (or "braves") meet Ahab's, "as the bloodshot eyes of the prairie wolves meet the eye of their leader, ere he rushes on at their head in the trail of the bison; but, alas! only to fall into the hidden snare of the Indian." Again and again in these figures hunter and hunted coalesce, comprehending the complex predatory history of America's continental culture, and ominously hinting further traps to be sprung.

Moby-Dick is a point-by-point refutation of practically everything in Parkman.

Melville's most inclusive intention is constantly to insinuate some sort of sly connection between Ahab's business with the White Whale and America's business with the Far West; and indeed we must never forget that his whole early career (1846-1851) coincided with the most dramatic phase of American expansion, an expansion that in these years carried well beyond the West Coast into what was popularly called the Western Ocean. In the earlier encounter, when Moby Dick took his leg, Ahab "had dashed at the whale, as an Arkansas duellist at his foe, blindly seeking with a six inch blade to reach the fathom-deep life of the whale. . . . He piled upon the whale's white hump the sum of all the general rage and hate felt by his whole race from Adam down; and then, as if his chest had been a mortar, he burst his hot heart's shell upon it."[4] Ahab is also the *Pequod*, as the *Pequod* is in certain respects the ship of American state: "The rushing Pequod, freighted with savages, and laden with fire, and burning a corpse, and plunging into that blackness of darkness, seemed the material counterpart of her monomaniac commander's soul. . . . Uppermost was the impression, that whatever swift, rushing thing I stood on was not so much bound to any haven ahead as rushing from all havens astern." That is also my uppermost impression of the mid-nineteenth-century American craft Melville was so dangerously steering.

In *Israel Potter* (1855), Melville briefly presents his frontiersman as a temporary harpooneer, "whose eye and arm had been so improved by practice with his gun in the wilderness, [and who] now further intensified his aim, by darting the whale-lance"; he also listed, as if they were virtual equivalents, "wandering in the wilderness, and wandering upon the waters . . . felling trees, and hunting, and shipwreck, and fighting with whales, and all his other strange adventures." That is backwash from *Moby-Dick*, whose controlling metaphor—the image in which the other

---

[4] Cf. Parkman: "I made an attempt to ride up and stab her [a buffalo] with my knife; but the experiment proved such as no wise man would repeat" (quoted in Melville's review).

images swim, or upon which they float, or try to float—is the ocean (pre-eminently the Pacific) as American West.[5] This is the obvious explanation for all the Western references, and for the various identifications of Ahab as Grisly Bear, Logan, prairie wolf, and Arkansas duellist. "Across the wide trance of the sea, east nodded to west, and the sun over all." As always, the world is bipolar; unity, in this instance, derives from the sun, Melville's common symbol for reason. In the context of this central but relatively simple orientation, Melville is at liberty to regard any nautical action, person, or thing as if it were Western; conversely, he is free to regard any Western action, person, or thing as if it were oceanic. Thus he Americanizes— imaginatively speaking, he conquers—the world for his novel, while simultaneously he universalizes the sign in which he conquers. His exploits begin in the "Extracts," where "From 'Something' unpublished" (and obviously nonexistent) Melville quotes a passage alleging whalemen "to have indirectly hit upon new clews to that same mystic North-West Passage"; the preceding extract, from *McCulloch's Commercial Dictionary*, obliquely glanced at the same possibility. Then the whaleship is called "the pioneer in ferreting out the remotest and least known parts of the earth," best interpreter between civilization and savagery; hence, another frontiersman. Later still it is the whale himself who is superstitiously thought to have discovered a North-West Passage. As Babbalanja had remarked in *Mardi*: " 'Vainly, we [men] seek our North-West Passages—old alleys, and thoroughfares of the whales.' "

Such fancies, primarily aesthetic in intention, though historical in origin, spring endlessly from Melville's basic metaphor. The harpooneer snatches up his weapon "as readily from its rest as a backwoodsman swings his rifle from the wall"; the whaleman "goes and hunts for his oil,

[5] For earlier treatments of Melville's Western Ocean, see Constance Rourke, *American Humor* (New York, 1931), p. 192; Charles Olson, *Call Me Ishmael* (New York, 1947), pp. 12-13, 23, 114, 117; and Richard Chase, *Herman Melville* (New York, 1949), pp. 67-68.

so as to be sure of its freshness and genuineness, even as the
traveller on the prairie hunts up his own supper of game";
the whaleboat rides "light as a birch canoe." Everything
follows from the initial interchangeability of sea and West,
as if one transparent map were superimposed upon another,
but with an even more perfect mutuality than that comparison might suggest, for in Melville's major metaphor
neither term is permitted to dominate the other. It is quite
impossible to say whether ocean or West is tenor or vehicle,
just as it is impossible to say whether *Moby-Dick* is "really"
about whaling or about America's imperial thrust into the
waters beyond California. Both sides of the comparison are
geographies. Both geographies are vast, uncertain, and relatively immune to intellectual subjugation; they are irre-
ducible to each other or to anything else, but anything else
in the universe is reducible to them. This is a far grander
game than Poe's, who for the most part simply wrote
"South" when he meant "West." Melville means "ocean"
and he means "West"; further, he means each as each defines, identifies, and extends the other; finally, he means this
interacting extension to include, as imaginative probability,
the entire imaginable cosmos.

"The Town-Ho's Story," the main point of which comes
to the *Pequod* through the Indian Tashtego, is the almost
perfect illustration of this perfect ambiguity. Melville's
conception of Steelkilt as backwoods mariner, fusing in a
single personal image ocean and West, lies at the axis of the
novel:

> "This Lakeman, in the land-locked heart of our America,
> had yet been nurtured by all those agrarian freebooting
> impressions popularly connected with the open ocean.
> For in their interflowing aggregate, those grand fresh-
> water seas of ours,—Erie, and Ontario, and Huron, and
> Superior, and Michigan,—possess an ocean-like expan-
> siveness, with many of the ocean's noblest traits; with
> many of its rimmed varieties of races and of climes.
> They contain round archipelagoes of romantic isles, even

as the Polynesian waters do; in large part, are shored by two great contrasting nations, as the Atlantic is; they furnish long maritime approaches to our numerous territorial colonies from the East, dotted all round their banks; here and there are frowned upon by batteries, and by the goat-like craggy guns of lofty Mackinaw; they have heard the fleet thunderings of naval victories; at intervals, they yield their beaches to wild barbarians, whose red painted faces flash from out their peltry wigwams; for leagues and leagues are flanked by ancient and unentered forests, where the gaunt pines stand like serried lines of kings in Gothic genealogies; those same woods harboring wild Afric beasts of prey, and silken creatures whose exported furs give robes to Tartar Emperors; they mirror the paved capitals of Buffalo and Cleveland, as well as Winnebago villages; they float alike the full-rigged merchant ship, the armed cruiser of the State, the steamer, and the beech canoe; they are swept by Borean and dismasting blasts as direful as any that lash the salted wave; they know what shipwrecks are, for out of sight of land, however inland, they have drowned full many a midnight ship with all its shrieking crew. Thus, gentlemen, though an inlander, Steelkilt was wild-ocean born, and wild-ocean nurtured."

Steelkilt is further associated with two other frontier types from the Erie Canal, and later he calls himself a buffalo. His enemy Radney (alternately a Vineyarder or from Nantucket) is also "as vengeful and full of social quarrel as the backwoods seaman, fresh from the latitudes of buck-horn handled Bowie-knives." Radney is only a derivative or analogous Westerner, however, less heroic than Steelkilt. Not unexpectedly, Steelkilt's insulted manhood is vicariously revenged by Moby Dick—as West, not as divine justice—killing the tyrannical Radney.

In the light of Melville's interfusing Western Ocean, many watery phenomena assume clearer outline. In "The Spirit-Spout," for instance, "some thought there lurked a devilish charm, as for days and days we voyaged along, through seas so wearily, lonesomely mild, that all space, in repugnance to our vengeful errand, seemed vacating itself of life before our urn-like prow." The "Spirit-Spout" is conceivably related to the Western spirit, luring, receding, vacating, "treacherously beckoning us on and on, in order that the monster might turn round upon us, and rend us at last in the remotest and most savage seas." But still in American seas. Perhaps following Camoens, the *Pequod* sails East around the Cape of Good Hope—whereas the *Acushnet* went the other way, around Cape Horn—only to arrive at her Western Pacific by the backdoor. Melville's elementary geography lesson demonstrates that the farthest East is but the farthest West. When he conjectures that a stone lance embedded in the corpse of a captured whale "might have been darted by some Nor' West Indian long before America was discovered," or when he informs us that 13,000 whales are annually killed by Americans "on the nor' west coast," he means to suggest the West Coast from San Diego to Alaska and the ocean from California to China.[6] The *Pequod* suffers a typhoon in Japanese waters, but for Melville that is merely a hop, skip, and a jump past

[6] In Melville's day, "Northwest Coast" normally meant California, the Oregon Territory, and an indeterminate area farther on. How much the whole Pacific had come to seem an American lake, under the aegis of whaling, which was obviously an extension of pioneering, is nakedly revealed in (for example) Henry Wise, *Los Gringos* (New York, 1849), p. 391. For the "Western" implications of the chief whaling grounds, see the map from Commodore Charles Wilkes, *Narrative of the United States Exploring Expedition* (Philadelphia, 1844), conveniently reprinted in Howard P. Vincent, *The Trying-Out of Moby-Dick* (Boston, 1949), facing p. 113. Wilkes's own discussion (*Narrative*, v, 517-519) is also suggestive. In *Western America* (Philadelphia, 1849), he recommended a railroad from Lake Michigan to Oregon, so that whaling might be conducted directly from the West Coast (p. 113). In *The Whale and His Captors* (New York, 1850), Henry T. Cheever told how "the *northwest*, as all men know, became a very El Dorado to the intrepid American whalers" (p. 104). Melville later blamed the possibility of America's annexing Hawaii and other Pacific islands on "the whalemen of Nantucket and the Westward ho! of California." Merton M. Sealts, Jr., *Melville as Lecturer* (Cambridge, 1957), p. 179.

Sausalito, which at the time went by the name of Whalers' Harbor. Had the White Whale not interposed, the *Pequod* might have wrecked off Monterey.

Melville's fondness for figures blending prairie and ocean is only a special case of his generally identifying Pacific and West.[7] "There is, one knows not what sweet mystery about this sea," one of the sweetest passages begins, going on to St. John's imaginary Ephesian sod, and then returning to "these sea-pastures, wide-rolling watery prairies . . . for here, millions of mixed shades and shadows, drowned dreams, somnambulisms, reveries; all that we call lives and souls, lie dreaming, dreaming, still; tossing like slumberers in their beds; the ever-rolling waves but made so by their restlessness." The Pacific, so this meditation continues, "rolls the midmost waters of the world, the Indian ocean and Atlantic being but its arms. The same waves wash the moles of the new-built Californian towns, but yesterday planted by the recentest race of men, and lave the faded but still gorgeous skirts of Asiatic lands, older than Abraham. . . . Thus this mysterious, divine Pacific zones the world's whole bulk about; makes all coasts one bay to it. . . . Lifted by those eternal swells, you needs must own the seductive god, bowing your head to Pan." Under the coercion of prairie, the Pacific quietly takes the intentional shape of the Western frontier, all-embracing includer and reconciler of opposites, as it does in another magnificent prairie-sea passage, where Melville again meanders through verdant water and aqueous vegetation toward the metaphorical frontier:

[7] "For leagues and leagues . . . [vast meadows of brit] undulated round us, so that we seemed to be sailing through boundless fields of ripe and golden wheat"; or (immediately preceding the first day's encounter): "The ocean grew still more smooth; seemed drawing a carpet over its waves; seemed a noon-meadow." In "The Encantadas," Melville calls the view from Rock Rodondo "a boundless watery Kentucky. Here Daniel Boone would have dwelt content." *Piazza Tales*, ed. Egbert S. Oliver (New York, 1948), p. 163. All the popular Western writers worked the trope (sea-prairie-carpet) tirelessly.

These are the times, when in his whale-boat the rover softly feels a certain filial, confident, land-like feeling towards the sea; that he regards it as so much flowery earth; and the distant ship revealing only the tops of her masts, seems struggling forward, not through high rolling waves, but through the tall grass of a rolling prairie: as when the western emigrants' horses only show their erected ears, while their hidden bodies widely wade through the amazing verdure. . . . And all this mixes with your most mystic mood; so that fact and fancy, half-way meeting, interpenetrate, and form one seamless whole.

Not very mystically, but much in the manner of Hawthorne's great definition in "The Custom-House," the standard American metaphor identifies the prevailing aesthetic mode of *Moby-Dick*—reciprocal interpenetration of fact and fiction—or, for that matter, the aesthetic mode of American literature in its formative phase.

But the sea is prairie in only one of her several moods. Other times, she is undeniably "savage." So are killer whales, the Algerine porpoise, the harpooneers (who respond more fiercely and more knowingly to mention of the White Whale than the other men, as if they remember something), the entire crew, their language, their captain, and their crazy ship. According to Queequeg, even the god who created sharks " 'must be one dam Ingin.' " Queequeg himself is part Ingin. His "poncho" is decorated "with little tinkling tags something like the stained porcupine quills round an Indian moccasin." He carries a tomahawk-pipe, wears a scalp knot, and is alternatively described as in "the transition state" from savagery to civilization, or as "George Washington cannibalistically developed." In keeping with the literary traditions of his adopted land, Queequeg hails from an imaginary island "far away to the West and South. It is not down in any map; true places never are."[8] Actually

---

[8] In his lecture on the South Seas, Melville "mentioned several groups of islands that are not down on the maps." Newspaper report

he comes from the double map (watery West) and is only the last and most memorable of Melville's favorite Polynesian-Indians, engagingly idealized. His famous friendship with Ishmael appears to reflect the customs of both peoples, about which Melville would have read in his Western as well as in his South Sea sources. Clean, comely, delicate, polite, sensible, brawny, sagacious, devout, this "soothing savage" dominates the novel's opening movement, and inspires its finest speech: " 'We cannibals must help these Christians.' " With renewed gusto, Melville has returned to the firing line of *Typee*, and to the fascinatingly "wicked" idea of savagism, the *ne plus ultra* of humanity, modern man on or beyond the frontier of his own soul: "Long exile from Christendom and civilization inevitably restores a man to that condition in which God placed him, *i.e.* what is called savagery. Your true whale-hunter is as much a savage as an Iroquois. I myself am a savage." So is the artist of the beautiful, in this context a Hawaiian paddle-carver. So to Melville is Achilles, or perhaps he who carved the shield (Hephaistos-Homer). So is Albert Durer. Or as Thoreau said in *A Week on the Concord and Merrimack Rivers*, which Melville borrowed from his friend Evert Duyckinck in 1850: "Inside the civilized man stands the savage still in the place of honor."

Queequeg is an ideological link between Melville's old Polynesians with Indian qualities and his new Indians with universal qualities. For the archetypal hunting tale, American Indians were indispensable. "Where else but from Nantucket did those aboriginal whalemen, the Red-Men, first sally out in canoes to give chase to the Leviathan?" The rhetorical question indirectly dignifies the Red-Men more than Nantucket, and the word "aboriginal" is designedly ambiguous. "All whaleboats," we learn later, "carry certain curious contrivances, originally invented by the Nantucket Indians, called druggs." (Melville's whaling sources—espe-

---

quoted by Merrell R. Davis in "Melville's Midwestern Lecture Tour, 1859," *Philological Quarterly*, xx (1941), 49.

cially Henry Cheever, *The Whale and his Captors*—included such facts, but drew no special conclusions from them.) In technology as in prowess, the Indian is at the bottom of this affair called in modern times "whaling." There is also "the wondrous traditional story of how this island was settled by the red-men" (in the chapter on "Nantucket"), an Indian legend involving eagle and ocean and canoe and coffin and skeleton and bereaved parents, which evidently foreshadows the denouement of *Moby-Dick*.[9] The name of that "cannibal of a craft," the *Pequod*, "you will no doubt remember, was the name of a celebrated tribe of Massachusetts Indians, now extinct," another example of the hunter-hunted theme, and of the Anglo-Americans' way with the natives. On deck the Quaker owners drive their dubious bargains in what is repeatedly called a "wigwam," with a tufted top "where the loose hairy fibres [whale jaw-bones] waved to and fro like the top-knot on some old Pottowotamie Sachem's head." Pottowotamie was the name of a celebrated tribe not quite extinct in Melville's day, but only removed.

Because he appears first on the scene, Queequeg appropriates to himself nearly all the attention a modern reader is inclined to bestow upon mere savages. This is a pity, for in some ways Tashtego is more important to the book's economy; certainly, during the *Pequod*'s long cruise, he is more often present, and is usually glimpsed in attitudes isolated, contemplative, critical. "TASHTEGO (*Quietly smoking*.) That's a white man; he calls that fun: humph! I save my sweat." Like his fellow-savage, he is favored with great lines. To Stubb's " 'What d'ye say, Tashtego' "? he replies: " 'I say, pull like god-dam.' " He has a chapter all

[9] In a note to *Journal of a Visit to London and the Continent by Herman Melville, 1849-1850* (Cambridge, 1948), Eleanor Melville Metcalf reports that among the Gay Head Indians of Martha's Vineyard "the most important legends, including those about *a great white whale*, are still alive" (p. 170). In *Etchings of a Whaling Cruise* (New York, 1846), J. Ross Browne promised, but failed to deliver, "a marvelous yarn in relation to the capture of a white whale," presumably off "the Northwest Coast" (p. 448).

to himself, four lines long, and wholly impenetrable. Tashtego sights the first whale, and a number of others; if Stubb is the first to slaughter a Leviathan, that is because Tashtego is the *Pequod*'s ablest and most ardent harpooneer. " 'Woo-hoo! Wa-hee!' screamed the Gay-Header . . . raising some old war-whoop to the skies; as every oarsman in the strained boat involuntarily bounced forward with the one tremendous leading stroke which the eager Indian gave." Toward the end of this first kill, sunset makes all the sailors look like "red men," a detail conceivably drawn from Cooper's description of Leatherstocking in *The Pathfinder*. In another emblematic tableau, Tashtego sights the White Whale only a split second after Ahab, with whom he is so often closely associated, "Tashtego standing just beneath him . . . so that the Indian's head was almost on a level with Ahab's heel." Always he occupies a privileged-ironic position in the physical action, as fundamental hunter, fundamental victim, unitary and unifying; after all, it is *his* West, the particular home of the Indian (where his benefactors temporarily placed him, out of harm's way), which he pathetically helps Ahab destroy.[10] Sometimes he is a comic Indian, self-consciously playing the role, as when he pretends to scalp Dough-Boy. At other times, he is savage enough for anybody's taste. Only with the greatest regret, and on Stubb's orders, does he spare Pip. "He was full of the fire of the hunt. He hated Pip for a poltroon."

Tashtego chiefly represents the subterranean continuities of America's hunting culture. He is an "unmixed Indian from Gay Head, the most westerly promontory of Martha's Vineyard, where there still exists the last remnant of a village of red men, which has long supplied the neighboring island of Nantucket with many of her most daring harpooneers." Rising from logistic to historical considerations,

[10] In *Moby-Dick* hunting a particular whale is compared with hunting a particular Indian (p. 203). Flask also derives from popular legends of Indian-hating: "very pugnacious concerning whales, who somehow seemed to think that the great Leviathans had personally and hereditarily affronted him; and therefore it was a sort of point of honor with him, to destroy them whenever encountered."

Melville calls him "an inheritor of the unvitiated blood of those proud warrior hunters, who, in quest of the great New England moose, had scoured, bow in hand, the aboriginal forests of the main. But no longer snuffing in the trail of the wild beasts of the woodland, Tashtego now hunted in the wake of the great whales of the sea; the unerring harpoon of the son fitly replacing the infallible arrow of the sires." In somewhat the same fashion, Melville in *Moby-Dick*, dragging the native culture with him, passed from the backwoods to the open sea—or from the practicalities of American life to its poetics—while retaining and transforming the characteristic dynamics of the hunt, which are sometimes disastrous. The most notorious action performed by "Tashtego, that wild Indian," is unluckily falling into a whale's severed head, which in turn drops "like Niagara's Table-Rock into the whirlpool." The sinking head throbs and heaves, "as if that moment seized with some momentous idea; whereas it was only the poor Indian unconsciously revealing by those struggles the perilous depth to which he had sunk." It sounds a little like a parody of the ambivalences customarily displayed by humanitarian tracts about the helpless savage. But Tashtego is quickly delivered by the ever-helpful Queequeg, and soon afterward, Ishmael begins to call him "Tash"—as Ahab and Stubb previously do—an affectionate liberty he takes with no other man's name. The chapter concludes in high comedy, of the frontier variety, the poor Indian's peril finally suggesting the predicament of an Ohio honey-hunter who fell into the empty crotch of a tree and "died embalmed. How many, think ye, have likewise fallen into Plato's honey head, and sweetly perished there?"

Tashtego is most conspicuous at the end. On the first day, after Moby Dick has sounded, he sees the birds who see the whale. The third day a sea-hawk—the same hawk who stole Ahab's hat, and was elaborately compared with a Roman eagle?—carries off the *Pequod*'s whaling pennant.[11]

[11] For hawks and eagles, see the anti-patriotic proclamation in *Mardi*: " 'The eagle of Romara [Rome] revives in your own moun-

Tashtego is replacing it when the great whale nears, and "the red flag . . . then streamed itself straight out from him, as his own forward-flowing heart." Tashtego is the last person to whom ungodly, god-like Ahab speaks, turning away from sun and humanities, to address the White Whale only. And he is the last man on the *Pequod* to go down:

> But as the last whelmings intermixingly poured themselves over the sunken head of the Indian at the mainmast, leaving a few inches of the erect spar yet visible, together with long streaming yards of the flag, which calmly undulated, with ironical coincidings, over the destroying billows they almost touched;—at that instant, a red arm and a hammer hovered backwardly uplifted in the open air, in the act of nailing the flag faster and yet faster to the subsiding spar. A sky-hawk that tauntingly had followed the main-truck downwards from its natural home among the stars, pecking at the flag, and incommoding Tashtego there; this bird now chanced to intercept its broad fluttering wing between the hammer and the wood; and simultaneously feeling that etherial thrill, the submerged savage beneath, in his death-gasp, kept his hammer frozen there.

Exit Melville's first ship of fools, carrying Old Glory[12] and the screaming imperial eagle into the white vortex, her representative calamity hammered home by the submerging savage, the American Indian. Ishmael's is inevitably the final word ("orphan"); Tashtego's is the penultimate action (destruction).

---

tain bird, and once more is plumed for her flight. Her screams are answered by the vauntful cries of a hawk; his red comb yet reeking with slaughter. And one East, one West, those bold birds may fly, till they lock pinions in the midmost beyond.'" Here the hawk is probably France.

[12] So I suspect the flag should be interpreted, though in the text it is literally "the flag of Ahab" in which the drowning bird is wrapped, and it is only in the next sentence that the sea is a "shroud." In *Israel Potter* the American flag is a "glorified shroud" (ch. 17), and in "America" (*Battle-Pieces*) "the shining shroud" and "that starry shroud."

Of course, Ishmael does most of the talking, and what he talks about most is whales. He is always the cetological pioneer—he uses that word—who tries all things, and achieves what he can. With his Transcendental captain, he thinks that " 'not the smallest atom stirs or lives on matter, but has its cunning duplicate in mind.' " But his cunning mind is no duplicate of schematic Ahab's. To consider the whale from Ishmael's angle is to entertain a multiplicity of linked analogies, many of them too intangible for clear expression, some of them frankly contradictory or incoherent. But through all possible wallows of interpretation, one point is clear enough: the whale is the king of creation (province of the Pacific), and consequently king of the West.[13] As Melville's brother Allan said, he is "the hero of the volume";[14] more accurately, he shares this honor with Ishmael; and of course he wins. Ishmael also wins. "Such, and so magnifying, is the virtue of a large and liberal theme!" The hero's mighty bulk is the body of America, extended in a Westerly direction. His stomach is "the great Kentucky Mammoth Cave." His teeth are extracted by the three savage harpooneers, "as Michigan oxen drag stumps of old oaks out of wild woodlands." His brow is "full of a prairie-like placidity"—"I but put that brow before you. Read it if you can." His windpipe is "like the grand Erie Canal" (standard symbol of "internal improvements"). Most comically, his penis ("that unaccountable cone") is "longer than a Kentuckian is tall." Over-all, he is "wrapt up in his blubber . . . [as if] an Indian poncho [were] slipt over his head." Stepping into the Right Whale's mouth, Ishmael declares: "Upon my word were I at Mackinaw, I should take this to be the inside of an Indian wigwam." In a number of physiological

[13] Moby Dick is a little more than whale and a little less than God. As Melville definitively explains: "Human or animal, the mystical brow is as that great golden seal affixed by the German emperors to their decrees. It signifies—'God: done this day by my hand.' "

[14] Quoted in Jay Leyda, *The Melville Log* (New York, 1951), I, 427.

HERMAN MELVILLE

details, the whale appears to correspond with details of Melville's 1840 Western tour.

If the whale, or typifying creature of the Pacific, resembles the continental West, he also resembles the West's typifying creature, the buffalo. Whale and buffalo are repeatedly compared and identified. The whale "is the great prize ox of the sea, too fat to be delicately good. Look at his hump, which would be as fine eating as the buffalo's (which is esteemed a rare dish), were it not such a solid pyramid of fat." Or again: "But this occasional timidity [of the whales] is characteristic of almost all herding creatures. Though banding together in tens of thousands, the lion-maned buffaloes of the West have fled before a solitary horseman." But there is also a crucial difference, movingly revealing Melville's determination to provide himself a West beyond the ravages of time and the depredations of man. "Does the Whale's Magnitude Diminish?—Will He Perish?" or "the moot point is, whether Leviathan can long endure so wide a chase, and so remorseless a havoc." At first blush, it might seem not, "comparing the humped herds of whales with the humped herds of buffalo, which, not forty years ago, overspread by tens of thousands the prairies of Illinois and Missouri, and shook their iron manes and scowled with their thunder-clotted brows upon the sites of populous river-capitals, where now the polite broker sells you land at a dollar an inch." On a closer view, the slaughter of whales is perhaps less amenable to New World greed than some might wish; for "the far different nature of the whale-hunt peremptorily forbids so inglorious an end to the Leviathan. . . . Whereas, in the days of the old Canadian and Indian hunters and trappers of the West, when the far west (in whose sunset suns still rise) was a wilderness and a virgin, the same number of moccasined men, for the same number of months, mounted on horse instead of sailing in ships, would have slain not forty, but forty thousand and more buffaloes." The whale will "outlast all hunting," Melville happily concludes, "immortal in his species, however perishable in his individuality," and will always "spout his

274

frothed defiance to the skies." The whale is to the buffalo as *Moby-Dick* is to the West which was so rapidly vanishing before Melville's eyes, even while his pen raced over the paper. As a clever parody of Job makes clear—"Oh! that unfulfilments should follow the prophets"—Melville was well aware that within inconsequential limits man can and does conquer nature; and if even his temporary failure to do so entails the disaster of an Ahab, what might his success portend? Aesthetically and philosophically, *Moby-Dick*, the indestructibility of the whale, is Melville's "insular Tahiti, full of peace and joy, but encompassed by all the horrors of the half known life," which "half known life" some of his contemporaries called "progress" and some "the frontier." A man could always retire to another kind of interior; beginning with Cooper, or perhaps with Charles Brockden Brown, the great American writers have regularly done so. "And thus, though surrounded by circle upon circle of consternations and affrights, did these inscrutable creatures at the centre freely and fearlessly indulge in all peaceful concernments; yea, serenely revelled in dalliance and delight. But even so, amid the tornadoed Atlantic of my being, do I myself still for ever centrally disport in mute calm; and while ponderous planets of unwaning woe revolve round me, deep down and deep inland there I still bathe me in eternal mildness of joy." In the next paragraph, the outermost circle of hysterically circling whales is called "the frontier of the host." But some interiors are more delightful than others. After the first day, "far inland, nameless wails" issue from Ahab.

We must own the whale, but may never know him. Like the West we hope to win, the whale we desire is either a dead whale, in which case he isn't a whale any more, or a fatal whale: "The wisest thing the investigator can do then, it seems to me, is to let this deadly spout alone." The West was West only so long as a man wasn't there; so long, really, as *no* man was there. "Thou shalt see my back parts, my tail, he seems to say, but my face shall not be seen. But I cannot completely make out his back parts; and hint

275

what he will about his face, I say again he has no face."
But if "he" (the West) has no face, he assuredly has a
"front," i.e., the battering-ram that wrecks Ahab and his
ship: "This aspect is sublime." Even the back parts disappear when scrutinized too closely; as Pip observes:
" 'Unscrew your navel, and what's the consequence?' "
"Your back parts fall off"[15] is the unstated answer and the
point of the joke. This ambiguous face-rump (front-back)
joking begins in "Going Aboard," where Queequeg sits on
a sleeping sailor, and it reappears strangely metamorphosed
in Stubb's dream ("Queen Mab"). Having killed a whale,
the dreamer stands "thoughtfully eying the vast corpse he
had made." Such is creation, American style, where vast
corpse equals—in the delightful language of Western historians—continental destiny.

In contrast, Ishmael's intuitions of the whale are im-
peccably modest. "I am horror-struck at this antemosaic,
unsourced existence of the unspeakable terrors of the whale,
which, having been before all time, must needs exist after
all humane ages are over." The "mystic-marked whale remains undecipherable" as "the old Indian characters
chiselled on the famous hieroglyphic palisades on the banks
of the Upper Mississippi"; here is the same ominous language discovered near the end of *Pym*. Up to a point, the
whale can be sniped at, or whittled away, but it is only
his need to surface for air which enables man to take his
pot shots. "Not so much thy skill, then, O hunter, as the
great necessities that strike the victory to thee!"—a sample
of the kind of sentiment Melville hands Daniel Boone, and
other representative types, to put in their pipes and smoke.
Boone himself turns up a few chapters later, as a lonely
old whale, or reformed and jaded voluptuary, "moss-
bearded," uxoriously bound to Mother Nature "in the
wilderness of waters," fancying himself free, very much as
Parkman had described "the last buffalo, a miserable old

[15] See John D. Seelye, "The Golden Navel: The Cabalism of
Ahab's Doubloon," *Nineteenth-Century Fiction*, xiv (1960), 353-355.

bull, roaming over the prairie alone and melancholy."[16]
Ishmael's complexity of attitude is further illustrated in
"The Honor and Glory of Whaling," where all the great
whalers—Perseus, St. George, Jonah, Vishnoo (Second Person in the Hindoo Trinity, and "our grand master")—are
indirectly pioneers, engaged in winning one or another
analogous West. Hercules is specifically "that antique
Crockett and Kit Carson," the latter of whom Parkman had
rated "pre-eminent in running buffalo."[17] Sometimes it seems
as if everything in American literature through Melville
and Whitman were built on analogy, and the analogy were
always the same. "I do not know that the subject treated
of has ever been worked up by a romancer," Melville de-
viously informed his British publisher.[18]

Why should the whale be white? The easiest and most
probable answer is simple. Moby Dick is a whale, and hence,
in general extension, nature. Nature in America is (or was)
practically equivalent to the West. The West is (or was)
practically equivalent to the American future. The future is
by definition the not yet determined, the page not yet
written on, and thus, by way of unavoidable association
with John Locke's *tabula rasa* (America's favorite epistemological concept), white. Melville's whale could hardly
have been red, or green, the alternative Western shades.
(It might conceivably have been black.)[19] To be sure, Melville took more than one hint from Rabelais. It is far more
significant that whiteness suggests the white man's bewildered defeat by white nature, i.e., himself. This, and

---

[16] *The California and Oregon Trail*, pp. 440-441.

[17] *Ibid.*, p. 388. For Henry Chatillon (according to Parkman pre-
eminent in "approaching" buffalo), Melville wrote in his review,
"we feel a fresh and unbounded love. He belongs to a class of men,
of whom Kit Carson is the model; a class, unique, and not to be
transcended in interest by any personages introduced to us by Scott."

[18] *The Letters of Herman Melville*, ed. Merrell R. Davis and William H. Gilman (New Haven, 1960), p. 109.

[19] And perhaps it is. "May we not surmise that Ishmael's whiteness, by virtue of a culminating paradox, is blackness in perversely
baffling disguise?" Harry Levin, *The Power of Blackness* (New
York, 1958), p. 222.

more, we may learn from Ishmael's prolonged meditation on "The Whiteness of the Whale," or, in Captain Ahab's somewhat too vivid language, " 'the white fiend!' "

Apart from a vague indefiniteness, suggestions of annihilation, ambiguity of colorless all-color, and the deceptive "mystical cosmetic" of a Newtonian universe, what chiefly intrigues and appalls is the Westness behind the whiteness—or, more accurately, the Westness *of* the whiteness. Ishmael has hardly opened his mouth to allege that white gives "the white man ideal mastership over every dusky tribe," when his mind is unaccountably thronged with associations from a little lower layer: "Among the Red Men of America the giving of the white belt of wampum was the deepest pledge of honor," a pleasant reminder of the Anglo-Americans' corresponding deficiency. The white wampum is quickly followed by the sacred White Dog of the noble Iroquois, whose sacrifice "was by far the holiest festival of their theology, that spotless, faithful creature being held the purest envoy they could send to the Great Spirit with the annual tidings of their own fidelity." However sublime these references, still—or consequently—there "lurks an elusive something in the innermost idea of this hue, which strikes more of panic to the soul than that redness which affrights in blood." As in *Pym*, and doubtless for the same ethnological reasons, red is thematically the complement of white.

"Most famous in our Western annals and Indian traditions," and most famous in this chapter, is the White Steed of the Prairies, who by native right commanded pastures that "in those days were only fenced by the Rocky Mountains and the Alleghanies," trooping at the flaming head of the herds like the "chosen star" of the chosen people, "a most imperial and archangelical apparition of that unfallen, western world, which to the eyes of the old trappers and hunters revived the glories of those primeval times when Adam walked majestic as a god." To the Indians, "he was the object of trembling reverence and awe." Ishmael is gradually approaching his dualistic metaphysical climax, "this visible world seems formed in love, the invisible spheres were formed in fright." On the way his argument appropriately shifts from honor to terror, the West continuing to furnish more than its fair share of examples, "the backwoodsman of the West" for one, who indifferently, because ignorantly and insensitively, views his "unbounded prairie sheeted with driven snow."

But the most telling evidence is the Vermont colt (respectable New England dupe). "Shake a fresh buffalo robe behind him," and he goes wild, proving "the instinct of the knowledge of the demonism in the world. Though thousands of miles from Oregon, still when he smells that savage musk, the rending, goring bison herds [black bison are specified] are as present as to the deserted wild foal of the prairies, which this instant they may be trampling into dust."[20] Revealed by multiple signs of fidelity and betrayal, between man and man, race and race, humanity and God; intimately associated with blood and the blackness of darkness; imperial and archangelical (are they in apposition or conflict?); unfallen and unredeemed; ancient and uncontaminated (the usual ambivalence for "primeval"); boundless, terrifying, violent: "of all these things," these secondary qualities, as one might say, "the Albino whale was the symbol. Wonder ye then at the fiery hunt?" The White

[20] Melville's sources for the Western materials in "The Whiteness of the Whale" are extensively treated in the explanatory notes of the Mansfield-Vincent edition, and include Poe, Lewis Henry Morgan, James Hall, and, possibly, Parkman. Morgan's account of the White Dog contains the curiously Poe-like detail (controverted by Melville) of the victim's being "spotted" with red paint. *Literary World*, VII (December 28, 1850), 522. Morgan also explains that "the fidelity of the dog, the companion of the Indian, as a hunter, was emblematical of their fidelity. . . . They hung around his neck a string of white wampum, the pledge of their faith" (523). For the White Steed, Hall's story "The Black Steed of the Prairies"—in *The Wilderness and the War Path* (New York, 1846)—seems the most likely source of details not invented by Melville, who may also have seen "The White Steed of the Prairies," a poem by "J. Barber" (John Warner Barber?) in the *Democratic Review*, XII (1843), 367. In *The California and Oregon Trail*, Parkman told of a white dog (p. 235), a white buffalo who turned out to be only an ox (p. 398), and a white wolf (p. 412).

Whale was Melville's symbol of the essential, universal West, which had always held the clue to the suicidal American future; at the mid-century mark, it held more secrets of the past than most Americans were ready to bargain for.

3. THE DISPUTED FRONTIER

In *Moby-Dick*, Melville had been genuinely ambiguous about America's Western destiny, a destiny with which, until then, he had felt so entirely at home that it was practically synonymous with his early career. For all his doubts, Melville in *Moby-Dick* dominated America. Then, almost overnight, he suffered a loss of confidence, perhaps caused by an awareness that there was no longer an America worth dominating. Now he would treat "with all Powers upon an equal basis," as he wrote Hawthorne while *Moby-Dick* was still in process.[1] The language of that letter appears in the novel, and carries over to *Pierre* (1852), whose protagonist declares himself "an equal power" with both God and man.[2] But there was a devastating anomaly concealed behind Melville's lordly independence. He had to have a country to dominate and quarrel with, and the America he had been especially treating with since 1846 was now—having come to the end of its aggressions, evasions, and postponements— flying apart. Nothing he had been saying quite made sense in the new context, and a protracted period of suffering necessarily followed. Melville was in somewhat the same dilemma as his new hero, "profoundly sensible that his whole previous moral being was overturned, and that for him the fair structure of the world must, in some then unknown way,

[1] *The Letters of Herman Melville*, ed. Merrell R. Davis and William H. Gilman (New Haven, 1960), p. 125.

[2] Unless otherwise specified, quotations in this section are from *Pierre; or, The Ambiguities*, ed. Henry A. Murray (New York, 1949) ; *Moby-Dick; or, The Whale*, ed. Luther S. Mansfield and Howard P. Vincent (New York, 1952) ; *The Piazza Tales*, ed. Egbert S. Oliver (New York, 1948) ; and *Battle-Pieces and Aspects of the War*, ed. Sidney Kaplan (Gainesville, Florida, 1960). Quotations from *Israel Potter* may be found in *The Works of Herman Melville* (London, 1922-1924).

be entirely rebuilded again, from the lowermost corner stone up. . . . He seemed to feel that in his deepest soul, lurked an indefinite but potential faith, which could rule in the interregnum of all hereditary beliefs, and circumstantial persuasions." Significantly, it is an "infant Ishmael," or "magazine contributor to Juvenile American literature," whom Melville once more has on his hands, almost as if he were deliberately reverting to the puerilities of Wellingborough Redburn.

Melville can always be counted on to ask the leading question, and it is perhaps no accident that he asks it in connection with Pierre's book, which seems to resemble his own: "In the heart of such silence, surely something is at work. Is it creation, or destruction?" It is precisely the question one would most like to ask the America of 1852. Initially, one can only say that the American West looms out of the quiet recesses of *Pierre* with an exasperating ambiguity—or even, to coin a Melvillean term—non-Meaning. There seems no compelling reason for Plotinus Plinlimmon to be "a Tennesseean by birth," nor for Pierre in his garret to wear moccasins over his boots, nor for Merry Christmas to steal upon the world "on tinted Indian moccasin." *Pierre* also contains what looks like intentional mystification, such as the "S. ye W." inscription on the Memnon stone, which to any ordinary reader (unblocked by the senseless "y^e") would seem rather obviously geographical, but whose national significance, if any, Melville ostentatiously avoids and then misinterprets.[8] Another granitic passage (Enceladus) is embellished with description suspiciously suggesting an oceanic prairie, and, further on, cluttered with similes "like bridging rifts of logs up-jammed in alluvial-rushing streams of far Arkansas." In the course of a long meditation commencing in the Alps and ending

---

[8] Otherwise the Memnon Stone suggests Melville's literary achievement, with special emphasis on *Moby-Dick*, perhaps, since the shape is very like a whale. "Not only might this stone well have been the wonder of the simple country round, but it might well have been its terror."

in an empty sarcophagus ("appallingly vacant as vast is the soul of a man!"), we are unaccountably asked to advert to the Rocky Mountains; elsewhere to consider (Cooper-style) New York patroons "surviving, like Indian mounds, the Revolutionary flood"; or to ponder the visible truth that "a true gentleman in Kentucky would cheerfully die for a beautiful woman in Hindostan."

We should probably take more seriously the many allusions to emigration, which range from hints of an entangling alliance between Pierre's father and a lovely French émigrée to recollection of the angels' divinely dallying with the daughters of man, a liaison equally unsusceptible of verification. The sewing circle where Pierre first sees "that face" is organized "for the benefit of various settlements of necessitous emigrants." Isabel herself comes to Saddle Meadows after previous employers " 'broke up their household and departed for some Western country.' " Behind all the secretive masochism of Melville's bizarre psychological narrative, the course of empire drags its slow length along. But from another angle, the West and the psyche (its inevitable American development) appear to be one and the same. "Watch yon little toddler, how long it is learning to stand by itself! . . . But, by-and-by, grown up to man's estate, it shall leave the very mother that bore it, and the father that begot it, and cross the seas, perhaps, or settle in far Oregon lands. There now, do you see the soul. . . . It shall yet learn to stand independent, though not without many a bitter wail, and many a miserable fall." We also see lingering traces of the Pacific-West equation which informed Melville's earlier works, an equation which also sustains the otherwise inexplicable passage about the frontier man "seized by wild Indians, and carried far and deep into the wilderness"; there he is "held a captive," and several sentences later mysteriously finds "a continent and an ocean between him and his wife." The frontier man appears to have been transported to the Marquesas, where Tommo had once "thought of the loved friends who were thousands and thousands of miles from the savage island in which I was held a captive."

Pierre's family background, presumably congruent with American history (a brief tale), is suitably if somewhat imprecisely derived from an earlier frontier. Saddle and all, the great-grandfather was fatally unhorsed—thus anticipating the disasters of his heir, and bequeathing a name to the estate—in the French and Indian Wars. During the Revolution, the grandfather defended a "rude but all-important stockaded fort" against British and Indians, including Joseph Brant, "the gentlemanly, but murderous half-breed," who subsequently came to dinner.[4] Somewhat as in *The House of the Seven Gables*, Saddle Meadows is held by deed from Indian kings, "the aboriginal and only conveyancers of those noble woods and plains."[5] But are these Glendinning ancestors heroic or disgusting or ridiculous or, more likely, a little of each? "In a night-scuffle in the wilderness," the grandfather—"the mildest hearted, and most blue-eyed gentleman in the world"—"annihilated two Indian savages by making reciprocal bludgeons of their heads," as his grandson is now to annihilate two girls. Pierre is a parodic continuator of these noble ancestors, "Life his campaign"— behaviors violent, ludicrous, and destructive may well be imagined of him. He is also a pathetic comedown from the kind of character once defined as aboriginal with his country. "Oh, I hear the leap of the Texan Camanche, as at this moment he goes crashing like a wild deer through the green underbrush; I hear his glorious whoop of savage and un-

[4] Brant was thus entertained by General Peter Gansevoort, Melville's grandfather, according to William L. Stone, *Life of Joseph Brant* (New York, 1838), II, 460. Doubtless the entire book was gratifying to Melville, for Stone was a stout defender of the Indian from his despoilers, the American people, and his traducers, the popular Western writers.

[5] In his parody-tirade about American genealogies, Melville makes a great point of the Randolphs having in their blood through Pocahontas "an underived aboriginal royalty." No such specific honor is claimed for the Glendinnings, but a number of subliminal innuendoes may conceivably hint Indian qualities in mysteriously dark Isabel, who is allegedly half-French.

tamable health; and then I look in at Pierre [writing]. If physical, practical unreason make the savage, which is he? Civilization, Philosophy, Ideal Virtue! behold your victim!" As usual, Melville wants it both ways—Pierre is too "civilized," Pierre is too "savage," depending on which meaning we assign to which word. (He is repeatedly called both.) Pierre rejects, or thinks he rejects, his family heritage, but like a young nation, the more he asserts his independence, the more he resembles his relatives; and under the veneer of their moneyed manners, these relatives are a rough and hard-bitten lot.

The idyllic haze bathing Saddle Meadows is deceptive; this is still wild country. Lucy may emigrate inland like an inspired linnet, but more disturbing voices proceed from Isabel's " 'furthest inland soul,' "; throughout *Pierre*, Melville keeps up this saccharine-sardonic inner-inmost-interior-inland kind of talk. Thoreau-like, Pierre broods by a "primeval pine-tree . . . luckily left standing by the otherwise unsparing woodmen, who long ago had cleared that meadow," or wanders in the primeval woods "as the only fit prelude to the society of so wild a being as his new-found sister." All the natural scenes and objects betoken moral or emotional values; as in a Hawthorne tale, "from out the infinite inhumanities of those profoundest forests, came a moaning, muttering, roaring, intermitted, changeful sound," culminating in "devilish gibberish of the forest-ghosts." And as to Hester Prynne, "there came into the mind of Pierre, thoughts and fancies never imbibed within the gates of towns; but only given forth by the atmosphere of primeval forests, which, with the eternal ocean, are the only unchanged general objects." At the very start of his quest, Pierre thinks the ambiguous "chair-portrait" of his father taunts him: "Probe, probe a little—see—there seems one little crack there, Pierre—a wedge, a wedge. Something ever comes of all persistent inquiry; we are not so continually curious for nothing, Pierre; not for nothing, do we so intrigue and become wily diplomatists, and glozers with our own minds, Pierre; and afraid of following the Indian trail from the open plain into the dark thickets, Pierre." The metaphor seems more mixed than it really is, for to follow the Indian trail into the dark thickets ("truth") is more or less equivalent to driving wedges into the cracks of America's disintegrating structure.

Either way, we are led to confront an almost classic case of epistemological-ontological collapse, on the part of Isabel and Pierre, if not of Melville or even America.[6] For years he had tended to go along with the literary crowd; but like his friends, the Indians, Melville was a hopeless Manichee, and therefore unable indefinitely to live at peace with the metaphysical implications ("bipolar unity") of the metaphorical frontier. *Moby-Dick* is full of contradictory transitional evidence on this point. Pagans happily dream of death as floating off "to the starry archipelagoes," where "their own mild, uncontinented seas, interflow with the blue heavens," a figure of speech innocuously conventional; but essentially the same metaphor is also used to explain Ahab's derangement: "His torn body and gashed soul bled into one another; and so interfusing, made him mad." Except in Melville's earliest days—and not always then—the image of the interfusing frontier rarely suggested to him peace, mediation, and richness of inclusion, as it was supposed to, but rather chaos, hemorrhage, insanity, hostility, horror, or an inscrutable disjunction (vague ellipsis, the region of the everlasting lull) in the affairs of men and worlds. The first movement of *Moby-Dick* begins with "inlanders" happily heading for water's edge ("Nothing will content them but the extremest limit of the land. . . . They must get just as

---

[6] "Moral conflict, if radical and stubborn, results in a division, an inflexible dualism, in all branches of feeling and thought, which so influences the sufferer's apperceptions, that every significant object becomes *ambivalent* to him. . . . The whole long sequence of antinomies, or pairs of opposites, which constitute the structure of this novel are but products of one nuclear conflict." Henry A. Murray's introduction to *Pierre*, pp. xv-xvii. But if Melville's problems were shared at different degrees of depth by his entire generation, his nuclear conflict must be understood in cultural as well as in psychological terms, unless the entire generation is to be understood as neurotic.

nigh the water as they possibly can without falling in"),
which again sounds reassuring, especially as swathed in
references to the Great American Desert, the flowery
prairies, Niagara, and Tennessee; and perhaps equally traditional is Ishmael's wild conceit about "processions of the
whale," *two and two*, resolving into the image of *one* "grand
hooded phantom." But this first movement of the novel
ends with "The Lee Shore," Melville's personal contribu-
tion to literary frontiersmanship, an elaborate figure of
speech built on an ocean-land (soul-nature) dualism, in
which all the expected associations of reconciliation and
harmony are rudely shelved, and replaced by ignominious
disaster at the point of meeting, "the treacherous, slavish
shore."[7] Not surprisingly, Melville sometimes tries to rid
himself of the whole dualistic problem, as when he jettisons
Locke (the Transcendentalists' whipping boy) and Kant
(their unread Savior), after mutual cancellation, so he can
"float light and right."

Much more characteristically, he evades the problem of
bipolar unity by pressing his antitheses as wide apart as he
can. The whale, he says, possesses a double perspective, seeing "one distinct picture on this side, and another distinct
picture on that side; while all between must be profound
darkness and nothingness to him." All between was the neutral territory where Cooper, Hawthorne, Poe, and Thoreau,
employing a single unified vision, magnanimously resolved
their splintered heritage. Melville would not have it that
way. The whales' "divided and diametrically opposite powers of vision" are the source of "timidity and liability to
queer frights," and a "helpless perplexity of volition," a
description equally suggestive of Melville's mental state as
it was coming to be, and of American sectional politics as
they inescapably had become. Shortly after completing

[7] "Pyramids still loom before me—something vast, undefiled, incomprehensible, and awful. Line of desert & verdure, plain as line
[*emended to* plainer than that] between good & evil. An instant
collision of the two [*emended to* alien] elements." *Journal of a Visit
to Europe and the Levant*, ed. Howard C. Horsford (Princeton,
1955), p. 119. These are the very tones of Melville's mind and heart.

Pierre, he sketched for Hawthorne the tale of "Agatha": "Suddenly she catches the long shadow of the cliff cast upon the beach 100 feet beneath her; and now she notes a shadow moving along the shadow. It is cast by a sheep from the pasture. It has advanced to the very edge of the cliff, & is sending a mild innocent glance far out upon the water. Here [There?], in strange & beautiful contrast, we have the innocence of the land placidly eyeing the malignity of the sea."[8] No reciprocating adjustments could possibly flow from a situation thus defined. Melville has made sure of it, as he did later with his emblematic tortoises in "The Encantadas": "The tortoise is both black and bright."[9] (Still, we notice that black side up is "natural.") These images are entirely too schematic, and, in that degree, ominous.

During Melville's most desperate period—which not very miraculously coincided with the closing of the frontier and the approach of the Civil War—he increasingly safeguarded himself against the customary victories. In *Pierre*, especially, he fended off (at the same time courting) the perils of ambivalence; consequently, this dubious novel must share with *The Confidence-Man* the honor of signalizing the moment in American literary history when all the values the national culture had been optimistically attributing to the Western frontier were suddenly inverted, and harmony and reconciliation were revealed to be chaos and nightmare. Several times in *Pierre* we encounter the anticipated trope, or at least its tawdry remnants: in the hero's interior susceptibility to Isabel's mysterious power, "a power so hovering upon the confines of the invisible world, that it seemed more inclined that way than this"; in the surly auctorial comment, "But here we press upon the frontiers of that sort of wisdom,

---

[8] *Letters*, p. 156.

[9] Cf. the Mealy-mouthed Porpoise in *Moby-Dick* (p. 141); Hautboy in "The Fiddler"; Derwent and Rolfe in *Clarel*, ed. Walter E. Bezanson (New York, 1960):

> "Man has two sides: keep on the bright."
> "Two sides imply that one's not right;
> So that won't do."—"Wit, wit!"—"Nay, truth."

(IV, xxiii)

which it is very well to possess, but not sagacious to show that you possess"; and at the end, when mystical-suicidal Isabel desires to be " 'out there! where the two blues [sky and ocean] meet, and are nothing.' " (In popular poems and tales, bereft Indian maidens always sought death by water.) But such explicit figures count for little. In order to read this novel at all, we must descend to a darker level, where the frontier has all but vanished, whelmed in Melville's agonistic intelligence, but still phosphorescently proclaims its whereabouts in such recurrent and revelatory language as "melt," "blend," and "intermarry."

All these key words are ironically intended, for in Melville's compulsive pursuit of the ambiguities he feared, the submerged traditional metaphor was the symbol of his dread.[10] Isabel is more than Isabel when she tells Pierre: " 'Always in me, the solidest things melt into dreams, and dreams into solidities. . . . A second face, and a third face, and a fourth face peep at me from within thy own. . . . I go groping again amid all sorts of shapes, which part to me; so that I seem to advance through the shapes; and yet the shapes have eyes that look at me.' " This latter-day Yillah lives in a surrealistic borderland between the Actual and the Imaginary, where each world tortures itself with the emerging forms of the other, not, as in the earlier writers, to the greater glory of America, but to her (and our) confusion and sorrow. It is no accident that the most con-

[10] Although *Pierre* is presumably about moral ambiguity, the hero loudly declares (Melville to a considerable extent sympathizing) that virtue, vice, and man himself are " 'nothing. It is all a dream— we dream that we dreamed we dream.' " Yet the official epistemological doctrine of the book is Emersonian correspondence (however distorted): "From without, no wonderful effect is wrought within ourselves, unless some interior, responding wonder meets it. . . . Wonder interlocks with wonder; and then the confounding feeling comes." *Pierre* is compounded of what Melville calls "these mutually neutralizing thoughts," conflicts of attitude and belief impossible to reconcile. "In this little nut," Melville explains about one of his little nuts, "lies germ-like the possible solution of some puzzling problems; and also the discovery of additional, and still more profound problems ensuing upon the solution of the former."

spicuous verbs in *Pierre* are "glide," "slide," and "displace," and that they nearly always suggest the impossibility of intelligent volition. Isabel's problem is clearly related to Melville's; he was now too much indulging in a single direction those short, quick probings at the axis of reality for which he had so warmly commended Shakespeare and Hawthorne. By 1852 he had arrived at the point of uncertainty whence Hawthorne set out, or pretended to set out, a debilitating skepticism about the reliability of experience and the validity of fictive truth. But as Melville's and Hawthorne's directions were opposite, Melville only exacerbated his torment with Hawthorne's solutions. *Pierre* is the record of his struggle to prevent the Actual and the Imaginary from coming together, as well as his self-tormenting campaign to discover what happens when they do.

Throughout the novel, everything falls apart into pairs, as the North and South were concurrently doing; and then, worse, the pairs intermarry. "For an instant, the fond, all-understood blue eyes of Lucy displaced the as tender, but mournful and inscrutable dark glance of Isabel. He seemed placed between them, to choose one or the other; then both seemed his; but into Lucy's eyes there stole half of the mournfulness of Isabel's, without diminishing hers." Pierre's memory of his father's face similarly blends with the distinctly different portrait of him: "By some ineffable correlativeness, they reciprocally identified each other, and, as it were, melted into each other, and thus interpenetratingly uniting, presented lineaments of an added supernaturalness." With this result: "On all sides, the physical world of solid objects now slidingly displaced itself from around him, and he floated into an ether of visions"—at which point certain lines from the *Inferno*, violently wrenched from context, obligingly float upon the page, reciprocally to identify the political and philosophical horrors of the day:

> "Ah! how thou dost change,
> Agnello! See! thou art not double now,
> Nor only one!"

So sang Emerson and his friends, not foreseeing a world in which Idealism, as it appeared in 1842, and by which they primarily meant "America," would become another word for Hell, or a nation neither two nor one. "Nature intended a rare and original development in Pierre. Never mind if hereby she proved ambiguous to him in the end." After a later bout with Dante, Pierre falls "dabbling in the vomit of his loathed identity."

This is the turning-point of *Pierre*, and indeed of Melville's passion. Not content with subverting the literary West and the figurative frontier, with all their political-philosophical implications of unity to be won from dualism, Melville in one of his greatest moments proceeds to destroy a figure basic to his own apprenticeship (as in *Mardi* and *Redburn*). In "More Light, and the Gloom of that Light. More Gloom, and the Light of that Gloom," the compass spins wildly, and the American West is slidingly displaced, though not without many a visible sign of Melville's close attention to the nation's favorite section:

> In those Hyperborean regions, to which enthusiastic Truth, and Earnestness, and Independence, will invariably lead a mind fitted by nature for profound and fearless thought, all objects are seen in a dubious, uncertain, and refracting light. Viewed through that rarefied atmosphere the most immemorially admitted maxims of men begin to *slide and fluctuate*, and finally become wholly *inverted*; the very heavens themselves being not innocent of producing this confounding effect. . . .
>
> It is not for man to *follow the trail of truth* too far, since by so doing he entirely loses the directing compass of his mind; for arrived at the Pole, to whose barrenness only it points, there, the needle indifferently respects all points of the horizon alike.[11]

[11] Cf. Hawthorne in "The Artist of the Beautiful" (1844): "To persons whose pursuits are insulated from the common business of life—who are either in advance of mankind or apart from it—there often comes a sensation of moral cold that makes the spirit shiver

But even the *less distant regions of thought* are not without their singular introversions. . . . After all, what is so enthusiastically applauded as the *march of mind,* —meaning *the inroads of Truth into Error* . . . a tremendous mistake may be lurking here, since *all the world does never gregariously advance to Truth, but only here and there some of its individuals do; and by advancing, leave the rest behind.* . . . What wonder, then, that those advanced minds, which in spite of advance, happen still to remain, for the time, ill-regulated, should now and then be goaded into turning round in acts of wanton aggression upon *sentiments and opinions now forever left in their rear* . . .

One way or another, the phrases I have italicized hint of Melville's commerce with the prairies, to the end of which he had plainly come, and contain in fewest words the explanation of what happened to him after *Moby-Dick*. Most crucially, the trail of truth, or Westward course of empire, is a trail of error, a continental mistake, the way to insanity. Perhaps on closer inspection the dubious, uncertain, refracting light will be found to emanate less from the Hyperborean regions than from the kind of truths Melville's fellow-Americans held to be most self-evident. Perhaps—to risk a final conjecture—the ill-regulated mind turning round in acts of wanton aggression has advanced less by choice than by necessity. The mind is obviously a pioneer (Melville). Is it also the pioneer's pioneer, the defeated, retreating Indian, who had always been the *alter ego* of the American writer, once again having a final ominous word?

Melville was lured to the Northern lights by the presumed necessity of involving God in his sliding and monstrous world, and perhaps by political considerations also. The incestuous union, not unexpectedly, proves misfortunate in the extreme, and from this dire calamity the remainder of

---

as if it had reached the frozen solitudes around the pole." *The Complete Works of Nathaniel Hawthorne*, ed. George P. Lathrop (Cambridge, 1883), II, 518.

the novel inexorably proceeds. The more Melville contemplates the idea of mediation, the more he hastens the collapse he fears. "In the soul of the enthusiast youth two armies come to the shock; and unless he prove recreant, or unless he prove gullible, or unless he can find the talismanic secret, to reconcile this world with his own soul, then there is no peace for him, no slightest truce for him in this life. Now without doubt this Talismanic Secret has never yet been found; and in the nature of human things it seems as though it never can be." The more we look at such passages, the more they slide and fluctuate. But if the enthusiast youth is America, then the Talismanic Secret is in the final analysis America's future identity and Western destiny. In political terms, this involves the undiscovered solution of the slavery issue in the Western territories, now recoiling upon the horrified East from California's *ne plus ultra*. Only in some such terms as these can the sudden eruption of military imagery be explained. Conscious or unconscious, this is prophecy, and, like most prophecy, unpalatable and threatening. To speak plainly, the Civil War was about to begin, and Melville knew it.[12] But the implications of this final showdown were to be far more than political, for the epistemological and ontological problems of American thought had for decades been blended—by "some ineffable correlativeness" (analogy), and by reciprocally identifying each other—with the beloved imagery of the West, and with a desperately held faith that there, if not here, all would yet be well; hence the standard confusion, in antebellum American writing, between "the West" and "Heaven." All was not well, however, and was not going to be well, say what some poets would, and the West itself—first as a temptation to evasion and greed, and then as an uncontrollable irritant to sectional arrogance—was the chief cause of disaster.

In the early fifties, Hawthorne turned away from the

[12] So did a few other people. See such contemporary titles as William A. Phillips, *The Conquest of Kansas, by Missouri and Her Allies* (1856), and George D. Brewerton, *The War in Kansas* (1856), republished in 1859 as *Wars of the Western Border*.

American past, for the first time seriously to confront the contemporary scene; but as Hawthorne's New England past was at the same time his contemporary West, the new departure was rather an abdication of responsibility than a renewed dedication to it. Thoreau was meanwhile fortifying himself with an aesthetic West beyond time, a basic model of attitude and behavior which might survive the holocaust. Melville had already so fortified himself, and now he alone faced the American tragedy head-on. When he speaks of "two armies come to the shock" ("in the soul of the enthusiast youth," who is not merely America but Young America), promising "no peace," and "no slightest truce," he can only be understood as hinting the scarcely-to-be-imagined yet increasingly threatening collapse of the Union. Along with it would go—and did go—all the related unities with which the Americans had so anxiously striven to furnish themselves against "a new world, material without being real" (Fitzgerald's phrase in *The Great Gatsby*), Union and unities alike symbolized and validated by the imagined West, the figured frontier.[13] As Melville was later to remark, in a poem revealingly entitled "On the Slain Collegians":

> . . . what troops
> Of generous boys in happiness thus bred—
> Saturnians through life's Tempe led,
> Went from the North and came from the South,
> With golden mottoes in the mouth,
> To lie down midway on a bloody bed.

The time-honored neutral territory could not stand so much reality. It was "time-honored," of course, only in the context of American history, where nothing lasts very long; from *The Pioneers* to *Pierre* was less than thirty years.

---

[13] In "Dupont's Round Fight," Melville writes "Unity" and means "the Union":

> The rebel at Port Royal felt
> The Unity overawe,
> And rued the spell. A type was here,
> And victory of LAW.

The philosophical center of *Pierre* is located in Plotinus Plinlimmon's ridiculous pamphlet, "Chronometricals and Horologicals," which resolves none of these cultural issues or even encourages their elucidation. Deliberately Melville thrusts his warring terms asunder and holds them there, partly by making the essay (suggestively built on irreconcilable antagonism between principle and expediency) ambiguous beyond any possibility of interpretation. Its argument is simple, but we can take no simple attitude toward an argument at once so irrefutable, so contemptible, and so irrelevant. (Naturally, its "conclusion was gone.") Melville implies that by settling for nothing we avoid something worse. This most difficult of all his novels—perhaps the most difficult novel in American literature—seeks to blur actuality, or cancel it altogether, and is maddening as a work of art precisely in the degree that it achieves that perverse intention. And yet, in a way, Melville's intention was the proper one, and his achievement indirectly the historian's best index to crucial aspects of the American mind in the years preceding the Civil War, for truly the native culture hovered over vortices. "But while this sleep, this dream is on ye," warned the canny Ishmael, "move your foot or hand an inch; slip your hold at all; and your identity comes back in horror." *Pierre* is Melville's horrified glance at the experience of self-knowledge returning upon a nation, as upon a man falling to his death, too late. " 'Enceladus! it is Enceladus!'—Pierre cried out in his sleep. That moment the phantom faced him; and Pierre saw Enceladus no more; but on the Titan's armless trunk, his own duplicate face and features magnifiedly gleamed upon him with prophetic discomfiture and woe. With trembling frame he started from his chair, and woke from that ideal horror to all his actual grief."

Further evidence in support of such ambiguous readings is found in *Israel Potter: His Fifty Years of Exile* (1855). Toward the end, and however briefly, appears Ethan Ticonderoga Allen, "like a great whale breaching," to shatter the placid surface of Melville's last potboiler with a magnificent symbolic splash. Most of Allen's rodomontade is cribbed from his own *Narrative* (1779), but not this: "Though born in New England, he exhibited no trace of her character. He was frank, bluff, companionable as a Pagan, convivial, a Roman, hearty as a harvest. His spirit was essentially Western; and herein is his peculiar Americanism; for the Western spirit is, or will yet be (for no other is, or can be), the true American one." So, apparently, Melville still, or once again, hoped. Or perhaps he felt obliged to make a public profession of faith, in the expectation that the profession would revive the faith.[14] "Outlandishly arrayed in the sorry remains of a half-Indian, half-Canadian sort of a dress," Allen is another tardy Leatherstocking (whom Whitman, as late as 1888, said was "from everlasting to everlasting"[15]—only a slight exaggeration). Or perhaps Allen more nearly resembles young Edwards in *The Pioneers*, for according to an English lady, he " 'talks like a beau in a parlour, this wild, mossed American from the woods.' " Whatever his origins, Allen as outsize ring-tailed roarer has effectually displaced the other historical frontiersman whom Melville found in *Life and Remarkable Adventures of Israel R. Potter* (1824), but was unable to energize.[16] Ideally,

[14] Melville's tales and sketches (1853-1856) contain a number of perfunctory Western allusions, usually to prairies, Kentucky, and Indians. "Cock-A-Doodle-Doo!" and "The Tartarus of Maids" involve rudimentary East-West symbolism, but the data are too slight for interpretation; perhaps intentionally so. "The Piazza" is charmingly constructed upon a more conspicuously Western quest, which begins on one domesticated metaphorical frontier ("I like piazzas, as somehow combining the coziness of in-doors with the freedom of out-doors") and ends on another ("a small abode—mere palanquin, set down on the summit, in a pass between two worlds, participant of neither"), also described as " 'An old house. They went West, and are long dead, they say, who built it.' "

[15] Horace L. Traubel, *With Walt Whitman in Camden*, I (Boston, 1906), 454.

[16] At first glance, Israel Potter seems more Western than he is. Melville sets the stage with a nostalgic account of pioneering in his beloved Berkshires; but readers unduly impressed with the other frontier details of these early chapters should check his source. Sometimes he copies; sometimes he embellishes, drawing on the

Melville was more than ever concerned with the West; actually, he was unable to derive any fresh meaning from it, except sporadically and obliquely. He needed a new conception, something to supersede the gigantic negations of *Pierre*.

Almost miraculously, the new conception was already gestating within *Israel Potter* itself. "Ambassador, projector, maxim-monger, herb-doctor, wit: Jack of all trades, master of each and mastered by none—the type and genius of his land. Franklin was everything but a poet." The last sentence was not a minor concession, but a sweeping condemnation. The walls of Poor Richard's Paris apartment have "a necromantic look, hung round with . . . [various devices and] wide maps of far countries in the New World, containing vast empty spaces in the middle, with the word DESERT diffusely printed there, so as to span five-and-twenty degrees of longitude with only two syllables,—which printed word, however, bore a vigorous pen-mark, in the doctor's hand, drawn straight through it, as if in summary repeal of it." In the 1770's, as in the 1850's, twenty-five degrees of American longitude amounted to a stretch of land from, say, Boston to Lawrence, Kansas, over which cultural desert two new syllables (FRANKLIN) were by Melville's time spread perilously thin. From the cultural past of this curious desert, Melville is obviously delighted to quote such typical inanities as "God helps them that help themselves" (pun on "help yourself," as quoted by Melville); "Never joke at funerals, or during business transactions"; or, most sharply directed toward the new and improved point, "An indiscriminate distrust of human nature is the worst con-

---

public stockpile of standard Western material. Only occasionally does he achieve a powerful and apparently original image, as of alien Israel in London suffering a vision of home, "like some amazed runaway steer, or trespassing Pequod Indian, impounded on the shores of Narragansett Bay, long ago." Back in America, Potter discovers the last survivor of his family has "sold out and removed to a distant country in the West"; in the source, it is merely to "a distant part of the country."

sequence of a miserable condition." The new and improved pen-mark was Melville's, and what it summarily repealed was AMERICA.

" 'Untrammelled citizen and sailor of the universe,' " fighter, outlaw, revenger, rake ("All barbarians are rakes"), Indian, *poet*, John Paul Jones is Allen's cousin, Franklin's foil, and a third stab at defining the national character— a far more attractive figure, though also a more ominous prototype of the confidence-man. "So at midnight, the heart of the metropolis of modern civilization [Paris] was secretly trod by this jaunty barbarian in broadcloth; a sort of prophetical ghost." Prophetical, certainly, of the next book: "So easily may the deadliest foe—so he be but dexterous— slide, undreamed of, into human harbors or hearts," as, in- deed, Melville was increasingly sliding into the great demo- cratic heart of his witless audience, or what was left of it. Jones is—for the most part, in the best sense—a "savage," who looks and acts like "a disinherited Indian chief in European clothes"; is variously a prophetic Iroquois, "a parading Sioux demanding homage to his gewgaws" (like the *Red-Hot Coal*), a "prowling *brave*"; and he is seen "wrapped in Indian meditations," or "waving his solitary hand, like a disdainful tomahawk." This Rob Roy of the American Revolution has captured Melville's imagination, and taken over the book. Even more important, perhaps, through rhythm and rhetoric he is inseparably linked with the Western spirit: "Intrepid, unprincipled, reckless, preda- tory, with boundless ambition, civilized in externals but a savage at heart, America is, or may yet be, the Paul Jones of nations." It is impossible to say of the 1855 Melville whether he more feared or desired the validation of this particular national image.

For all their three-way richness of ironic implication, Allen, Franklin, and Jones conspicuously fail to coalesce, or even add up to a coherent and compelling syndrome for American civilization, perhaps because Melville was still too contradictory in his own mind, or perhaps because America was. The superficial truce of the 1850 Compromise had now been completely disrupted by the inflammatory Kansas-Nebraska Act of 1854; by spring of the year following *Israel Potter*'s publication in book form, open hostilities would commence in Kansas. Melville's sense of the connection between West and War is simply inescapable. And with some justice: was not the Kansas-Nebraska Act contrived by a Western Senator, and its specious theory of "popular sovereignty" a typical expression of "frontier democracy"? After Jones has done his work, the *Drake* looks "like a piece of wild western woodland into which choppers had been" (not quite the woodcutters of *The Pioneers*, whose wasty ways Natty Bumppo so eloquently but ineffectually deplored), which is about the way the United States will look when Melville is through with them. In recounting the battle between the *Serapis* and the *Bon Homme Richard*—commanded by that wild Indian Jones—Melville is as explicit as we could wish: he positively leers. This "unparalleled deathlock" is "indicatory" (he says twice), and "may involve at once a type, a parallel, and a prophecy," a series of ascriptions conceivably dependent upon his readers' recognition that the American Revolution was a civil war, while the Civil War (were there to be one) would also be a revolution. "Never was there a fight so snarled. The intricacy of those incidents which defy the narrator's extrication, is not illy figured in that bewildering intertanglement of all the yards and anchors of the two ships, which confounded them for the time in one chaos of devastation." Dead and dying drop through the "long lane of darkling water" which "lay wedged between" the ships, locked side by side, hulls not touching, not double now, nor only one. "As some heaving rent coinciding with a disputed frontier on a volcanic plain, that boundary abyss was the jaws of death to both sides."

But who, precisely, is disputing that scoriac frontier? According to Melville's literal statement, the British and Americans. And yet: "It seemed more an intestine feud, than a fight between strangers. Or, rather, it was as if the

Siamese Twins, oblivious of their fraternal bond, should rage in unnatural fight." *Israel Potter* has much to say about relations between a mercantile tyrant and her hapless colonies, and little of it suggests fraternity; neither does anything else in the book support an interpretation of the American Revolution as "unnatural," except insofar as the American Revolution may be considered a rehearsal for the hostilities ahead. "The belligerents were no longer, in the ordinary sense of things, an English ship and an American ship. It was a co-partnership and joint-stock combustion-company of both ships; yet divided, even in participation. The two vessels were as two houses, through whose party-wall doors have been cut; one family (the Guelphs) occupying the whole lower story; another family (the Ghibelines) the whole upper story." There is no conceivable "party-wall" between England and her overseas possessions, several thousand miles of water being in the way; neither does the Guelph-Ghibelline lower story-upper story imagery fit this particular case in international relations. The "party-wall" can only be the Mason-Dixon line running through a house divided, and perhaps also the Missouri Compromise line, only recently abrogated; both lines were uneasily related in the American imagination to the half-analogous Western frontier, to which boundary (any of these boundaries) each of Melville's sly comparisons perfectly applies, even, or especially, the "joint-stock combustion-company." "It seemed as if in this fight, neither party could be victor. Mutual obliteration from the face of the waters seemed the only natural sequel to hostilities like these."

Immediately preceding the "disputed frontier" passage, Melville compares the neutral territory between ships to "that narrow canal in Venice which dozes between two shadowy piles, and high in air is secretly crossed by the Bridge of Sighs. . . . The six yard-arms reciprocally arched overhead, three bridges of sighs." Years later in *Clarel* (1876) he was to explicate his feeling toward this strange image, speaking of:

That evil day,
Black in the New World's calendar—
The dolorous winter ere the war;
True Bridge of Sighs—so yet 'twill be
Esteemed in riper history—
Sad arch between contrasted eras;
The span of fate; that evil day.

From the beginning, the Border States derived their name from Scott's terminology for a line of division running between areas marked by strong differences of culture (Highlands-Lowlands), but not quite separate nations. As the American situation worsened, the inherited terminology became ever more appropriate. In *Uncle Tom's Cabin; or, Life Among the Lowly* (1852), Mrs. Stowe claimed to have lived "for many years, on the frontier-line of slave States." During the war, Oliver Wendell Holmes told of "approaching the perilous borders, the marches where the North and the South mingle their angry hosts, where the extremes of our so-called civilization meet in conflict." In the same essay ("My Hunt After 'The Captain'") he referred to the battlefield where the "fierce centripetal forces have met and neutralized each other," and described Philadelphia as "the great neutral centre of the Continent, where the fiery enthusiasms of the South and the keen fanaticisms of the North meet at their outer limits, and result in a compound." In a Fourth of July address (1863), he asked: "Whom have we then for our neighbors, in case of separation,—our neighbors along a splintered line of fracture extending for thousands of miles,—but the Saracens [i.e., Savages] of the Nineteenth Century . . . a people whose existence as a hostile nation on our frontier is incompatible with our peaceful development?"[17] In a note to "The Frenzy in the Wake," Melville observed that "the war of Pompey and Caesar divided the Roman people promiscuously; that of the North and South ran a frontier line between what for the time

[17] *The Writings of Harriet Beecher Stowe* (Cambridge, 1896), II, 247. *The Writings of Oliver Wendell Holmes* (Boston, 1891), VIII, 23, 29, 71, 106.

were distinct communities or nations." Even more hor-
rendously, he jeered in "The Armies of the Wilderness":

> The Indian has passed away,
>   But creeping comes another—
> Deadlier far. Picket,
>   Take heed—take heed of thy brother!

"There were excesses which marked the conflict," he added
drily in his prose "Supplement," "most of which are perhaps
inseparable from a civil strife so intense and prolonged, and
involving warfare in some border countries new and imperfectly civilized." Since the fourteenth century (according
to the *Oxford English Dictionary*), "front" has been the
common term for a battle-line, but it took the Americans
a long time to realize it.

In sober fact, little of the Civil War was fought in the
West. But to dwell on this fact is utterly to miss the much
more important point that the Civil War destroyed the final
vestiges of the American frontier, and thus brought to an
end the first great period of American history and literature.
Ironically, the mediatorial West was in this sense the instrument of its own undoing—as its "winning" was also the
primary cause of its loss—for it was the increasingly
determined fight to control the Western territories that
irrevocably divided North from South in the 1850's. All
along, the bitterest irony had been the existence of two
Western "frontiers," the Romantic boundary between East
and West, and the far more dangerous boundary between
North and South, free states and slave states. But only the
Romantic boundary was widely known as "the frontier." By
the terms of the Missouri Compromise, however, a line
between North and South (36° 30′) was run to the Rocky
Mountains, continuing the separation of sections which
geographically and historically began on the Atlantic seaboard, and for decades this line was one of the sacred objects
of American politics, dearly beloved by the American people,
whose indefinitely Westward progressivism blinded them to
the obvious truth that the Compromise solved no problems,

but merely perpetuated them, or "removed" them farther West, with the Indian. Although this line was legislated out of existence in 1854, it did not therefore cease to exist; it merely exploded. The traditional political parties cracked and reformed, such diverse types as John Brown and Abraham Lincoln emerged from obscurity, and Bleeding Kansas replaced the neutral territory as the national emblem. The West had always been cherished by the quarreling sections as the one part of the country which might hopefully be kept free of sectional conflict, ultimately to work for national resolution and harmony; at the same time, each section was desperately trying to grab the West for itself. The admission of California to the Union as a free state in 1850, and Lincoln's election in 1860, were only the most dramatic incidents in the long last act of the national tragedy. The West had been "won" by the North, and the South was outflanked and contained. Her choices were now limited to acceptance of beleaguered status, or open rebellion; she chose the latter, and the first American republic was wrecked. Perhaps there had never been any such thing, for the failure to extirpate slavery, either immediately or gradually, must ultimately be referred to our Founding Fathers.

Melville's awareness of this developing calamity is the key to his best writing between *Moby-Dick* and *The Confidence-Man*. His frontiers are realistically enough both East-West and North-South, as if he had in mind a metaphorical model of what Faraday called diamagnetism, where the official frontier was split into two lines, lying at right angles to each other, self-neutralizing. Keeping these two frontiers simultaneously in view, he achieved without effort the most painful fusions of wildly contradictory ideas and emotions. So the *Serapis* - *Bon Homme Richard* conflict ends with Melville asking in its most memorable and sarcastic form a question raised for him initially by the white man's behavior in the South Seas, subsequently reinforced by his literary knowledge of the Indian's comparable fate, and now conceivably sharpened by observation of civilized savages in Charleston and Boston: "In view of this battle one may ask—What separates the enlightened man from the savage? Is civilization a thing distinct, or is it an advanced stage of barbarism?" The fundamental American problem was arising more urgently than ever, but in a shockingly altered context, and for nearly the last time. It was arising, of course, from considerations of the West, and of the frontier which represented the West, the frontier as a figure of speech, the hopefully dynamic metaphor comprehending the dialectic of civilization (such as it was) and nature (or the new start). By 1855, American nature was practically gone; it was daily becoming plainer that the new start was over; and now, as Melville was on the verge of realizing, the Americans' language also began to fail. With it, the American writer would sink toward silence, for as old Bardianna, the quotable wise man of Mardi had long since observed, " 'Truth is in things, and not in words: truth is voiceless.' "

4. THE CONFIDENCE-MAN

Melville's last completed novel sums up the age, but it is not an easy summary, and has never been popular. Quite obviously, *The Confidence-Man* (1857) is about the West, and constitutes on Melville's part a vote of no confidence in the nation. Practically everything else in it is deliberately obscure, and some things are almost hopelessly so. At the very beginning, for example, the "mysterious impostor" advertised on the placard is "supposed to have recently arrived from the East; quite an original genius in his vocation . . . though wherein his originality consisted was not clearly given." Nothing is clearly given. Only a few pages later, the all-white lamb-like deaf-mute (the first of the metaphysical scamps who inhabit the novel) is said to look as if he has traveled "from some far country beyond the prairies."[1] These directions are presumably significant, but how? What

[1] Unless otherwise indicated, quotations in this section are from *The Confidence-Man: His Masquerade*, ed. Elizabeth S. Foster (New York, 1954).

is the point of the impostor's being thought to have arrived from the East, when he also appears to have come from the Far West? If, indeed, that is what "beyond the prairies" means, and if the impostor and deaf-mute are the same man, and if any of these statements is reliable. Perhaps Melville wishes to suggest the dual "originality" of American civilization in Europe and in nature, which of course met in the middle of the country. In any case, this representative American national—busily entering St. Paul's predications about "charity" one after another on the right-hand half of his slate, while to the left the key word remains unaffected, for all the world as if he were dashing off a string of bad checks—is a wolf in sheep's clothing, and will soon, in St. Matthew's words, be known by his fruits.

Whatever manifold autobiographical or allegorical intentions may ultimately be involved, the immediate purpose of *The Confidence-Man* is to achieve high comedy through running contrast between all imaginable sorts of "confusion"—in facts, deductions, implications, generalizations, metaphors, analogies, evaluations, motives—and Melville's disciplined skeptical intelligence, as subsumed and displayed by the best prose he ever wrote. " 'I have confuted you, my dear barber,' " says the cosmopolitan, " 'I have confounded you' "; but as he must use Melville's tongue to say so, no reader need be as confounded as the barber, unless he wants to be. In other words, the content is negative, the attack affirmative, which is the customary procedure of the satirist, or of the early American writer lighting out from the actual West toward an aesthetic Territory. So viewed, at least the setting of *The Confidence-Man* begins to make sense (assuredly it has nothing to do with "local color"): Melville's election of the Mississippi River is once again his sardonic inversion of the values his culture conventionally attributed to the frontier. For a generation or more, that mighty and mythical river had been a synecdoche for the West, as had the frontier; Melville was neither the first nor the last to use them interchangeably. The West was in turn metonymous for America, as America (the New World) indirectly meant the Humanity of the Future. To speak of one was to speak of all, and thus automatically to entertain delectable visions of mediation, harmony, inclusion, and synthesis, to be achieved by means of the reconciliation of opposites, whether in literature, philosophy, or politics, on the happy hunting-ground, or neutral territory, of American wish-fulfillment.[2]

In a preliminary sketch, not used in the novel, but surviving in manuscript, Melville spread a rich palette:

As the word Abraham means the father of a great multitude of men so the word Mississippi means the father of a great multitude of waters. His tribes stream in from east & west, exceeding fruitful the lands they enrich. In this granary of a continent this basin of the Mississippi must not the nations be greatly multiplied & blest?

. . . Undisturbed as the lowly life in its bosom feeds the lonely life on its shores. . . . Wood & wave wed, man is remote. The Unsung time, the Golden Age of the billow.

. . . The unhumbled river ennobles himself now deepens now purely expands, now first forms his character & begins that career whose majestic serenity if not overborne by fierce onsets of torrents shall end only with ocean.

Like a larger Susquehannah like a long-drawn bison herd he hurries on through the prairie, here & there expanding into archipelagoes cycladean in beauty, while fissured & verdant, a long China Wall, the bluffs sweep bluely away. Glad & content the sacred river glides on.

But at St: Louis the course of this dream is run.

---

[2] Normally the Mississippi was known as "the aorta of the continent," or words to that effect. Parkman had recently written of it at length and in language that may have suggested Melville's inversions, in *The Conspiracy of Pontiac* (Boston, 1851), pp. 513-514. For another probable source of Melville's Mississippi, see John D. Seelye, "Timothy Flint's 'Wicked River' and *The Confidence-Man*," *Publications of the Modern Language Association of America*, LXXVIII (1963), 75-79.

Down on it like a Pawnee from ambush foams the yellow-jacket Missouri. The calm [?] is gone, the grouped [?] isles disappear, the shores are jagged & rent, the hue of the water is clayed, the before moderate current is rapid & vexed. The peace of the Upper River seems broken in the Lower, nor is it ever renewed.

The Missouri sends rather a hostile element than a filial flow. Longer stronger than the father of waters like Jupiter he dethrones his sire & reigns in his stead. Under the benign name Mississippi it is in short [no other?] the Missouri that now rolls to the Gulf, the Missouri that with the snows from his solitudes freezes the warmth of the genial zones, the Missouri that by open assault or artful sap sweeps away fruit & field grave-yard & barn, the Missouri that not a tributary but a murderer enters the sea, long disdaining to yield his white wave to the blue.[3]

Just as the devious Missouri underflows the benign Mississippi, so this passage reveals Melville in the act of subverting the traditional gestalt of the West. "Wood & wave wed" is the conventional frontier metaphor, but used, as in *The Marble Faun*, for a pre-human state of affairs. The Mississippi as ostensible harmonizer of East and West (North and South), happily irrigating the "granary of a continent," is also orthodox. But the secondary figures are more ambivalently balanced: innocent (Mississippi as bison herd) and ominous (Missouri as Pawnee from ambush). And finally, the juncture between the two rivers, their point of meeting or frontier, is "hostile" (disputed), and from it the Missouri (disguised as the Mississippi) rolls like a murderer, or John Paul Jones of nations, to the Gulf of extinction. At the hostile juncture (St. Louis), the course of the American dream is run. And St. Louis is precisely where *The Confidence-Man* begins—that is, after a period of his-

---

[3] More or less as transcribed in *The Confidence-Man*, ed. Foster, pp. 379-380. I have simplified her text, while questioning a few of her readings, and have emended "an outlaw" in the last sentence to "a murderer."

tory in which the American dream has been subtly replaced by an inverted double. The *Fidèle*'s destination is New Orleans; significantly, she never arrives.[4] " 'In general,' " Melville says in the novel, allegedly quoting Tacitus, " 'a black and shameful period lies before me.' " The word "before" is ambiguous.

The setting is no mere setting, then, but an ironic compendium and critique of Western clichés, appropriately enacted in the American heartland on April Fool's Day. So much carries over from sketch to novel, which discriminates these various figures far more rigorously, and deploys them far more dramatically, whether in the comedy of thought or the comedy of action. In the sketch, the frontier metaphor is alternately good and bad (weddings vs. hostilities); in the novel, it is invariably bad. Platitudinously considered, the frontier metaphor meant inclusive harmony; in *The Confidence-Man*, it means preposterous confusion. The Mississippi which is not the Mississippi is simultaneously the national mode of definition and the satiric vehicle of the novel's central theme, as we are surely supposed to infer from the passage in chapter 2 about "the dashing and all-fusing spirit of the West, whose type is the Mississippi itself, which, uniting the streams of the most distant and opposite zones, pours them along, helter-skelter, in one cosmopolitan and confident tide." Every word is ironic, but readers entrapped by conventional attitudes will miss the point—Melville was increasingly fond of leading bad readers into temptation—that all this confident fusing and uniting (the mission of the age and of America, according to the tireless publicists) served primarily to conceal the basest ends with the emptiest rhetoric. So far as reconciliation and mediation were concerned, the intransigent Melville now believed in the frontier as the indispensable setting for his final onslaught against stupidity and meanness. " 'You fools! . . . you flock of fools, under this captain

[4] There was actually a Western steamboat named "Fidelity," and it was listed in James Hall, *Statistics of the West* (Cincinnati, 1836), as "destroyed" (p. 255).

307

of fools, in this ship of fools!' " snarls an exasperated man early in the game; but then, as one of the confidence-men confidently remarks, a few pages later: " 'Along the Mississippi, you know, business is not so ceremonious as at the East.' " All the novel's themes must ultimately be interpreted in the context of this symptomatic setting; if, for example, *The Confidence-Man* secretly hints the betrayal and death of Christianity, the more comprehensive and realistic point is the exquisite propriety of the American frontier for such a denouement.[5]

And yet, paradoxically, there are clarities and even positive values within the confusions, as in Melville's passenger list, which immediately precedes the "all-fusing spirit of the West" passage, and which, like the rest of the novel, is dominated by Western people:

As among Chaucer's Canterbury pilgrims, or those oriental ones crossing the Red Sea towards Mecca in the festival month, there was no lack of variety. Natives

[5] Melville's main source for the religious consequences of American intellectual collapse was probably a passage in Swift's "Mechanical Operation of the Spirit," which purports to examine "the fundamental Difference in Point of Religion, between the wild *Indians* and Us," with respect to worship of God and Devil. "What I applaud them for," Swift comically remarks, "is their Discretion, in limiting their Devotions and their Deities to their several Districts, nor ever suffering the Liturgy of the *white* God, to cross or interfere with that of the *Black*. Not so with Us, who pretending by the Lines and Measures of our Reason, to extend the Dominion of one invisible Power, and contract that of the other, have discovered a gross Ignorance in the Natures of Good and Evil, and most horribly confounded the Frontiers of both." *A Tale of a Tub*, ed. A. C. Guthkelch and D. Nichol Smith (Oxford, 1920), p. 276. Melville may also have been reading Orestes Brownson's "novel" *The Spirit-Rapper* (1854), a caustic anatomy of mid-nineteenth-century American religion and philosophy, in which the Devil appears as a sentimental or humanitarian "philanthropist." Chapter titles include "A Lesson in Philanthropy," "A Lesson in World-Reform," "Worth Considering," "Sheer Deviltry," and "Left in the Lurch." Under the name of "Mr. Winslow" (Melville's Mark Winsome) Emerson is devastated by Brownson in a typically Melvillean fashion. Melville conceivably offers a clue to this source in the mélange of ejaculations commencing ch. 2.

of all sorts, and foreigners; men of business and men of pleasure; parlor men and backwoodsmen; farm-hunters and fame-hunters; heiress-hunters, gold-hunters, buffalo-hunters, bee-hunters, happiness-hunters, truth-hunters, and still keener hunters after all these hunters. Fine ladies in slippers, and moccasined squaws; Northern speculators and Eastern philosophers; English, Irish, German, Scotch, Danes; Santa Fé traders in striped blankets, and Broadway bucks in cravats of cloth of gold; fine-looking Kentucky boatmen, and Japanese-looking Mississippi cotton-planters; Quakers in full drab, and United States soldiers in full regimentals. ... In short, a piebald parliament, an Anacharsis Cloots congress of all kinds of that multiform pilgrim species, man.[6]

Despite an air of reckless exuberance, this passage is patterned on a multiplicity of contrasts, of which one—the contrast between the genuine and the spurious—is crucial. Backwoodsmen vs. parlor men, farm-hunters vs. fame-hunters, moccasined squaws vs. fine ladies in slippers: although the West is the appropriate scene of all this confusion, and the frontier the inevitable habitat of fraud, we are also asked to discriminate the genuine from the false through identifying the genuine with the West. This kind of reversing perspective, or involuted irony, is the chief formal principle of *The Confidence-Man*, whose leading moral intention is to teach the pleasures of close discrimination. *The Confidence-Man* is deliberately and markedly anti-syncretic.

If that passenger list, closely scrutinized, reveals strange commitments beneath an apparently senseless surface, so do many of the other Western references. The recurrent joke about the "Widow and Orphan Asylum recently founded among the Seminoles," is not really much of a joke, if we pause to inquire why widows and orphans are so numerous

[6] This potpourri originated in Melville's review of Parkman, where Melville was following a particular passage in *The California and Oregon Trail* (New York, 1849), p. 10, and enriching it with details found elsewhere (pp. 11, 49).

among that unhappy people, or reflect upon the secret motives of those who belatedly find it desirable to assist them. " 'And now let me give you a little history of our asylum,' " says the man in gray, " 'and the providential way in which it was started.' " Chapter break. "At an interesting point of the narration, and at the moment when, with much curiosity, indeed, urgency, the narrator was being particularly questioned upon that point, he was, as it happened, altogether diverted both from it and his story." So the reader must supply his own history, and what he supplies will depend on what he thinks about the relations between "Providence" and America's "continental destiny." Nearly always, the jokes are satiric, and satire demands a butt, or, on this occasion, a whole society of butts:

> Another peddler, who was still another versatile chevalier, hawked, in the thick of the throng [full of "chevaliers," or pickpockets], the lives of Measan, the bandit of Ohio, Murrel, the pirate of the Mississippi, and the brothers Harpe, the Thugs of the Green River country, in Kentucky—creatures, with others of the sort, one and all exterminated at the time, and for the most part, like the hunted generations of wolves in the same regions, leaving comparatively few successors; which would seem cause for unalloyed gratulation, and is such to all except those who think that in new countries, where the wolves are killed off, the foxes increase.

Suddenly the irony triples to include the West of the past (violent), the West as subsequently misrepresented by Eastern hacks (fraudulent), and the contemporary West, full of the outlaws' heirs and the writers' counterparts.[7]

Especially in the first half of *The Confidence-Man*, Melville displays a jeering and often hilarious attitude toward

[7] For the proportional relations between wolves and foxes, see Edmund Spenser, *The Shepheardes Calender*, "September," ll. 150-161, and the corresponding notes in the "Glosse." Predictably, James Hall wrote about Measan and the Harpes—in *Letters From the West* (London, 1828)—indulging unalloyed gratulation over their disappearance (p. 281).

certain sacred assumptions his countrymen regularly made about the West. " 'Open their eyes?' echoed the cosmopolitan, slowly expanding his; 'what is there in this world for one to open his eyes to?' " Actually, hints of this attitude are found in many a native humorist. As one of them remarked in his preface: "The west abounds with incident and humor, and the observer must lack an eye for the comic who can look upon the panorama of western life without being tempted to laugh. . . . I have wondered why the finished and graphic writers of our country so seldom sought material from this inviting field."[8] His query was more than answered, and long before Mark Twain began to enrich himself from other men's diggings. On the other hand, to return to the paradox which emerges from Melville's passenger list, it is hardly ever the real West—as marginally defined by the author for the purposes of this book—which Melville ridicules, but a false-front, travesty West, conventional and stereotyped, analogous with all the other false fronts in the novel, plausible and fake. Apart from the prose style (always the safest indication), and its underlying conception of "the open ground of reason," together with its near analogue the "natural heart," this peculiarly Melvillean West is the most certain aid to interpretation of *The Confidence-Man.* Eruption of the real West into the gilded saloons of the *Fidèle* is nearly always the sign for the eruption of some unpleasing, disquieting fact (such as the fact of the defrauded Indian) into the novel's world of discourse, which is more or less equivalent to a tour of American civilization. Somehow, since the writing of *Pierre,* Melville has discovered a new rock on which to build his faith, for the West of *The Confidence-Man*—such glimpses as we get of it —is strikingly different from the West in any of his earlier books. This is a hardpan West, grim, dirty, threatening, diseased, disagreeable; and grimness, dirt, etc. are not to

[8] John S. Robb, *Streaks of Squatter Life, and Far-West Scenes* (1847), ed. John F. McDermott (Gainesville, Florida, 1962), p. viii.

be despised in a world dedicated to the smiling contemplation of their opposites.[9]

This typical movement of the action is easy to isolate in the incident of the wretched, morose Westerner who comes aboard in chapter 17 to refute the herb-doctor's argument about the automatic beneficence of nature. Like a toxic exhalation, or ailing nature-god, the frontiersman seems to emanate from the aguish Western landscape:

> For just then the boat touched at a houseless landing, scooped, as by a land-slide, out of sombre forests; back through which led a road, the sole one, which, from its narrowness, and its being walled up with story on story of dusk, matted foliage, presented the vista of some cavernous old gorge in a city, like haunted Cock Lane in London. Issuing from that road, and crossing that landing, there stooped his shaggy form in the door-way, and entered the ante-cabin, with a step so burdensome that shot seemed in his pockets, a kind of invalid Titan in homespun; his beard blackly pendant, like the Carolina-moss, and dank with cypress dew; his countenance tawny and shadowy as an iron-ore country in a clouded day. In one hand he carried a heavy walking-stick of swamp-oak; with the other, led a puny girl, walking in moccasins, not improbably his child, but evidently of alien maternity, perhaps Creole, or even Camanche. Her eye would have been large for a woman, and was inky as the pools of falls among mountain-pines. An Indian blanket, orange-hued, and fringed with lead tassel-work, appeared that morning to have shielded the

[9] Melville's sentiments about the West as a place of relief are of course standard; his tone is not. Cf. Josiah Gregg, *Commerce of the Prairies* (1844): "This passion for Prairie life . . . will be very apt to lead me upon the Plains again, to spread my bed with the mustang and the buffalo, under the broad canopy of heaven,—there to seek to maintain undisturbed my confidence in men, by fraternizing with the little prairie dogs and wild colts, and the still wilder Indians." *Early Western Travels, 1748-1846*, ed. Reuben G. Thwaites (Cleveland, 1904-1907), xx, 221.

child from heavy showers. Her limbs were tremulous; she seemed a little Cassandra, in nervousness.[10]

As always, Melville's sympathies lie with the weary and heavy-laden, and as he turns to consider them, his prose accommodates itself to the reversed current of feeling. In contrast to the "dashing and all-fusing spirit of the West," father and daughter are as stark and incontrovertible as natural fact. This is the realism of specification, best antidote to the confidence-man's dubious prescriptions. " 'Some pains cannot be eased but by producing insensibility,' " this saturnine frontiersman informs the herb-doctor, " 'and cannot be cured but by producing death.' " But human fatuity is not easily silenced; the herb-doctor resumes his spiel, until "a sudden side-blow all but felled him"; the invalid Titan departs the windy cabin, followed by the benediction of all quackery: " 'Regardless of decency, and lost to humanity!' "

At the novel's center is a long sequence (chapters 21-27) in which the confidence-man battles another crotchety frontiersman (or Ishmael) named Pitch: " 'My name is Pitch,' " as he is always saying, " 'I stick to what I say.' " This sequence properly comes to an end with the notorious Indian-hating story. Like Pitch, the Indian theme has been often foreshadowed, as in the Seminole joke, or in the story of Goneril (who is said to resemble "the women of savage life" —an unwarranted slander of savage women, perpetrated conjointly by "two" of the confidence-men), and equally though oppositely in the herb-doctor's attempt to dignify his calling by associating himself with Indian doctors. Like the obvious spoofing of Emerson, in whose rainbow Melville did not oscillate, most of what follows is literary satire;[11]

[10] This would seem to be Melville's development, and fundamental reversal, of a passage in Charles Fenno Hoffman, *A Winter in the West* (New York, 1835), II, 118-119.

[11] Emerson as "mystical master" (chs. 36-37) is fairly obvious, and Thoreau as "practical disciple" (chs. 37-41) nearly as indisputable. Whitman is probably represented in chs. 29-30 by " 'a kind of poetry, but in a form which stands in something the same rela-

most of what precedes is preliminary testing of theme in a wide variety of applications. In the first half of the novel Melville develops various facets of the confidence-man one by one; in the middle he fuses them in the cosmopolitan; then he brings into contact with the cosmopolitan a series of characters who are figuratively but not literally confidence-men; most of them are writers. The joke is that both figuratively and literally, all the confidence-men are only one.

Suddenly, with no warning, Pitch is aboard; we hear him, before we see him, sounding like an irascible Natty Bumppo: " 'Yarbs, yarbs; natur, natur; you foolish old file you! He diddled you with that hocus-pocus, did he?' " Immediately, Melville interpolates a pointedly functional description of Pitch's appearance and quality: "It was a rather eccentric-looking person who spoke; somewhat ursine in aspect; sporting a shaggy spencer of the cloth called bear's-skin; a high-peaked cap of raccoon-skin, the long bushy tail switching over behind; raw-hide leggings; grim stubble chin; and to end, a double-barreled gun in hand—a Missouri bachelor, a Hoosier gentleman, of Spartan leisure and fortune, and equally Spartan manners and sentiments; and, as the sequel may show, not less acquainted, in a Spartan way of his own, with philosophy and books, than with woodcraft and rifles."

---

tion to blank verse which that does to rhyme.' " Poe turns up in ch. 36, "peddling a rhapsodical tract [doubtless *Eureka*; Emerson refuses to buy it], composed by himself, and setting forth his claims to some rhapsodical apostleship. Though ragged and dirty, there was about him no touch of vulgarity; for, by nature, his manner was not unrefined, his frame slender, and appeared the more so from the broad, untanned frontlet of his brow, tangled over with a disheveled mass of raven curls." Hawthorne, I conjecture, is Orchis, or Doleful Dumps, in "The Story of China Aster," a rather transparent allegorical parody of Melville's disastrous literary career and of its relation to Hawthorne's. The story takes place at Marietta, on the "banks of the inland Ohio," and is told, or re-told, by "Thoreau," who complains about its "maudlin" style. Only one major writer remains unaccounted for—unless, as is sufficiently likely, Pitch is Cooper, or, more subtly stated, the spirit of Cooper reaffirming itself through Melville.

Pitch is by far the most complicated and broadly human character in the book, and the ambassador from the real West to the world of American cant, as derived from popular contemplations of the West.[12] His costume constitutes his credentials, nearly every item in it plainly won from nature through practical effort and at ascertainable risk. Everything about him represents do-it-yourself American pragmatism, as everything about the confidence-man suggests American flatulence. The point about Pitch's clothing is driven home by the attempts of the man with the brass-plate to befuddle him with false analogies between costume and cast of mind (later, that spurious Westerner Charlie Noble tries to discredit him as an Easterner by birth): " 'When I behold you on this mild summer's eve, thus eccentrically clothed in the skins of wild beasts, I cannot but conclude that the equally grim and unsuitable habit of your mind is likewise but an eccentric assumption, having no basis in your genuine soul, no more than in nature herself.' " What Melville means by these outrageous puns is that Pitch's habit of mind is as direct and forthright as his clothing, which in his case seems no clothing at all (in the Carlylean sense of false appearances and stock responses) but the inevitable integument of character, just as his speech is the transparent skin of thought. He is unsuitable only in relation to a sham society, eccentric only in being genuine.

Although ultimately defeated, Pitch causes the confidence-man more trouble than anyone else—Emerson and Thoreau possibly excepted—and at one point is complacently told: " 'The back-woods would seem to have given you rather eccentric notions.' " Almost invariably his notions resemble the author's. Significantly, it is Pitch who utters Melville's anti-confidence prayer—the most important speech in the book, and closely resembling the much better-known prayer in *Moby-Dick* ("Bear me out in it, thou great democratic God!"): " 'Now the high-constable catch and confound all knaves in towns and rats in grain-bins, and if in this boat,

[12] Late in the novel, Melville sports with Emerson for knowing the West mostly by hearsay.

which is a human grain-bin for the time, any sly, smooth, philandering rat be dodging now, pin him, thou high rat-catcher, against this rail.' " Is that spare eloquence surpassed by anything in Melville, or even matched for close propriety to the nation that wrecked him? Few American writers, surely, have so inventively extended the attributes of God. Pitch is only human, and therefore errs, betrayed by a false analogy or a mixed metaphor. For all that, he wins and retains our amused and affectionate regard. His folly is neither wilful nor ungenerous nor confirmed. He is also Melville's private salvation, for in artlessness as in integrity (time, perhaps, will make him all right) he represents an altogether new West, arising, however fitfully, and apparently through a kind of unanticipated and almost inexplicable attainment of perspective, from the catastrophes of the 1850's.

Melville's fullest meditation on the necessity for skepticism ("In which the powerful effect of natural scenery is evinced in the case of the Missourian, who, in view of the region round about Cairo, has a return of his chilly fit") is appropriately centered on Pitch, and introduced as well as occasioned by another of those unpicturesque, unliterary landscapes which weave their threads so strikingly through the novel's deliberately flimsy verbal fabric. This landscape is even more complex than that whence the invalid Titan emerged; each represents the intrusion of reality, but in the present instance the reality happens to be the certainty of false appearances:

> In the dank twilight, fanned with mosquitoes, and sparkling with fire-flies, the boat now lies before Cairo. She has landed certain passengers, and tarries for the coming of expected ones. Leaning over the rail on the inshore side, the Missourian eyes through the dubious medium that swampy and squalid domain; and over it audibly mumbles his cynical mind to himself. . . . He bethinks him that the man with the brass-plate was to land on this villainous bank, and for that cause, if no

other, begins to suspect him. Like one beginning to rouse himself from a dose of chloroform treacherously given, he half divines, too, that he, the philosopher, had unwittingly been betrayed into being an unphilosophical dupe.

Poor Pitch! unknowingly, he merely rests for a minute before his encounter with the greatest—because much the most magnificently multifarious—of all confidence-men.

The cosmopolitan, who slides into the action at Cairo (as the sun sets), from the East, along with *la Belle Rivière*, bringing further confusion, and inspiring the novel's one notable change of direction, is the eternal enemy of Pitch—enemy of precision, definition, particularity—and his exact antithesis. Their opposition is immediately established in terms of apparel. Pitch is speaking:

> "And who of my fine-fellow species may you be? From the Brazils, ain't you? Toucan fowl. Fine feathers on foul meat."
>
> This ungentle mention of the toucan was not improbably suggested by the parti-hued, and rather plumagy aspect of the stranger, no bigot it would seem, but a liberalist, in dress, and whose wardrobe, almost anywhere than on the liberal Mississippi, used to all sorts of fantastic informalities, might, even to observers less critical than the bachelor, have looked, if anything, a little out of the common; but not more so perhaps, than, considering the bear and raccoon costume, the bachelor's own appearance.

The various items of this costume derive from various cultures, as in the theory of the American melting-pot; the cosmopolitan is further armed with a pipe (which he wields like a scepter or wand) whose "great porcelain bowl [is] painted in miniature with linked crests and arms of interlinked nations"; he is a kind of parody Anacharsis Cloots. We appear to have returned to the characteristic language of *Pierre*, where words like "link" and "interlink" revealed the secret presence of the frontier metaphor. Like the false Mississippi, where business is not so ceremonious as at the East, the liberalist cosmopolitan is the false spirit of the West, and therefore the false American spirit, as we may guess from his Franklinesque self-description as " 'a catholic man; who, being such, ties himself to no narrow tailor or teacher, but federates, in heart as in costume, something of the various gallantries of men under various suns. Oh, one roams not over the gallant globe in vain. Bred by it, is a fraternal and fusing feeling.' " The spirit of the West is "all-fusing," and the tide it pours along "confident" (fraudulent) and "cosmopolitan" (confusing), though of course another reason for the cosmopolitan's "catholicity" is his role as comprehender of all previous confidence-men. "Cosmopolitan" (like "genial") suggests false synthesis, false reconciliation, false harmony, false inclusiveness—as, for example, between good and evil, being and nothing, truth and lie. (For these antitheses the figurative frontier was useless, even in friendly hands.) " 'Ah, now,' deprecating [to Pitch] with his pipe, 'irony is so unjust; never could abide irony; something Satanic about irony. God defend me from Irony, and Satire, his bosom friend.' " *The Confidence-Man* is a fight to the finish between that prayer and the rat-catching prayer, and an indispensable, if perplexing, guidebook for those who live in new countries.

What such people evidently need most is elementary instruction on the subject of the natives, in this case Indians —a clearly integral part of the West, and increasingly synonymous with that section as the aboriginal population, together with the West's square miles, was annually squeezed into narrower and narrower compass. The story grows both more farcical and more deadly as we approach its problematic center, the interpolated tale of a famous Indian-hater; this is the final incarnation of *Gun-Deck*, that repulsive sailor in *Redburn* who so thoroughly enjoyed himself in Florida "popping off Indians," and who called his pastime "a rat-killing war." But if God is the "high rat-catcher," occasionally delegating authority to writers of Melville's

persuasion, and the cosmopolitan a "sly, smooth, philandering rat," then the Indian-hater, above and beyond his obvious inhumanity, is obscenely parodic of the true Christian:
under the prejudicial metaphor of rat, he hunts, not lies, or
confidence-men, as he ought, but human beings. He refuses
to conceive them as people, perpetually figuring them to himself, and to his audience, as beasts to be exterminated or
fiends to be exorcised. He is only another confidence-man,
and thus another pathological symptom of American civilization, over against whom stand, in all the naked splendor
of irrefutable and embattled indignation, nature, Indian,
writer, truth. And truth, as one of Melville's minor heroes
aptly remarks, " 'will *not* be comforted.' "

That this Indian-hating story is told—by Charles Arnold
Noble, a small-time operator and log-cabin critic—with the
intention of discrediting Pitch, lest his skepticism prove con-
tagious, is clear from the outset. Noble's first words to the
cosmopolitan, approaching him "with the bluff *abord* of
the West," immediately establish a disparaging relationship between the difficult Missourian and a notorious Indian-
hater: " 'Queer 'coon, your friend. Had a little skrimmage
with him myself. Rather entertaining old 'coon, if he wasn't
so deuced analytical. Reminded me somehow of what I've
heard about Colonel John Moredock, of Illinois, only your
friend ain't quite so good a fellow at bottom, I should
think.' " The cosmopolitan, who specializes in a good word
for everyone, genially comes to the defense of Indians, with
his vague, sentimental palaver: " 'Hate Indians? Why
should he or anybody else hate Indians? *I* admire Indians.
Indians I have always heard to be one of the finest
of the primitive races, possessed of many heroic virtues.
Some noble women, too. When I think of Pocahontas, I
am ready to love Indians. Then there's Massasoit, and
Philip of Mount Hope, and Tecumseh, and Red-Jacket,
and Logan—all heroes; and there's the Five Nations, and
Araucanians—federations and communities of heroes.' " The
cosmopolitan is not praising the Indian, of course, about
whom he knows nothing, and cares less, but waving away

the disquieting information that Indian-haters exist; partly because it suits his ends to deny evil altogether, partly because this particular evil—the systematic extirpation of inconvenient fact—constitutes his own mode of being, or non-being. Characteristically, he confuses the issue.

Charlie Noble then claims to have been as a boy " 'westward a long journey through the wilderness' " with his father, and to have seen Moredock's cabin on the West bank of the Wabash River, though not the great man in person, who was sleeping late, after an all-night Indian-hunting expedition. Still, he knows all about Moredock— Melville's confidence-men always know everything about everything—having heard " 'his history again and again from my father's friend, James Hall, the judge, you know. In every company being called upon to give this history, which none could better do, the judge at last fell into a style so methodic, you would have thought he spoke less to mere auditors than to an invisible amanuensis; seemed talking for the press; very impressive way with him indeed.' " It is from Hall's foxy *Sketches of History, Life, and Manners, in the West* (1835), and especially from "Indian hating.—Some of the sources of this animosity.— Brief Account of Col. Moredock," that Charlie Noble claims to have the story " 'almost word for word.' "[13] Actually,

[13] Perhaps he also drew on the works of such notorious Indian-haters as Robert Montgomery Bird and Parkman (see Miss Foster's explanatory notes, pp. 338-339), but of all the popular writers about the West, Hall was clearly pre-eminent in making literary capital of the national disgrace. Melville may have come to him via Hoffman; see *A Winter in the West*, I, 226-227; II, 28-34, 275. In addition to the story of Col. Moredock, Hall gave the public two further tales and innumerable shorter passages on the subject: "The Indian Hater" (in *Legends of the West*, and elsewhere), and "The Pioneer": "In killing a savage . . . I served my country as a citizen" (*Tales of the Border*, Philadelphia, 1835, p. 86). His most extensively devious treatment of the Indian, which he reprinted several times with minor variations, is "Intercourse of the American People With the Indians," Part I of *Sketches of History, Life, and Manners, in the West* (Philadelphia, 1835), and in this context the Moredock tale must finally be placed. The basic argument is sustained by a hidden pun on "progress": the morally superior nation

Melville supplies a loose and murderous paraphrase-parody of which perhaps half is sheer fabrication. He loads the sketch with additional aspersions of Indian character, and interpolates into it every known or imaginable cliché about the innate superiority of Western pioneers. The technique is simplicity itself: Melville merely makes explicit, or hyperbolic, what in Hall is understated, implied, or concealed. He had only to transpose into this context passages from Hall's other writings, or burlesques of his own along the same lines. " 'Indian-hating, then, shall be my first theme,' " says the operator—following Hall's practice, if not his language, for "border warfare" was clearly his favorite topic —" 'and Colonel Moredock, the Indian-hater, my next and last.' " For Melville, Hall replaced Parkman as a target, as Hawthorne once replaced Dana as an inspiration.

Part of the alteration in Hall's text may be attributed to Charlie Noble, who argues for Pitch's being worse than—not merely as bad as—Moredock, on the typically American grounds that Pitch distrusts men in general (men being "good"), while Moredock hated only Indians (a venial sin, if sin it be) but showed himself notably "humane," "convivial," and even "benevolent" (that "loving heart") toward his own people.[14] Moredock is of course the grossest racial bigot, and it is to an anticipated correspondence of prejudice in the cosmopolitan that Charlie Noble hopes to appeal, as James Hall appealed to the same prejudice in his readers. Independent, self-reliant, philosophical, "the backwoodsman would seem to America what Alexander was to Asia—captain in the vanguard of conquering civilization.

---

is obliged to expand geographically, inevitably pushing the pioneers, who in turn push the Indians, until obviously, although this is not mentioned by Hall, pioneers and Indians are pushed into the water. The best scholarly treatments of literary Indian-hating are Roy Harvey Pearce, *The Savages of America* (Baltimore, 1953), esp. pp. 225-236, and Arthur K. Moore, *The Frontier Mind* (Lexington, 1957), esp. pp. 95-99.

[14] In these and subsequent quotations from the Indian-hating story I have simplified the quotation marks, which are unduly complicated.

. . .Worthy to be compared with Moses in the Exodus"—typical Melvillean reductions to absurdity. Indians can never be civilized, and must therefore be removed, or obliterated; kindness is wasted on savages, who always repay it with treachery; Indian evaluation of these matters is never disinterested, and may therefore be ignored. All these preposterous opinions—widely shared by the American people, and in the last analysis the justification for their national behavior—Melville attributes to Hall, and he ends with an even more spectacularly diabolical hoax, which is of course his own delicious invention: "To be a consistent Indian-hater involves the renunciation of ambition, with its objects—the pomps and glories of the world; and since religion, pronouncing such things vanities, accounts it merit to renounce them, therefore, so far as this goes, Indian-hating, whatever may be thought of it in other respects, may be regarded as not wholly without the efficacy of a devout sentiment." Or, as he has said earlier: "Upon the whole, the judge, by two and thirty good and sufficient reasons, would maintain that there was no known vocation whose consistent following calls for such self-containings as that of the Indian-hater *par excellence*. In the highest view, he considered such a soul one peeping out but once an age." This is pure and corrosive farce.

When it is plain that the story about Moredock has inexplicably failed of its desired effect, Charlie Noble quickly evades responsibility for it, again emphasizing its origins with another writer, as Hall regularly evaded responsibility for such views by quoting them as the pioneers', and then pretending to be shocked. The story is " 'not my story, mind, or my thoughts, but another's,' " he says, and goes on to make Hall responsible even for the Pitch-Indian-hater equation. " 'And now, for your friend Coonskins, I doubt not, that, if the judge were here, he would pronounce him a sort of comprehensive Colonel Moredock, who, too much spreading his passion, shallows it.' " According to Judge Hall—according to Charlie Noble, according to Melville—it is a terrible thing to be "misanthropic" (" 'so

deuced analytical' ") about the motives of men (especially
Americans), but quite acceptable " 'never [to] let pass an
opportunity of quenching an Indian.' " The technique is the
same as that used to discredit Emerson, whose benevolism
(as exemplified in Thoreau) that benevolent cynic, the cosmopolitan, finds too cynical to bear.

Why did Melville desire to make Hall appear so ridiculous and so inhumane? There is only one possible answer:
Melville thought he was. Through the genial façade of
Hall's genteel narration, behind the protestations of
morality and piety, Melville detected the fundamental barbarism of his eminently respectable views. Hall was not
merely Hall, of course, but the representative writer of the
West—" 'Not that the backwoodsman ever used those words,
you see, but the judge found him expression for his meaning' "—the confidence-man himself, the seamy underside of
whose conventionally progressive admiration of the "civilizing process" (destruction, loot, and manslaughter) Melville
was now determined to lay bare once and for all. His comic
additions to Hall's story were designed to expose what
Melville had decided was the real motivation behind this
writer, and this kind of writing—whitewash—and thus to
damn the good literary judge, cultural arbiter of Ohio and
Illinois, out of his own mouth. As the narrator-once-removed
of Melville's ridiculous version, Hall is pompously fat-
headed and stupidly cruel, as indeed he looks in the standard
portrait, whereas his tales and sketches remarkably resemble
Melville's description of Charlie Noble, exuding a "warm
air of florid cordiality, contrasting itself with one knows
not what kind of aguish sallowness of saving discretion lurking behind it. Ungracious critics might have thought that the
manner flushed the man." Ungracious critics might even
have thought that the manner flushed the entire nation.
After all, Melville's bitter burlesque rests squarely on the
recognition of a tragic anomaly inherent in the Westward
Movement: the impossibility of being simultaneously pro-
Indian and pro-American in the usual, patriotic sense. The
American writer was ultimately compelled to elect Indian-

hating or a radical re-definition of what it meant to be an American, a re-definition in which (by definition) he would stand outside American civilization and opposed to it; with, in fact, the Indian. Hall's and Melville's choices were antithetical and mutually exclusive.

Even the cosmopolitan detects the basic incoherence of "Hall's" story (the benevolent Indian-hater, or "Leather-stocking Nemesis"), and correctly notes its lack of application to Pitch. All the Indian-hating story adds up to, as a thing in itself, is the indisputable truth that there was frequently bad blood between frontiersmen and Indians. It tells us absolutely nothing about Melville's attitude toward Indians that we did not know before, except that his attitude is precisely what it always was. What really matters is the reason—sufficiently obvious—for retelling this nasty little tale. The story was included in *The Confidence-Man*, and placed in the central position, because the Indian was the crucial and intractable fact of American history, the primary fact that all good American confidence-men were most anxious to conceal. Not merely another man, the Indian was fundamental humanity (as Melville had said or implied in book after book), in a relatively helpless posture. The Americans had cheated, hunted, destroyed, or exiled him— into, of all places, the West; if the West were also their future, the Humanity of the Future would some day pay for it.[15] The Indian was also, in the poet's vision, the embodiment of the land, the human manifestation of the New World. This, too, the Americans had exploited and lost. Finally, as we have seen time and again, at least as early as

[15] "Civilization," wrote Lewis Henry Morgan in *League of the . . . Iroquois* (Rochester, 1851), "is aggressive, as well as progressive—a positive state of society, attacking every obstacle, overwhelming every lesser agency, and searching out and filling up every crevice, both in the moral and physical world; while Indian life is an unarmed condition, a negative state, without inherent vitality, and without powers of resistance" (p. 444). Therefore, "it cannot be forgotten, that in after years our Republic must render an account, to the civilized world, for the disposal which it makes of the Indian. It is not sufficient, before this tribunal, to plead inevitable destiny" (pp. 459-460).

in *The Last of the Mohicans*, the Indian was the major American writer in his usual spiritual warfare with the James Halls of this world. No wonder the Indian was still, for Melville's generation—as indeed he is for ours—an awe-inspiring, or even a fearful figure. At any moment, he might come to life—cease to be "literature," as in *The Song of Hiawatha* (1855)—and emerge into actuality, to oppress the conscience. And then what would happen to the confidence-man's little game?

By the time of *The Confidence-Man*, Melville's picture of the Westward Movement was harshly realistic, and qualified only by the detachments inherent in the comic mode; this picture was quite a different picture from that of *Moby-Dick*, as *Moby-Dick* was in turn different from *Mardi*. Yet these differences were perhaps more of tone than of substance; from the beginning, Melville had been intermittently critical, showing himself skeptical both toward the social-stages-of-history theory and the kind of romance which that theory supported, where Natty Bumppo and Indian John Mohegan sat down together on the frontier, each imbuing himself with the nature of the other. Melville had himself worked in the tradition, and I think he never objected that such theories lacked meaning, nor that such romances failed in nobility; the difficulty lay rather in their inadequacy to the facts. Together with the other best minds of his time, Melville was also more charitably disposed (more Rousseauistic, if one likes) toward the Indian than the generality of his countrymen; to such effect as we have seen. He was also less inclined to let these countrymen slur over their crimes, whether past, present, or merely projected; no American historian has ever exhibited nearly so great a talent for nosing out what is called in *The Confidence-Man* "sinning by deputy." "How shocking would that be! But it is not permitted to be; and even if it were, no judicious moralist would make proclamation of it." And few have.

But Melville was nothing if not a moralist, and he remained a moralist to the bitter end, improving all the time. In *Moby-Dick*, a book which is possibly greater, but for certain purposes less instructive as well as less entertaining, he had laid down the lines along which, after the collapse of *Pierre*, he would at length fight through to a second magnificent triumph (the interpolated tale of Charlemont may be taken as a parable of the return) : " 'Delight is to him, who gives no quarter in the truth, and kills, burns, and destroys all sin though he pluck it out from under the robes of Senators and Judges.' " Did Melville already suspect from under which Judge's robe he would pluck it out? (To think of particular Senators opens another rich field of speculation.) " 'Delight,—top-gallant delight is to him, who acknowledges no law or lord, but the Lord his God, and is only a patriot to heaven.' " Unlike most Americans, Melville never forgot the First Commandment, which is also the First Commandment for the writer; under its unremittent and arduous discipline, he scrutinized the frontier, the West, and the United States of America, as popularly conceived, until they faded into the most ambiguous and diaphanous of existences, while from the heart of the confusion certain stirrings of the whole truth about real things began to put forth their live, unmistakable signs.

Indian Summer of the
Literary West

1. THOREAU'S UNWRITTEN EPIC

ACCORDING TO LEGEND and Ellery Channing, Thoreau's last words were "moose" and "Indian." Perhaps he was only delirious, and his mind wandered backward along the trail of his beloved excursions to the Maine woods; or perhaps, as has also been conjectured, and as I should naturally prefer to believe, his mind wandered forward, and thus bore final witness to his long-standing determination to write a great book about the natives of America. The book itself, unquestionably, remained unwritten at his early death, though he had labored toward its composition for at least twelve years, collecting in the process over 2800 pages of notes and excerpts from other writers on the subject. Unfortunately, these "Indian Notebooks" reveal little about Thoreau's literary intentions, except as their bulk and doggedness convince us he meant business. Most of the entries are factual and bare, most of the excerpts direct quotation, close paraphrase, or careful translation. Only a few penciled notes (added later) represent the stirrings of an organizing impulse, and a couple of references to the *Journal* the rudiments of a correlating instinct. From this evidence, his critics have tended to draw certain inferences: Thoreau was written out after *Walden*, or he was increasingly bogged down in the collection of meaningless data, or the Indian as a literary problem was insoluble. None of these inferences is provable or even plausible. Thoreau's later writing will not support any theory of creative exhaustion. And there is an inherent absurdity in charging with an abject surrender to data the man of the age most sensitive to that particular disaster of the spirit, the man who regularly guarded himself against it by emulating the unscientific sensibility of the Indian.

In any case, Thoreau's customary processes of composition almost automatically rule out any possibility of reconstructing his literary intentions through a study of the Indian Notebooks. They are only raw material; not proximate but initial sources. Doubtless their contents were continuously passing into his *Journal* as they were assimilated by his literary intelligence. Doubtless they would have passed through many another stage, now impossible to reconstruct, both before and after their appearance in the *Journal*. In fact, there was no earthly reason why Thoreau should have entered in the Indian Notebooks indications of attitude toward his subject, or speculations concerning the general nature of the book he meant to write. The first were in his mind always; the second would emerge, organically, as his images took shape. He was not gathering data in the hope that he might ultimately discover their meaning, nor in the wilder hope that they might of themselves compose; to say so is utterly to miss the point of what "inspiration" meant, in a practical sense, to a writer of Thoreau's particular bent. He was collecting further evidence to underwrite and embody convictions he already possessed.

What would Thoreau's Indian book have been like? That question can only be answered by reference to what he had already written. His *Journal*, and his published writings from *A Week on the Concord and Merrimack Rivers* to *The Maine Woods*, are full of passages about the Indian. From this material, it is not only possible but relatively easy to project the unborn soul of the book itself. "The future reader of history will associate this generation with the red man in his thoughts," Thoreau wrote in an 1839 diary, "and give it credit for some sympathy with his race. Our history will have some copper tints and reflections at least." That was Thoreau's ambition, considerably antedating his first public appearance as a serious writer. From the outset he recognized the extent of the challenge: "The Indian has vanished as completely as if trodden into the earth; absolutely forgotten but by a few persevering poets."[1] Thoreau was required to attain an almost unattainable empathy by means of—not by avoidance of—the facts of the case; in short, his was the usual difficulty of the poet, only in this case aggravated, to engender the poetic image from the coupling of exact knowledge and rectitude of heart. Thoreau had also to divest himself of parochial prejudices—a few of them personal, most of them national; from some of his youthful utterances, it seems he had much to learn. Fortunately, he was a diligent scholar.

Thus he resolutely went to school to Cartier, Champlain, the compilers of the Jesuit *Relations*, Gookin, Lewis and Clark, Heckewelder, Schoolcraft, Lewis Henry Morgan, and the countless other authorities in whom he sought particularities for the incarnation of his personal response to the idea of the Indian. His remarks in the *Week* on Alexander Henry's *Travels and Adventures* may well represent his attitude toward them all: "It reads like the argument to a great poem on the primitive state of the country and its inhabitants, and the reader imagines what in each case, with the invocation of the Muse, might be sung, and leaves off with suspended interest, as if the full account were to follow."[2] Thoreau as poet was to invoke the Muse, supply the song; the full account would follow perforce. He worked at it all his life, for the great poem he was writing—*Walden* is the most impressive part he was able to finish—must be envisaged as nothing less than the epic of the New World, the same epic that all the major American writers of the age were in their various ways approaching.

The crucial step in cultivating a sense of Thoreau's unwritten epic is taken the minute we begin to perceive how regularly his remarks about the Indian group them-

---

[1] *The First and Last Journeys of Thoreau*, ed. Franklin B. Sanborn (Boston, 1905), I, 36.
[2] *The Writings of Henry David Thoreau* (Boston, 1906), I, 231. Unless otherwise indicated, quotations in this section are from that edition, and from *The Journal of Henry D. Thoreau*, ed. Bradford Torrey and Francis H. Allen (Boston, 1906).

selves into a small number of surprisingly clear and closely connected categories. In the terminology of Emerson's *Nature*, we might say that Thoreau apprehended the Indian according to one or another of five "uses."[3] Systematically to run through them, attempting to understand by them what Thoreau understood, is to fill the mind with the richest awareness of what possibilities in form and development awaited only the stylistic cunning of that inveterately cunning hand.

The Indian as the Past. Facing the problem of the Indian, the representative man of the New World inevitably confronted his deepest historical necessity and sternest historical challenge. "What happened here before I arrived?" The answer to that question would plainly affect the answer to the question always raised by the West for all the persevering poets: "Who shall I be tomorrow?" Thoreau especially was a narrowly vertical historian, an ecologist of the human condition passionately committed to the vision of one place through all time. Despite the Romantic extravagances of "Walking," he was basically indifferent to man's Westward migrations from a European past; rather, to seek the past of where he lived was increasingly what he lived for.

Yet he was also unusually aware how new and raw his country was, how much it lacked in lacking all that the ancient and medieval worlds had deposited on European soil. He set himself the task of supplying their nearest equivalent, knowledge of what was in those far-off times actually going on in the Western Hemisphere. After all, his favorite idea of *strata* applied to man, and to man's history, quite as well as to nature; in either realm, what was wanted was a sense of something firm under foot, a solid ground formed by the bequests of the dead past. The plowing up of bones was for Thoreau the necessary reassurance

[3] These "uses" are not to be confused with the "list of subjects" found in the Indian Notebooks and published in Albert Keiser, "Thoreau's Manuscripts on the Indians," *Journal of English and Germanic Philology*, XXVII (1928), 197.

that he was currently at home where other men had made themselves at home. But it was extraordinarily difficult for Thoreau or any other American to achieve this sense of a continuous human community extending indefinitely backward, partly for want of historical records, partly for want of a dependable channel of sympathy. As conceived by the vertical ecologist, the American past was by no means the relatively single historical development displayed by Western Europe, but a story broken in the middle by a conflict of two races, two forms of human consciousness and sensibility and culture, opposing faces of man—in one light the same, in other lights tragically disjunct. In order to write the natural and human history of the New World, Thoreau must himself become something of an Indian. As he reminded himself in an early *Journal*, "there is only so much of Indian America left as there is of the American Indian in the character of this generation."

Even the contemporary Indian was sufficiently bewildering. No matter what he asked, Thoreau was answered "out of that strange remoteness in which the Indian ever dwells to the white man." A number of anecdotes in *The Maine Woods* illustrate this point. Much more overwhelming was the difficulty of acquiring accurate knowledge of the Indian in his proper state, before contact with Europeans ruined his type. Speaking in the *Week* of Lovewell's Fight and other early frontier skirmishes, Thoreau indirectly defined his problem as a writer: "I think that posterity will doubt if such things ever were,—if our bold ancestors who settled this land were not struggling rather with the forest shadows, and not with a copper-colored race of men. They were vapors, fever and ague of the unsettled woods. . . . In the Pelasgic, the Etruscan, or the British story, there is nothing so shadowy and unreal." Obviously, this unreality is the historian's or poet's special experience of unreality—not an inherent quality of the object but a symptom of his present inability to lay his hands on the object.[4] And of course there

---

[4] Attempting to bring the Indian into sharper focus, Thoreau sometimes cultivated a sense of unreality in the opposite direction,

were minor compensations: if the Indian's past was thus obscure, then Thoreau's very inability to apprehend the real Indian enabled him to supply the Americans their wistfully desired "antiquity," and even arm them with an ancient world more primitive, more mythical, more shadowy and unreal than anything the upstart Europeans could boast.[5]

Yet even though the New World's antiquity happily managed to straggle down to the present moment, Thoreau to the end despaired of grasping it fully. The Indian, he said in *The Maine Woods*, "lives three thousand years deep into time, an age not yet described by poets," by implication identifying his theme as more primitive and archaic than his favorite Homer's. But only if he could realize the phantom, "dim and misty to me, obscured by the æons that lie between the bark canoe and the batteau. . . . He glides up the Millinocket and is lost to my sight, as a more distant and misty cloud is seen flitting by behind a nearer, and is lost in space. So he goes about his destiny, the red face of man." I am far from thinking the Indian's elusiveness would have prevented Thoreau's writing about him; in dozens of passages like these, he is already doing so, and as well as he ever wrote. On the other hand, the Indian as literary subject would clearly have imposed certain tones, among them paradox. The Indian was all paradox. In Thoreau he would have met the master of paradox.

"Wherever I go, I tread in the tracks of the Indian," he wrote in 1842, before he knew how far those tracks were to lead or how difficult they would be to follow. As he learned these things, he increasingly cultivated the retro-

---

making the present seem as shadowy and unreal as he could: "The hooting of the owl! That is a sound which my red predecessors heard here more than a thousand years ago. It rings far and wide, occupying the spaces rightfully,—grand, primeval, aboriginal sound. There is no whisper in it of the Buckleys, the Flints, the Hosmers who recently squatted here." *Journal*, IX, 182.

[5] "Who has not heard of the *Antiquities of the West?*" rhapsodically inquired progressive James Hall. "Who that has heard, has not listened with admiration or incredulity?" *Letters From the West* (London, 1828), p. 12.

spective glance. In one remarkable vision, the sort of passage that might well have formed an imaginative node in the Indian book, as comparably imagined passages do in *Walden*, he even persuaded time to reverse itself, turning the civilized landscape of his own day backward, stage after stage, until at last the Indian reappeared, true to life, in his unspoiled habitat:

> At first, perchance, there would be an abundant crop of rank garden weeds and grasses in the cultivated land,—and rankest of all in the cellar-holes,—and of pinweed, hardhack, sumach, blackberry, thimble-berry, raspberry, etc., in the fields and pastures. Elm, ash, maples, etc., would grow vigorously along old garden limits and main streets. Garden weeds and grasses would soon disappear. Huckleberry and blueberry bushes, lambkill, hazel, sweet-fern. . . . Finally the pines, hemlock, spruce, larch, shrub oak, oaks, chestnut, beech, and walnuts would occupy the site of Concord once more. The apple and perhaps all exotic trees and shrubs and a great part of the indigenous ones named above would have disappeared, and the laurel and yew would to some extent be an underwood here, and perchance the red man once more thread his way through the mossy, swamp-like, primitive wood.[6]

Such fantasies are never idle, as the remarkable list of plants—so cautiously ordered along a scale from domestic to wild—sufficiently indicates.

Thoreau's ability to render the Indian—and the literary

---

[6] *Journal*, XIV, 262-263. "As the aboriginal, or poetic period of our territorial history recedes from us, each passing year both deepens the obscurity upon the Indian's footsteps, and diminishes the power of the imagination to recall the stupendous forest scenery by which he was surrounded. To obtain a glance at the face of nature during the era of Indian occupation, the wave of improvement must be rolled backward, not only displacing, in its recession, the city and the village which have sprung up in the wilderness; but restoring, also, by a simultaneous effort, the original drapery of nature, when clothed in her wild attire." Lewis Henry Morgan, *League of the . . . Iroquois* (Rochester, 1851), pp. 37-38.

situations involving the Indian—in metaphor is our best warrant for thinking him readier to compose his vaunted book than some of his more skeptical readers are willing to allow. "Another species of mortal men," begins another attempt at figurative definition and embodiment, "but little less wild to me than the musquash they hunted. Strange spirits, dæmons, whose eyes could never meet mine; with another nature and another fate than mine. The crows flew over the edge of the woods, and, wheeling over my head, seemed to rebuke, as dark-winged spirits more akin to the Indian than I. Perhaps only the present disguise of the Indian. If the new has a meaning, so has the old."[7] Once again—but not this time by way of paradox—Thoreau's humility in the face of the inscrutable leads him straight to the mark. The image of the wheeling crows (perhaps only the Indian in disguise) flying over the woods (that interminably Western emblem) summons up nearly everything he most wished to say about the Indian: his dark elusiveness, his dæmonic sympathy with nature, his contiguity with and alienation from the white man's life, his eternal presence in nature as warning and inspiration.

Again and again, on those walks which were the source and structure of all Thoreau wished to be, to know, and to write about, his eye would light on an arrowhead or potsherd, which his companion almost as invariably failed to notice. He even developed a personal *mystique*—the same as for the finding of rare plants—to account for his luck. But of course he perfectly well understood, and was sometimes willing to explain, that these wonderful discoveries depended on his extraordinarily close knowledge of local conditions and Indian habits. He knew upon what kind of ground the Indians customarily had encamped, and what kinds of soil and site they had selected for crops, as he also knew at what time of year and in what climate the relics were likely to rise to the surface. The quest for arrowheads

[7] *Journal*, I, 337. This long entry (March 19, 1842), from which I have already quoted twice, is one of Thoreau's more telling performances.

was not literal but mimetic, a representative action analogous to the quest of the historian, so curiously blended of active search and a habit of patience. In *Walden*, Thoreau wished to anticipate if possible nature herself. But in his passion for Indian relics he desired to anticipate something altogether more wraith-like, the re-emergence of the past, the imaginative return of the dead. He was chanticleer only when occasion demanded, as in *Walden*; otherwise, it was more and more the past he tried to recapture.[8] For this attempt he was remarkably gifted, though receiving little enough credit for it; had he lived to complete the Indian book, he would probably have been remembered as, among other things, the greatest historian of the age.

Because he depended upon poetry, or the exact imitation of real life in the right images, he would have written more useful history than Prescott or Parkman. He was always chiding his contemporaries for their indifference to the evidence (not only arrowheads) lying before their eyes: "On the sandy slope of the cut, close by the pond, I notice the chips which some Indian fletcher has made. Yet our poets and philosophers regret that we have no antiquities in America, no ruins to remind us of the past."[9] Ruins would find a second life through form and style—in the perfect present of art—in such passages as this:

As I drew a still fresher soil about the rows [of beans] with my hoe, I disturbed the ashes of unchronicled nations who in primeval years lived under these heavens, and their small implements of war and hunting were brought to the light of this modern day. They lay mingled with other natural stones, some of which bore the marks of having been burned by Indian fires, and

[8] As he succeeded, the past was compelled to furnish him with one more reason for abstaining from the Westward Movement of his busy compatriots. "I feel no desire to go to California or Pike's Peak, but I often think at night with inexpressible satisfaction and yearning of the *arrowheadiferous* sands of Concord." *Journal*, XII, 175.

[9] *Journal*, XI, 212.

some by the sun, and also bits of pottery and glass brought hither by the recent cultivators of the soil. When my hoe tinkled against the stones, that music echoed to the woods and the sky, and was an accompaniment to my labor which yielded an instant and immeasurable crop. It was no longer beans that I hoed, nor I that hoed beans.

Thus in *Walden* Thoreau cultivated timelessness; not, as his fellow Transcendentalists were prone to do, by asserting a childish independence of history, but by incorporating so much of the essential past, so much of the essential future into his present consciousness that history ceased to matter. It ceased to matter when it became real. Insofar as history became real, Thoreau might save his own soul and thereby gain the whole New World. Unavoidably, then, the Indian book would have owed much to Thoreau's special sense of the past and his specific identification of the Indian with the American past. The sense of the past would have furnished the underlying structure of the book; that structure would have been integral, thematic, pervasive, and compelling.

The Indian as Fundamental Man. This use of the Indian is less uniquely Thoreau's, and comes closer to representing that aspect of his attitude shared with the other major writers, most notably Cooper, Hawthorne, and Melville. It is to be understood in all four as primarily the ironic consequence of regarding the Indian from a fundamentally Christian point of view—that is, with both realism and charity—in a fundamentally non-Christian society. To most nineteenth-century Americans, the savage and heathen Indian was outside the purview of their ordinary religious obligation, too different from themselves to touch the conscience. The way to deal with Indians was to root them out, and then bewail their disappearance in sentimental plays and novels. The major writers insistently declared that if the Indian was different, he was also the same. Doubtless they meant to irritate; they were all of them

336

moralists. Their attitudes also entailed striking literary repercussions: witness the outraged cry (chiefly from the Western states) that Cooper's Indians were "idealized." What hurt was their being human.

According to the prevailing idealism of mid-nineteenth-century American thought, the concept of the Indian as fundamental man might mean either the Indian as one of several expressions of the general idea of humanity (as in Thoreau's superb formula, "the red face of man"), or it might mean the Indian as embodying the essence of humanity, an essence common to all, but more conspicuous in primitive man, whose basic nature is not yet overlaid with civilization (as when Thoreau says: "Inside the civilized man stands the savage still in the place of honor").[10] Thus the Indian could suggest, alternately or concurrently, the richly various possibilities of human life, or, more simply, humanity itself. Either way, Thoreau was further encouraged to express the Indian through metamorphosis or metaphorical action, the Indian suddenly erupting into the present, the spirit of the past entering and animating the heavy body of the contemporary: "In the musquash-hunters I see the Almouchicois still pushing swiftly over the dark stream in their canoes. These aboriginal men cannot be repressed, but under some guise or other they survive and reappear continually."[11] If the American thought he was replacing the Indian, he was wrong. Dispossession was a reciprocal process, and more complicated than anyone but poets suspected. The Indian was not gone, but had merely taken another form.

There is no question of the humility and decency with which the author of *Walden* approached the Indian, nor that these qualities would have informed every page of this even more ambitious book. Naturally, he thought most American

[10] As in *Walden*, such visions might be either satiric or heroic: "Who are the inhabitants of London and New York but savages who have built cities, and forsaken for a season hunting and war? Who are the Blackfeet and the Tartars but citizens roaming the plains and dwelling in wigwams and tents?" *First and Last Journeys*, I, 95.

[11] *Journal*, XI, 424-425.

historians as contemptible (on this subject) as they obviously thought the Indian. In a crucial *Journal* passage, Thoreau worked out a careful indictment of their inhumanity, and proposed an altogether different attitude:

> Some have spoken slightingly of the Indians, as a race possessing so little skill and wit, so low in the scale of humanity, and so brutish that they hardly deserved to be remembered,—using only the terms "miserable," "wretched," "pitiful," and the like. In writing their histories of this country they have so hastily disposed of this refuse of humanity (as they might have called it) which littered and defiled the shore and the interior. But even the indigenous animals are inexhaustibly interesting to us. How much more, then, the indigenous man of America! If wild men, so much more like ourselves than they are unlike, have inhabited these shores before us, we wish to know particularly what manner of men they were, how they lived here, their relation to nature, their arts and their customs, their fancies and superstitions.

In short, the questions Thoreau would ask about the Indian, thereby eliciting a novel kind of American history (still unwritten), are precisely the questions he asked about himself and his countrymen in *Walden*.

Continuing in the same passage his indictment of "historians," Thoreau proceeds to define their activity through a comparison even more suggestive to the student of American civilization: "It frequently happens that the historian, though he professes more humanity than the trapper, mountain man, or gold-digger, who shoots one [an Indian] as a wild beast, really exhibits and practices a similar inhumanity to him, wielding a pen instead of a rifle." This observation is dated February 3, 1859.[12] The central episode of *The*

[12] *Journal*, XI, 437-438. Eight months later, Thoreau returned to this matter of Indian-hating. "In California and Oregon, if not nearer home, it is common to treat men exactly like deer which are hunted, and I read from time to time in Christian newspapers how

Confidence-Man—the American edition of which was published on April Fool's Day, 1857—is a radical attack on the frontier attitude of Indian-hating, defined there and elsewhere in Melville as hunting one's fellow man as if he were an animal; this crime against humanity is ultimately attributed, not only to the pioneers themselves, but indirectly to writers, and specifically to that popular chronicler of the West, James Hall. Of course, it makes little difference whether Thoreau read *The Confidence-Man* and was influenced by it. The important point is the obvious meeting of minds, and the way it supplies another lively perspective on the potentialities inherent in Thoreau's unwritten book. At any moment, it might have veered in the direction of Melville.

The passage about historians concludes more broadly and affirmatively: "It is the spirit of humanity, that which animates both so-called savages and civilized nations, working through a man, and not the man expressing himself, that interests us most. The thought of a so-called savage tribe is generally far more just than that of a single civilized man." To such a state of humility had the youthful egotist arrived, doubtless instructed by his perpetually difficult meditation on the Indian. For all their apparent difference and disjunction in time and culture, that Indian was only another man like himself. Thoreau's simplest insight into the life of the Indian was also the most extraordinary, and surely it promised well for his literary ambitions, which were just and capacious beyond the comprehension of all except

---

many 'bucks,' that is, Indian men, their sportsmen have killed." *Journal*, XII, 416-417. The next day he added, in defense of John Brown's exploits: "For once the Sharp's rifle and the revolver were employed in a righteous cause. . . . I know that the mass of my neighbors think that the only righteous use that can be made of them is to fight duels with them when we are insulted by other nations, or hunt Indians, or shoot fugitive slaves with them." In "Civil Disobedience," he says that only in jail can the fugitive slave, the Mexican prisoner, "and the Indian come to plead the wrongs of his race," find the just man. But in "Walking," Thoreau seems strangely insensitive to the horrors of Indian Removal.

339

a small handful of other writers. But Thoreau had one advantage over them: he had learned the hard way what he was talking about, whereas Cooper, Hawthorne, and Melville, for all their magnanimity, were only guessing.

The Indian as Nature. That the Indian's contact with nature was closer than ours scarcely needs arguing; that this was a fact of cardinal importance to Thoreau scarcely needs discussing. Like Melville—but with less ambiguity of attitude and a more accomplished control of image—Thoreau persistently sees the Indian as an emanation of nature.[13] Again and again, this aspect of Thoreau's vision leads to metaphors between the Indian and his environment in which the terms of comparison practically coalesce. "They seem like a race who have exhausted the secrets of nature, tanned with age. . . . Their memory is in harmony with the russet hue of the fall of the year." In that image Indian and autumn foliage are almost indistinguishable. The memory of the Indian (his memory, and perhaps also our memory of him) resembles the russet leaves because he is "tanned with age" as they are; tanned with nature, too, for in exhausting her secrets he has taken on her color. A much later notation repeats substantially the same image: "Many trunks old and hollow, in which wild beasts den. Hawks nesting in the dense tops, and deer glancing between the trunks, and occasionally the Indian with a face the color of the faded oak leaf." (Deer and Indian additionally fuse in "glancing.") Alternatively, Thoreau's comparisons show the natural object gradually turning into a red man: "The pine stands in the woods like an Indian,—untamed, with a fantastic wildness about it, even in the clearings. If an Indian warrior were well painted, with pines in the background, he would seem to blend with the trees, and make

[13] Thoreau took great pleasure in noting that *savage* was in the seventeenth century spelled *salvage*, and thus derived from *sylva.* "The savages they described are really *salvages*, men of the *woods*." *Journal*, IV, 494. He was equally pleased with the discovery that *forest* is related to (Saxon) *faran* 'to go,' "as if this newer term were needed to describe those strange, wild woods furthest from the centres of civilization." *Journal*, XI, 386.

a harmonious expression. The pitch pines are the ghosts of Philip and Massasoit. The white pine has the smoother features of the squaw."[14] These metaphors rest upon close correspondence between significant visual aspects of Indian life and details from nature observed with equal accuracy; nearly always they also insinuate a more general point, most frequently the Indian's harmonious identification with his setting.

The Indian was the *native*—a word of remarkable force in Thoreau—of the New World. After listing indigenous animals threatened with extinction, he adds: "With these, of course, is to be associated the Indian." If the Indian were to be associated with nature historically and realistically, he could be associated with nature in metaphor. Then Thoreau could disregard as irrelevant his annoyance with Indians who lived in town, got drunk, accumulated property, and went to church on Sunday. Some of the passages I have been quoting are early and some are late; in every one, Thoreau is obviously trying to particularize in poetic terms his general response to the Indian. The idea he had all the time; for example, in 1841: "The charm of the Indian to me is that he stands free and unconstrained in Nature, is her inhabitant and not her guest, and wears her easily and gracefully. But the civilized man has the habits of the house. His house is a prison."[15] If in *Walden* Thoreau imitated the pioneer, he was also imitating the Indian whom in real life the pioneer imitated. Nature-Indian-pioneer-poet, poet-pioneer-Indian-nature: that is the reversible series of meanings organizing the single work Thoreau spent his life preparing to write. The reversible series is essentially the social-stages-of-history theory, with poet replacing merchant, or capitalist, as final term. None of Thoreau's subversions of American assumption was more radical, and none was more needed.

The Indian's use as nature sufficiently explains Thoreau's distaste for the idea of "civilizing" him. "We talk of civiliz-

---

[14] These *Journal* passages are at I, 444; XIV, 231; and I, 258.
[15] The list is in *Journal*, III, 72; the prison-house passage in I, 253.

ing the Indian," he wrote in the *Week*, "but that is not the name for his improvement. By the wary independence and aloofness of his dim forest life he preserves his intercourse with his native gods, and is admitted from time to time to a rare and peculiar society with Nature. He has glances of starry recognition to which our saloons are strangers." Then to the main point: how would Thoreau himself utilize the Indian for poetry? "There are other, savager and more primeval aspects of nature than our poets have sung. It is only white man's poetry. . . . If we could listen but for an instant to the chant of the Indian muse, we should understand why he will not exchange his savageness for civilization. Nations are not whimsical. Steel and blankets are strong temptations; but the Indian does well to continue Indian." Thoreau likewise did well to continue Thoreau, for the essential paradox was that he (who must fight his way back to nature) was a poet, and the Indian (who was nearly nature herself) was not. Like the pioneer, he was a forerunner of the poet, a savage John the Baptist, and Thoreau intended to profit from him as much as he could, in order that his own life, a poet's life, might be continuous with primitive life on the new continent. By sympathetic communion with the Indian, Thoreau might some day escape the bounds of white man's poetry and realize such an art as one might reasonably look to the West for. But poetry was the expression of civilization, and would only be written by civilized man.

The Indian as Language. Naturally, the Indian as language was also of crucial concern to the writer intending to derive from him substance and style for an epic about nature and man in the New World. To know the Indian was to know what he knew; to know what he knew was to know how to say it in words of one's own. In this respect, as in others, Thoreau conceived the two races as complements: the Indian remembered what the white man had forgotten, spoke what the white man could no longer comprehend. To master the whole meaning of life on this continent, Thoreau must join, in the mind, by means of poetic images, what the course of history, and maybe the will of God, had put asunder.

Especially as a point of entry into that primitive past he longed to penetrate, the Indian's language was so central to Thoreau's literary problem that the mere sound of it was enough to evoke all his deepest responses. "It took me by surprise," he reported in *The Maine Woods*, "though I had found so many arrowheads, and convinced me that the Indian was not the invention of historians and poets. It was a purely wild and primitive American sound. . . . These were the sounds that issued from the wigwams of this country before Columbus was born. . . . I felt that I stood, or rather lay, as near to the primitive man of America, that night, as any of its discoverers ever did." Wildness, remoteness, mystery, simplicity, purity—these were the tones of voice Thoreau was always listening for, in the hope of modulating the language he inherited. The English of *his* past was the English of another place, however estimable, and must needs accommodate itself to the new life. How better than by contact with the Indian, whose language was not only the language of the American past, and thus the speech of the fundamental American miraculously surviving into the present, but the very language of nature in these parts? To discover and assimilate some of its meaning and manner would be indispensable. But it would not be easy. Nor in a literal way were Thoreau's accomplishments in "Indian" remarkable. But a literal command of the language was not what he required.

The main thing about the Indian's way with words, as with things, was its organic quality, the sympathetic closeness to nature, reality. As Thoreau worried it out in the privacy of his study (*Journal*, x, 294-295):

> We would fain know something more about these animals and stones and trees around us. We are ready to skin the animals alive to come at them. Our scientific names convey a very partial information only; they suggest certain thoughts only. . . . How much more con-

versant was the Indian with any wild animal or plant than we are, and in his language is implied all that intimacy. . . . It was a new light when my guide gave me Indian names for things for which I had only scientific ones before. In proportion as I understood the language, I saw them from a new point of view.

Few expository passages in Thoreau more clearly suggest the directions he was intending to go. Still, it is not exposition alone that will enliven our understanding of what this ambitious man was projecting. The perpetually pertinent questions are: could he have realized such ideas in poetry, and how? Once again, the answers are "yes," and "the way he had always done."

The little narrative concluding his observations for July 24 in "The Allegash and East Branch" affords a satisfying example; as usual in Thoreau, it is *multum ex parvo*, realistic, lyric, witty, devout, nocturnal, prophetic, and passionate. The story opens quietly with simple narration of the fact that his Indian guide "cut some large logs of damp and rotten hard wood to smoulder and keep fire through the night." (But in Thoreau's writing the simplest fact turns figurative as soon as we look at it.) Thoreau rises in the middle of the night, to find the fire out, but the logs still shining in "a perfectly regular elliptical ring of light." He decides this must be phosphorescent wood, which he has heard about but never seen. "It could hardly have thrilled me more," he tells us, revealingly moving from science to significance, "if it had taken the form of letters, or of the human face." The literary importance is further emphasized by his receiving next morning from his favorite guide Joe Polis the Indian word for the phenomenon, together with the information that Indians frequently see this and similar sights. "Nature must have made a thousand revelations to them which are still secrets to us."

Consequently Thoreau transforms this anecdote into a parable for the acquisition of a more important kind of knowing than the white man's "science." ("I let science slide, and rejoiced in that light as if it had been a fellow creature.") Merely the possibility of such knowledge renews the world, recreating it as sentience:

> I believed that the woods were not tenantless, but choke-full of honest spirits as good as myself any day,—not an empty chamber, in which chemistry was left to work alone, but an inhabited house,—and for a few moments I enjoyed fellowship with them. . . . It suggested, too, that the same experience always gives birth to the same sort of belief or religion. One revelation has been made to the Indian, another to the white man. . . . [But now both have been made to Thoreau.] Long enough I had heard of irrelevant things; now at length I was glad to make acquaintance with the light that dwells in rotten wood. Where is all your knowledge gone to? It evaporates completely, for it has no depth.

But not Thoreau's kind of knowledge, which is solidly grounded, like the Indian's, in the accurate apprehension of apprehensible things. Recognizing the necessary transcience of this particular kind of thing, Thoreau with a final flourish "destroys" it, thereby putting it forever beyond the temptations of overstatement or undue perpetuation: "I kept those little chips and wet them again the next night, but they emitted no light."

The Indian as the Frontier. At the risk of imperiling his other views of the Indian, Thoreau was also drawn by the common obsession of the age to the traditional neutral ground of the frontier, thereupon to arrange a mutual and presumably beneficent confrontation of white man and red. Yet that mutual confrontation having been in history so cruelly destructive, and so apparently without benefit to either party, it is not at first easy to imagine how Thoreau would have achieved those affirmative resolutions of polar opposition which the shape and purpose of the frontier metaphor imperiously demanded. One way out of the impasse was to concentrate on exceptional moments in history; thus in the narrative of the phosphorescent wood, we find the following reflections about Joe Polis: "His singing carried me back to the period of the discovery of America, to San Salvador and the Incas, when Europeans first encountered the simple faith of the Indian. There was, indeed, a beautiful simplicity about it; nothing of the dark and savage, only the mild and infantile." That Thoreau is thinking of the point of meeting between Indian and European—not of the Indian in his primeval state—is confirmed by his guess that the song "probably was taught his tribe long ago by the Catholic missionaries." Perhaps it was because they concentrated on the first encounters of European and Indian, but in a rare spirit of charity, that the Jesuit *Relations* were Thoreau's favorite source for Indian materials.

Another way out was to envisage Indian and white man as complements within a larger harmony. Within the more comprehensive frame, Thoreau might conceive the Indian as mediating the major contradiction of life in the New World; as redefined, that contradiction would be between man and nature, rather than between white man and Indian. Thus Thoreau argued the case of the Indian against Alcott's simplistic and genteel plea for civilization: "Thoreau defends the Indian from the doctrine of being lost or exterminated, and thinks he holds a place between civilized man and nature, and must hold it."[16] *He must hold it* because the most urgent need of the American writer and people then and always was the integration of a world split in two in nearly every conceivable direction (Indian and European, past and future, civilization and nature; not to mention the epistemological, ontological, and aesthetic dualisms that also harassed the American Romantic). For Thoreau, the point of meeting between these various antitheses is the Indian himself. The frontier is the Indian, the Indian is the frontier. Whenever Thoreau, the civilized poet, turns to nature—his best word for the Being he needed to propitiate—he finds a personal intercessor, the American Indian.

Hence the anxiety of his excursions to the Maine woods,

[16] *The Journals of Bronson Alcott*, ed. Odell Shepard (Boston, 1938), p. 325.

the all-importance of securing the right Indian guides, and, especially after the third excursion, the happy conclusion (often reiterated): "I have now returned, and think I have had a quite profitable journey, chiefly from associating with an intelligent Indian."[17] It was wonderful that Joe Polis should be so unspoiled by civilization; it was even better that he should so marvelously combine "civilized" and "savage" virtues. In *The Maine Woods*, Thoreau concludes an account of Polis' hunting prowess with the triumphant assertion: "Thus you have an Indian availing himself cunningly of the advantages of civilization, without losing any of his woodcraft, but proving himself the more successful hunter for it." That was the Indian on whose backward trail Thoreau had been following so long. If we follow it far enough, we once again come to the Leatherstocking Tales and then to the basic conditions of American life lying behind them.

But Joe Polis was a special case. Most of the Indians Thoreau knew grievously disappointed him. This was partly his own fault. The great thing about the Maine woods, *his* wilderness, was not really its wildness but its closeness. "Some hours only of travel in this direction will carry the curious to the verge of a primitive forest, more interesting, perhaps, on all accounts, than they would reach by going a thousand miles westward." Persistently he declined the popular attractions of the Far West, where, it was said, the progress of the human race was spread open like a book, earliest pages nearest the Pacific, and where, if anywhere in America, relatively uncorrupted Indians were still to be found. Thoreau preferred a handier pamphlet. Yet in going to Maine he was also putting himself on the trail of the wrong Indian. "Met face to face, these Indians in their native woods looked like the sinister and slouching fellows

[17] *The Correspondence of Henry David Thoreau*, ed. Walter Harding and Carl Bode (New York, 1958), p. 491. In the same letter: "I have made a short excursion into the new world which the Indian dwells in, or is. He begins where we leave off." That was a backward glance with a vengeance.

whom you meet picking up strings and paper in the streets of a city. . . . The one is no more a child of nature than the other." As the great book on the primitive state of the country came down to the present, it would have drawn to itself some curious ironies.

Thoreau's story must also be tragic, or at least elegiac. Somehow he would have to explain the fate of this savage who was the oldest inhabitant of the Western Hemisphere, the common element in the species man, the *confidant* of nature in the New World, the potential source of a renewed poetic language, and the primary human fact confronting the European in America—and who was, for all that, plainly dying. The easiest answer was fatalistic, as when Thoreau untypically generalizes: "There is always a slight haze or mist on the brow of the Indian. The white man's brow is clear and distinct." Such a view, however, met neither the facts nor Thoreau's real sentiments. Alternatively, he might "explain" Indian decline in terms of the social-stages-of-history doctrine: "If he would not be pushed into the Pacific, he must seize hold of a plow-tail and let go his bow and arrow." Unfortunately, an Indian so saved was hardly worth saving. A few paragraphs later, Thoreau is saying: "The Indian, perchance, has not made up his mind to some things which the white man has consented to; he has not, in all respects, stooped so low."[18] The Indian was of value only so long as he remained true to his nature; remaining true to his nature, he guaranteed his destruction. Paradox, elegy, irony—these are the literary tones that would have contributed most to the shaping of Thoreau's epic. Imagining the various uses under which his responses to the Indian were organically arranged, formed and styled by these predominant and inherent tones, we perhaps come closest to a sound guess as to the probable nature of the prospective work.

One consideration would have controlled all the rest. The book about the Indian would have been a work of lit-

[18] *Journal*, X, 77; I, 444-445.

erary art. It is entirely predictable, then, that Thoreau must finally have explained the decline of the Indian in terms of his wanting art. The central point of view must needs have been something like this: Thoreau, the writer, the highest expression of civilized value, confronting the Indian, in order to derive from his experience whatever was most required by civilized men, together with the realization, urgent and ironic, that it is the Indian's inability to express himself in art that has caused his extinction and at the same time necessitated this poem, which is now the only way he can be saved. Thoreau must do for the Indian what he cannot do for himself—leave his mark—by means of the civilized attribute, art, or the ability of the mind to affect nature, which the Indian lacks, yet the very lack of which strangely constitutes his value for us. As the pre-artistic, the Indian is the primary challenge for the poet of the New World.[19]

So in his effort to redeem the Indian, if in memory only, Thoreau was always searching for evidence of an aesthetic sensibility which, sufficiently developed, might have saved the race; but he was for the most part compelled to conclude that the Indian's response to nature was utilitarian, inadequately conscious. Thoreau's most important evaluation of the Indian's fate is thus centrally stated in a summary passage about relics (*Journal*, v, 526):

> As long as I find traces of works of convenience merely, however much skill they show, I am not so much affected as when I discover works which evince the exercise of fancy and taste, however rude. It is a great step to find a pestle whose handle is ornamented with a bird's-head knob. It brings the maker still nearer to the races which so ornament their umbrella and cane handles. I have, then, evidence in stone that men lived here who

[19] In *Walden*, Thoreau had identified himself as a writer—and particularly as the writer of *A Week on the Concord and Merrimack Rivers*—with a local Indian who was bewildered when white men did not invariably wish to buy his baskets. "I too had woven a kind of basket of a delicate texture, but I had not made it worth any one's while to buy them. Yet not the less, in my case, did I think it worth my while to weave them." *Writings*, II, 20-21.

had fancies to be pleased, and in whom the first steps toward a complete culture were taken. It implies so many more thoughts such as I have. The arrowhead, too, suggests a bird, but a relation to it not in the least godlike. But here an Indian has patiently sat and fashioned a stone into the likeness of a bird, and added some pure beauty to that pure utility, and so far begun to leave behind him war, and even hunting, and to redeem himself from the savage state. In this he was leaving off to be savage. Enough of this would have saved him from extermination.

No man had learned better how long art was, nor what demands it made upon intelligence, knowledge, discipline, and perseverance. Toward the successful completion of his task, Thoreau possessed every necessary gift but time. Suddenly, at the age of forty-four, he died, and what should have been an American masterpiece absolutely *sui generis* was forever lost, except as it can now be partially reconstructed for a purely speculative profit and delight.

2. HAWTHORNE'S LAST STAND

In the entire story of early American literature—broadly speaking, a story of sudden, unexpected achievement, followed by a disintegration nearly as sudden—perhaps no chapter is more pathetic or problematical than Hawthorne's career after *The Scarlet Letter*. A variety of reasons can be, and has been, offered in explanation of his gradually declining creative success; among them, it is necessary to find room for the fact that, commencing with *The House of the Seven Gables*, Hawthorne abandoned, or was evicted from, the profound though indirect and ambivalent concern with the American West which had sustained his one really distinguished novel and so many of his finest tales and sketches. The change in direction proved increasingly disastrous, for the West was not a literary subject like any other, to be taken up or dropped at the writer's pleasure, but the Talismanic Secret (Melville's phrase) of the national experience.

Deprived of the Talismanic Secret, and yet confined to a civilization which so far possessed no other, the American writer lacked a working definition of the civilization defining him, and thus, ultimately, of his own identity and purpose as a writer.

Between 1850 and 1852 Hawthorne's passionate involvement with the West cooled to indifference, frivolity, and irrelevance. In *The House of Seven Gables* (1851), the earliest Maule is a pioneer who builds his "hut" (thatched, like Hester's) by a "natural spring" or "gem of the wilderness," at a distance (again, like Hester's) from the center of town, and until the time of the witchcraft madness manages to retain "the acre or two of earth, which, with his own toil, he had hewn out of the primeval forest."[1] As usual, the ground is "bestrewn with the virgin forest-leaves," which Maule sweeps away. When this yeoman-pioneer is by Colonel Pyncheon dispossessed of his holdings, the spring loses "the deliciousness of its pristine quality," yet even so survives two centuries in the back yard as an object which "Nature might fairly claim as her inalienable property." In addition to this first piece of frontier land, the Pyncheon family acquires through an Indian deed an insufficiently documented claim to "vast" and "unexplored" tracts in Maine, the course of whose anticipated development falls into another typical American pattern: "When the pathless forest that still covered this wild principality should give place . . . to the golden fertility of human culture, it would be the source of incalculable wealth." But the territory is re-granted to actual settlers, who "would have laughed" at the Pyncheons' pretensions to lands "they or their fathers had wrested from the wild hand of nature." All the Pyncheons really possess of the wilderness is an old map—

[1] Unless otherwise indicated, quotations in this section are from *The Complete Works of Nathaniel Hawthorne*, ed. George P. Lathrop (Cambridge, 1883). For *Doctor Grimshawe's Secret*, I use the modern edition by Edward H. Davidson (Cambridge, 1954). The notes, scenarios, and early drafts of that novel are from the same edition; those for the other fragments are from Davidson, *Hawthorne's Last Phase* (New Haven, 1949).

somewhat resembling those fraudulent maps that used to accompany speculative land purchases in the West—"grotesquely illuminated with pictures of Indians and wild beasts," and as "fantastically awry" with respect to geography as all this wilderness of allusion is to the central purposes of the novel. In connection with Phoebe's domestic virtues, Hawthorne wanders so far afield from modern Salem as to imagine how readily she might bestow a "home aspect" upon "a wild hut of underbrush, tossed together by wayfarers through the primitive forest."

In *The Blithedale Romance* (1852), New England farmers are said to cherish each stick of firewood "as if it were a bar of California gold"; the Blithedale people want to adopt "the old Indian name of the premises" (unfortunately not euphonious); in a fit of boredom, Coverdale thinks of going "across the Rocky Mountains," or quite preposterously imagines himself approaching the Farm, "resolving to spy out the posture of the Community, as craftily as the wild Indian before he makes his onset"; "The Masqueraders" include "an Indian chief, with blanket, feathers and war-paint, and uplifted tomahawk" (complete with a Diana, or "woodland-bride"), as well as a "Kentucky woodsman in his trimmed hunting-shirt and deerskin leggings"; in the back garden of Coverdale's Boston hotel dwells a cat "who evidently thought herself entitled to the privileges of forest-life in this close heart of city conventionalisms." One or two details are perhaps more organic. The main characters frequently resort to "Eliot's Pulpit," a pocket of "wilderness" which will never be entirely tamed, and where Zenobia behaves with a suitable wildness. A decade earlier, Emerson and Hawthorne had discussed the need for a history of Brook Farm;[2] perhaps by way of compliment, the utterances of Emerson, Carlyle, and the *Dial* are now said to resemble "the cry of some solitary sentinel, whose station was on the outposts of the advance-guard of human progression," and to be "well adapted" to the Blithedale beat-

[2] *The American Notebooks*, ed. Randall Stewart (New Haven, 1932), p. 176.

niks, who in turn somewhat vaguely resemble pioneers. The experiment itself is briefly brought within the traditional purview of the social-stages-of-history theory when Coverdale, from the safe perspective of Boston, calls it "part of another age, a different state of society . . . a leaf of some mysterious volume interpolated into the current history which time was writing off." But as he fails to specify whether the page be past or future, the point of this subsumption—like so much else in *The Blithedale Romance*—remains charmingly inexact.

Perhaps in these two novels following *The Scarlet Letter* Hawthorne was indirectly or unconsciously responding to the disappearance of the frontier; if so his response was—compared, for example, with Melville's—feeble and irrelevant. Conspicuously running down, Hawthorne now turned from fiction to fact with a campaign biography of Franklin Pierce (1852). Except in conducting his nationally emblematic operations on a smaller and more democratic scale, Pierce's father is another Judge Temple: "In 1785, being employed as agent to explore a tract of wild land, he purchased a lot of fifty acres in what is now the town of Hillsborough. In the spring of the succeeding year, he built himself a log hut, and began the clearing and cultivation of his tract." Here the father—and by implication Pierce—grew up with the country, in "the mansion which he built, after the original log-cabin grew too narrow for his rising family and fortunes. The mansion was spacious, as the liberal hospitality of the occupant required, and stood on a little eminence, surrounded by verdure and abundance, and a happy population, where, half a century before, the revolutionary soldier had come alone into the wilderness, and levelled the primeval forest trees." From 1853 to 1858 Hawthorne wrote almost nothing.

If my conjectures about loss of purpose and identity are correct, then his sudden resumption of productivity in the late fifties was an act of desperation, its nature determined by the previous lapse.[3] Yet although *The Marble Faun*

[3] In the fourth preliminary study for *The Dolliver Romance,*

(1860) is derived from the metaphor of the frontier, and *Our Old Home* (1863) decked out with ill-fitting allusions to the West, Hawthorne's belated effort is not comprehensible from these books alone. The conclusive evidence is in the uncompleted romances, or fragments, as they are called, about which he was so secretive. What they reveal is a feverish determination to make one last stand on the matter of the West, and, at the same time, to write an international novel. At first glance, the first of these motives is scarcely visible, and when visible scarcely credible. Yet all the fragments are shaped by an attempt to join two disparate fictive worlds, past and present, England and America; the two halves originate in Hawthorne's guilty infatuation with life abroad and his longing for something reassuringly American at home;[4] and the most American thing at home is still the West, especially the Indian with whom he had confederated his literary destinies so many years before in "The Seven Vagabonds."

In *The Ancestral Footstep*—the titles of all these fragments were supplied by editors—written in April and May of 1858, the recrudescence of images and motifs from Hawthorne's literary youth is already evident. A seventeenth-century Englishman decides to "bury himself in the Western wilderness," desiring to "disconnect himself with all the past, and begin life quite anew in a new world." Two cen-

---

Hawthorne wrote of his elderly hero: "He has been long regretting some error in middle life, or earlier, which, he thinks, has caused a long ill success through subsequent years; he wishes now to return and retrieve that error, in the hope of living to some purpose thereafter?"

[4] Hawthorne is forever discussing his fictional halves, perhaps most often and most explicitly in *The Ancestral Footstep*; e.g.: "Thus he arrives, bringing half of a story, being the only part known in America, to join it on to the other half, which is the only part known in England." The entire situation is painfully autobiographical: "My ancestor left England in 1635. I return in 1853. I sometimes feel as if I myself had been absent these two hundred and eighteen years." *The English Notebooks*, ed. Randall Stewart (New York, 1941), p. 92. But see also Melville, *Pierre*, ed. Henry A. Murray (New York, 1949), p. 323.

turies later his modern American descendant returns, establishes his claim to family title and fortune, yet relinquishes
both, "feeling that it is better to make a [words evidently
omitted here] virgin soil than to try to make the old name
grow in a soil that had been darkened with so much blood
and misfortune." This hero is a product of frontier conditions: "The plastic character of Middleton was perhaps
a variety of American nature only presenting itself under
an individual form; he could throw off the man of our day,
and put on a ruder nature, but then it was with a certain
fineness." After all, the ancestor's grave "was first made
under the forest leaves, though now a city had grown up
around it," a detail returning us to the literary scene of the
1830's and Hawthorne's customary imagery for the metamorphosis of American landscape into American civilization. A later entry reveals the hero, now joined by a " 'wild,
free spirit' " of an American sweetheart, again relinquish-
ing his English claims.[5] "Thus he and his wife become the
Adam and Eve of a new epoch, and the fitting missionaries
of a new social faith, of which there must be continual hints
through the book." There are few such hints, however, except in Hawthorne's instructions to himself,[6] as how could
there be? The renunciation-reawakening is a simple contradiction of the entire projected plot line. "After all those
long, long wanderings,—after the little log-built hut of the
early settlement, after the straight roof of the American
house, after all the many roofs of two hundred years, here

[5] Middleton's renunciations and feelings of guilt often sound like
Hawthorne's. "He [Middleton] found himself strangely disturbed
with thoughts of his own country, of the life that he ought to be
leading there, the struggles in which he ought to be taking part;
and, with these motives in his impressible mind, the motives that
had hitherto kept him in England seemed unworthy to influence
him."

[6] For instance, "Middleton shall not come to the decision to resign
it, without having to repress a deep yearning for that sense of
long, long rest in an age-consecrated home, which he had felt so
deeply to be the happy lot of Englishmen. But this ought to be
rejected, as not belonging to his country, nor to the age, nor any
longer possible."

he was at last under the one which he had left, on that fatal night, when the Bloody Footstep was so mysteriously impressed on the threshold." Hawthorne evidently acquired the legend about the Bloody Footstep in England. Did he then conceivably fuse it with unconscious remembrance of some such Western passage as the following, from John Filson? "Brother," says an Indian to Daniel Boone, "we have given you a fine land, but I believe you will have much trouble in settling it." "My footsteps," Boone goes on, "have often been marked with blood, and therefore I can truly subscribe to its original name," which was, of course, "the Dark and Bloody Ground, and sometimes the Middle Ground."[7] But how was the Bloody Footstep of Kentucky related to the Bloody Footstep imprinted upon the threshold of an English country mansion, and why is it the English soil which is "darkened with so much blood" while the American soil remains "virgin"? These are questions more easily asked than answered.[8]

Doctor Grimshawe's Secret (1860-1861) is *The Ancestral Footstep* all over again. "The English and American ideas to be brought strikingly into contrast and contact. . . . It must be shown, I think, throughout, that there is an essential difference." But if the essential difference, which had also been insisted on in *The Ancestral Footstep*, sprang from the American frontier, how could Hawthorne bring the two ideas together? Perhaps through the analogy between seventeenth-century and nineteenth-century conditions that had

---

[7] *The English Notebooks*, pp. 106, 194-195; Filson, *The Discovery, Settlement and Present State of Kentucke* (Wilmington, Del., 1784), pp. 8, 80.

[8] Throughout the fragments we hear notes of desperation. In *The Ancestral Footstep*: "I have not yet struck the true key-note of this Romance, and until I do, and unless I do, I shall write nothing but tediousness and nonsense"; "I do not at present see in the least how this is to be wrought out." In *Doctor Grimshawe's Secret*: "It is not possible to work this out; the idea does not take to itself representative form"; "Oh, Heavens! I have not the least notion how to get on. I never was in such a sad predicament before"; "So easily said—so impossible to do. Try back!" More of the same in the preliminary studies for *Septimius Felton* and *The Dolliver Romance*.

paid off so handsomely in *The Scarlet Letter*. Again, Hawthorne works up Western background for his emigrating Englishman, who trails through the novel, and the notes for the novel, depositing bloody footprints on America's forest leaves. (Still the blood is English, not American.) Clutching for a reason to prevent his inconveniently returning home, Hawthorne imagines him "carried away by the Indians, &c." Even in the nineteenth-century action, New England is called "these western shores."

Partly, as I think, with the intention of pulling the plots together, but partly, too, because Western reference was habitual and instinctive with Hawthorne, *Doctor Grimshawe's Secret* is full of brief, and usually disconnected, allusions to Western matters. " 'That tree,' observed the Warden, [']is well worth the notice of such an enthusiastic lover of old things; though I suppose aged trees may be the one ⟨thing⟩ antiquity that you do not value, having them by myriads in your primeval forests.' "[9] Along with English specimens, there are in the Warden's garden "all the modern and far-fetched flowers from America, the East [the Orient, or the Eastern United States?], and elsewhere; even the prairie flowers, and the California blossoms were represented here." For the Warden's banquet, Etherege supplies "some of the western wines of America." For the heroine, Hawthorne supplies "some peculiar little handwork, which enables her to get a living; something that she had learnt in America. Indian manufactures, with beads? No. She sells Indian meal, done up in neat packages, for washing hands. Oh, the devil!" The old Western magic has deteriorated into parlor tricks, and even Hawthorne knows it. (Yet a few lines later he thinks "the Indian beadwork may do.") This young heroine is also proficient in a kind of embroidery combining "wild, barbarian freedom with cultivated grace." At a point of especially intense frustration, Hawthorne reaches for one of his earliest Western symbols: "He shall have inherited the Great Carbuncle, and shall be forbidden

[9] Angle brackets indicate canceled word.

357

to show it to any mortal. 'Twon't do." The same must be said of nearly everything in the book. Possessing a "vein of wildness and romance ... characteristic of his country," Etherege is further defined by "imaginative and poetic tendencies; but yet young America shall show a promising blossom in him—there shall be a freedom of thought, a carelessness of old forms of things." Hawthorne's curious adversative is explained by the fact that "imaginative and poetic tendencies" have now hooked themselves onto such old forms of things as genealogy, ancient custom, and the like, and thus suddenly stand opposed to "wildness and romance" and "freedom of thought," which were once associated with the Western frontier.

Again, as in *The Ancestral Footstep*, Hawthorne thinks to fuse disparate times of action—and their places also?— by collapsing two hundred years' history into a factitious present identity: "The thought thrilled his bosom, that this [English mansion] was his home;—the home of the wild western wanderer, who had gone away centuries ago, and encountered strange chances, and almost forgotten his origin, but still kept a clue to bring him back, and had now come back and found all the original emotions safe within him." This is no wild Western wanderer, but a confused American author. In the native context, "Western" meant "changing." Evidently sensing the impasse, Hawthorne shifts to another mode of imaginative and poetic synthesis: "Musing upon this mysterious circumstance [being shot], and how it should have happened in so orderly a country as England, so tamed and subjected to civilization—an incident to happen in an English park, which seemed better suited to the Indian-haunted forests of the wilder parts of his own land . . ." Afterwards: "There should be a slight wildness in the patient's remark to the surgeon, which he cannot prevent, though he is conscious of it. 'It was an Indian bullet,' said the patient, still fancying himself gone astray into the past, 'shot at me in battle, two or three hundred years hereafter.' " So far as we are informed by the narrative, Etherege spends his time between Salem, Mass. and Washington, D.C.; yet somehow he is "long accustomed . . . to the hasty and rude accommodations, if so they were to be called, of log-huts and hasty, mud-built houses, in the western states of America."

In the Western direction, this representative young American is indeed mobile; immediately before the shooting, he makes a tour more astonishing still:

> As he walked along—he could not tell exactly where —the path had somewhat lost its distinctness; and it did not seem so much like one that was constantly trodden. It did not exactly grow wild; for it was the character of this scenery that there was no wildness about, everything seeming to have been touched, handled, arranged, at some period or other, by man. But it seemed to be getting remote; the path led him into plashy places where he had to pick his way; and it seemed, he thought, to be on the point of leaving him altogether, when he should be at a distance from habitation. Still; this would be no great hardship or peril, in a neighborhood which man had got so completely within his control, and where the fiercest wild beast that leapt across his path, or sat up at a distance to gaze at him, was a hare; no peril, surely, to him, who had wandered heretofore in wild primeval forests, and had seen the red Indian in his original haunts, and coped both with bear and buffalo. And so he walked cheerily on, finding a sort of nameless charm in this wandering, when, having no certain aim, he could not go astray. And we will let him go on, and not follow him, but remain behind listening to what we may hear . . . because there is a foreboding, a sense within us, that this traveller is not going the right way . . .[10]

The hero's path is the lost thread of Hawthorne's story. Like a sleepwalker, Etherege wanders backward and West-

[10] In the second draft, Hawthorne made this passage longer, dreamier, and yet more explicitly English, less blatantly Western (pp. 58-59 vs. pp. 275-276). The revised version is also more fretful—full of variants, false starts, and so forth.

ward out of the actual English scene, onto the fabulous ground of the frontier, or conditioned reflex of the American writer. In sober fact, Etherege has no more business in England than Middleton, but is only (like Hawthorne) on vacation. "With a little play moment," Hawthorne obligingly tells us, "in what had heretofore been a turbulent life, he felt an inclination to follow out this dream, and let it sport with him, and by-and-by to awake to realities. . . . It seemed just the thing for him to do—just the fool's Paradise for him to be in." Not even a wildly Romantic fiction could survive such a locale and such a motive. In the midst of a tortured second draft, Hawthorne abandoned *Doctor Grimshawe's Secret* and turned to a new venture.

For all its sporadic, unseemly flirtation with what Hawthorne apparently considered the necessary emblematic apparatus of international fiction—coffers of hair, for example, and gigantic spiders—*Septimius Felton; or, The Elixir of Life* (1861-1863) is much more firmly anchored in the American scene. It is anchored, in fact, in Hawthorne's house at Concord, which he bought from Bronson Alcott before going to Europe, and to which he returned in 1860; in 1852 or 1853 Thoreau had told him a story about a previous inhabitant of this house, who thought he would never die. "I staid here but a little while," Hawthorne mused, in his first set of notes for the novel, "but often times, afar off, this singular idea occurred to me, in foreign lands, when my thoughts returned to this place which seemed to be the point by which I was attached to my native land." In a subsequent letter to Fields, Hawthorne declared his intention of prefixing "a little sketch of Thoreau" to his newest romance, "because, from a tradition which he told me about this house of mine, I got the idea of a deathless man, which is now taking a shape very different from the original one. It seems the duty of a live literary man to perpetuate the memory of a dead one, when there is such fair opportunity as in this case: but how Thoreau would scorn me for thinking that *I* could perpetuate him!"[11] This "romance of im-

[11] James T. Fields, *Yesterdays With Authors* (Boston, 1871), p.

mortality," upon which Hawthorne expended so much ink, and which at first seems such a foolish scheme, evidently supplied him a fair opportunity to deal with a number of considerably more significant matters: Thoreau's final place in literature, his own capacity to secure and enhance it (in England he had always shown a proprietary interest in Thoreau's literary success),[12] a conviction that Thoreau's reputation could take care of itself, and perhaps also an unconscious conviction that his own reputation might be the safer attached to Thoreau's, or at least that his reputation and Thoreau's somehow belonged together.

With the new novel, Hawthorne would enshrine a friend and refurbish his own dwindling fame. Neither writer had been notably productive in the last few years, which painful truth may have sent Hawthorne's mind back to a Notebook entry on immortality—or, more accurately, inordinate longevity—made about the time he first met Thoreau: "The advantages of a longer life than is allotted to mortals—the many things that might then be accomplished;—to which one life-time is inadequate, and for which the time spent is therefore lost; a successor being unable to take up the task when we drop it."[13] Hawthorne began writing *Septimius Felton* early in 1862; Thoreau died in May of that year; sometime in the middle of the year Hawthorne commenced a total revision (abandoned early 1863). Did this early

---

110. The letter appears to refer to *The Dolliver Romance*, but as *Septimius Felton* commenced with the same idea, and Thoreau was repeatedly named in the preliminary notes for that novel, it seems reasonable to suppose that Hawthorne's intention of commemorating his friend in a prefatory sketch originated with the earlier work and, when that work failed (in Hawthorne's estimation), was simply passed along to the next. In the same way, the "pleasant and familiar summary of my life in the Consulate at Liverpool," once designed as "an integral and essential" introduction to *The Ancestral Footstep*, was eventually transferred to *Our Old Home*.

[12] *The English Notebooks*, pp. 316, 351. For Hawthorne boosting Thoreau in America more than a decade earlier, see Edward C. Sampson, "Three Unpublished Letters by Hawthorne to Epes Sargent," *American Literature*, XXXIV (1962), 102-103.

[13] *The American Notebooks*, p. 100.

concern over the relation between longevity and accomplishment recur—or, already swirling around in his mind, take more realistic shape—when Thoreau suddenly died at the age of forty-four, losing the greater number of years in which he might reasonably have been expected to make his literary mark, and leaving his book about the Indian undone?

A trip to wartime Washington in March may also have affected Hawthorne's plans. Having seen cartoons and sketches of Emmanuel Leutze's grandiose Capitol mural, he wrote (in "Chiefly About War Matters") with an obvious wistfulness and a probably unconscious anachronism: "The work will be emphatically original and American, embracing characteristics that neither art nor literature have yet dealt with [!], and producing new forms of artistic beauty from the natural features of the Rocky-Mountain region, which Leutze seems to have studied broadly and minutely. . . . It looked full of energy, hope, progress, irrepressible movement onward, all represented in a momentary pause of triumph; and it was most cheering to feel its good augury at this dismal time, when our country might seem to have arrived at such a deadly stand-still." It was Hawthorne himself who had arrived at a "deadly stand-still," while his country moved irrepressibly onward and downward through the final disasters. Observing the hordes of commissioned officers, many of them greenhorns, some of them fakes, he nostalgically fixed his attention on the kind of man he had years before learned to find true, a "grizzly veteran among this crowd of carpet-knights . . . who had spent his prime upon the frontier, and very likely could show an Indian bullet-mark on his breast." So rapidly had changed the American scene! "If such decorations, won in an obscure warfare, were worth the showing now," added this grizzly veteran of an American writer, whose warfare was not the warfare of the 1860's, although it was sufficiently obscure. On the previous page Hawthorne was wondering where all the loiterers in bars came from, and conjecturing that their "strange figures" were perhaps disgorged about equally from the decaying (depopulated) villages of the North and the

"forest-nooks of the West," no longer Romantically heroic
—"so that men long hidden in retirement," like Hawthorne
turning into Rip Van Winkle, "put on the garments of their
youth and hurry out to inquire what is the matter." The
matter was the death of the first American republic, and of
the Western dream which was its life-principle, as it was the
life-principle of the writers who dreamed and were dreamed
by that republic.

Many of Hawthorne's early notations about the protagonist of *Septimius Felton* sound curiously like descriptions of
Thoreau. By his neighbors, Septimius is thought to be an
infidel, but is probably not. "He had merely taken himself
out of the category of the rest of the human race. . . . His
lot was not with theirs. It was with the rich, beautiful earth
where they all dwelt. . . . Something there was, that daily
and continuously separated him more and more from his
kind." Far more seriously than Septimius Felton, Thoreau
was in fact "aiming at something removed from them, unexampled; and yet pretending to seek it in no remote way,
but only to take this birthright which any other might have
as well, if the force were in him to claim it and make it
good." We are told further of Felton's "stern emphasis and
faith in himself," of "certain queernesses," and of "strong
affinities for earth, a love of the soil, of this particular spot."
At one point Hawthorne thinks the narrative might begin
with a discovery of Septimius Felton's journal, "extending
over a long series of years."[14] Occasionally an elaborate
passage sails even closer to the personal biography of the
man who went to the woods to live deliberately:

> He shall grow apart from the world, hard, selfish, iso-
> lated, estranged from his nearest and dearest. Perhaps
> he shall lose the first love of his youth for this passion;
> the woman for whom he built his house—the building
> of which shall be described, and how he thought it
> would be but like a hut of boughs, so transitory as com-

[14] It is impossible to be certain how much Hawthorne knew about
Thoreau's journal. But as early as 1842 he knew that Thoreau kept
it, and what he used it for. *The American Notebooks*, p. 167.

pared with his long duration. . . . He shall discover that any engagement of the affections draws off his mind from its intentness, and makes him grow progressively older; so he gives up all that, for he is determined to live.

Granted, many of the details in the early sketches for *Septimius Felton* make no sense applied to Thoreau; Hawthorne was already spinning Romantic webs around his victim. For the same reason, none of his tentative, fictional descriptions, but only the general drift of the whole performance, should be taken as shedding any light on Hawthorne's attitude toward Thoreau. Still, it seems obvious that Thoreau was not merely to be the subject of a prefatory essay, but was from the outset an integral, if not wholly integrated, element in Hawthorne's conception of the novel.

Thoreau's ghostly presence probably explains the conspicuous increase, in this third fragment, of Indian materials. Hawthorne not only liked to identify himself with the dispossessed native; from the beginning, he identified Thoreau the same way: "For two or three years back, he has repudiated all regular modes of getting a living, and seems inclined to lead a sort of Indian life among civilized men. . . . It is a characteristic trait, that he has a great regard for the memory of the Indian tribes, whose wild life would have suited him so well."[15] By the time of his fifth set of preliminary notes, Hawthorne was in serious danger of being altogether overwhelmed by the literary Indian, no longer very reliably informed by the sane and imaginative views of his youth, or by Thoreau's views either, but bedizened with a trashy Gothicism. "Traditions of the temptation—the Divine [one of the earlier Feltons, presumably] used to have to go into the Forest and meet the Devil, and his wizard ancestor." More significantly, the central emblem of *The Ancestral Footstep*, which had also appeared in *Dr. Grimshawe's Secret*, appears once more, and this time in an unmistakably American context: "Aunt K has some strange

[15] *The American Notebooks*, pp. 166-167.

story about a bloody footstep's being seen round the door of the wigwam."

In the same set of notes, the emigrating ancestor arrives in the New World ahead of the Puritans, "betakes himself to the wilderness," and becomes chief (also "a great medicine man, or prophet and priest") of an Indian tribe. Naturally, the Puritans think him a wizard. "Possibly they slay him." His son they rear, however, and partially tame; through him mysterious family heirlooms, legends, traditions, documents, and secrets, are transmitted to the present. Such is the background of Septimius' "wild" ideas. Wild as they are, they are also related to Thoreau's vocation—and one of Hawthorne's avocations—around Concord. "The place where Septimius now lives was that where his ancestor, the wizard, had his wigwam; and there, perhaps, he finds a spear or arrow-head, which may have been his. . . . Bloody footstep." (It will be remembered that in "The Old Manse" Hawthorne spoke of Thoreau and himself as arrowhead-collectors; he also said that finding an arrowhead "builds up again the Indian village and its encircling forest, and recalls to life the painted chiefs and warriors," etc.) Hawthorne will render the New World half of his story indigenous by imbuing it, as quickly as possible, with actual Indian associations; simultaneously, he will fuse the two halves of his story through tribal adoption and racial mingling.

By the seventh set of preliminary notes, the hero has become even more melodramatic, and correspondingly more remote from Thoreau, who, had he known, would probably have declined the honor of commemoration. At the nadir of Hawthorne's conception, "Septimius has a wild genealogy. . . . This mixture of bloods had given him a strange and exceptional nature; and he had brooded upon the legends that clung around his line, following his ancestry, not only to the English universities, but into the wild forest, and into hell itself. The mixed race had probably made him morbid, in reality, besides giving his dark imagination this unwonted scope & lawlessness. His mind and character had a savage and fiendish strain, intermixed with its Puritan characteristics." It reads like an unkind parody of *The Scarlet Letter*, and of the variously brilliant Western speculations that led to it. Yet beneath the surface folly, it is impressive, and even moving, to see how inexorably Hawthorne gravitates toward the earliest and richest sources of his literary career. Most amazing of all, as he works into the novel itself he begins to make, from time to time, a strange kind of sense.

For one thing, Thoreau is definitely—if only intermittently, and never very profoundly—lodged in the novel. Septimius Felton is a Harvard graduate who helps support himself in college by schoolkeeping; later, in order to furnish himself "all possible quantity of scientific knowledge of botany," he walks to Cambridge, searches the college library, and borrows books to study at home. Doubtless it is Thoreau as well who is seen "brooding, brooding, his eyes fixed on some chip, some stone, some common plant, any commonest thing, as if it were the clew and index to some mystery." The doctrines of *Walden* appear regularly, as when Septimius improbably rhapsodizes: " 'How wonderful it is to see it all alive on this spring day, all growing, budding! . . . The whole race of man, living from the beginning of time, have not, in all their number and multiplicity and in all their duration, come in the least to know the world they live in!' " To which the minister replies: " 'But the lesson is carried on in another state of being!' "—so that Felton may crush him with such a retort as the one-world-at-a-time man would have relished: " 'Not the lesson that we begin here. . . . We might as well train a child in a primeval forest, to teach him how to live in a European court.' " One of the hidden processes of *Septimius Felton* is a running dialogue between Thoreau and Hawthorne, perhaps not unrelated to their actual conversations. Septimius raving (until his voice echoes "out of the woods") to the memory of the dead British officer is Hawthorne talking to Thoreau, in sorrow and admiration and reluctance: " 'I see, it requires a strong spirit, capable of much lonely endurance, able to be sufficient to itself, loving not too much, dependent on no sweet ties of affection, to be capable of the mighty trial which now devolves on me. . . . Yet thou, I feel, hast the better part, who didst so soon lie down to rest, who hast done forever with this troublesome world, which it is mine to contemplate from age to age, and to sum up the meaning of it.' "

Even more frequently than he is Thoreau, Septimius is the man writing about Thoreau, withdrawn from the life around him, especially as it takes the form of war.[16] "And then, perchance,—perchance,—there was destined for him some high, lonely path, in which, to make any progress, to come to any end, he must walk unburdened by the affections. Such thoughts as these depressed and chilled (as many men have found them, or similar ones, to do)." As Hawthorne remarks, a few pages on, all things "set themselves against man's progress in any pursuit that he seeks to devote himself to. It is one struggle, the moment he undertakes such a thing, of everything else in the world to impede him." In *Septimius Felton* a variety of signs indicates what price Hawthorne was willing to pay in order to crown his career. Some of his noblest prose is wrung from the usual agonies of guilt, but he is also, sustained by Thoreau, uncharacteristically aggressive about his right to isolate himself from society in favor of a higher end. "The people have a little mistaken the character and purpose of poor Septimius," he tells us, resolutely flying in the face of common sense, "and remember him as a quack doctor, instead of a seeker for a secret, not the less sublime and elevating because it happened to be unattainable." The secret referred to is no trivial "elixir of life," but something more akin to the Great Carbuncle. As Hawthorne says of his hero's conviction that he

---

[16] "Our story is an internal one, dealing as little as possible with outward events [the Revolutionary War for Septimius Felton, the Civil War for Hawthorne], and taking hold of these only where it cannot be helped, in order by means of them to delineate the history of a mind bewildered in certain errors. We would not willingly, if we could, give a lively and picturesque surrounding to this delineation."

will never die: "The feeling was not peculiar to Septimius. It is an instinct, the meaning of which is mistaken. We have strongly within us the sense of an undying principle." Behind the idea of fame lies the undying principle of significant achievement permanently recorded. "He would write a poem," Hawthorne reminds himself in a note, "or other great work, inappreciable at first, and live to see it famous, —himself among his own posterity."

For all its obvious inadequacies of execution, such is the work before us. If it reveals Hawthorne's determination to get one more solid piece of writing on the record, it also reveals his longing to be released from a lifelong obligation. " 'That is an awful idea that you present,' " Sybil replies to Felton's visions of their indefinitely prolonged future, " 'doing this till these trees crumble away, till perhaps a new forest grew up wherever this white race had planted, and a race of savages again possess the soil.' " The conceit is Thoreauvian, but its doctrinal content chimes rather with the minister's assurance that the " 'importance of death at any particular moment' " is overestimated. Yet Hawthorne never seems quite pacified. He talks about his hero's indecipherable manuscript as if it were a screen for his own compositional desires and difficulties. Septimius is Hawthorne, worrying over "the document that had so possessed him, turning its crabbed meanings every way, trying to get out of it some new light, often tempted to fling it into the fire," and then he would have to "try back," again like Hawthorne, "rising out of that black depth of despair, into a determination to do what he had so long striven for." It is a wonder, Hawthorne concludes, "that its essence did not arise, purified from all alloy of falsehood, from all turbidness of obscurity and ambiguity, and form a pure essence of truth and invigorating motive, if of any it were capable." This is more the language of literary analysis than of alchemy. Approaching his denouement, Hawthorne ecstatically describes Septimius' final delusory success: "Everything became facile to his manipulation, clear to his thought. . . . That is to say, he had succeeded in amalgamating his materials so that they acted upon one another, and in accordance; and had produced a result that had a subsistence in itself, and a right to be." That is no elixir of life either, but a novel.

Of the various materials constituting *Septimius Felton*, the Indian was central, because to him Thoreau, Hawthorne, and their America might each and all be accommodated. With varying degrees of success, Hawthorne tried to invest his hero with Indian qualities sufficiently realized to achieve this personal and national accommodation. He was not invariably successful. Septimius' "fierce Indian blood stirred in him, and gave a murderous excitement," or "that Indian fierceness that was in him arousing itself, and thrusting up its malign head like a snake"—these are further examples of Septimius considerately dropping out of character to suit Hawthorne's devious ends. He is said to have the "Indian nature of revenge," when obviously he is the least bloodthirsty man in Revolutionary America. At one point, Hawthorne grotesquely attributes to him a "customary American abhorrence for any mixture of blood." Upon another occasion, Hawthorne sees him as Dimmesdale, "none the worse, as a clergyman, for having an instinctive sense of the nature of the Devil." Septimius further bears false witness in announcing: " 'There is in me the wild, natural blood of the Indian, the instinctive, the animal nature, which has ways of warning that civilized life polishes away and cuts out.' " The young enthusiast possesses no such instincts, and few fictional characters have ever displayed less animal nature.

Yet Hawthorne also manages to move from the clichés of American thought about savagism toward a limited and therefore a convincing reality. Preserving "a true Indian composure of outward mien" at Aunt Keziah's deathbed, Septimius is perfectly in character, but still exhibits an undeniable "racial" trait. At the same time, the old woman fights "with her anguish, and would not yield to it a jot, though she allowed herself the relief of shrieking savagely at it,—much more like a defiance than a cry for mercy." This, too, is believable human behavior. Hawthorne even makes

a start toward furnishing Septimius a physique and a physical manner recognizably American, and plausibly related to
American encounter with, and imitation of, the Indian: "His
apparel took an unsought picturesqueness that set off his
slender, agile figure, perhaps from some quality of spon-
taneous arrangement that he had inherited from his Indian
ancestry." This nervous informality was quite likely derived
from the gestures and gait of Thoreau, who had all his life
re-enacted in reverse the process by which Felton's half-breed
ancestor was domesticated by the Puritans, and induced to
build "a house among them, with a good deal of the wigwam, no doubt, in its style of architecture, but still a permanent house, near which he established a corn-field. . . .
There he spent his life, with some few instances of temporary relapse into savage wildness, when he fished in the
river Musquehannah, or in Walden, or strayed in the
woods."

Aunt Keziah says she can leave Septimius only the recipe
of her outrageous ancestral drink, and (possibly) relatives
still living among the Cape Indians. She expires "in a great
sigh, like a gust of wind among the trees," but first delivers
her nephew a farewell address containing many a curious
literary echo:

> If you could be an Indian, methinks it would be better
> than this tame life we lead. . . . Oh, how pleasant 't
> would have been to spend my life wandering in the
> woods, smelling the pines and the hemlock all day, and
> fresh things of all kinds, and no kitchen work to do . . .
> but to sleep on fresh boughs in a wigwam, with the leaves
> still on the branches that made the roof! And then to
> see the deer brought in by the red hunter, and the blood
> streaming from the arrow-dart! Ah! and the fight too!
> and the scalping! and, perhaps, a woman might creep
> into the battle, and steal the wounded enemy away of
> her tribe and scalp him, and be praised for it! O Seppy,
> how I hate the thought of the dull life women lead! . . .
> Thank Heaven, I'm done with it! If I'm ever to live
> again, may I be whole Indian, please my Maker!

Apparently Hawthorne thought that would be a good idea too; in the scenario he wrote as a guide for revision, he instructed himself: "Dwell upon Aunt Nashoba's [Keziah's] Indian love of the woods," as if he had still not said enough.

From his Indian ancestry Septimius receives gifts of the spirit magnificently comprehensive. His "paternal inheritance"—land and more than land—has been in the family "since the world began (for they held it by an Indian deed)." But the prospect of landed estate bores him—not merely or even mainly because he expects to live forever. " 'That strain of Indian blood is in me yet,' said Septimius, 'and it makes me . . . reject for myself what you [an English eccentric] think so valuable. I do not care for these common aims. I have ambition, but it is for prizes such as other men cannot gain, and do not think of aspiring after. . . . It would suit me well enough to try that mode of life, as well as a hundred others, but only for a time. It is of no permanent importance.' " So speaks the American, this new man. In another remark the voice of America asserts itself even more unmistakably: " 'My destiny is one which kings might envy, and strive in vain to buy with principalities and kingdoms.' "

In the course of the narrative Septimius hears two legends, one from Aunt Keziah, one from Sybil Dacy, the English girl. Understandably he is impressed by their coincidence, for Hawthorne is one more weary time trying to connect Old World and New through the adventitious intricacies of genealogical plot. Yet the legends themselves contain linked allegories anything but superficial. "Strangely wild and uncouth, and mixed up of savage and civilized life," Aunt Keziah's story is about one of their forefathers, a wild Indian king, wise and good, so old his people feared he would live forever, thereby disturbing "the whole order of nature," and who could "foretell as far into the future as he could remember into the past." The king is the historical-prophetic American writer, or, more simply, Hawthorne-Thoreau. Having learned of the world all it has to teach, and having taught his people all they are willing to know, he agrees to be killed. He proves impervious to ordinary weapons, however, and must be dispatched by having his nose, and his mouth ("which kept uttering wisdom to the last"), plastered with clay. To a chosen one he transmits the secret of a fabulous drink, the same inherited by Keziah, Septimius, and Hawthorne. The legend is a parable about the working imagination, its sources and ends, and the hazards of literary mortality.

The matching legend is about an English lord, Sir Forester, who also possesses a secret of longevity. In his case, the boon must be purchased each generation with the sacrifice of another life. His choice falls on the "one human being whom he cared for;—that was a beautiful kinswoman, an orphan, whom his father had brought up, and, dying, left her to his care." He kills and buries her "in the wood," thereafter leaving a bloody track in college, street, and "wilderness," increasingly "sick to death of the object that he had pursued," a "horror-stricken man, always looking behind him to see the track." Home from his world-wide wandering, he finds on the threshold a Bloody Footstep and in the wood a "beautiful crimson flower," the final ingredient needed for his elixir, which he forthwith prepares and drinks, becoming "immortal in woe and agony, still studying, still growing wiser and more wretched in every age." This legend cunningly turns up the other side of the American coin. The orphan is the Indian, the father is God, the track is the white man's record of guilt, the red flower is American culture, springing from the grave of a race and retaining the telltale color.[17] The English lord's name perhaps goes back to one of the earliest American "novels," Jeremy Belknap's *The Foresters, An American Tale* (1792), an allegory representing Revolutionary patriots as "foresters," and America as "the forest." By Hawthorne's time, "forester" had become a common synonym for "pioneer."

[17] Cf. Margaret Fuller, in *Summer on the Lakes* (1844): "Kishwaukie is according to tradition the scene of a famous battle, and its many grassy mounds contain the bones of the valiant. On these waved thickly the mysterious purple flower of which I have spoken before. I think it springs from the blood of the Indians." *The Writings of Margaret Fuller*, ed. Mason Wade (New York, 1941), p. 47.

Septimius Felton opens with three young people conversing on a hillside where, "according to tradition, the first settlers of the village had burrowed in caverns which they had dug out for their shelter." It concludes with Hawthorne's visit to Smithell's Hall in England, where he meets a baron identifiable as the son of Septimius "by the thin, sallow, American cast of his face, and the lithe slenderness of his figure," together with, possibly, "a certain Indian glitter of the eye and cast of feature." How is he here? His father had believed his own lot to be in the lowest of the social stages: " 'I must be, of necessity, a wanderer on the face of the earth, changing place at short intervals, disappearing suddenly and entirely.' " Yet probably he brought to England more than he received. It is well for an English line to become extinct, Hawthorne patriotically informs us, because the family stock is doubtless "flourishing in the New World, revived by the rich infusion of new blood in a new soil, instead of growing feebler, heavier, stupider, each year by sticking to an old soil." *Pace* Buffon, Sydney Smith, and the American abhorrence for any mixture of blood. The "new birth" idea is back, with a further implication: having achieved his proper New World identity, the American may inherit and enjoy what he likes. Yet the "new flower" (American culture) born from a corpse, while the hero is poring over his manuscript, is poisonous, however "like a person, like a life!" (This is practically the same language used for Pearl in *The Scarlet Letter*.) On the other hand, to consider the matter still more closely, the same fatal draught intuitively discovered by the savages of America was also "contrived by the utmost skill of a great civilized philosopher [Friar Bacon], searching the whole field of science for his purpose." The blood guilt has now been distributed equally to the United States and England, as seems to have been Hawthorne's inchoate intention all along. According to tales told by Robert Hagburn's aged mother, Septimius might at any time have returned to England and found an estate prepared for him. Equally, " 'if Felton chose to strike into the woods, he'd find a tribe of wild In-

373

dians there ready to take him for their sagamore, and conquer the whites.'" Hawthorne was never fully to realize
the action implicit in *Septimius Felton*, but its tendency is
to say that our crazy protagonist encompasses both extremes.
Septimius Felton is the American hero as Indian as citizen
of the world. He is victor and victim, bloody and bleeding,
immersed in gloomy wrongs both ancient and modern. What
more was there to say?

In 1863 Hawthorne collected as *Our Old Home* the English sketches he had been transferring from his Notebooks to
the immaculate page of the *Atlantic* since 1860. The sketches
bear marks of his concurrent labors on *Doctor Grimshawe's
Secret* and *Septimius Felton*. Americans are "Western people," with a "Western love of change" befitting "Western
wanderers." Half facetiously, Hawthorne proposes annexing
England, then, for the benefit of both parties, "transferring
their thirty millions of inhabitants to some convenient wilderness in the great West"—as in "Earth's Holocaust" practically synonymous with empty space—"and putting half or
a quarter as many of ourselves into their places." Lost on
Blackheath, Hawthorne finds that the "solitude is as impressive as that of a Western prairie or forest," or says he
does. "For aught I know," he goes on, "the Western prairie
may still compare favorably with it as a safe region to go
astray in," a sentiment doubtless owing something to Cooper's enchanted West, where Natty Bumppo and his friends
drifted about interminably, and for the most part safely.
Obviously Hawthorne relishes these comparisons between
the exotic West and the colorfully sordid aspects of England: "The wild life of the streets has perhaps as unforgettable a charm, to those who have once thoroughly imbibed it,
as the life of the forest or the prairie." Then he catches himself: "But I conceive rather that there must be insuperable
difficulties, for the majority of the poor." This general reciprocity between the fragmentary romances and *Our Old
Home* is not, however, invariable. Apparently forgetting
his fictional involvement with Thoreau, Hawthorne ostentatiously declares: "A lodging in a wigwam or under a tent

has really as many advantages, when we come to know them, as a home beneath the roof-tree of Charlecote Hall. But, alas! our philosophers have not yet taught us what is best, nor have our poets sung us what is beautifullest, in the kind of life that we must lead." Our philosophers and poets had been doing little else since the 1820's.

Of *The Dolliver Romance* (1863-1864), which proved to be the final fragment, Hawthorne was able to complete only three graceful, inconsequential chapters. From the preliminary studies, we gather that two of the characters were to flee to the wilderness, there to find shelter "with an Indian Doctress," and that after they "have dwelt there some time, it turns out this [another elixir] was an old family recipe. A great deal of wild Indian traditions shall be introduced here and told by the old herb-woman." A few paragraphs later, we find a far more significant entry: "The title to an estate in England?" Immediately preceding that entry, we find the most significant revelation of all: "The central thought; the central thought." There was, of course, no central thought, as the published draft makes abundantly clear. At Hawthorne's funeral, the first chapter of this dying effort was placed on the coffin, in an action unconsciously betokening New England's increasing literary sentimentality. Even this gesture was superfluous. Like the Westward-moving American people, Hawthorne had long before death left his neighbors—and even his own best self—far in the rear, an ambiguous and ironic accomplishment worthy of his genius, for at the time of his death he was not quite sixty years old, and his nation, constitutionally considered, only seventy-five.

3. MELVILLE AS POET

Except for Whitman, Western poetry (however loosely defined) hardly existed, which is perhaps merely to say that the great achievements of American writing in its formative phase were almost entirely in prose, with the finest moments of American verse coming later. Of Western jingling there was more than enough.[1] But during the whole period in which our literature was dominated by social, political, and philosophical considerations arising from contemplation of the West, the serious poets were struggling, unsuccessfully, with a special problem of their own—the conflict between their zeal to be American at all costs, and the necessity of writing in an artistic medium (the English language and its poetic tradition) which in technique, sensibility, and cultural assumption was preponderantly alien to them. Until this problem was solved—and it was not even near solution until 1855—the American poet would egregiously fail to get the West or anything else into major poetry, for no matter how significant his subject it was never matched by a correspondingly significant rhythm.[2] And by the time this technical obstacle was more or less removed, the West was as good as gone.

It is to specific conditions connected with the poetic situation, then, rather than to causes mystic and metaphysical, that we must attribute the dearth of Western poetry in early American literature. Certainly there was nothing inherently anti-poetic in the idea of the West, which was both a metaphor (especially as the frontier) and an action (especially as the Westward Movement); it ought to have been as amenable to treatment in lyric poetry as to treatment in narrative prose, but in fact it was not. Even in the poetry of Melville—who almost certainly commanded more poetic talent than Poe, Emerson, Thoreau, or any of the lesser songsters—metric all too frequently wars with meaning. For this reason, among others, Melville's career as Western poet was marginal, even though poetry of one sort or another occupied him for about thirty-five years. He wrote practically all his prose in a little over ten.

---

[1] Run-of-the-mill frontier poetizing may be surveyed in such representative anthologies as William D. Gallagher, *Selections From the Poetical Literature of the West* (Cincinnati, 1841), and William T. Coggeshall, *The Poets and Poetry of the West* (Columbus, 1860).

[2] For a more extensive discussion of this problem, see my essay, "The Meter-Making Argument," in *Aspects of American Poetry*, ed. Richard M. Ludwig (Columbus, 1962), pp. 3-31.

"Storms at the West derange the wires," is an unconsciously ironic line in *Battle-Pieces* (1866). In this first volume of verses, Melville more than once descended to doggerel, perhaps in part because at first he found it so difficult to think in the medium of poetry, except off and on:

> But, full of *vim* from Western prairies won,
> They'll make, ere long, a dash at Donelson.[3]

In view of the fact that the prairies traditionally belonged to the whole nation, Melville's identification of them as a training-ground for Union troops (even with respect to an obviously Western victory) rings hollow; apparently he was half-automatically trying to invoke the old magic of the West for the new cause (Civil War, poetry), but the two worlds simply declined to lie down together. In the same poem, Indians linger like ghosts, or as Melville prefers to say, "Our fellows lurk/ Like Indians that waylay the deer/ By the wild salt-spring." The battle is "an Indian fight,/ Intricate, dusky, stretching far away." Where it stretched was into the dusky past, as Melville admitted in "Apathy and Enthusiasm":

> But the elders with foreboding
> Mourned the days forever o'er,
> And recalled the forest proverb,
> The Iroquois' old saw:
> *Grief to every graybeard*
> *When young Indians lead the war.*

To some graybeards, perhaps, the most exasperating fault of the young bucks who came of age during the Civil War was their ignorance of being Indians. Melville's tribute to "The College Colonel"—"An Indian aloofness lones his brow" —was a compliment conceivably less gratifying to the young brave in question than to the mature writer bestowing it. In

[3] Quotations in this section are from *Battle-Pieces and Aspects of the War*, ed. Sidney Kaplan (Gainesville, Florida, 1960); *Clarel, A Poem and Pilgrimage in the Holy Land*, ed. Walter E. Bezanson (New York, 1960); and *Collected Poems of Herman Melville*, ed. Howard P. Vincent (Chicago, 1947).

"The Muster: Suggested by the Two Days' Review at Washington. (May, 1865)," Melville went so far as to imagine the antebellum Mississippi performing a miracle of reconciliation which he himself, years earlier, had exposed as mere sentimentality:

> The Abrahamic river—
>   Patriarch of floods,
> Calls the roll of all his streams
>   And watery multitudes:
>   Torrent calls to torrent,
>   The rapids hail the fall;
>   With shouts the inland freshets
>   Gather to the call.
>
>   The quotas of the Nation,
>   Like the water-shed of waves,
>   Muster into union—
>   Eastern warriors, Western braves. . . .
>
> The Abrahamic river
>   To sea-wide fullness fed,
> Pouring from the thaw-lands
>   By the God of floods is led:
>   His deep enforcing current
>   The streams of ocean own,
>   And Europe's marge is evened
>   By rills from Kansas lone.

From the author of *The Confidence-Man*, such innocence seems scarcely believable; but the sad truth is that Melville, of all people, had fallen into both platitude and anachronism. The Civil War had temporarily outflanked him, which may explain his appearing to age so fast. When Fort Sumter fell, he was only forty-one.

The modes of historical consciousness in which he grew up were shattered; and unless he were able to exchange them for new—which, for the time being, he was not—contemporary topics must elude his grasp. Western allusions in Melville's poems are nearly always retrospective, as indeed most of the poems are. "Trophies of Peace: Illinois in 1840" was probably suggested by his 1858-1859 lecture tour to the Midwest, with its reminders of the earlier journey.[4] Understandably, the poem reveals a great weariness with war and heroism, preferring instead "Files on files of Prairie Maize," even though the final stanza concedes that this choice of natural cycle over human striving is tantamount to a rejection of fame and even of history. "Old Counsel of the Young Master of a Wrecked California Clipper" dwells on the disparity between youthful daring and middle-aged dubieties, and conceivably also hints the wreck of the American ship of state. It was probably written in 1860, when Melville sailed to San Francisco in a ship commanded by his much younger brother Tom, and almost upon arrival nervously turned on his heel and went home:

> Come out of the Golden Gate,
> Go round the Horn with streamers,
> Carry royals early and late;
> But, brother, be not over-elate—
> *All hands save ship!* has startled dreamers.

In "Rip Van Winkle's Lilac," a transitional Western reference serves primarily to remind us, as it doubtless reminded the author, that Western references had gone out of style:

> It came to pass as years went on
> (An Indian file in stealthy flight
> With purpose never man has known) . . .

And in "After the Pleasure Party," which deals in an old man's way with a young man's passion, Melville likewise returned to the literary milieu of his earlier days for a favorite image:

[4] Leon Howard, *Herman Melville: A Biography* (Berkeley, 1951), p. 265. For further details of these later Western travels, see Merton M. Sealts, Jr., *Melville as Lecturer* (Cambridge, 1957), the indispensable study of Melville's transition from prose writer to poet. It seems obvious, however, that this second Western trip, or trips, provided little in the way of literary stimulus not already available to him. As might have been anticipated, Melville was something less than a howling success as a lecturer in the West, whose log-cabin critics worked him over more harshly than their Eastern colleagues.

379

Hence the winged blaze that sweeps my soul
Like prairie fires that spurn control,
Where withering weeds incense the flame.

First by the passing of the frontier, and then by the War which was the final spasm of that passing, Melville had been almost completely divorced from the world of his young manhood. In fact, not one major writer who grew up before these abruptnesses and dark transitions really survived them intact, so that in retrospect it may even seem a kind of fated cultural action which prophetically sent Poe to his premature death in 1849; which wasted and ruined Thoreau (d. 1862) and Hawthorne (d. 1864); which ultimately left Emerson senile, and Whitman a paralytic. Whether paralyzed in body or in spirit, Melville and Whitman were condemned to live on and on, and to write as long as they lived.

Only belatedly did Melville achieve (more or less) a genuine poetic style. And he achieved it by learning to make much of a diminished thing. As one of his best biographers says of the trip to Palestine (1856-1857), and of the long poem that finally emerged from that experience: "It was as if, having spent his youth voyaging westward, toward the spaces that lay beyond America, to the islands that had no history and were still pristine, he were under a compulsion now to reverse that movement and voyage eastward and backward, to retrace the Asiatic and the European currents to their headwaters, to immerse himself in scenes that, as he may well have felt, were *only* history, only memory, only the source and not the future. The nostalgia for the primitive had yielded in him to the nostalgia for the venerable and the moribund."[5] So, in their different ways, were Thoreau and Hawthorne inundated by obsessive concern with one or another aspect of the Western past. With all three writers, perhaps, *compulsion* is the word to underline, for there was little or no choice in the matter. The reversion from futurism to ennui was national—or simply human—and Melville conformed with it only insofar as he had to; from his own

[5] Newton Arvin, *Herman Melville* (New York, 1950), p. 212.

personal stake in the national experience, he salvaged what
he could. Thus *Clarel* (1876)—his major literary work after
The Confidence-Man—is at once a poem and pilgrimage
in Palestine, and a poem and pilgrimage *toward* a vanished
America. Consequently, the strictly subdued tone of Melville's verse is flecked with Western highlights (but not nearly so many as glint from the sea), from an early reference
to " 'The breath of Sharon's prairie land!' " to Don Han-
nibal's jaunty self-description:

> "A poor one-legged pioneer;
> I go, I march, I am the man
> In fore-front of the limping van
> Of refluent emigration."

In between, a bright barrage of allusions keeps us ever alert
to superficial differences and basic similarities between Old
World and New. Rustlings from the shadowy spaces of the
Church of the Holy Sepulcher steal upon the ear "Like steps
in Indian forest deep." Palestine's deserts ironically unroll

> Like Western counties all in grain
> Ripe for the sickleman and wain.

Man's skull, or the intimations of mortality it enforces,
becomes

> "That sachem old
> Whose wigwam is man's heart within—
> How taciturn, and yet can speak,
> Imparting more than books can win."

Clad in a costume which reveals him as bewilderingly old
and new at the same time, patriarchal Abraham roves from
Ur of the Chaldees, "Priest, shepherd, prince, and pioneer."
More extensively, Vine (almost certainly Hawthorne) rumi-
nates on the mother of Ishmael (and, it may be, on "the *Red-
Hot Coal*" of *White-Jacket*):

> "Clan of outcast Hagar,
> Well do ye come by spear and dagger!
> Yet in your bearing ye outvie

> Our western Red Men, chiefs that stalk
> In mud paint—whirl the tomahawk.—
> But in these Nimrods . . ."

and thence to the Holy Land again. The narrator himself speculates on the ancient vegetative possibilities of the Mar Saba desert:

> Or, earlier yet, could be a day,
> In time's first youth and pristine May
> When here the hunter stood alone—
> Moccasined Nimrod, belted Boone . . .

Thus the near past—what in Melville's first youth was still the Far West—was in his poetic imagination projected backward upon the almost unimaginably farthest past and the Near East.

Versions of the frontier metaphor, of which Melville had never been overfond, once more appeared in *Clarel*, one of them in a passage controlled by the conceit of Theocritus' line threading "dark Joel's text of terror." In Melville's text, the terminology of the Age of Arnold is threaded by imagery from the Age of Cooper and the historical facts of an age previous to either, reminding us that even the Old Dominion was once the hither edge of free land (these lines immediately precede the first appearance of Vine, and perhaps help define that "funeral man, yet richly fair" as Hawthorne):

> Yes, strange that Pocahontas-wedding
> Of contraries in old belief—
> Hellenic cheer, Hebraic grief.

Although less explicit in reference, another figure is even more old-fashioned in metaphorical form:

> But what's evoked in Clarel's mien—
> What look, responsive look is seen
> In Celio, as together there
> They pause? Can these a climax share?
> Mutual in approach may glide

Minds which from poles adverse have come,
Belief and unbelief? may doom
Of doubt make such to coincide—
Upon one frontier brought to dwell...[6]

(Out of the corner of the eye, we catch a glimpse of Natty Bumppo and the Sarpent.) Perhaps because the War was now so well behind him, Melville occasionally risks even a metaphor suggestive of the old East-West North-South diamagnetism which so tormented him in the 1850's:

" 'Lulled by tinklings at the side,
I, along the taffrail leaning,
Yielding to the ship's careening,
    Shared that peace the upland owns
Where the palm—the palm and pine
Meeting on the frontier line
    Seal a truce between the zones.' "

In antebellum American literature, palm and pine had been standard symbology for South and North; that incorrigibly Western river, the Mississippi, it was often said, embraced both extremes.

Three characters especially are defined in terms of the fading or faded West. "Rolfe—capricious man" (almost certainly the poet) is first presented as a lone survivor from Melville's early travels in the West and on the Western Ocean:

Trapper or pioneer
He looked, astray in Judah's seat—
Or one who might his business ply
On waters under tropic sky.

Everything in his manner—which is notably imaginative, skeptical, self-reliant, inventive, hardheaded—bespeaks the ideals of personal behavior and value derived from the wild West, or from the literary confrontation of it in the earlier nineteenth century:

[6] In this and the next quotation, "frontier" is stressed on the first syllable. Melville's pronunciation of the word apparently follows British rather than American usage.

> With equal pace
> Came Rolfe in saddle pommeled high,
> Yet e'en behind that peaked redoubt
> Sat Indian-like, in pliant way,
> As if he were an Osage scout,
> Or Gaucho of the Paraguay.

High-riding Rolfe is no mere Osage scout, of course, for as occasionally in Melville's earlier writing, and so often in Whitman's, "the West" (Western part of America) is interchangeably "the West" (Western civilization). Westerner Rolfe is the quintessential modern. So when the poem speaks of religious faith dissolved "In laboratories of the West," it is doubtless both Wests in concatenated relationship which are in question, as the general drift of the subsequent commentary indicates:

> But in her Protestant repose
> Snores faith toward her mortal close?
> Nay, like a sachem petrified,
> Encaved found in the mountain-side,
> Perfect in feature, true in limb,
> Life's full similitude in him,
> Yet all mere stone—is faith dead *now*,
> A petrifaction? Grant it so,
> Then what's in store?

Conceivably that passage looks backward toward Hawthorne's "Man of Adamant"; but what's in store is a typical American flood of abuse against the United States of America, which Melville had long since suggested might be held responsible for the decline of Christianity. Vine-Hawthorne, in his resurrected and ambiguously glorified state, has already been persuaded to join Melville in voicing resentment for the long struggle to define and establish an American sensibility:

> "But, as men stray
> Further from Ararat away
> Pity it were did they recede

384

In carriage, manners, and the rest;
But no, for ours the palm indeed
In bland amenities far West!
Come now, for pastime let's complain;
Grudged thanks, Columbus, for thy main!
Put back, as 'twere—assigned by fate
To fight crude Nature o'er again,
By slow degrees we re-create."

Full circle for the idea of an American literature—from Freneau's rising glories ("empires rising where the sun descends!") to Melville's bland amenities, and the back of our hand to him who stretched his vans from Palos.

The second conspicuous Westerner is Nathan, father of the fated heroine, an adamantine son of the Puritans, doomed to another in a series of tree-chopping self-engendering encounters with the wilderness:

Those primal settlers put in train
New emigrants which inland bore;
From these too, emigrants again
Westward pressed further; more bred more . . .

On and on they go, those dying generations, until they reach the oceanic prairies of Illinois, where Nathan's father sinks to rest with sachems and mound-builders. Soon the son begins to suffer from "his grave life, and power/ Of vast space, from the log-house door/ Daily beheld," together with mounds like pyramids, crowned with trees which seem to grow from the planted corpses of "red sagamores." Challenged by isolation and by multiple reminders of death, he thinks too much, reads too much (Tom Paine, very likely), and then temporarily settles for a pantheism appropriate to "our maiden hemisphere." Years later, he abandons "Doubt's freezing pole," where "He wrestled with the pristine forms/ Like the first man," and falls in love with Agar, whom he meets in a lake-port. Thence he is converted to Judaism: farthest West Nathan finds certainty antedating Rome and Luther. Unfortunately, a Puritan heritage (parody-Hebraic to begin with) is not so easily jettisoned; Nathan at length becomes the most crackpot of Zionists, devoting himself henceforth to the agricultural redemption of Palestine, where he inevitably stands toward the hostile Arabs exactly as

> His sires in Pequod wilds immersed.
> Hittites—foes pestilent to God
> His fathers old those Indians deemed:
> Nathan the Arabs here esteemed
> The same.

With the usual results: "Events shall speak." The entire story of Nathan is an impressively imaginative elaboration of one way the recoil might come. In its spare detail, it comprehends over three centuries' experience in the American West, and well over three thousand years' experience in Western civilization; for each of these two distinct but clearly connected dimensions, it is the fundamental narrative of backtrailing.

The third notable Western character in *Clarel* is one of the most prophetic figures in all Melville's *dramatis personae*, and a more than adequate refutation of the common notion that he never recovered from the Civil War. Ungar is everything an American should not be—Southern, Indian, essentially Catholic, unpatriotic—and he is obviously (after Rolfe) Melville's darling. This "native of the fair South-West" even refuses to conform to the national haircut, but wears his hair long, "much like a Cherokee's." His face is copper, with high cheekbones, and his "forest eyes" are as sad as his "forest name." Ungar, "wandering Ishmael from the West," is the New World's surly answer to the Old, the butt-end of European Romantic projection. His bitterness is the inevitable product of the white man's perpetually sentimental aggressions: *"Indian's* the word." Equally aghast at Southern slavery and the subtler exploitations of the North, Ungar especially despises Anglo-Saxons:

"lacking grace
To win the love of any race;
Hated by myriads dispossessed
Of rights—the Indians East and West.
These pirates of the sphere! grave looters—
Grave, canting, Mammonite freebooters,
Who in the name of Christ and Trade
(Oh, bucklered forehead of the brass!)
Deflower the world's last sylvan glade!"

Against shallow good-natured Anglican Derwent, he argues
(as Gertrude Stein was to argue) that the New World, having endured fierier furnaces, is by now older than the Old:

"*Old* World? if age's test
Be this—advanced experience,
Then, in the truer moral sense,
Ours is the Old World. You, at best,
In dreams of your advanced Reform,
Adopt the cast skin of our worm."

In the face of such tirades, Rolfe is finally driven to play
advocatus diaboli in feeble defense of the indefensible (virgin land will indefinitely postpone class conflict), to which
Ungar replies with a withering denunciation, in the course
of which he touches upon the perennial fall of Adam, the
debasements of equality, the horrors of civic barbarism, the
brutalizations of popular science, the smatterings of atheists,
and a number of other related matters. The narrator quietly
broods:

America!
In stilled estate,
On him, half-brother and co-mate—
In silence, and with vision dim
Rolfe, Vine, and Clarel gazed on him;
They gazed, nor one of them found heart
To upbraid the crotchet of his smart,
Bethinking them whence sole it came,
Though birthright he renounced in hope,

Their sanguine country's wonted claim.
Nor dull they were in honest tone
To some misgivings of their own:
They felt how far beyond the scope
Of elder Europe's saddest thought
Might be the New World's sudden brought
In youth to share old age's pains—
To feel the arrest of hope's advance,
And squandered last inheritance;
And cry—"To Terminus build fanes!
Columbus ended earth's romance:
No New World to mankind remains!"

Although everybody senses that Ungar's charges are intemperately expressed, nobody can refute him. Nobody even wants to.

But the central dilemma of the poem is occasioned by Vine, Melville's most tortured encounter with the ghost of Hawthorne. "The Recluse"—or "Paul Pry? and in Gethsemane?"—is alienated, neutral, pessimistic, unhappy, yet almost always darkly right; some of these qualities he shares with Rolfe (those which are stigmata of genius). The two aristocrats are obviously "peers," and "needs that these must pair," for to Clarel theirs are "Exceptional natures, of a weather/ Strange as the tropics." Yet if ordinary people can never entirely be brought to dwell on one frontier, "How with the rarer in degree?" The problem is exacerbated by Hawthorne's idiosyncrasies—his inveterate glancing away from present reality toward specters of the past, his phantasmal moralizing, his rigid repression of presumably warm sympathies (is this from fear?), his distaste for speculative thought; these faults seem all the more deplorable in the light of Melville's portrayal of himself as a genius in full rapport with humanity. If between Hawthorne and Melville had once existed the deepest friendship possible to such natures, there was also, and unavoidably, mutual distrust and disapproval—in real life, probably related to their competitive situation. The only ultimate reconciliation be-

388

tween any two men, Melville hints, is in retrospective
understanding:

> Whom life held apart—
> Life, whose cross-purposes make shy—
> Death yields without reserve of heart
> To meditation.

Obviously, such a retrospective understanding is possible
only in the imagination of the survivor, where the man
memorialized has lost the right to talk back. In *Clarel*, Melville somewhat outrageously informs us that Rolfe exhibits
"A gleam of oneness more than Vine's"; that Vine is
probably unknowable; that perhaps in that granitic stolidity
there was little to know:

> Near, in the high void waste advanced,
> They saw, in turn abrupt revealed,
> An object reared aloof by Vine
> In whim of silence, when debate
> Was held upon the cliff but late
> And ended where all words decline:
> A heap of stones in arid state.

> The cairn (thought Clarel), meant he—yes,
> A monument to barrenness?

Certainly the monument is Hawthorne's, and is emblematic
of his stony life or works or both, as is borne out by his
subsequent ambiguous confession: "And is it I/ (He muses),
I that leave the others,/ Or do they leave me?" On the
other hand, these reservations are also paradoxically the
highest conceivable praise, for the dilemma of Hawthorne's
presence in *Clarel* is precisely the dilemma of God's presence
in Melville's world; the result, in either case, was adoration,
dubiety, and irritable frustration.

More than a decade later, Melville published in a limited
edition of twenty-five copies, for family and friends, *John
Marr and Other Sailors* (1888). For the title poem he supplied, as was his wont, an introductory prose sketch four or

five times as long as the poem, and a hundred times as valuable. Possibly this sketch commemorates perpetually hopeful uncle Thomas, who in 1837 removed to Galena, where nephew Herman three years later "was anew struck by the contrast between the man and his environment," in "what was then the remote West."[7] Perhaps the John Marr sketch also glances obliquely at Melville's unfortunate son Stanwyx, who, after several false vocational starts, and as many continental wanderings, died in a San Francisco hospital in 1886. Certainly, the sketch and the poem are as autobiographical as anything Melville wrote—though the allegorically-minded will search them in vain for easy and obvious equivalents—and indispensable for an understanding of his later career. John Marr is Herman Melville's elderly view of young Herman Melville, who might have been America's greatest writer, defeated, exiled, and hopeless, in the heart of his own country, on the prairie, on the frontier, at the West. This is the final turn of Melville's ironic and self-mutilating knife, and it delivers to us all we need know about the sorrow with which he was finally compelled to regard his heroic efforts to create the high art his country so desperately needed.

"From boyhood up to maturity a sailor under divers flags," John Marr is wounded in a fight with pirates, disabled, and retired to life ashore. "There, too, he transfers his rambling disposition acquired as a sea-farer," as Melville relinquished his own roving propensity, first to domestic life and then to the New York Custom House. After several attempts to earn a living as a sailmaker in seaports, staying as close as possible to the sources of his youthful life, John Marr moves "adventurously inland" as a carpenter, and finally settles "upon what was then [c. 1838] a frontier-prairie," in a sparse community of emigrants "from one of our elder inland States." He marries, but a malignant fever ("the bane of new settlements on teeming loam") kills his wife and infant child. (This identification of West and disease had been firmly asserted in *The*

---

[7] "Sketch of Major Thomas Melville Junior By a Nephew."

Confidence-Man, but as a blessing compared with the nauseous verbiage of American Babbitry.) Their graves make a small mound "in the wide prairie, nor far from where the mound-builders of a race only conjecturable had left their pottery and bones, one common clay." John Marr decides to spend the remainder of his life in this country where his closest domestic affections lie buried; and that is his disaster. The sketch becomes a more and more transparent vehicle for Melville's soliloquizing on frustration, futility, isolation, boredom, and the torment of being left behind. "The void at heart abides."

John Marr tries to make friends with his neighbors, but finds it impossible to go beyond "that mere work-a-day bond arising from participation in the same outward hardships," the prime social bond of the frontier (and conceivably of the Custom House), almost universally remarked in books about the West as early as Crèvecœur's *Letters From an American Farmer*. It is never easy to talk about the present, much less the future; and what common past does John Marr share with these inlanders? No more than the man who created *Moby-Dick* with the men who were corrupting Hadleyburg. "The past of John Marr was not the past of these pioneers," who more closely resemble the Western farmers of *fin de siècle* realistic fiction than the benevolent settlers of the first Leatherstocking Tale. "So limited unavoidably was the mental reach, and by consequence the range of sympathy, in this particular band of domestic emigrants, hereditary tillers of the soil, that the ocean, but a hearsay to their fathers, had now through yet deeper inland removal become to themselves little more than a rumor traditional and vague."

These pioneers are staid, industrious, respectable, ascetic, pietistic, unimaginative, and unforgivably dull. Inevitably they mean little to John Marr; once when he dares allude to his former life, a kindly old soul tells him, " 'Friend, we know nothing of that here.' " So a new America, whose spirit had once been "essentially Western"—the term meaning next to nothing now that the megalomaniac standardized nation sprawled from coast to coast, crisscrossed by transcontinental railroads, only a short century since ratification of the Constitution—this new America, with a population of about sixty million (compared with fewer than ten million, when Melville was born), knew, of that writer who had once tried to pluck out her innermost secrets, nothing except (as he had feared) that he was a man who had once lived among cannibals, and had spun some good sea yarns. In New York, old-timers pointed him out to the young literati, explaining who he was.[8]

Worse than the spiritual poverty of the pioneers is the hideous perfection with which they embody a landscape equally futile. To John Marr, his Western neighbors "seemed of a piece with the apathy of Nature herself as envisaged to him here on a prairie where none but the perished mound-builders had as yet left a durable mark." The two eras—1838 and 1888—fuse and contrast in a wild lament:

> The remnant of Indians thereabout—all but exterminated in their recent and final war with regular white troops, a war waged by the Red Men for their native soil and natural rights—had been coerced into the occupancy of wilds not very far beyond the Mississippi— wilds *then*, but now the seats of municipalities and States. Prior to that, the bisons, once streaming countless in processional herds, or browsing as in an endless battleline over these vast aboriginal pastures, had retreated, dwindled in number, before the hunters, in main a race distinct from the agricultural pioneers, though generally

[8] "The further our civilization advances upon its present lines," Melville wrote James Billson in 1885, "so much the cheaper sort of thing does 'fame' become, especially of the literary sort. This species of 'fame' a waggish acquaintance says can be manufactured to order, and sometimes is so manufactured thro the agency of a certain house that has a correspondent in every one of the almost innumerable journals that enlighten our millions from the Lakes to the Gulf & from the Atlantic to the Pacific." *The Letters of Herman Melville*, ed. Merrell R. Davis and William H. Gilman (New Haven, 1960), p. 281.

their advance-guard. Such a double exodus of man and beast left the plain a desert, green or blossoming indeed, but almost as forsaken as the Siberian Obi.

This is metaphorical desert, of course—the land was well enough populated, except that Melville didn't like the people—a figurative setting expressive of cultural aridity and aesthetic insignificance, utterly lacking the lonely grandeurs of ocean. Under the beating sun of unrelieved boredom, the flowery prairies of an earlier time have long since withered away. "Blank stillness would for hours reign unbroken on this prairie," as it never does at sea, where a "stir . . . animates at all times the apparent solitudes of the deep." Melville's prairie has all the marks of a late-Victorian Waste Land; and indeed it is pleasant to recall that T. S. Eliot was born in St. Louis the year Melville published this sketch.

The only solace the prairie offers is through reminders of a better world. " 'It is the bed of a dried-up sea,' " thinks John Marr ("no geologist"). Or he indulges in useless fancies: "A scene quite at variance with one's antecedents may yet prove suggestive of them. Hooped round by a level rim, the prairie was to John Marr a reminder of ocean."

But from tidings of anybody or any sort he, in common with the other settlers, was now cut off; quite cut off, except from such news as might be conveyed over the grassy billows by the last-arrived prairie-schooner—the vernacular term, in those parts and times, for the emigrant-wagon arched high over with sail-cloth and voyaging across the vast champaign. There was no reachable post-office as yet; not even the rude little receptive box with lid and leather hinges, set up at convenient intervals on a stout stake along some solitary green way, affording a perch for birds, and which, later in the unintermitting advance of the frontier, would perhaps decay into a mossy monument, attesting yet another successive overleaped limit of civilized life; a life which in America can to-day hardly be said to have any western bound but the ocean that washes Asia. Throughout these plains, now in places overpopulous with towns overopulent; sweeping plains, elsewhere fenced off in every direction into flourishing farms—pale townsmen and hale farmers alike, in part, the descendants of the first sallow settlers; a region that half a century ago produced little for the sustenance of man, but to-day launching its superabundant wheat-harvest on the world;—of this prairie, now everywhere intersected with wire and rail, hardly can it be said that at the period here written of there was so much as a traceable road.

Melville's mood is anything but progressive, and yet his view of the traceable road running through American civilization is closer to Sinclair Lewis's *Main Street* than to Hawthorne's sketch of the same name, his prose style closer to Faulkner than to Cooper.

If there was heroism in the Westward Movement (*Mardi, Moby-Dick*), terror (*Moby-Dick, Pierre, Israel Potter*), and folly (*The Confidence-Man*), so was there personal waste, cultural deprivation, unutterable weariness, and, worst of all, at the end, a sense of total irrelevance. In *Moby-Dick* Melville had delightfully compared a hull-down ship with emigrants' horses showing only their ears above the "amazing verdure." Now he once again tells how Western travel is "much like navigation." The bare lines of comparison are the same as in 1851, but the feeling is reversed. The "amazing verdure" has changed into "rank vegetation."[9] So of course "the growing sense of his environment threw him [John Marr] more and more upon retrospective musings," as it must have more and more thrown Melville. It is no accident, then, but the heart's logic, that in the same sentence Melville falls into the characteristic rhythms and ruminations of his old friend Hawthorne, now a quarter century

---

[9] Melville had always been intermittently skeptical about those Pacific-West equations of his. "Go visit the Prairies in June," he wrote at the outset of *Moby-Dick*, "when for scores on scores of miles you wade knee-deep among Tiger-lilies—what is the one charm wanting?—Water—there is not a drop of water there!"

dead, and even in life estranged (as long since commemorated in "Monody," presumably composed shortly after Hawthorne's final disappearance, and then again in *Clarel*). "These phantoms," John Marr's shipmates, either deceased or forever incommunicado, "next to those of his wife and child, became spiritual companions, losing something of their first indistinctness and putting on at last a dim semblance of mute life; and they were lit by that aureola circling over any object of the affections in the past for reunion with which an imaginative heart passionately yearns." Melville was almost certainly recapturing Hawthorne's description of himself sitting in the moonlit, firelit parlor, evoking the "illusive guests" of *The Scarlet Letter*. In the "Inscription Epistolary" to this volume, Melville also worked in a final tribute to Dana (d. 1882), "our own admirable '*Man before the Mast*.'"

The poem, John Marr's imagined invocation of these "visionary ones," is finally allowed to proceed. For a few lines, Hawthorne's presence is felt, for the last time:

> I yearn as ye. But rafts that strain,
> Parted, shall they lock again?
> Twined we were, entwined, then riven,
> Ever to new embracements driven,
> Shifting gulf-weed of the main!
> And how if one here shift no more,
> Lodged by the flinging surge ashore?
> Nor less, as now, in eve's decline,
> Your shadowy fellowship is mine.

But now everything was passing. Melville's long traffic with the West, so complicated, subtle, and intense, so private and so universal, so intelligent and so moving, was over.[10] "John

[10] From *The Confidence-Man* to the end, Melville had continued to venerate the relics and reminiscences of his Western youth. In his 1856-1857 *Journal of a Visit to Europe and the Levant*, ed. Howard C. Horsford (Princeton, 1955), he instinctively reached for the old comparisons: at Pigeon Mosque in Constantinople he was reminded of pigeons flying in hosts in the West (p. 83); the Bosporus was "clear as Ontario" (p. 93); Constantinople dogs roamed "in bands

Marr" is a weak poem, yet in the light of this introductory
sketch—and all the more in the light of Melville's forty-
plus years' contemplation of the New World, the United
States, the American West, the Western frontier—sufficiently affecting. For this is the set of sun of the noblest
spirit yet to arise from American democratic culture. No
previous thinker had looked so hard and long at the national
experience, nor at the West, where that experience concentrated itself in clearest meanings. None had seen so much.
And none had been so hurt by what he saw, nor made of his
dismay a legacy so valuable to posterity.

---

like prairie wolves" (p. 102); the Tiber was "primeval as Ohio
in the midst of all these monuments of the centuries" (p. 194); the
Po was "very turbid & rapid. Yellow as Mississippi" (p. 225);
the Grand Canal of Venice "winds like a Susquehanna" (p. 234).
In "Portrait of a Gentleman," Major Jack Gentian deliberately
uses in mixed company language as "startling to the ladies as
Brandt's flourished tomahawk at the London masked ball long
ago"; his freedom of speech is subsequently attributed to "adventures in early life among our frontiersmen." *The Works of Herman Melville* (London, 1922-1924), XIII, 354-355. In "Daniel Orme,"
the old veteran "might have suggested an image of the Great Grizzly
of the California Sierras, his coat the worse for wear, grim in his
last den awaiting the last hour." *Works*, XIII, 119. Since Ahab's day,
this bear has moved from Missouri to the West Coast, and is pro-
portionately more beleaguered. Two of Steelkilt's companions in
"The Town-Ho's Story" were Canallers, and the Canal itself was
a transitional ground between "Christian corn-field" and "the most
barbaric seas." Canallers reappear at the beginning of *Billy Budd,
Sailor (An Inside Narrative)* (left unfinished 1891; first published
1924; re-edited by Harrison Hayford and Merton M. Sealts, Jr.,
Chicago, 1962), with a radically altered tonality: "The Handsome
Sailor of the period in question [presumably 1797] evinced nothing
of the dandified Billy-be-Dam, an amusing character all but extinct
now [1891], but occasionally to be encountered, and in a form yet
more amusing than the original [1840? 1851?], at the tiller of
the boats on the tempestuous Erie Canal or, more likely, vaporing
in the groggeries along the towpath" (p. 44). In the same tale,
Claggart's chin is "beardless as Tecumseh's" (p. 64), and the hero
is an Adamic noble savage—"a sort of upright barbarian" (p. 52).
But the Western references in *Billy Budd* are few.

Walt Whitman's Leaves of Grass

D. H. LAWRENCE called Whitman "a very great poet, of the end of life. A very great post mortem poet, of the transitions of the soul as it loses its integrity. The poet of the soul's last shout and shriek, on the confines of death." Whitman was "the one pioneer. . . . Ahead of Whitman, nothing. Ahead of all poets, pioneering into the wilderness of unopened life, Whitman. . . . It is a dead end." Yet Lawrence also felt that Whitman had "the true rhythm of the American continent speaking out in him. He is the first white aboriginal."[1] The bewildering multiple paradoxes are more apparent than real, and are sustained by a more complicated and specific cultural dilemma than Lawrence knew. For one thing, Whitman grew up in the decades preceding the Civil War, when American literature and the American West were practically synonymous terms; Whitman as poet was formed by his idea of the West, and his poetic talents were consecrated to that idea. Then, soon after he had crossed the threshold of the great career Emerson predicted for him in 1855, the West disappeared. As a Western poet, Whitman was in serious difficulty only a few years after he began.

From the beginning he was "morbid about geography," as Van Wyck Brooks was to complain,[2] unless it be more accurate to say that in the early years Whitman was wonderfully superficial, conventional, and chauvinistic about geography, and especially about the geography of Western America. In the 1855 letter of welcome and tribute, Emer-

---

[1] *Studies in Classic American Literature* (New York, 1923), pp. 252, 253-254, 257.
[2] *America's Coming-of-Age* (New York, 1915), p. 124.

son correctly surmised that the great career "must have had a long foreground somewhere, for such a start." But Emerson could not have known how confused that foreground had been, how barren, and how banal. One way or another, Whitman was in these early years busy trying to prove himself a Westerner of sorts, and thus perhaps to ingratiate himself with the Young America wing of Knickerbocker literary influence; such a motive would at least account for his heavily facetious description of New York City as itself the frontier, "the focus, the main spring, the pinnacle, the extremity, the no more beyond, of the New World."[3] In his temperance novel, *Franklin Evans; or, The Inebriate. A Tale of the Times* (1842), he interpolated a conventional tale of "the primitive inhabitants who formerly occupied this continent," introduced by lines about the Indian from Bryant's poem "The Ages," and by a brief but ardent disquisition concerning the effects of rum upon the savages of America. The novel as a whole Whitman called "a pioneer in this department of literature," and the growth of the temperance movement he enthusiastically traced, through reports from "the Western mail," as far as Illinois.[4]

Three years later he published his second-longest work of fiction, and his most elaborately Western performance before 1855, *The Half-Breed: A Tale of the Western Frontier* (1845). As in a Hawthorne sketch, the scene is a little town

[3] *Walt Whitman of the New York Aurora*, ed. Joseph J. Rubin and Charles H. Brown (State College, Pa., 1950), p. 19. Assaulting Bishop John Hughes during a local controversy over parochial schools, editor Whitman urged his side to behave like Western vigilantes (above the law) since the Catholic side was behaving like Indians (sneaky); pp. 58, 67.

[4] Whenever possible, quotations in this chapter are from *The Collected Writings of Walt Whitman*, general ed. Gay Wilson Allen and Sculley Bradley (New York, 1961-). For material not yet available in that edition, I quote from *The Complete Writings of Walt Whitman*, ed. Richard M. Bucke, Thomas B. Harned, and Horace L. Traubel (New York, 1902). Passages from early editions of *Leaves of Grass* are from modern facsimile editions: the 1855 text, ed. Clifton J. Furness (New York, 1939); the 1860 text, ed. Roy Harvey Pearce (Ithaca, 1961); *Drum-Taps and Sequel to Drum-Taps* (1865-1866), ed. F. DeWolfe Miller (Gainesville, Fla., 1959).

"on one of the upper branches of the Mississippi," which
"seven years previously . . . had been a tangled forest,
roamed by the savage in pursuit of game." The town is
populated by "adventurers," for the West is full of adventurers and there "all men are comrades." All white men,
anyway; for ultimately, the tale rests on American racism
and horror of miscegenation. The villain is (of course) the
half-breed of the title, and his motive is (of course) undying
revenge. By a not very ironic irony, his victim is Arrow-Tip,
a "good Indian" (friendly to the whites) who is "one of
the finest specimens of the Red People." In connection with
Arrow-Tip's unjust and partly accidental hanging, Whitman condescendingly, and at the same time condoningly,
discusses Western modes of law enforcement and justice.
And after the hanging, the victim's brother, Deer, obligingly
leads "his tribe still farther into the west, to grounds where
they never would be annoyed, in their generation at least,
by the presence of the white intruders." In the literary sense,
Walter Whitman is the obvious intruder, in a literary situation where he knows not what he does. His prose is in
every bad sense conventional, and in the worst of all possible
senses urban:

A hunt in the western forests! To those who have
tasted of the fun, and know its pleasures, we need say
but little! With the great woods all about, and no sign
of man's neighborhood except the cheerful voices of your
companions; with the wide, solemnly wide, stretching
of unpeopled territory to a distance which it would take
the journey of months to compass; with the blue sky
overhead, clear, and not murky from the smoke of a
million chimneys; with that strange, and exhilirating,
and pervading sense of *freedom*, which strikes into all
your sense and body, as it were, from the illimitable, and
untrammelled, the boundless nature of every thing about
you—is it not a right manly and glorious sport? There
are no appearances of the artificial about such a hunt—
no park walls and no cultivated and regularly-laid-out

grounds to be crossed. It is all nature—all wild, beautiful, and inspiriting business, which no systematic chasing of a poor deer, within fences, and by trained packs,
can equal! One week of such fine and wholesome
recreation would do more good to our enervated city
gentry, than a hundred gymnasiums, or all the medicines
of the drug-shop!

It is conceivably worth meditating, though not very long,
whether the crucified hero is unconsciously a spokesman for
the author. " 'I am silent,' " he says in the novella's one
revealing speech, " 'because I have seen no fit occasion to
speak. What would you have me say?' "

If young Walter Whitman had little to say, and saw no
fit occasion to speak, that seems to have been quite irrelevant
to his literary activities. By March 1846 he was editing the
Brooklyn *Daily Eagle*, and during that year and the next
reviewing in it such titles as Thomas J. Farnham, *Life and
Adventures in California, and Scenes in the Pacific Ocean*
(1846); Mrs. Mary (Robson) Hughs, *Julia Ormond; or,
The New Settlement* (1846); Charles Edwards Lester, *Sam
Houston and his Republic* (1846); and Samuel Parker,
Journal of an Exploring Tour Beyond the Rocky Mountains
(5th ed., 1846). With respect to Parker, Whitman was
several editions behind Poe, and even less aware how much
too late he was. To the public school boards, Whitman
warmly recommended such Western staples as Mrs. Eliza
W. Farnham's *Life in Prairie Land* (1846). What, he rap-
turously inquired, "can be more fit for 'general circula-
tion' "? After all, the book was (or Whitman apparently
thought it was) "on a new rich theme—and the authoress
writes from actual knowledge."[5]

Even in the early years, it is not always easy to tell
exactly what Whitman means by the West. As a favorite
phrasing—"the great FUTURE of this Western World!"—
reveals, the West was sometimes as comprehensive as Amer-

[5] *Walt Whitman Looks at the Schools*, ed. Florence B. Freedman
(New York, 1950), p. 110.

ica, or even Western civilization; this pleasing confusion of terms Whitman would never abjure. "We must be constantly pressing onward," he was constantly saying, "and carrying our experiment of democratic freedom to the very verge of the limit." The effect of a double limit was apparently like that of a double negative; in another editorial Whitman speaks of "the boundless democratic free West!— We love well to contemplate it, and to think of its future." Whitman loved to contemplate it so well that he could bring himself to say that "there is something refreshing even in the extremes, the faults, of Western character." The West was somehow more real and more central than the other sections, and therefore Whitman's own East Brooklyn was, or was to be, to the rest of the city, "somewhat as the valley of the Mississippi is to the other part of the Union."

He wrote endlessly and recklessly of American expansion Westward, political, military, and demographic; he endorsed government land grants (or sales at low prices) to soldiers and civilians; he urged congressional purchase of George Catlin's Indian paintings (a lifelong object of admiration); and he argued for American acquisition, not necessarily by purchase, of California: "The daring, burrowing energies of the Nation will never rest till the whole of this northern section of the Great West World is circled in the mighty Republic—there's no denying that fact!" He wrote elegiacally of the Indians on Long Island, while also encouraging accelerated emigration from Europe. (This anomaly, too, he persisted in all his life.) He advocated, as everybody did, an independent American literature, and research into "Indian Life and Customs" as a means to that lofty end ("fit themes for poetry and imagination here"). He expatiated on the wonders of Western pioneering ("There is a fascination in such an existence").[6] Ironically, Whitman was fired from the *Eagle* for his uncompromising stand on a Western issue, the Wilmot Proviso, which sought to prohibit the spread of slavery into the annexed territories

[6] *The Gathering of the Forces*, ed. Cleveland Rodgers and John Black (New York, 1920), I, 4, 10, 25, 27, 122; II, 122, 137, 140.

for which the *Eagle* was so stridently screaming. By a further irony, the loss of employment contributed to the making of a major writer.

Out of work, and having made almost no dent at all in the New York literary world, Whitman undertook a Western tour. Specifically, he accepted a position as editor of the New Orleans *Daily Crescent*. In order to arrive at the Southern metropolis—which, as the outlet for the entire Mississippi Valley, was also a quintessentially Western metropolis— he had to travel through the West.[7] He spent approximately 90 days in New Orleans, and 35 days coming and going, traveling West and South through the Cumberland Gap and down the Ohio and Mississippi Rivers, and returning up the Mississippi and then East across the Great Lakes.[8] Literary results, although at first small, were not slow in declaring themselves. "The Mississippi at Midnight" is surely Whitman's best poem thus far, though characteristic of *Leaves of Grass* only in its Poesque obsession with disaster and death; some of the ghostly imagery later made its way into "A Child's Reminiscence" (eventually "Out of the Cradle Endlessly Rocking") in 1859, but was subsequently deleted. In the *Crescent*, Whitman also published a number of prose sketches, most notably "Excerpts From a Traveller's Note Book," which included "Crossing the Alleghanies," "Western Steamboats—The Ohio," and "Cincinnati and Louisville." The sketches are characterized by specificity and realism, idiomatic diction and phrasing, and plentiful drafts on native wit and humor—all of these qualities contrasting with the sentimental strains and ponderous facetiousness (however sincere) of the earlier writing. For the first time, Whitman had at his disposal fresh and direct impressions of Western life, and under their influence the American literary

[7] At one time he may even have thought of settling there. In *New York Dissected* (New York, 1936), Emory Holloway and Ralph Adimari cite a diary in the Library of Congress to support their contention that "in 1848 he was dreaming of taking up another and cheaper homestead in the still freer West" (pp. 87 and 216, n. 1).

[8] For details of the trip see Gay Wilson Allen, *The Solitary Singer: A Critical Biography of Walt Whitman* (New York, 1955), pp. 92-100.

tradition began to come alive in his hands. He was pleased
to discover and to proclaim that the distinguishing characteristic of young men in the West was precisely their greater
attention "to the *realities* of life, and a habit formed of
thinking for one's self; in the cities, frippery and artificial
fashion are too much the ruling powers."[9] These attitudes
Whitman was in the process of appropriating to himself and
assimilating in his writing: the Ohio, he reported, was a
beautiful word but a muddy river. Whitman's 1848 prose
sketches also show once again how much the West was a
habit of mind rather than a place: for all his effort to *be* the
West, or at least to wear it, the itinerant New Yorker,
writing in New Orleans of the West to a New Orleans
audience, writes as if Cincinnati and Louisville were more
Western than New Orleans.

"The important fact," as Emory Holloway says about a
passage from one of these sketches, "is that Whitman has
begun his war on the conventionality of existing poetry.
The early notebook specimens belong to this period."[10] By
"this period" we must understand a period possibly just
preceding and certainly just following Whitman's Western
tour, and by "early notebook specimens" poetic fragments
clearly anticipating the 1855 breakthrough. The only reasonable conclusion is that there was a direct and powerful
relationship—though certainly it would not have been a
simple relationship, as of mechanical cause and effect—
between the 1848 Western tour and the gradual emergence
of the developed poet. Sometimes in verse and sometimes
in prose, these fragmentary jottings are in essence parts of
the first *Leaves of Grass*, and indeed a few of them appear
in it, with relatively little change:

> When I see where the east is greater than the west . . .
> or where a father is more needful than a mother to
> produce me—then I guess I shall see how spirit is greater
> than matter.

[9] *The Uncollected Poetry and Prose of Walt Whitman*, ed. Emory
Holloway (London, 1922), I, 185.
[10] *Uncollected Poetry and Prose*, I, 183, n. 1, and II, 63, n. 1.

If I walk with Jah in Heaven and he assume to be
intrinsically greater than I it offends me, and I shall
certainly withdraw from Heaven,—for the soul prefers
freedom in the prairie or the untrodden woods . . .

In vain were nails driven through my hands.
I remember my crucifixion and bloody coronation
I remember the mockers and the buffeting insults
The sepulchre and the white linen have yielded me up
I am alive in New York and San Francisco . . .

What the rebel felt gaily adjusting his neck to the rope
noose,
[What Lucifer cursed when tumbling from Heaven]
What the savage, lashed to the stump, spirting yells
and laughter at every foe
What rage of hell urged the lips and hands of the victors.

However mysterious, the gist of the matter was simply expressed: the poet "drinks up quickly all terms, all languages,
and meanings.—To his curbless and bottomless powers, they
be like ponds of rain water to the migrating herds of buffalo,
who make the earth miles square look like a creeping
spread.—See! he has only passed this way, and they are
drained dry."[11] So a number of later nineteenth-century
American poets were to discover.

By about 1850 Whitman had adopted, and was in the
process of perfecting (if that is the word for it), his notorious
cataloguing device as a central poetic technique. In the
unpublished "Pictures," his most ambitious poem before
Leaves of Grass, the realistic West vigorously pressed for
entry among the miscellaneous images ransacked from all
times and places. Whitman included the West he had seen
with his own eyes, and then moved on to the West which
that seeing enabled him now to imagine, or at least to
imagine that he imagined:

[11] *Uncollected Poetry and Prose*, II, 66, 68, 74, 82, 84-85. Square
brackets in the rebel-savage quotation indicate deleted words.

And there hang scenes painted from my Kansas life—
and there from what I saw in the Lake Superior
region.

Other pictures are of woodcutters "cutting down trees in
my north coast woods," an Oregon hunting-hut ("See me
emerging from the door"), "rude grave-mounds in California," Chicago ("my great city"), "a string of my Iroquois, aborigines," "a husking frolic in the West," "a deckhand of a Mississippi steamboat," and "my treeless llanos,
where they skirt the Colorado, and sweep for a thousand
miles on either side of the Rocky mountains." As the personal and possessive pronouns sufficiently indicate, the
problem was to establish an organic relationship between
the Great West and America's first Great Western Poet,
"cicerone himself."[12]

By 1855 the relationship was worked out. It variously
consisted, as it was always to consist, of a poetic theory
drenched with the Western spirit, and in parallel with the
fascinating and representative American action of pioneering; of poetry subsuming Western themes and implications
for more than Western ends; and, inevitably, of Western
themes and implications which Whitman was unable to
transform into poetry. "The United States themselves are
essentially the greatest poem," he wrote in the preface,
obviously glancing at the West, which had always been the
greater part of the United States. "Here at last is something
in the doings of man that corresponds with the broadcast
doings of the day and night. Here is not merely a nation
but a teeming nation of nations." The nation of nations is
further distinguished by the "space and ruggedness and
nonchalance that the soul loves"; obviously, these virtues are
at once sectional epithets and analogues of the new American poetry. "As if it were necessary to trot back generation
after generation to the eastern records! . . . As if the open-

---

[12] *Pictures*, ed. Emory Holloway (New York, 1927), pp. 13, 19,
21, 22, 23, 24, 26-27. Oddly enough, the most beautiful picture
of all is apparently of "Death" (p. 14). The phrase "my great
city" (of Chicago) was later deleted.

ing of the western continent by discovery and what has transpired since in North and South America were less than the small theatre of the antique or the aimless sleepwalking of the middle ages!" The American "bard is to be commensurate with a people. . . . His spirit responds to his country's spirit . . . . he incarnates its geography and natural life and rivers and lakes." The list of rivers and lakes which follows is designedly national and preponderantly Western; so is the scope of Whitman's poetic ambition, which must not be taken literally: "When the long Atlantic coast stretches longer and the Pacific coast stretches longer he easily stretches with them north or south. He spans between them also from east to west and reflects what is between them." He reflects "agriculture and mines—the tribes of red aborigines," "the first settlements north or south," "the perpetual coming of immigrants," "the unsurveyed interior —the loghouses and clearings and wild animals and hunters and trappers," "whaling and gold-digging—the endless gestation of new states," "the fluid movement of the population." All these details are hopefully metaphors of the spirit, and especially of the spirit which is moved to discover itself in poetry. And because Whitman's poetic spirit was so ecstatically and confidently sustained by the American West, and thus by the American future, he could proclaim that for poetry in this country "the theme is creative and has vista. Here comes one among the wellbeloved stonecutters and plans with decision and science and sees the solid and beautiful forms of the future where there are now no solid forms." And indeed this much was clearly true, that before 1855 there had been in America no solid and beautiful poetic forms. In 1855, and for a few years thereafter, they began to emerge, dimly, like Western states.

The poet is a pioneer who "leaves room ahead of himself," taking a temporary stand on the moving figurative frontier: "He places himself where the future becomes present . . . he glows a moment on the extremest verge." As "the age transfigured," he "makes the present spot the passage from what was to what shall be," and "projects himself centuries ahead": "Whom he takes he takes with firm sure grasp into live regions previously unattained . . . . thenceforward is no rest." The strength of Whitman's aesthetic program lay in the forceful alignment of American poetry with what had been and perhaps might still be thought of as the dominant historical experience of the age. The corresponding weakness lay in Whitman's all but inevitable unawareness that the historical experience of the age was on the very verge of the limit, and about to pass away forever. (Except for Melville's sardonic and subversive *Confidence-Man*, all the Western classics of early American literature had been published before the first edition of *Leaves of Grass*.) Still, Whitman's new American poetic was in 1855 essentially right for his time and place, and it is impossible to imagine him achieving either the poetic theory or the poems in quite the way he did without the prior model of Westward expansion, adventure, and innovation. However belatedly, major American poetry began when Whitman, carrying to a logical conclusion in literary form and style the Western themes of Cooper, Hawthorne, Poe, Thoreau, and Melville, announced that "a heroic person walks at his ease through and out of that custom or precedent or authority that suits him not. . . . Nothing is finer than silent defiance advancing from new free forms. . . . He is greatest forever and forever who contributes the greatest original practical example. The cleanest expression is that which finds no sphere worthy of itself and makes one."

In the 1855 poems, Whitman worked hard to realize his theory of Western poetry, but the results were not invariably impressive. In this first of the many editions of *Leaves of Grass*, Whitman's poetic argument (like Cooper's in the Leatherstocking Tales) was always moving away from culture (as particularized, articulated) toward nature (as the source of particular articulations), and in the light of that argument, nearly any detail drawn from the West might be presumed significant. Thus Whitman included images which were merely references, as in a line (which is also a stanza) from a poem subsequently known as "Song of the Answerer":

The engineer, the deckhand on the great lakes or on the
Mississippi or St Lawrence or Sacramento or Hudson
or Delaware claims him [the poet].

The deckhand (borrowed from "Pictures") is only a notation, an exhortation to the reader to imagine something
which the poet has not himself imagined, and to invest with
vast importance what has, in fact, no importance at all,
poetic or otherwise. A line in a poem later called "Faces"
is slightly more organized:

The faces of hunters and fishers, bulged at the brows . . . .
the shaved blanched faces of orthodox citizens.

Still, this is a conventional or even sentimental antithesis,
and nothing further comes of it. From 1855 to the end, when
Whitman fails as a Western poet he fails because he simply
shovels Western material into his poem, and expects it to
do his creative work for him:

The common people of Europe are not nothing . . . . the
American aborigines are not nothing.

Granted. But what then? There is no "then," except, apparently, "I swear I think there is nothing but immortality!"

The West figures more dynamically in the untitled vision
which became "Night Poem" in 1856, "Sleep-Chasings" in
1860, and eventually "The Sleepers." As the poet, like the
sun and the nation, descends his "western course," through
dreams of disaster, death, and burial into nocturnal glimpses
of the communal past, he comes at length to the American
aborigines and to a deliberately flat and baffling anecdote
of a beautiful red squaw who visited his mother (not his
actual mother, surely) at the "old homestead," stayed all
morning and half the afternoon, then went away, and
"never came nor was heard of there again."

Now Lucifer was not dead . . . . or if he was I am his
sorrowful terrible heir;
I have been wronged . . . . I am oppressed . . . . I hate
him that oppresses me,
I will either destroy him, or he shall release me.

The Western poet speaks the first line in sympathetic contrition for the national crime; the other two lines are spoken by the Indian, who is also the Western poet. In the next stanza, the Indian fuses with the equally wronged Negro (references to being sold down the river);[13] then the passage concludes:

> Now the vast dusk bulk that is the whale's bulk ....
>   it seems mine,
> Warily, sportsman! though I lie so sleepy and sluggish,
>   my tap is death.

And here the speaker is at once Whitman, Indian, Negro, Moby Dick, and, conceivably, a generic American dreamer, like the generic Irish dreamer or dreamers of *Finnegans Wake*. Later in the poem, another backward-flowing dream —a Thoreauvian dream with a difference—sends America's European immigrants home again; as an apparent consequence of this departure the poet swears that "they [all people, specifically including the red squaw] are averaged now," and that "the wildest and bloodiest is over and all is peace." In the final section the sleepers, like the sun, but not like the nation, come forward again in time and in space, to "flow hand in hand over the whole earth from east to west as they lie unclothed." Such poetry is a long way from *The Half-Breed*, and a longer way from the Mississippi deckhand.

Whitman's great poem of 1855—the untitled rhapsody which became "Poem of Walt Whitman" in 1856, "Walt Whitman" in 1860, and eventually "Song of Myself"— is even more abundantly supplied with Western matter; the Western matter which is poetically realized is almost invariably expressive of the poetic process. "I speak the password primeval," the speaker says, brilliantly bypassing Longfellow; or, as he elsewhere phrases his intention, in

---

[13] Whitman may well have had in mind Tocqueville's emphasis on "The Three Races in the United States." Cf. these revealing phrases in the 1855 *Leaves of Grass*: "Examine these limbs, red black or white" ("I Sing the Body Electric"), and "red white or black, all are deific" ("Faces").

the mode of Poe, and without irony, "I launch all men and women forward with me into the unknown." Again, this time rather in the mode of Thoreau, "I tramp a perpetual journey,/ My signs are a rain-proof coat and good shoes and a staff cut from the woods;/ . . . My right hand points to landscapes of continents, and a plain public road." The landscapes of continents are either poetic or "cosmic."

> This day before dawn I ascended a hill and looked at the
>   crowded heaven,
> And I said to my spirit, When we become the enfolders of
>   those orbs and the pleasure and knowledge of every
>   thing in them, shall we be filled and satisfied then?
> And my spirit said No, we level that lift to pass and con-
>   tinue beyond.

As the poet has repeatedly pointed out: "See ever so far . . . . there is limitless space outside of that." Whether inside or outside that space, the Indian is inevitably a commanding figure:

> The sentries desert every other part of me,
> They have left me helpless to a red marauder.

The red marauder, the attacking Indian, is in this context the sense of touch (the sentries are the other senses) preluding orgasm, which is the central metaphor of the poem, and which culminates in a vision of "Landscapes projected masculine full-sized and golden." And so, once again, the American Indian is also the American poet:

> The friendly and flowing savage . . . . Who is he?
> Is he waiting for civilization or past it and
>   mastering it?
>
> Is he some southwesterner raised outdoors? Is he
>   Canadian?
> Is he from the Mississippi country? or from Iowa,
>   Oregon or California? . . .

The poet is from anywhere and everywhere, but mostly from the metaphorical West, state or territory, "a wandering savage."

As in "The Sleepers," the poet is also the sun, in desperately successful competition with the real sun (obviously, the poet is only an analogous or second-hand "kosmos"). Sunrise is his special hour of agonizing ecstasy:

> Hefts of the moving world at innocent gambols, silently
>   rising, freshly exuding,
> Scooting obliquely high and low.

> Something I cannot see puts upward libidinous prongs,
> Seas of bright juice suffuse heaven.

> The earth by the sky staid with .... the daily close of
>   their junction,
> The heaved challenge from the east that moment over
>   my head,
> The mocking taunt, See then whether you shall be master!

As ex-cicerone adds, by way of clarification: "Dazzling and tremendous how quick the sunrise would kill me,/ If I could not now and always send sunrise out of me." Later in the poem, the friendly and flowing savage chaffs his cosmic competitor: "Flaunt of the sunshine I need not your bask . . . . lie over." At least temporarily, America's Western poet was in charge; as the sun, he imaginatively comprehended and therefore dominated such mere phenomena as America's Westward Movement. In the time it took the United States to inch forward another parallel of longitude, Whitman had circled the whole earth from East to West as many times as he liked.

Nearly always, his successful catalogues commence with poetical-personal hyperboles:

> I skirt the sierras .... my palms cover continents,
> I am afoot with my vision.

There follow several pages of things, places, people, and actions, plausibly including log-huts, forests, gold-digging, "girdling the trees of a new purchase," hunting, "the western persimmon," mountain-climbing, Niagara, "friendly bees and huskings and house-raisings," prairies, buffalo (who, as in the notebooks, make "a crawling spread of the square miles"), camp meetings, and a visionary poet "Far from the settlements studying the print of animals' feet, or the moccasin print." The catalogue ends as it began: "I am a free companion . . . . I bivouac by invading watchfires." "Song of Myself" is also full of interpolated vignettes of Western life—a hunter "choosing a safe spot to pass the night," "the marriage of the trapper in the open air in the far-west . . . . the bride was a red girl," "the western turkey-shooting" (conceivably from *The Pioneers*), the massacre at Goliad, Texas ("Hear now the tale of a jetblack sunrise"), a Western camp meeting. In the best of them, the poet fuses his experience of making poems with the experiences of these other, nationally representative lives, for "Song of Myself," like *Walden*, is constructed not only on the pioneer analogy but on the usual Romantic dualism between subject and object ("Out of the dimness opposite equals advance") and on its successful reconciliation and transcendence through sympathetic imagination in the neutral territory which is the poem itself:

> And these one and all tend inward to me, and I tend
> outward to them,
> And such as it is to be of these more or less I am.

The second line is divided into two equal distichs, each of three feet, and the corresponding third feet are reflexive toward the creation of a still further meaning, the inclusive meaning of the first *Leaves of Grass*: "to be" is the equivalent of "I am." And so, more or less, it was, in 1855, when Whitman was the West, i.e., the frontier between the American self and its imaginative New World.

In the next year, Whitman published a new and enlarged edition of *Leaves of Grass*, in which he saw himself lifting to the light "his west-bred face"; wrote an essay applauding

Indian names and the happy fact that language "appears to move from east to west as the light does"; journalistically, but with a proper regard for bipolar unity, described himself as "the sturdy, self-conscious microcosmic, prose-poetical author of that incongruous hash of mud and gold."[14] He received pilgrimages from Thoreau and from Bronson Alcott, who found Whitman "as hard to tame as Thoreau," and who portrayed the two would-be Western lions eyeing each other as warily as wild beasts.[15] The New York beast was apparently more intensely concerned with preparing a lecture (undelivered) or pamphlet (unpublished) stridently entitled: THE EIGHTEENTH PRESIDENCY! *Voice of Walt Whitman to each Young Man in the Nation, North, South, East, and West.* All his life, Whitman was fond of boxing the compass, and after each tour of the cardinal points he regularly found himself fronting in the Western direction: "I would be much pleased to see some heroic, shrewd, [fully-informed,] healthy-bodied, [middle-aged, beard-faced] American blacksmith or boatman come down from the West across the Alleghanies, and walk into the Presidency." Then the President would tally "the vast continental tracts of unorganized American territory, equal in extent to all the present organized States, and in future to give the law to all." The appeal was primarily directed toward, and was on behalf of, what Lincoln would call "free labor": "As the broad fat States of The West, the largest and best parts of the inheritance of the American farmers and mechanics, were ordained to common people and workmen long in advance by Jefferson, Washington, and the earlier Congresses, now a far ampler west is to be ordained. Is it to be ordained to workmen, or to the masters of work-

[14] *New York Dissected*, pp. 57, 130.

[15] *The Journals of Bronson Alcott*, ed. Odell Shepard (Boston, 1938), p. 294. "Whether Thoreau was meditating the possibility of Walt's stealing away his 'out-of-doors' for some sinister ends, poetic or pecuniary, I could not well divine . . . or whether Walt suspected or not that he had here, for once, and the first time, found his match and more at smelling out 'all Nature' " (pp. 290-291).

413

men?"[16] Fortunately, perhaps, for American poetry, if not for American politics, James Buchanan came down from Pennsylvania to be the eighteenth President of the North, South, East, and West.

In the years between the explosive and chaotic 1855 *Leaves of Grass*, and what might be called the zenith edition of 1860, Whitman was busy refining his relations with American politics and American poetry. In *An American Primer*—which he probably worked at, off and on, throughout the 1850's, but mostly after 1855—he meditated at length on the American language. Later he told Horace Traubel, who was finally to edit this posthumous work: " 'I sometimes think the Leaves is only a language experiment—that it is an attempt to give the spirit, the body, the man, new words, new potentialities of speech—an American, a cosmopolitan (the best of America is the best cosmopolitanism) range of self-expression. The new world, the new times, the new peoples, the new vista, need a tongue according.' " They needed the according tongue, apparently, in view of "American geography,—the plenteousness and variety of the great nations of the Union—the thousands of settlements . . . California and Oregon—the inland seas—the mountains—Arizona—the prairies—the immense rivers." Whitman was in love with words from all the states, and the states he alluded to were most of them Western, for even in politics "the western states have terms of their own."[17] While intermittently supporting himself with editorial labors for the Brooklyn *Daily Times*, in the course of which he repeated most of the Western opinions of his *Eagle* days, Whitman continued to daydream of a bardic lectureship: "I desire to go by degrees through all These States, especially West and South." In a note to himself, he inquired: "? Why not mention myself by name, Walt Wh - - - -, in my speeches

[16] *The Eighteenth Presidency!* ed. Edward F. Grier (Lawrence, Kansas, 1956), pp. 21, 25, 31. Square brackets signify intended deletions.
[17] *An American Primer by Walt Whitman* (Boston, 1904), pp. viii-ix, 7, 15.

—aboriginal fashion? as in the speech of Logan?" He even planned to develop a special style for Western audiences ("more declamatory and direct, with natural abandon and passion, the very intensity of rudeness, power, and natural meanings").[18]

In two senses the 1860 *Leaves of Grass* marks the culmination of Whitman's career as a Western (or any other kind of) poet: it contains nearly all the great poems he was ever to write, and it contains the announcement that his poetic creativity—which had only a few years earlier commenced—was already coming to an end. (American poetry was not seriously to resume until the publication in 1896 of Edwin Arlington Robinson's *The Torrent and the Night Before*.) When did he discover the trick American history had played him? Probably during the late stages of preparing the 1860 volume for publication.[19] His prepublication press-agentry seems untroubled by signs of the impending disaster. "The market needs to-day to be supplied," he wrote, "the great West especially—with copious thousands of copies." He proclaimed that "there will also soon crop out the true 'Leaves of Grass,' the fuller-grown work of which the former two issues were the inchoates." With triumphant irony, he described his aesthetic victories: "Is this man really any artist at all? Or not plainly a sort of naked and hairy savage, come among us, with yelps and howls, disregarding all our lovely metrical laws? How can it be that he offends so many and so much?" How indeed, except that he was the "bold American of the West," whose chants, or poetic analogues for "the broad continental scale of the New World," were to be "true pabulum of the children of the prairies"? A genteel reviewer in Cincinnati rose

---

[18] Quoted in *The Solitary Singer*, p. 219; *Walt Whitman's Workshop*, ed. Clifton J. Furness (Cambridge, 1928), p. 36; Thomas B. Harned, "Whitman and Oratory," in *Complete Writings*, VIII, 251.

[19] Many of the 1860 poems were of course also in the 1856 edition, but for want of a proper arrangement, and a suitable context, they failed to yield their full meanings. Almost certainly, Whitman himself at that time failed to recognize the symptoms of cultural collapse which his poems were ever more insistently revealing. By 1860, he evidently did.

to the bait: "And it is into this gentle garden of the Muses that that unclean cub of the wilderness, Walt Whitman, has been suffered to intrude, trampling with his vulgar and profane hoofs among the delicate flowers which bloom there."[20]

And so the 1860 *Leaves of Grass* was to have been, or at least started out to be, the Western edition.[21] The 1855 preface was replaced by a poem called "Proto-Leaf" (later "Starting From Paumanok"),[22] in which the Whitman program was promulged through some of the finest programmatic poetry ever written:

Free, fresh, savage,
Fluent, luxuriant, self-content, fond of persons and places,
Fond of fish-shape Paumanok, where I was born,
Fond of the sea—lusty-begotten and various,
Boy of the Mannahatta, the city of ships, my city,
Or raised inland, or of the south savannas,

[20] *A Child's Reminiscence*, ed. Thomas O. Mabbott and Rollo G. Silver (Seattle, 1930), pp. 19, 20, 21, 37.

[21] I use the term loosely and somewhat ironically, but Whitman did not. At one time or another, he evidently had in mind poetical promulgations East and West reminiscent of Poe's schemes for a doubly-published literary periodical a decade earlier. Thus Whitman wrote to himself: "N.B.—In Western edition don't make it *too* West —namely, it is enough if there be nothing in the book that is distasteful to the West, or is meaningless to it—and enough if there be two or three pieces, *first-rate*, applicable enough to all men and women, but *specially* welcome to Western men and women" (*Complete Writings*, IX, 201-202). Another prescription (X, 19) reads:

Poem of Wisconsin.
Poem of Missouri.
Poem of Texas.
Poem of Lake Superior.
Poem of the Rifle.

—*for Western Edition.*

See also *Complete Writings*, X, 28, and Edward G. Bernard, "Some New Whitman Manuscript Notes," *American Literature*, VIII (1936), 60, wherein it appears that the Western edition was to have been published in Chicago.

[22] In an earlier form, "Proto-Leaf" was suggestively entitled "Premonition." *Whitman's Manuscripts: Leaves of Grass (1860)*, ed. Fredson Bowers (Chicago, 1955), p. 2.

Or full-breath'd on Californian air, or Texan or Cuban air,
Tallying, vocalizing all—resounding Niagara—resound-
　ing Missouri,
Or rude in my home in Kanuck woods,
Or wandering and hunting, my drink water, my diet meat,
Or withdrawn to muse and meditate in some deep recess,
Far from the clank of crowds, an interval passing, rapt
　and happy,
Stars, vapor, snow, the hills, rocks, the Fifth Month flow-
　ers, my amaze, my love,
Aware of the buffalo, the peace-herds, the bull, strong-
　breasted and hairy,
Aware of the mocking-bird of the wilds at day-break,
Solitary, singing in the west, I strike up for a new world.

Whitman's new world is the world of the imagination, a
poetic world of rhythm, language, metaphor, syntax. It is
a world in which a daring simplicity alternates with the
most amazing metamorphoses, as bare prosaic statements
give way to poetic transformations wherein intransitive
verbs become transitive ("resound"), verbs become nouns
("amaze"), nouns hover between cases ("my amaze, my
love"). Whitman is absolute master of the "suspended predication":[23] everything preceding "I strike up" flows into an
attenuated introductory dependent clause in which the poet
works his way toward the invention of a new kind of epic
invocation. Whitman is absolute master of the pivot (technically, anacoluthon). What in the earlier poems had been
mere catalogue becomes a phantasmagorical grammar
through which phrasal shifts signal major shifts in form
and meaning: when Whitman shifts from "my city" to "Or
raised inland," he shifts from an autobiographical to a metaphorically national "I." Whitman is absolute master of the
internal fragment (which is also anacoluthon), as when he
moves from the adjectives "rapt and happy" to nouns illustrating his happiness and then to a series of adjectival

[23] The term is Gay Wilson Allen's, in *Walt Whitman as Man, Poet,
and Legend* (Carbondale, Ill., 1961), p. 56.

phrases defining the source of his awareness, namely himself as buffalo bull or mockingbird, powerful, destructive, lyrical, parodic. The West is America. The West ("some deep recess") is the poet's soul. West and West tally.

Despite an apparently miscellaneous content, the 1860 *Leaves of Grass* is informed by a more coherent pattern than any earlier or later edition. Specifically, it possesses an action, in the Aristotelian sense, with a beginning, a middle —a variety of middles, all of which amount to the same thing—and an end. "Proto-Leaf" is the beginning, *"So long!"* is the end. This concluding poem is carefully prepared for by "Sleep-Chasings" (later "The Sleepers"), which is about sleep and death; by "Burial" (untitled in 1855, later "To Think of Time"), a funereal poem followed by an emblem representing sunrise or sunset or both; and by "To My Soul" (later "As the Time Draws Nigh"):

> I shall go forth,
> I shall traverse The States—but I cannot tell whither or how long.

The tone of this sequence of poems is designedly antithetical to the tone (prophetic bravura) of "Proto-Leaf."

"So long!" begins on a guarded, time-bound note, as if Whitman, nearing the end, were unwilling or unable to look ahead: "All I know at any time suffices for that time only— not subsequent time." Therefore he invokes poets to come:

> I invite defiance, and to make myself superseded,
> All I have done, I would cheerfully give to be trod under foot, if it might only be the soil of superior poems.

For himself he claims only to "have pressed through in my own right" and to "have offered my style to every one." In effect, *"So long!"* proclaims the effective end of a poetic career. Something, Whitman says, is "crowding too close upon me!/ I foresee too much—it means more than I thought,/ It appears to me I am dying." Naturally, "My songs cease—I abandon them." In the final stanza, the poet

feels "like one who has done his work," and takes his farewell of the reader:

> Remember my words—I love you—I depart from
>   materials,
> I am as one disembodied, triumphant, dead.

These moving and enigmatic lines sufficiently reflect Whitman's personal situation, which was also the literary situation. Whitman's understanding of this situation, or at least
his intuition of it, which appears to be quite as sharp as
Melville's, and considerably sharper than, say, Hawthorne's,
is ultimately that on the dizzy verge of the Civil War the
literary West has to all practical intents and purposes come
to an end. Whitman had not set out to be a retrospective
poet—quite the contrary; but a retrospective (or post
mortem) poet was what the course of American history had
by 1860 constrained him to become. By the winning of the
West, the Western bard was at once triumphant and dis-
embodied. He had achieved the poetry of the West, savage
poetry, at precisely the moment when the West disappeared.
Naturally he departs from materials, unless it be more suggestive to say that materials depart from him. The emblem
following *"So long!"* and iconographically closing the
volume shows an outstretched finger with a butterfly poised
for flight, but not, of course, flying. The butterfly is no sign
of metamorphosis, which has already occurred, but of rest
and (possibly) escape.

Among the 1860 poems are many clues to what had happened to Whitman since 1855—for example, the almost
incessant references to frustrations, incapacities for expression, completions, ends. Significantly, the word which in "A
Word Out of the Sea" (later "Out of the Cradle Endlessly
Rocking") is given to "the outsetting bard of love" by his
"savage old mother" the sea is "the low and delicious word
DEATH,/ And again Death—ever Death, Death, Death,"
and even the memory of the gift of this key word must now
be grasped "ere all eludes me, hurriedly."[24] Still more ob-

---

[24] In *Specimen Days* (1882), Whitman implied that this, and other
seashore poems, were shaped by his special sense, or aftersense, of

vious clues are found in the "Calamus" sequence, which begins with a broad hint that the poet must henceforth escape "from the pleasures, profits, conformities,/ Which too long I was offering to feed to my Soul," and which ends with death, and with another presentation of the sunrise-sunset emblem.[25] To be sure, "Calamus" contains several Western poems and passages in the hortatory, optimistic manner of 1855 (or of "Proto-Leaf"), and it also contains warnings—superfluous, surely—that these poems are difficult of interpretation ("Here I shade down and hide my thoughts—I do not expose them"). But "Calamus 7" (later "Of the Terrible Doubt of Appearances") is clearly enough the work of a man trying to shift ground and plagued by uncertainties, and "Calamus 8," which reviews the poet's life, is as explicit as "Proto-Leaf" (which, in the fourth and sixth lines, Whitman echoes) and a good deal more explicit than *So long!* (whose mood it anticipates and justifies):

---

the old frontier metaphor: "Even as a boy, I had the fancy, the wish, to write a piece, perhaps a poem, about the sea-shore—that suggesting, dividing line, contact, junction, the solid marrying the liquid—that curious, lurking something, (as doubtless every objective form finally becomes to the subjective spirit,) . . . blending the real and ideal, and each made portion of the other." Even the language takes us back to Hawthorne's figure for creative process in "The Custom-House." For analysis of Whitman's seashore frontier metaphor shaping the entire poem, see Paul Fussell, Jr., "Whitman's Curious Warble: Reminiscence and Reconciliation," in *The Presence of Walt Whitman*, ed. R. W. B. Lewis (New York, 1962), esp. pp. 31-33, 50-51. Even Whitman's prosody may have been indirectly affected by the frontier metaphor; in "NEW POETRY—*California, Canada, Texas*," he declared: "In my opinion the time has arrived to essentially break down the barriers of form between prose and poetry." So, it might well be argued, were Thoreau and Melville during the 1850's approaching a comparable neutral ground from the opposite direction. See above, "Introduction" (p. 18), the passage from Orestes Brownson concerning prose, poetry, and the "disputed territory" between them.

[25] The third recurrent emblem in the 1860 *Leaves of Grass* depicts the Western Hemisphere emerging from or about to be engulfed by clouds. All three ambiguous emblems also appeared on the book's binding.

Long I thought that knowledge alone would suffice me—
O if I could but obtain knowledge!
Then my lands engrossed me—Lands of the prairies,
Ohio's land, the southern savannas, engrossed me—For
them I would live—I would be their orator;
Then I met the examples of old and new heroes—I heard
of warriors, sailors, and all dauntless persons—And it
seemed to me that I too had it in me to be dauntless
as any—and would be so;
And then, to enclose all, it came to me to strike up the
songs of the New World—And then I believed my life
must be spent in singing;
But now take notice, land of the prairies, land of the south
savannas, Ohio's land,
Take notice, you Kanuck woods—and you Lake Huron—
and all that with you roll toward Niagara—and you
Niagara also,
And you, Californian mountains—That you each and all
find somebody else to be your singer of songs,
For I can be your singer of songs no longer—One who
loves me is jealous of me, and withdraws me from
all but love,
With the rest I dispense—I sever from what I thought
would suffice me, for it does not—it is now empty and
tasteless to me,
I heed knowledge, and the grandeur of The States, and
the example of heroes, no more,
I am indifferent to my own songs—I will go with
him I love,
It is to be enough for us that we are together—We never
separate again.

"Him I love" may be a man, or all men, or God; in any
case, he is a metaphor for a centrally organizing form of
personal devotion superseding poetry. The pertinent question is whether Whitman at this time thought of himself
as choosing to abandon poetry or as forced to; from what
we know of his poetic ambitions, the second possibility seems

altogether more likely. As it turned out, he did not cease writing poems; but the unanticipated arrival of a new subject in the Civil War must be regarded as poetically adventitious and, in the light of Whitman's original intentions, gruesomely ironic. Significantly, when Whitman returned to *Leaves of Grass* after the Civil War—the fourth edition was in 1867—he omitted "Calamus 8" from the poems he wished to preserve.

In a section of "Proto-Leaf" which derives its basic form from "Pictures," Whitman exuberantly declares:

> See, in my poems immigrants continually coming and landing;
> See, in arriere, the wigwam, the trail, the hunter's hut, the flat-boat, the maize-leaf, the claim, the rude fence, and the backwoods village;

and so on for many lines. The progressive vista arriere is incompatible with the opening of the poem's final stanza:

> O a word to clear one's path ahead endlessly!

In poem after poem, Whitman surveyed the expanding United States, nearly always concentrating on the West (*the* word to clear one's path with). In passage after passage he closed in for a near look at the West, endlessly cataloguing details presumably suggestive of its essential life ("The unsurveyed interior, log-houses, clearings, wild animals, hunters, trappers," Whitman quoting himself almost verbatim from the 1855 preface). Neither the surveys nor the catalogues are poetically very impressive, partly for the reason that Whitman at his feeblest was always susceptible of the same error regularly made by the minor Western writers, the assumption that the West was intrinsically interesting, partly for a reason which comes to light in "Chants Democratic 4" (later "Our Old Feuillage"):

> Always the West, with strong native persons—the increasing density there—the habitans, friendly, threatening, ironical, scorning invaders.[26]

[26] In an earlier version, this line reads: "Always The West, with strong native persons, the increasing density, friendly, threatening,

But the West was the West only so long as its habitans remained unaffected by settling and civilizing from the East. Whitman, as a civilized Eastern poet bent on realizing the West through poetry, is in several ironic senses one of the invaders ironically scorned by the West. Conversely, Whitman as Western poet is in the process of being destroyed by the success of the Westward Movement: "the increasing density there" means, in effect, the loss of the West. Henceforth, Whitman's best poems were to be occasional—*Drum-Taps*, "When Lilacs Last in the Dooryard Bloom'd," "Passage to India," which insistently sounds a call, heard also in Thoreau and Melville, to "The Past! the Past! the Past!" More than ever, death became the key word of Whitman's poetry; it was the only good word he had left. The poet who so loved Cooper was even driven to glorify the broad-axe. In "Chants Democratic 2" (later "Song of the Broad-Axe"), Whitman whipped up a state of enthusiasm over America's arising "shapes" (states, poems, etc.), but the poem remains essentially destructive. The magnificent opening lines are sustained by feelings of monstrosity and horror:

> Broad-axe, shapely, naked, wan!
> Head from the mother's bowels drawn!
> Wooded flesh and metal bone! limb only one and lip only one!
> Gray-blue leaf by red-heat grown! helve produced from a little seed sown!

The typical instrument of national progress sounds like a deformed baby resulting from a scarcely imaginable perversion, perhaps from the union of the old American nature and the new American industrialism. In the "Apostroph" to "Chants Democratic," Whitman obliquely refers to "a wan and terrible emblem, by me adopted!"

---

ironical, scorning invaders"—as if the West, or its density, rather than its habitans, were the ironical, scornful threat. *Whitman's Manuscripts*, p. 124.

From time to time in the 1860 edition, Whitman kept up appearances as well as he could:

> As I sailed down the Mississippi,
> As I wandered over the prairies . . .
> As I bathed on the beach of the Eastern Sea, and again
> on the beach on the Western Sea,
> As I roamed the streets of inland Chicago—whatever
> streets I have roamed,
> Wherever I have been, I have charged myself with
> contentment and triumph.

But the tense of the verbs is conspicuously past tense; "charged" is an ambiguous word; and in the final lines of this poem ("Chants Democratic 8," later "Song at Sunset") the West appears to be synonymous with the setting sun, i.e., death—because, as "Chants Democratic 9" (later "Thoughts") confirms, "America illustrates birth, gigantic youth, the promise, the sure fulfilment." The fulfillment, unfortunately, was unanticipated and, in a very real sense, unwanted. It meant the end of easy, automatic progress. What would America do now, what would it think of itself, this nation which had all along been tempted to define itself in terms of progress? Frankly, it did not know, and perhaps does not know yet; it had never given the matter much thought.

In "Enfans d'Adam 10" (later "Facing West From California's Shores"), Whitman, like Melville, brooded on the mystery and futility of it all:

> Inquiring, tireless, seeking that yet unfound,
> I, a child, very old, over waves, toward the house of
> maternity, the land of migrations, look afar,
> Look off the shores of my Western Sea—having arrived
> at last where I am—the circle almost circled;
> For coming westward from Hindustan, from the vales
> of Kashmere,
> From Asia—from the north—from the God, the sage,
> and the hero,

From the south—from the flowery peninsulas, and the
  spice islands,
Now I face the old home again—looking over to it,
  joyous, as after long travel, growth, and sleep;
But where is what I started for, so long ago?
And why is it yet unfound?[27]

Only a century earlier, Crèvecœur had called the Americans
"the western pilgrims" who "will finish the great circle";
but Crèvecœur could not really imagine the great circle completed, and was not even sufficiently interested to inquire
what might happen next. Whitman was driven to the final,
completed vision (as in "Chants Democratic 11," later
"Thoughts"):

Of myself, soon, perhaps, closing up my songs by these
  shores,
Of California—of Oregon—and of me journeying hence
  to live and sing there.

He might as well have said "die there," for the poem ends:

(O it lurks in me night and day—What is gain, after
  all, to savageness and freedom?)

And of course there was no answer.
  By 1860 Whitman was well on the way toward becoming
a poet of pathos. "I but write one or two indicative words
for the future,/ I but advance a moment, only to wheel and
hurry back in the darkness." The headlong advance of 1855
had in five years turned into a forced retreat. In "Leaves of
Grass 1" (later "As I Ebb'd With the Ocean of Life"),
Whitman begs "You oceans both!" whom he had so often
apostrophized, "Be not too rough with me—I submit," and
in words susceptible of a cultural as well as a personal interpretation, reveals himself:

Oppressed with myself that I have dared to open my
  mouth,

---

[27] As originally conceived, this poem lacked the first line and the
last two lines, and thus celebrated triumph rather than defeat.
Whitman's Manuscripts, p. 66.

> Aware now, that, amid all the blab whose echoes recoil
> upon me, I have not once had the least idea who
> or what I am.

Now "the real ME" is "withdrawn far," mocking a superficial poem-writing "me" with "distant ironical laughter at
every word I have written or shall write." Another poem,
"Leaves of Grass 4" (later "This Compost") presupposes
a land thickly enough and long enough settled to be crowded
with corpses. It suggestively begins:

> Something startles me where I thought I was safest,
> I withdraw from the still woods I loved.

Whitman as Western poet is sadly identical with "the
despondent red man in the west" (in "Salut au Monde")
who "has heard the quail and beheld the honey-bee, and
sadly prepared to depart."

As "Poem of the Road" (later "Song of the Open Road")
sufficiently demonstrates, Whitman's tendency toward un-
substantiated symbolic statement began as early as 1856,
and was at least partly caused by his loss of the public half
of his fundamental comparison. With the disappearance of
the actual pioneer, pioneering was no longer a viable metaphor, but the merest sentimentality or empty rhetoric.
"Allons!" Whitman declaims, "To that which is endless,
as it was beginningless"—to that, in other words, which is
either God or nothing. Almost before it had time to clarify,
Whitman's vision began to fade, and he learned how to
dissemble (in "Thoughts 2"):

> Of vista—Suppose some sight in arriere, through the
> formative chaos, presuming the growth, fulness, life,
> now attained on the journey;
> (But I see the road continued, and the journey ever
> continued.)

The road continued is precisely what Whitman, and Whitman's America, did not and could not see; they had never
been educated to such difficulties of perception. Therefore
failure, disillusion, and despair are all over this 1860

Leaves of Grass, and especially all over its second half. "A Hand-Mirror," which purports to be a satiric sketch of a drunkard or "venerealee," concludes: "Such a result so soon—and from such a beginning!" Here in a single line is the acrid truth about Walt Whitman's ecstatic and foreshortened poetic career.

Now Whitman was not dead; or if he was, he was his sorrowful terrible heir. He continued to write poetry of a sort for thirty years, but, with a few notable exceptions, the poetry represented a Pyrrhic victory. (Another such victory and America may well be lost.) In *Drum-Taps and Sequel to Drum-Taps* (1865-1866), Western references are few, perfunctory, and repetitive of earlier poems; this volume also contains whole poems, usually brief and never good, on Western themes, such as "The Torch," "Others May Praise What They Like," or the wretched "Pioneers! O Pioneers!" which has always been Whitman's most popular poem. More significantly, the volume ends with "To the Leaven'd Soil They Trod," in which the poet praises "the general western world," "the Alleghanian hills," "the tireless Mississippi," "the prairie spreading wide,/ To the far-off sea," and then, in the final line, suddenly rejects all of these in favor of the nation's rejected section:

But the hot sun of the South is to ripen my songs.[28]

By identifying his poetic future with the political future of the devastated South, Whitman at once displayed a wonderful magnanimity, indulged in a justifiable self-pity, and indefinitely postponed the agony of his reconstruction.

[28] Later Whitman improved the rhythm (but not the grammar) of this line by changing it to read: "But the hot sun of the South is to fully ripen my songs." In view of the decline in his poetic abilities from the 1860 *Leaves of Grass* to *Drum-Taps*, it is pathetically ironic to find Whitman in 1863 writing in a personal letter: "I feel to devote myself more to the work of my life, which is making poems. I must bring out Drum Taps. I *must* be continually bringing out poems—now is the hey day. I shall range along the high plateau of my life & capacity for a few years now, & and then swiftly descend." *The Correspondence of Walt Whitman*, ed. Edwin Haviland Miller (New York, 1961-), I, 185. As it happened, Whitman's descent was extraordinarily slow and had already commenced.

The great poem in this volume is of course "When Lilacs Last in the Dooryard Bloom'd," an elegy both for an assassinated president and for a ruined poet who, by the harshest irony of all, and as if he were not already plagued with troubles enough, had been recently fired from his clerkship in the Indian Bureau of the Department of the Interior for having written an indecent book. The "great star" or "western orb" ("O powerful, western, fallen star!") that "early droop'd in the western sky in the night" may well be thought to suggest both Lincoln (who is not named) and Whitman—that is, Whitman's previous incarnation as Western poet. The poem is in several respects a compendium of earlier Whitman poems, ostentatiously invoking their special techniques (the pictorial form of "Pictures"), their imagery (the solitary singing bird from "Proto-Leaf"), and their lyric motifs (the carol of death from "A Word Out of the Sea"). Naturally the poem is about death, but it is about death more than it needs to be (unlike the traditional elegy, its "consolation" is also death), and it approaches its conclusion with a strange air of reluctance, as the poet once again addresses the western orb (himself his own lonely comrade) while ambiguities shower like starlight:

Must I pass from my song for thee;
From my gaze on thee in the west, fronting the west, communing with thee,
O comrade lustrous, with silver face in the night?

Not much remained—only "retrievements out of the night," as later versions of the poem were to have it (for Whitman's sunset had long since taken place, and was, in fact, implicit in his jetblack sunrise), and enough poetic realism to commit president, poet, and poem to "the large unconscious scenery of my land."

Whitman spent the best of his remaining years consolidating the poetic achievement of his one intensively productive period, and using that achievement as standing ground for vistas extending backward in time beyond the earliest written records and forward in time further than most of us dare imagine. Perhaps for this reason, his poetic decline was paradoxically accompanied by a wisdom and serenity rarely found in modern literature (Thomas Mann and James Joyce would be good examples of it) and practically never encountered in the United States—for reasons, as Whitman was always saying. In "Proud Music of the Storm" (1868), he returned to the painful recognitions of the 1860 poems with an altogether different attitude of acceptance, now celebrating:

> earth's own diapason,
> Of winds and woods and mighty ocean waves,
> A new composite orchestra, binder of years and climes, ten-fold renewer,
> And of the far-back days the poets tell, the Paradiso,
> The straying thence, the separation long, but now the wandering done,
> The journey done, the journeyman come home,
> And man and art with Nature fused again.

The frustrations of facing West from California's shores were exorcised by wit (the puns on journey and journeyman) and then subsumed in a vision of the age-old Westward Movement of humanity as, after all, only an episode, however diverting, a deflection from the centrally humane activities of self-definition, self-knowledge, confrontation, spiritual dominion. In "Passage to India" (1870),[29] the poet again initiates himself into a new role appropriate to the bard of a people whose frontier has closed, a role con-

---

[29] This is Whitman's most ambitious post-West poem. It was rejected by Bret Harte as editor of the *Overland Monthly*, published in San Francisco. Doubtless Whitman had Harte in mind when in 1874, after the usual jibes at aristocratic literature, he remarked: "There is, too, the other extreme,—the scene often laid in the West, especially in California, where ruffians, rum-drinkers, and trulls only are depicted. Both are insulting to the genius of These States." *Uncollected Poetry and Prose*, II, 58. See also Robert R. Hubach, "Three Uncollected St. Louis Interviews of Walt Whitman," *American Literature*, XIV (1942), 146.

ceivably more mature than any role available to the bards of that people during the pioneering period:

> Nature and Man shall be disjoin'd and diffused no more,
> The true son of God shall absolutely fuse them.

Among the great writers who came of age in antebellum America, Whitman alone carried through the Civil War with sufficient impetus to achieve in his best moments a vision of American literature directly leading to the twentieth century, and (it may be fondly thought) sufficiently realistic eventually to overcome the sentimental nostalgias and vexations trailing after Frederick Jackson Turner and the countless American historians bubbling in his wake. Whitman, of course, was to behold Canaan but not to enter it. He was too old to start over again writing the poetry he alone knew enough to look for from an entirely new America, an America which no longer could be defined, and therefore no longer need be defined, in terms of the West. As Whitman's literary vision kindled, his poetic powers continued to wane, and in the same poem he regrettably descended to bathos:

> I see over my own continent the Pacific railroad sur-
> mounting every barrier,
> I see continual trains of cars winding along the Platte
> carrying freight and passengers,
> I hear the locomotives rushing and roaring, and the
> shrill steam-whistle,
> I hear the echoes reverberate through the grandest scen-
> ery in the world.

Here is the well-beloved Whitman of platitude, stereotype, and cliché, darling of the modern American imagination as corrupted by its own egotism, aggression, and self-deceit. The grandest scenery in the world, seen from a railroad car, is neither what Whitman set out to celebrate, nor what he was now hoping to celebrate; it is merely the tawdry miracle to which the ruined poet—who, perhaps more than any other American writer, had sacrificed himself to the greater glory of American literature—was most grievously reduced.

Yet there were still great moments. Whitman's career had begun with journalism, and now he returned to a kind of journalism transfigured by the intervening years of poetic accomplishment. As if mysteriously returned to 1855, Whitman was once again, in a manner of speaking, the pioneer. "Democratic Vistas" (1870) was, he said, "an exploration, as of new ground, wherein, like other primitive surveyors, I must do the best I can, leaving it to those who come after me to do much better. (The service, in fact, if any, must be to break a sort of first path or track, no matter how rude and ungeometrical.)" The claim was unduly modest. No subsequent American criticism surpasses or even approaches Whitman's inspired survey of the relations among American literature, American civilization, and their underlying ground, or what metaphysicians like to call the intuition of being. It is worth emphasizing that Whitman's inspiration is great because it rests upon a full recognition of horrors, not only the actual horrors of American life but, even more, the American soul's nervous unnerving perception of the vacuums, non-entities, abysms, discontinuities which have always constituted the most formidable threat to human existence in the so-called New World and which remain, to this day, unexplicated and unappeased: "The fear of conflicting and irreconcilable interiors, and the lack of a common skeleton, knitting all close, continually haunts me." Although Whitman's language vaguely recalls the familiar problems of an earlier era, he had obviously moved through and out of the world of conflicting interior Wests, Northern and Southern, the old pre-War literary-political world in which spinal Mississippis and Rocky Mountains might be seriously envisaged as magical solutions for the Americans' spiritual torments.

The new vision was of course almost impossible to sustain, especially for a man who had grown up before the War. Elsewhere in "Democratic Vistas" Whitman once again falls to imagining that "the main social, political, spine-character

431

of the States will probably run along the Ohio, Missouri and Mississippi rivers," and so forth, piling section on section to achieve the same old boxing-the-compass *e-pluri-bus-unum* allegory: "From the north, intellect, the sun of things, also the idea of unswayable justice, anchor amid the last, the wildest tempests. From the south the living soul, the animus of good and bad, haughtily admitting no demonstration but its own. While from the west itself comes solid personality, with blood and brawn, and the deep quality of all-accepting fusion." At least in the back of his mind, the West was still for Whitman the reconciler of opposites, the old frontier metaphor expressive of bipolar unity.

Yet clearly, he had also learned something new. Reversing the position of the 1855 preface ("the United States . . . are essentially the greatest poem"), Whitman fought through to a demonstrably higher wisdom. "It may be argued that our republic is, in performance, really enacting to-day the grandest arts, poems, &c., by beating up the wilderness into fertile farms. . . . I too hail those achievements with pride and joy: then answer that the soul of man will not with such only—nay, not with such at all—be finally satisfied." The judgment was absolute and long overdue; it still merits (from American scholars and American laymen) close attention. "In vain have we annex'd Texas, California, Alaska," Whitman went on, salting the wound. "It is as if we were somehow being endow'd with a vast and more and more thoroughly-appointed body, and then left with little or no soul." In the light of that supposition, he mercilessly jeered at America's cultural pretensions: "Do you call those genteel little creatures American poets? Do you term that perpetual, pistareen, paste-pot work, American art, American drama, taste, verse? I think I hear, echoed as from some mountain-top afar in the west, the scornful laugh of the Genius of these States." (Leatherstocking, no doubt.) In his 1872 preface to *As a Strong Bird on Pinions Free*, Whitman once again spoke of the urgent necessity for "creating in literature an *imaginative* New World," and thus "delivering America, and, indeed, all Christian lands everywhere, from the thin moribund and watery, but appallingly extensive nuisance of conventional poetry." The issues were of course perpetual, but how long could this Last Survivor continue to cast them in the language and forms of the earlier nineteenth century?

At the beginning of 1873, Whitman suffered a paralytic stroke that left him more or less an invalid for the remainder of his life, and in the next year he published "Prayer of Columbus," wherein the ailing American poet achieved another of his many *personae*:

A batter'd, wreck'd old man,
Thrown on this savage shore, far, far from home.

Still, at the end of the poem, the aged admiral is blessed with the traditional American vision of Columbus: "And anthems in new tongues I hear saluting me." Whitman's anthems. In a prose note, he set the date in 1503 and Columbus' age at nearly 70. Whitman himself was only 55, and by now surely aware that the anthems in new tongues—the new American poetry in new American modes —which he had incessantly celebrated and predicted, would arrive well after his death, perhaps centuries after. Of "Song of the Redwood-Tree" (1874), a Danish admirer wrote Whitman: "It is your old great theme in a simple and powerful stile, embracing the holy and original nation of the far West." The long-suffering national poet noncommittally replied: "I myself have *pleased myself* more fully with *Redwood Tree* than any of my pieces of late years."[30] What pleased him so much is slightly mysterious— or perhaps not—since the poem is in so many ways the *inverse* of his old great theme. Despite a desperate and unconvincing satisfaction in California's "swarming and busy race settling and organizing everywhere," the poem's emotional center lies at the heart of the tree, doomed to a

[30] *Correspondence*, II, 309, and 309, n. 37. To the same friend, Whitman had previously described the poem as "a piece I have written to idealize our great Pacific half of America, (the future *better half*)" (II, 282).

433

senseless extinction to the tune of a "chorus of dryads, fading, departing, or hamadryads departing," as America's greatest Western poet was also in these years, and audibly in this poem, departing. "From Far Dakota's Cañons" (subtitled "June 25, 1876") celebrates Custer's last stand and identifies the anachronistic slaughtered Indian-fighter with the anachronistic wrecked old Western poet, "sitting in dark days,/ Lone, sulky, through the time's thick murk looking in vain for light."

After 1873—the date is arbitrary but useful—Whitman tended merely to repeat himself with dwindling force. In the 1876 preface (the perdurable *Leaves of Grass* had now reached a sixth edition) he said he was determined as ever "to re-occupy for Western tenancy the oldest though everfresh fields, and reap from them the savage and sane nourishment indispensable to a hardy nation, and the absence of which, threatening to become worse and worse, is the most serious lack and defect to-day of our New World literature." In a more retrospective mood, he said once again that his poetic form had "strictly grown from my purports and facts, and is the analogy of them. Within my time the United States have emerged from nebulous vagueness and suspense, to full orbic, (though varied,) decision." Three years later, during an interval of good health, Whitman made his second Western tour, and inspected with his own eyes the orbic decision. This time he sped through the grandest scenery in the world on the transcontinental railroad, viewing or visiting St. Louis, Kansas City, Lawrence, Topeka, Denver, Platte Canyon, Pike's Peak, Pueblo.[31] In *Specimen Days & Collect* (1882-1883), Whitman made much—much too much—of this trip.[32] At Lawrence, where

[31] Again, Gay Wilson Allen's summary of the basic facts (*The Solitary Singer*, pp. 486-490) is the most useful.

[32] In *Specimen Days*, Whitman practically ignored his early Western tour, perhaps because he wished to portray himself as an intuitive and indigenous genius mystically confirmed by the Western tour of 1879. For earlier statements admitting, and even exaggerating, the effect of the West on his poetry in the years after 1848, see *Walt Whitman's Workshop*, in which Whitman claims to have "ex-

he was an honored guest of the Old Settlers of Kansas Committee during the Quarter Centennial (!) celebration of the settlement of the state, he was expected to deliver a poem, which he neglected to provide; instead, he prepared a short speech, which he forgot to deliver, but unfortunately remembered to publish: "I wonder indeed if the people of this continental inland West know how much of first-class *art* they have in these prairies"—and so forth, from one gaucherie to the next. The country from Topeka to Denver, though varied, was "all unmistakably prolific, western, American, and on the largest scale." Under the heading, "An Egotistical 'Find,'" Whitman shamelessly announced that, in the Rocky Mountains, "'I have found the law of my own poems.'" Their law, according to this pathetically inept and practically posthumous view of them, was in effect lawlessness, tallying "all this grim yet joyous elemental abandon—this plenitude of material, entire absence of art, untrammel'd play of primitive Nature . . . the broad handling and absolute uncrampedness." (Whitman later versified these sentiments in "Spirit that Form'd This Scene," one of his weaker poems and a typical late Western poetic effusion. Others of the period—no better—include "The Prairie States" and "Italian Music in Dakota.") America's myriad anti-intellectuals—including Whitman critics to come—must have been gratified. Henceforth they could derogate art (Whitman's central virtue) in favor of spirit (their own emptiness) as much as they wished. Had they not the master's infallible imprimatur for their perpetual, pistareen, paste-pot, and appallingly extensive nuisances?

Twentieth-century sentimental-antiquarian West-mongering was just around the corner. Only eleven years later, Frederick Jackson Turner would make his astonishing confusion of cultural regression and "Americanization," and,

---

plored the west" (p. 152), and Richard M. Bucke, *Walt Whitman* (Philadelphia, 1883), in which Whitman claims to have jaunted through the South and West as far as Texas (p. 136). In both statements, he emphasized out of all proportion the Western quality of his trip and minimized, almost to the point of suppression, the facts of his sojourn and employment in New Orleans.

on the strength of that confusion, his definition of the American intellect as resulting from the frontier: "coarseness and strength combined with acuteness and inquisitiveness; that practical, inventive turn of mind, quick to find expedients; that masterful grasp of material things, lacking in the artistic but powerful to effect great ends," the great ends being, in the last analysis, only geographical expansion, "the advance of American settlement westward," which was tautologically supposed to "explain American development."[33] America's good gray poet was meanwhile busy contributing to the climate of opinion which made such confusions and reductions inevitable. In *Specimen Days*, he is forever identifying his poems with the Rocky Mountains or the prairies and then, not very subtly, preferring these mountains and prairies to any conceivable art, presumably not counting his own, which was artless. Everywhere in the West, he sees recent traces of pioneers—"dauntlessly grappling with these grisliest shows of the old kosmos"; yet even California, whose lovely shores Whitman in real life never managed to visit, had been a state of the Union for over three decades, or, indeed, since five years before the first edition of *Leaves of Grass*![34] "Talk, I say again, of going to Europe, of visiting the ruins of feudal castles, or Coliseum

___

[33] *The Frontier in American History* (New York, 1920), pp. 1, 37. Turner's fundamental definition of the frontier ("the meeting point between savagery and civilization") is of course no definition at all, but simply the age-old frontier metaphor. In one form or another—most often, perhaps, as "the Middle Region"—this metaphor pervades Turner's writings, though neither he nor his disciples seem ever to have recognized it as a metaphor or to have suspected its literary origins. For examples of Turner using, or, more properly, being used by, this metaphor, see *The Early Writings of Frederick Jackson Turner* (Madison, 1938), p. 79; *Rise of the New West, 1819-1829* (New York, 1906), pp. 28-30; *The Frontier in American History*, pp. 27-28, 29, 68, 129, 138, 151, 152, 161, 162, 175, 197-198, 219, 222, 236, 241-242, 351; *The United States, 1830-1850: The Nation and Its Sections* (New York, 1935), pp. 92, 145, 244, 324-325, 354.

[34] In "Some Diary Notes at Random," published in *November Boughs* (1888), Whitman was still wonder-struck at the idea of a plate glass factory near St. Louis, "in the wilds of the West."

remains, or kings' palaces—when you can come *here*. . . .
Yes, I think the chyle of not only poetry and painting, but
oratory, and even the metaphysics and music fit for the New
World, before being finally assimilated, need first and feeding visits here." For of course, and as ever, "grand as the
thought that doubtless the child is already born who will
see a hundred millions of people, the most prosperous and
advanc'd of the world, inhabiting these Prairies, the great
Plains, and the valley of the Mississippi, I could not help
thinking it would be grander still to see all those inimitable
American areas fused in the alembic of a perfect poem, or
other esthetic work, entirely western, fresh and limitless—
altogether our own, without a trace or taste of Europe's
soil, reminiscence, technical letter or spirit." What most impressed Whitman on the 1879 trip was the prairies and
plains; what failed to impress him at all was the analogy
between their most obvious characteristic—flatness—and
his own writing.

By 1882—or perhaps by 1879—Whitman had almost
completely lost his intellectual and aesthetic grip (except
for Mark Twain and Henry James, and the silent beleaguered Melville, America had lost *its* intellectual and
aesthetic grip much earlier); without realism or relevance,
the platitudes flowed uncheck'd:

> I stopp'd and laid down the book [Scott's poems], and
> ponder'd the thought of a poetry that should in due
> time express and supply the teeming region I was in
> the midst of, and have briefly touch'd upon. One's mind
> needs but a moment's deliberation anywhere in the
> United States to see clearly enough that all the prevalent
> books and library poets, either as imported from Great
> Britain, or follow'd and *doppel-gang'd* here, are foreign
> to our States, copiously as they are read by us all. But to
> fully understand not only how absolutely in opposition
> to our times and lands, and how little and cramp'd, and
> what anachronisms and absurdities many of their pages
> are, for American purposes, one must dwell or travel

437

awhile in Missouri, Kansas and Colorado, and get rapport with their people and country.

 . . . The pure breath, primitiveness, boundless prodigality and amplitude, strange mixture of delicacy and power, of continence, of real and ideal, and of all original and first-class elements, of these prairies, the Rocky mountains, and of the Mississippi and Missouri rivers—will they ever appear in, and in some sort form a standard for our poetry and art? (I sometimes think that even the ambition of my friend Joaquin Miller to put them in, and illustrate them, places him ahead of the whole crowd.)

Joaquin Miller, ahead of the whole crowd, was called to a ludicrously grandiose role, for all that Whitman wanted, really, was "a great throbbing, vital, imaginative work, or series of works, or literature, in constructing which the Plains, the Prairies, and the Mississippi river, with the demesnes of its varied and ample valley, should be the concrete background, and America's humanity, passions, struggles, hopes, there and now—an *eclaircissement* as it is and is to be, on the stage of the New World, of all Time's hitherto drama of war, romance and evolution—should furnish the lambent fire, the ideal." Indirectly, Whitman was talking about *Leaves of Grass* as the culmination of early American literature, as, indeed, he always had; and now he was talking nonsense. The metaphorical West, the figurative frontier, which in 1855 and 1860 had informed and sustained his major poems, were long since gone, and had been replaced, in the minds of most Americans, by the literal West. Whitman no longer seemed to know the difference.

 He had become—in W. H. Auden's phrase—his admirers. "Garrulous to the very last," as he observed in a late poem ("After the Supper and Talk"), he sat in his littered room delivering shifting, evasive, and contradictory opinions on all conceivable subjects, most of which he knew nothing about. "Bucke says in one of his letters that he is reading

438

Parkman and thinks a lot of him. W. nods: 'He ought
to if he thinks a lot of anybody: Parkman deserves it.' "
Four days later: "Bucke spoke in one of his letters [the same
letter?] of Parkman's histories. W. said: 'I never read
them—not one of them: yet by all accounts they are set
down as being strong and fascinating.' He had 'never met
Parkman'—in fact, knew 'little about him.' " Traubel, the
parody-Boswell reporting (or concocting) these conversations, was no help. " 'Walt, my idea of your idea is this—
that you are to write on and write on to the end, even if
in senility, so as to make the Leaves a complete record of
a life. Is that it?' " And of course, and sadly, it was. With
wonderful innocence, Hamlin Garland, a professional
Westerner whose name Whitman could never keep straight,
had written the old poet in 1886: "I am a border-man,—
born in Wisconsin and raised on the prairie frontier." In
1888, Whitman commented on the letter: " 'Did you
notice, too, that he speaks of himself as a borderman?'—
a child of the western prairies? That appeals to me—hits me
hardest where I enjoy being hit. That country out there
is my own country though I have mainly had to view it
from afar. I always seem to expect the men and women
of the West to take me in. . . . [Garland] ought to do something with the West—get it into great books.' " To which
the irrepressible Traubel, once more taking Whitman in,
added his usual banality: " 'The East is like hope and the
West is more like hope!' "[35]

In "A Backward Glance O'er Travel'd Roads," the
preface to *November Boughs* (1888), Whitman firmly asserted "that the geography and hydrography [the Western
waters upon which he had traveled in 1848] of this continent . . . are their [*Leaves of Grass*'s] real veins and
current concrete," which was true enough, if properly understood—and then he fussily deleted the passage in order to
make a page come out right.[36] In the preface as published,

[35] Horace Traubel, *With Walt Whitman in Camden*, II (New York,
1908), 161-163; III (New York, 1914), 356, 391, 419.
[36] *With Walt Whitman in Camden*, II, 108.

439

he alluded to "the uprisings of national masses and shiftings of boundary-lines—the historical and other prominent facts of the United States," and added, as always: "For all these new and evolutionary facts, meanings, purposes, new poetic messages, new forms and expressions, are inevitable." And so they were, or had been, and doubtless are and will be, though not the same facts, meanings, or purposes. Whitman's new and evolutionary facts were by now far, far back in the past. His poems, he admitted, were "in spirit the poems of the morning. (They have been founded and mainly written in the sunny forenoon and early midday of my life.)" Yet to the end, he simultaneously looked backward and forward, conceding failure, predicting success, not so much for himself as for American literature generally. His devotion to the national letters was the central motivation of his life and career, and so high was his estimate of its importance that he continually fell into a not altogether inexplicable despair. As he complained in *Good-Bye My Fancy* (1891): "All that has been put in statement, tremendous as it is, what is it compared with the vast fields and values and varieties left unreap'd? Of our own country, the splendid races North or South, and especially of the Western and Pacific regions, it sometimes seems to me their myriad noblest Homeric and Biblic elements are all untouch'd, left as if ashamed of, and only certain very minor occasional *delirium tremens* glints studiously sought and put in print, in short tales, 'poetry' or books." For a literature which in a span of about thirty-five years had produced in quick succession the Leatherstocking Tales, the sketches and stories of Hawthorne and Poe, *The Scarlet Letter*, *Moby-Dick*, *Walden*, *The Confidence-Man*, and finally, *Leaves of Grass*, Whitman's judgment seems unnecessarily harsh. Perhaps he was once again measuring American literary achievement by comparison with Homer, Dante, and Shakespeare. Or perhaps he was once again expressing in his own curious way his own curious blend of progressivism and reaction, so typically American, for in effect his remarks sound a paradoxical call to actions already concluded. It was

much too late, in 1891, for "Homeric and Biblic elements."
Such as they had been, they had been put in print as well
as they were ever to be put.

In 1893, Frederick Jackson Turner was wistfully (and
tardily) to announce: "And now, four centuries from the
discovery of America, at the end of a hundred years of life
under the Constitution, the frontier has gone, and with its
going has closed the first period of American history."[37] Living at the heart of such confusions as we have seen, energeti-
cally expressing and fostering them in an age which had almost totally lost the power or even the desire of thought, the
youthful Turner, like the elderly Whitman, was inevitably
bewildered about chronology and about more than chronology. Being human, Turner, like Whitman, was inevitably of
two minds about the passing of an old, familiar world, and
the advent of a new and unfamiliar world. And yet, as now
seems sufficiently obvious, the close of the first period of
American history and literature was not altogether a tragedy; not, in fact, a tragedy at all, but a simple condition of
existence (even leaving out of account the far more significant truth that "the soul of man will not with such only—
nay, not with such at all—be finally satisfied"), the condition of change. The West, the frontier, were long since
departed; change, and the ability to respond to change,
survive.

[37] *The Frontier in American History*, p. 38.

441

Index

Adams, James Truslow, 18n
Adams, John, 5-6
Aderman, Ralph M., 13n
Adimari, Ralph, 402n
Adkins, Nelson F., 78n
Alcott, Amos Bronson, 18, 20, 184, 190, 203, 360, 413; *Conversations With Children on the Gospels*, 103; *Journals*, 18, 20n, 184, 190, 346, 413, 413n; *Observations on the Principles and Methods of Infant Instruction*, 103
Allen, Ethan, 297; *Narrative*, 295
Allen, Francis H., 175n, 194n, 223n, 329n
Allen, Gay Wilson, 398n, 402n, 417n, 434n
American Magazine of Useful and Entertaining Knowledge, 71-73, 91
Anthon, Charles, 146
Aristotle, 19n
Arnold, Matthew, 215-16, 382
Arvin, Newton, 380n
Auden, W. H., 438

Baird, James, 242
Barber, John Warner [?], "The White Steed of the Prairies," 279n
Beard, James F., 29n
Belknap, Jeremy, 372
Bentley, Richard, 234n
Bernard, Edward G., 416n
Bezanson, Walter E., 287n, 377n
Billington, Ray Allen, ix, 75n, 148n
Billson, James, 392n
Bird, Robert Montgomery, 200, 320n
Black, John, 401n
Blake, Harrison, 188
Bleecker, Mrs. Ann Eliza, 10
Bode, Carl, 175n, 200n, 347n
Bowen, Francis, 42n, 154n
Bowers, Fredson, 92n, 114n, 416n
Brackenridge, Hugh Henry (with Philip Freneau), 5-6
Bradford, Alexander, 235n
Bradford, William, 92-93
Bradley, Phillips, 42n, 154n
Bradley, Sculley, 398n
Brainard, J. G. C., 139

Brewerton, George D., 292n
Brigham, Clarence S., 161n, 173n
Brooks, Van Wyck, 397
Brown, Charles Brockden, 6, 9-11, 275; *Clara Howard*, 10; *Edgar Huntly*, 9; "Memoirs of Carwin, the Biloquist," 10-11; *Ormond*, 9-10; *Wieland*, 10-11, 113
Brown, Charles H., 398n
Browne, J. Ross, 252n, 269n
Browne, Sir Thomas, 229
Brownson, Henry F., 18n, 31n
Brownson, Orestes A., 18, 31, 119, 129n, 420n; *New Views of Christianity, Society, and the Church*, 22; *The Spirit-Rapper*, 308n
Bruccoli, Matthew J., 92n, 114n
Bruno, Giordano, 21n
Bryant, William Cullen, 18n, 135n, 143; "The Ages," 398; "The Disinterred Warrior," 135-36; "Discourse on the Life and Genius of Cooper," 32; "The Hunter of the Prairies," 142; "Illinois Fifty Years Ago," 135n; *Letters of a Traveller*, 135n; "The Prairie," 135
Bucke, Richard M., 398n, 435n, 438-39
Buffon, Georges Louis Leclerc de, 373

Cabot, James E., 20n, 23n, 184n
Cameron, Kenneth Walter, 176n
Camoens, Luis de, 265
Campbell, Killis, 153n
Carlyle, Thomas, 19-20, 23, 191-92, 315, 352
Cartier, Jacques, 329
Catlin, George, 401; *Letters and Notes on the . . . North American Indians*, 3
Champlain, Samuel de, 329
Channing, William Ellery (the younger), 73, 88, 203, 327
Charvat, William, 92n, 114n
Chase, Owen, 154-55
Chase, Richard, 262n
Chaucer, Geoffrey, 308
Cheever, Henry T., 265n, 269
Chivers, Thomas Holley, 145-46